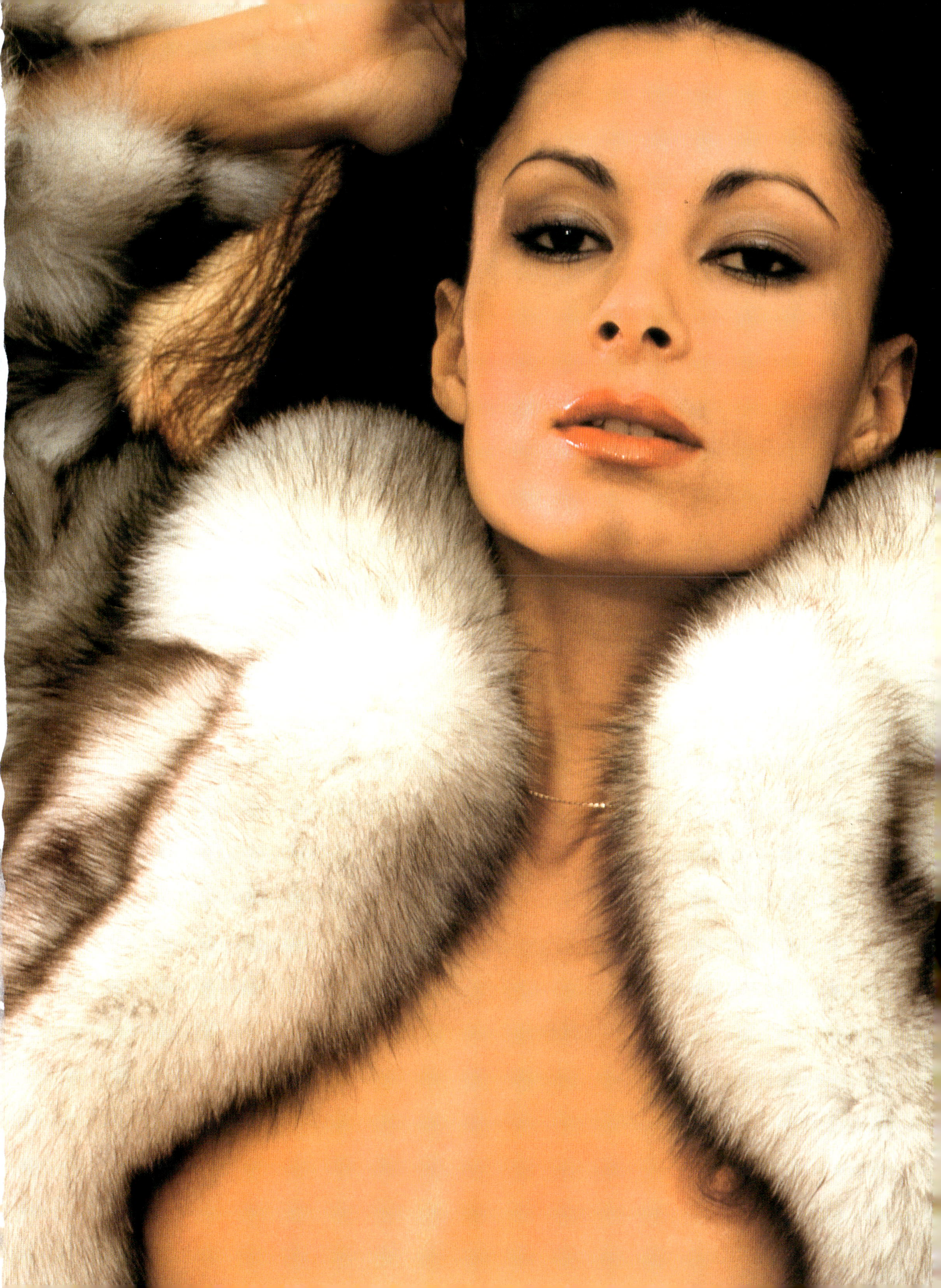

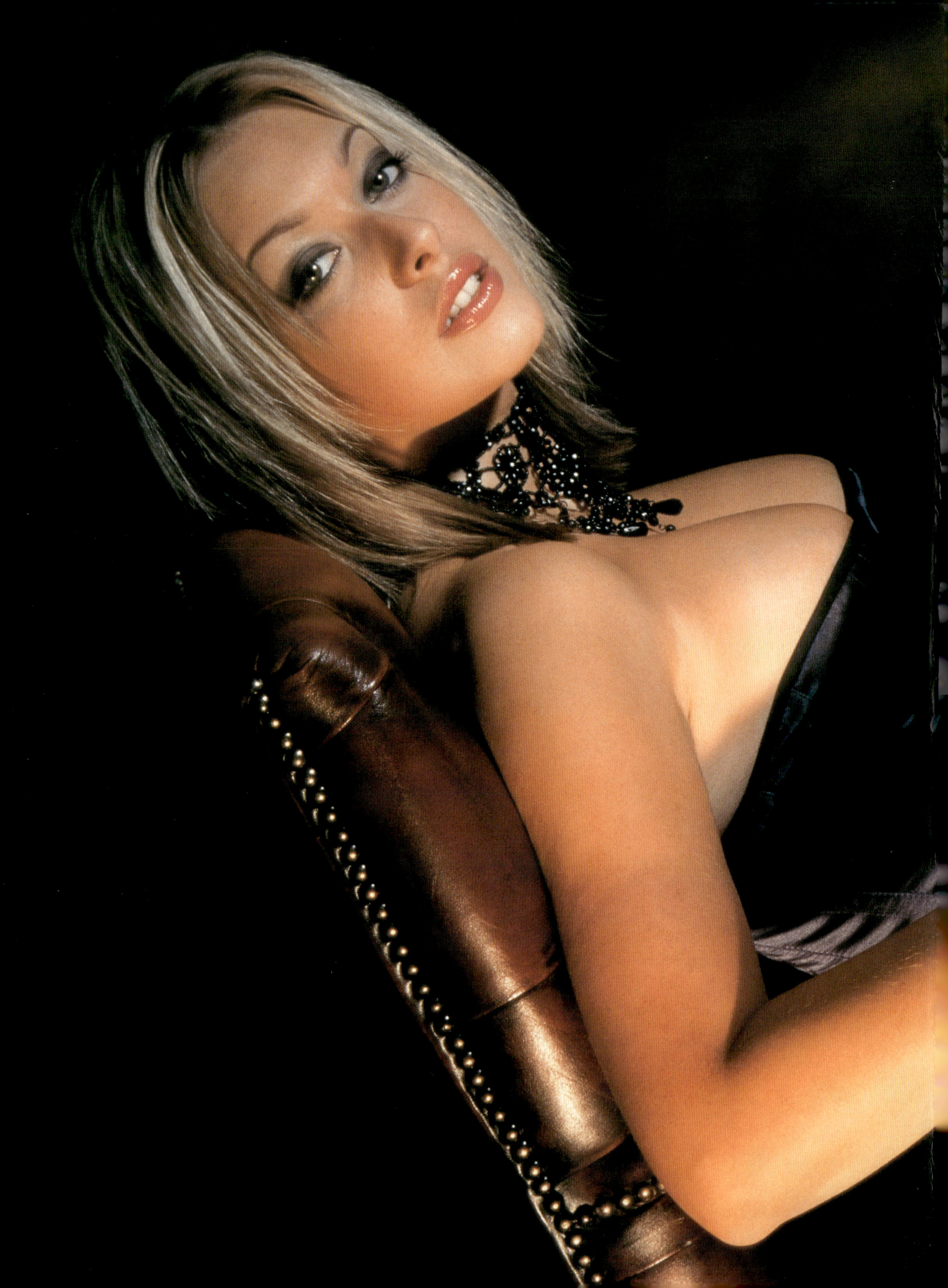

THE COMPLETE GUIDE TO BEAUTY & GLAMOUR PHOTOGRAPHY

Jon Gray

David & Charles

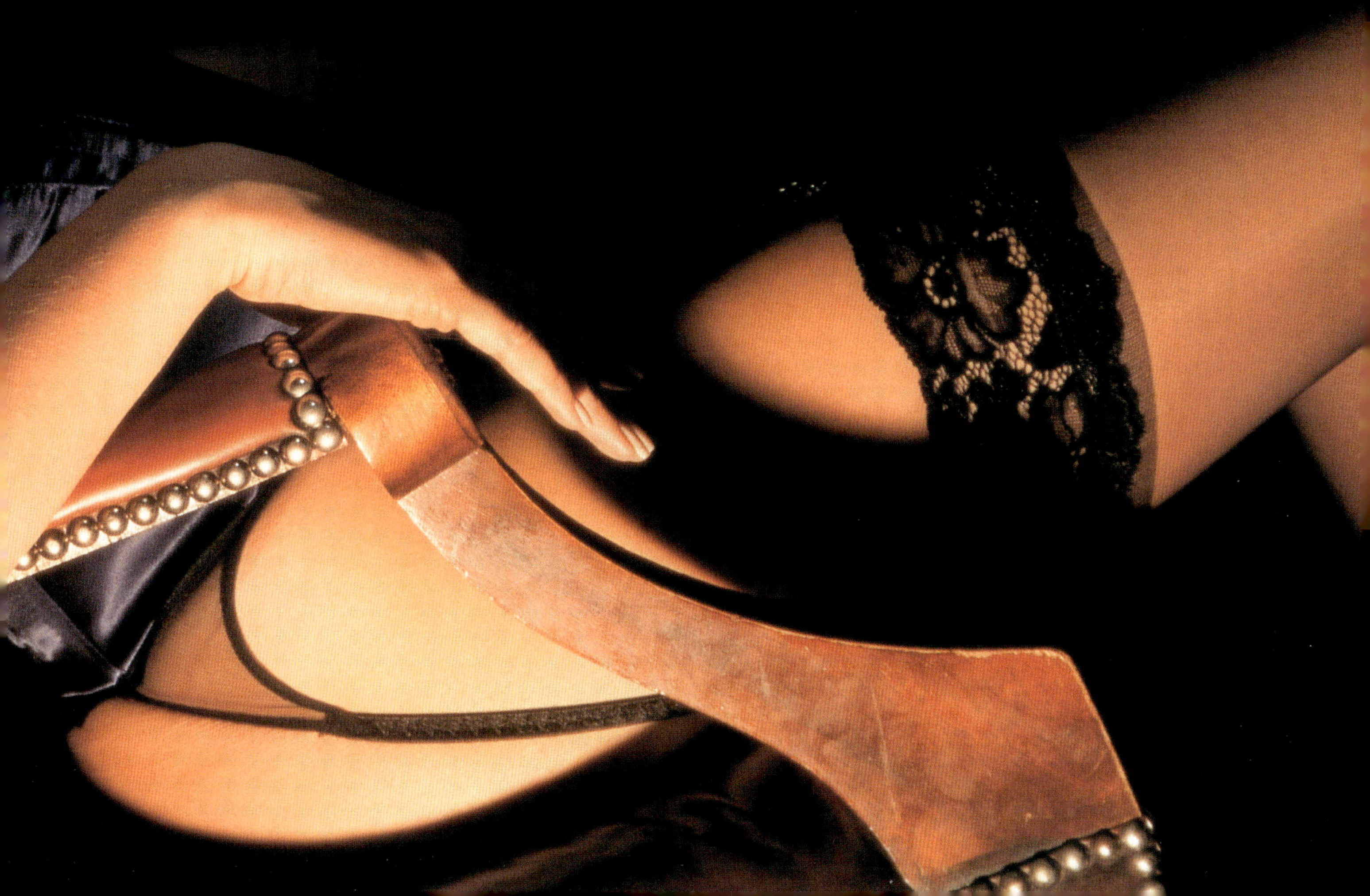

A DAVID & CHARLES BOOK

First published in the UK in 2003

Distributed in North America
by F&W Publications, Inc.
4700 East Galbraith Road
Cincinnati, OH 45236
1-800-289-0963

A catalogue record for this book is available from the British Library.

ISBN 0 7153 1404 1 hardback
ISBN 0 7153 1405 X paperback (USA only)

Printed in Hong Kong by
Dai Nippon Printing Co. Ltd
for David & Charles
Brunel House Newton Abbot Devon

Senior Editor Freya Dangerfield
Art Editor Sue Cleave
Project Editor Nicola Hodgson
Production Controller Kelly Smith

Visit our website at
www.davidandcharles.co.uk

David & Charles books are available from all good bookshops; alternatively you can contact our Orderline on (0)1626 334555 or write to us at FREEPOST EX2110, David & Charles *Direct*, Newton Abbot, TQ12 4ZZ (no stamp required UK mainland).

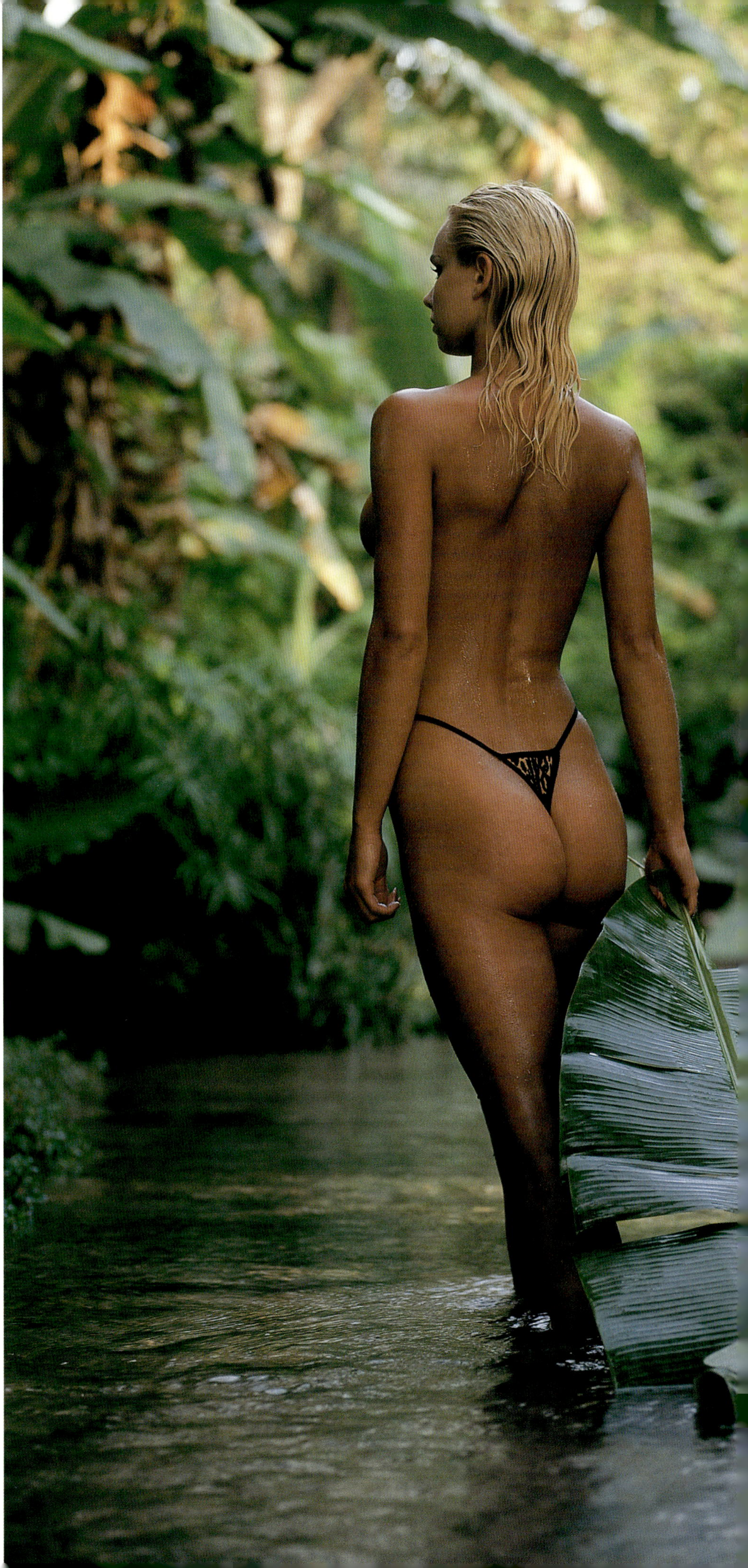

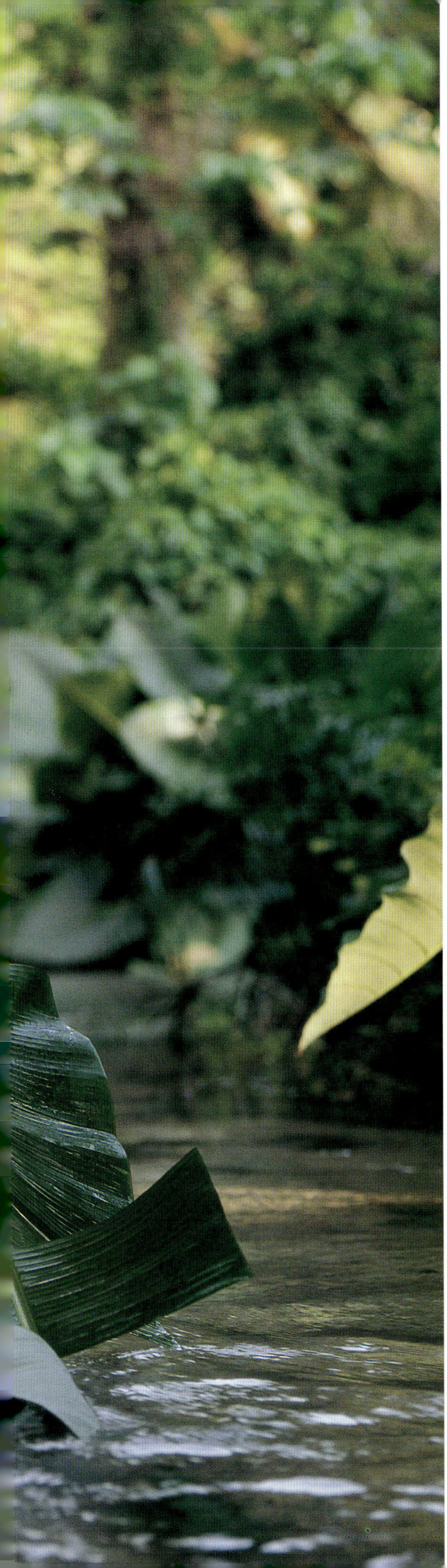

contents

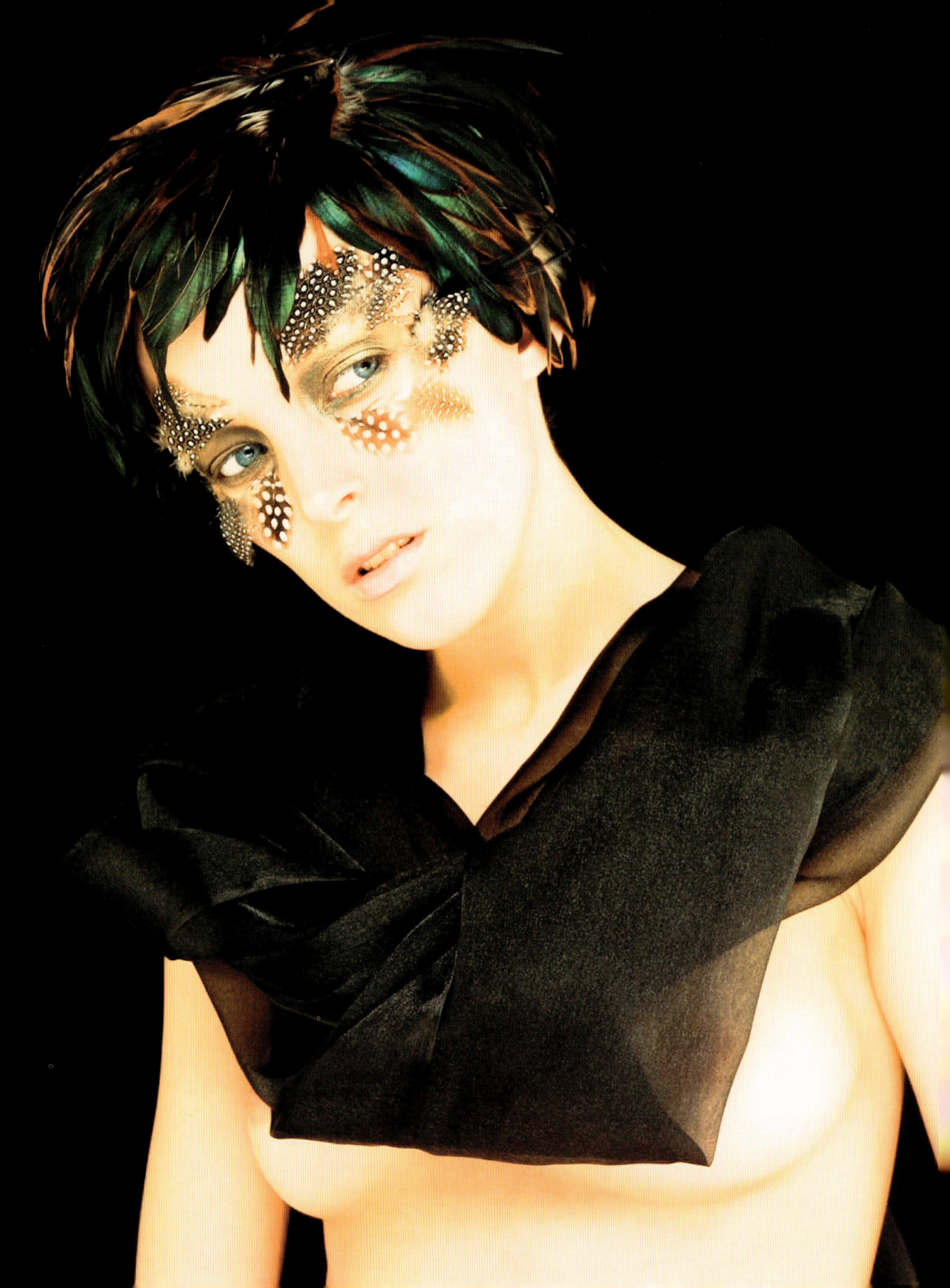

introduction

OPPOSITE: This creative portrait was taken as a test shot for a hairstyling company. The positioning of feathers on the face and in the hair was a lengthy, detailed process, but crucial to achieving the 'look' required by the client. The black material draped over the model's shoulders created a simple frame designed to emphasise the head further.
CANON D30; 100mm lens; 1/125 sec at f/8

Many would-be photographers have the illusion that being a photographer is a glamorous and lucrative way of life. My life as a beauty and glamour photographer has certainly given me the opportunity to work in many stunning locations around the world: Jamaica, Barbados, St Lucia, the United States, Brazil and Thailand among them, and it can be very rewarding – but make no mistake, it is always hard work. Take location shoots, for example: you may be working in beautiful surroundings, but you will also have to be up very early in the morning; keep everyone in your team – models, assistants, stylists, art directors – happy and motivated; and handle the complex logistics of how to get your equipment and your team to the location in good enough shape to achieve the images that your client wants.

There are thousands of things that can go wrong: you are vulnerable to the weather, even in tropical climates (I was once on a shoot in Jamaica where we caught the tail end of a hurricane that completely wrecked the beach where we wanted to shoot), models get sunburnt, people fall ill, equipment is stolen, you can even run into problems with local customs officials or the police because you need special permits to shoot in certain locations. However, when everything goes well – you achieve your goal with the minimum of hassle, the team works well together and you shoot strong images that the client is pleased with – it is all worthwhile.

The aim of this book

In putting this book together, I have tried to inspire and inform both the keen amateur photographer and the aspiring professional, using the experience I have gleaned in more than 25 years as a commercial glamour and beauty photographer. I have showcased a selection of my favourite images in the 'Portfolio' sections and explained the methods I used to create them. In each case, I discuss the equipment, the lighting set-up and other important factors, such as the commercial requirements for the image, or the particular challenges I faced to capture the shot. In some cases, I include 'before and after' examples and show the lighting set-up used. I also consider the essential tools of the trade of the professional glamour photographer – camera equipment, lights, backgrounds, props and special effects – and cover every aspect of a successful shoot, including composition, poses and working with models.

My aim has been to provide a useful guide to the equipment and techniques of glamour photography and examples of how I have put them into practice. There is plenty of practical information here that photographers of all standards should be able to put to good use and for the more serious enthusiast or aspiring professional, I hope I have provided lots of useful advice to help you take your photography as far as you want.

Making a start in professional photography

If you want to break into the world of professional photography, there is no substitute for possessing first-class technical skills. Only then would I advise that you start putting your portfolio together. The portfolio is your most important marketing tool and compiling it can be a time-consuming undertaking; I spent six months shooting non-stop in studios and on location to get mine together. It can also be expensive: ideally you should try to hire a photographic studio and work with professional models, as taking photographs in your living room using friends for subjects is unlikely to give you the calibre of shots that will get you taken seriously as a commercial photographer. Try contacting a good modelling agency to obtain models to build up a test-shot portfolio. Most will, of course, want payment, but it is possible to find models who will work for free if it means that they get test shots out of the session, in which case, they will require prints for their own portfolios. You may also want to think about hiring clothes and accessories, and using a make-up artist and hairstylist to obtain the necessary professional look to the shoot. You will also need to be aware of the photographic trends within your ideal market, whether these be *Vogue* magazine or the latest glamour calendars. Your portfolio should reflect these fashions and also show a wide range of styles to prove that you are versatile and creative.

Once you have your portfolio together, you can use your work to try to win a commission from a commercial client. Having a composite business card printed that displays samples of your work as well as your contact details is a good idea. When trying to identify potential clients, it is important to research them thoroughly and be sure that your images are appropriate for their needs – there is no point showing a range of glamour portfolio pictures to an advertising agency who don't have any glamour clients; and there is no point showing a client studio-based work if they exclusively use location pictures. Finally, when you have identified potential clients, make sure that you make contact with the right person within that company before you make an appointment to see them; it is easy to waste your time showing your portfolio to a person who is not directly responsible for commissioning photographers.

Whether it is your hobby or your profession, there are times when beauty and glamour photography can be a very challenging occupation. But when everything works out, it can also be a very rewarding one – seeing an image of mine blown up to the size of a billboard is very satisfying. But if you want your images to appear 15 metres (49 feet) high, then one thing is for sure: they had better be good ones in the first place.

OPPOSITE: This image was commissioned as a stock calendar shot. It was taken at 3p.m., and I used a little fill-in flash and a reflector to bounce more light into the image. The bright blue inflatable ring adds some vivid colour that helps to strengthen the overall image.
Mamiya RZ 6/7cm; 1/125 sec at f/16; 110mm lens; Fuji Provia 100

BELOW: This image was shot for a lingerie company who sell product on the internet. The poster was actually located near the MI5 building in London, and was subsequently reviewed in the press for being somewhat *risque*!
Mamiya RZ 6/7cm; 1/125 sec at f/16; 150mm lens; Fuji Provia 100

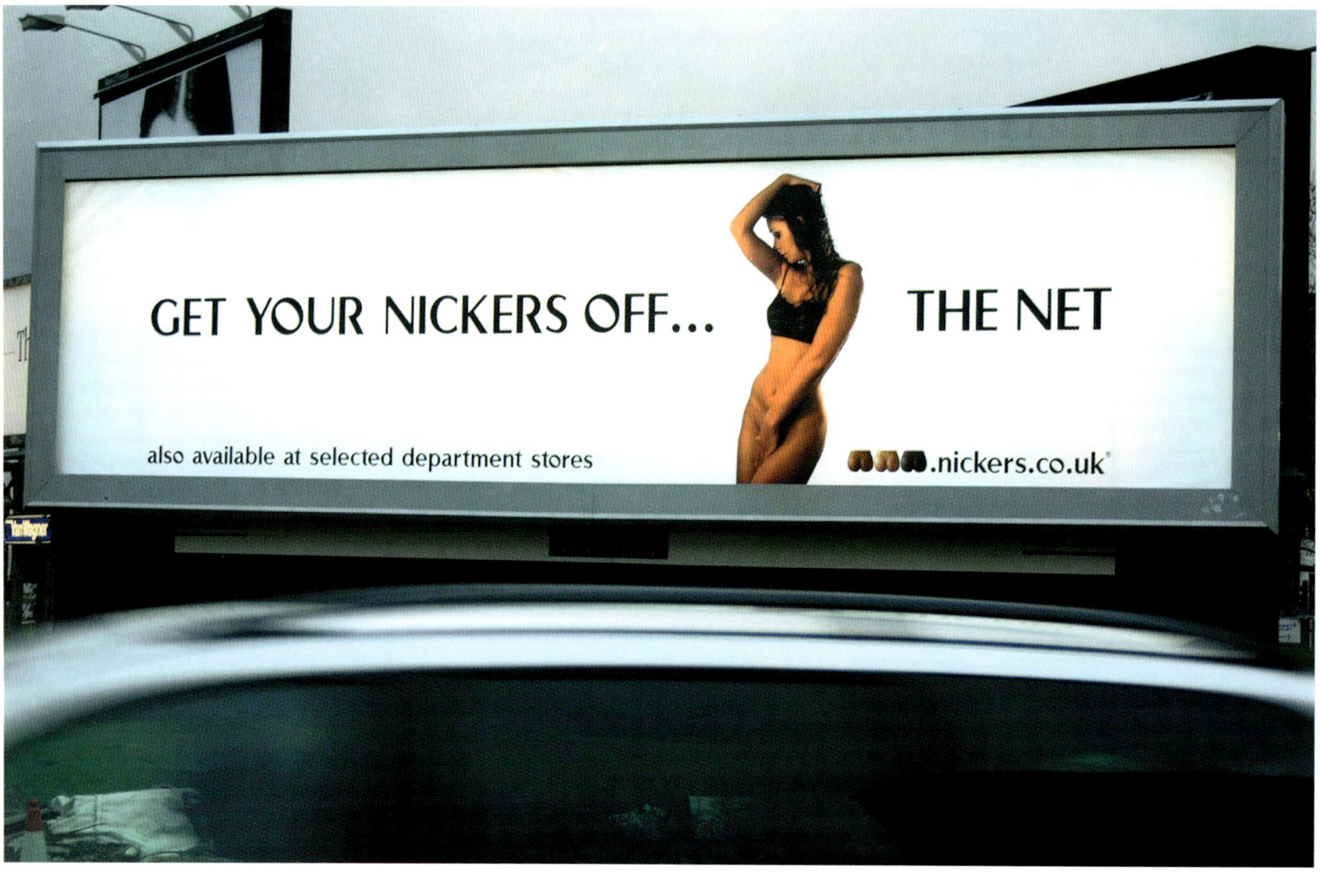

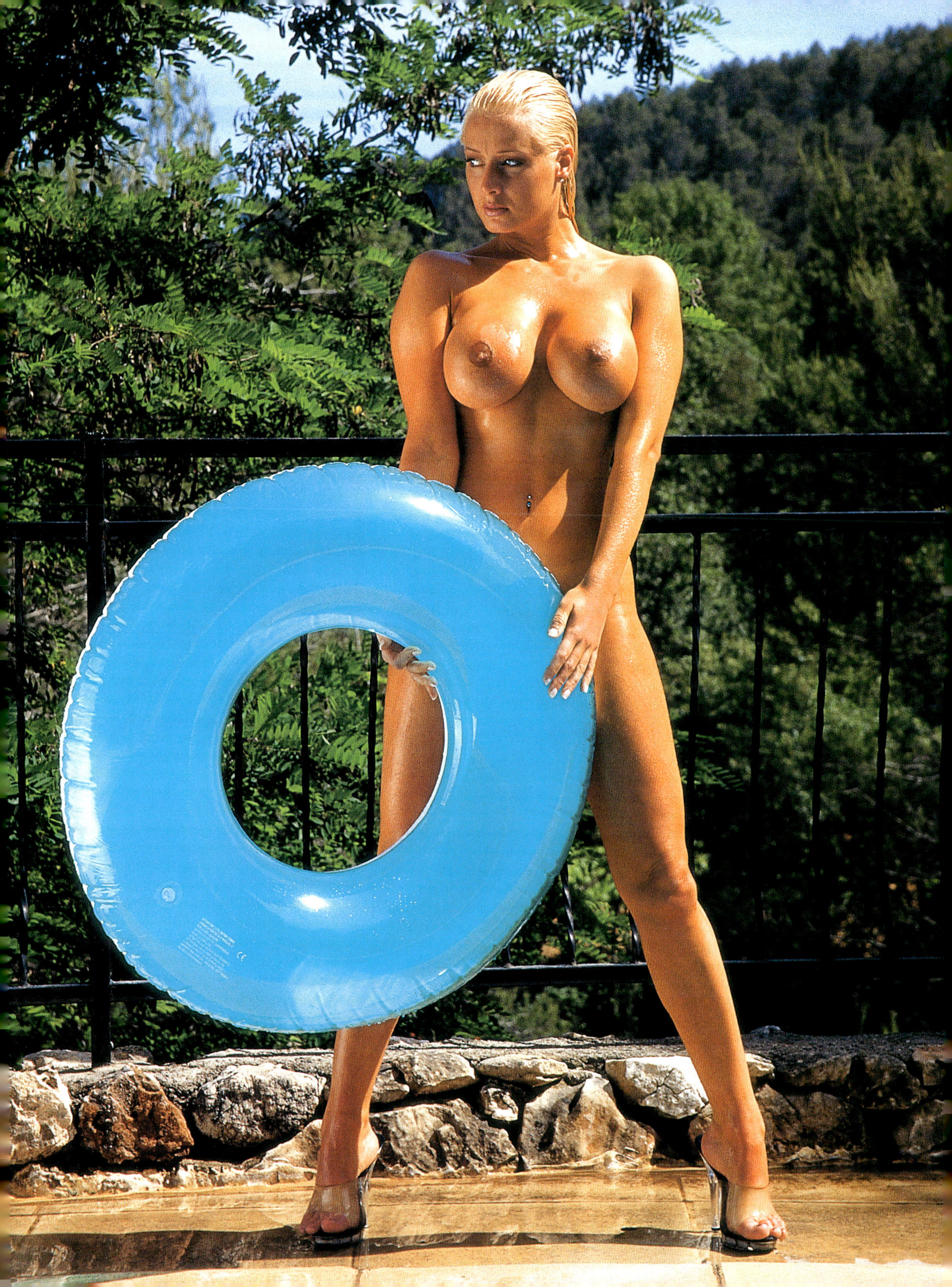

equipment

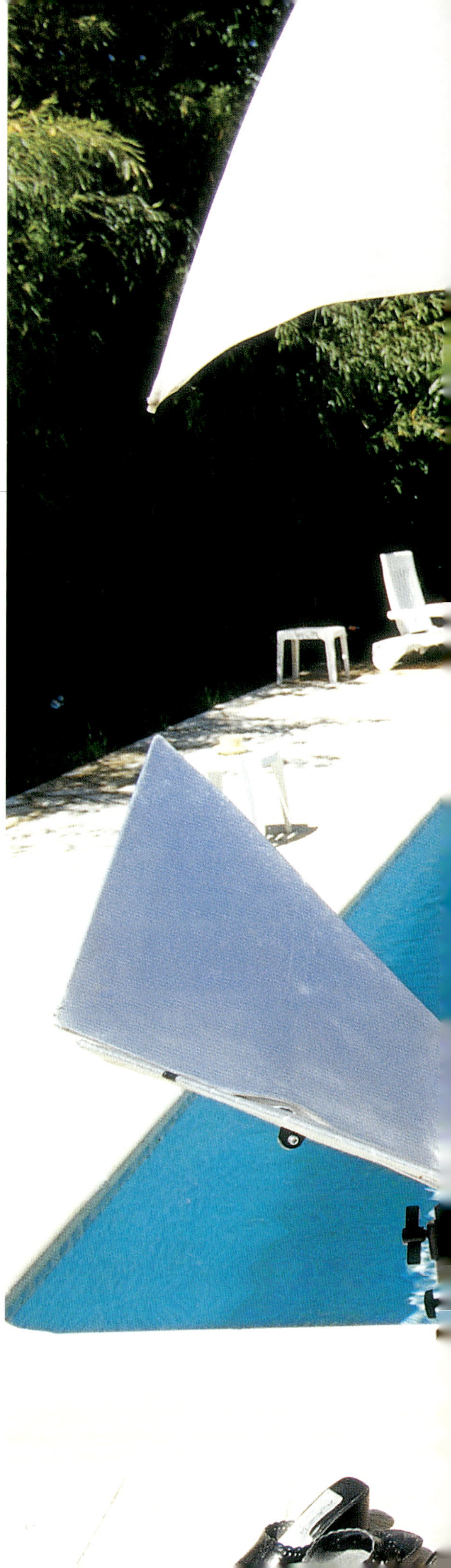

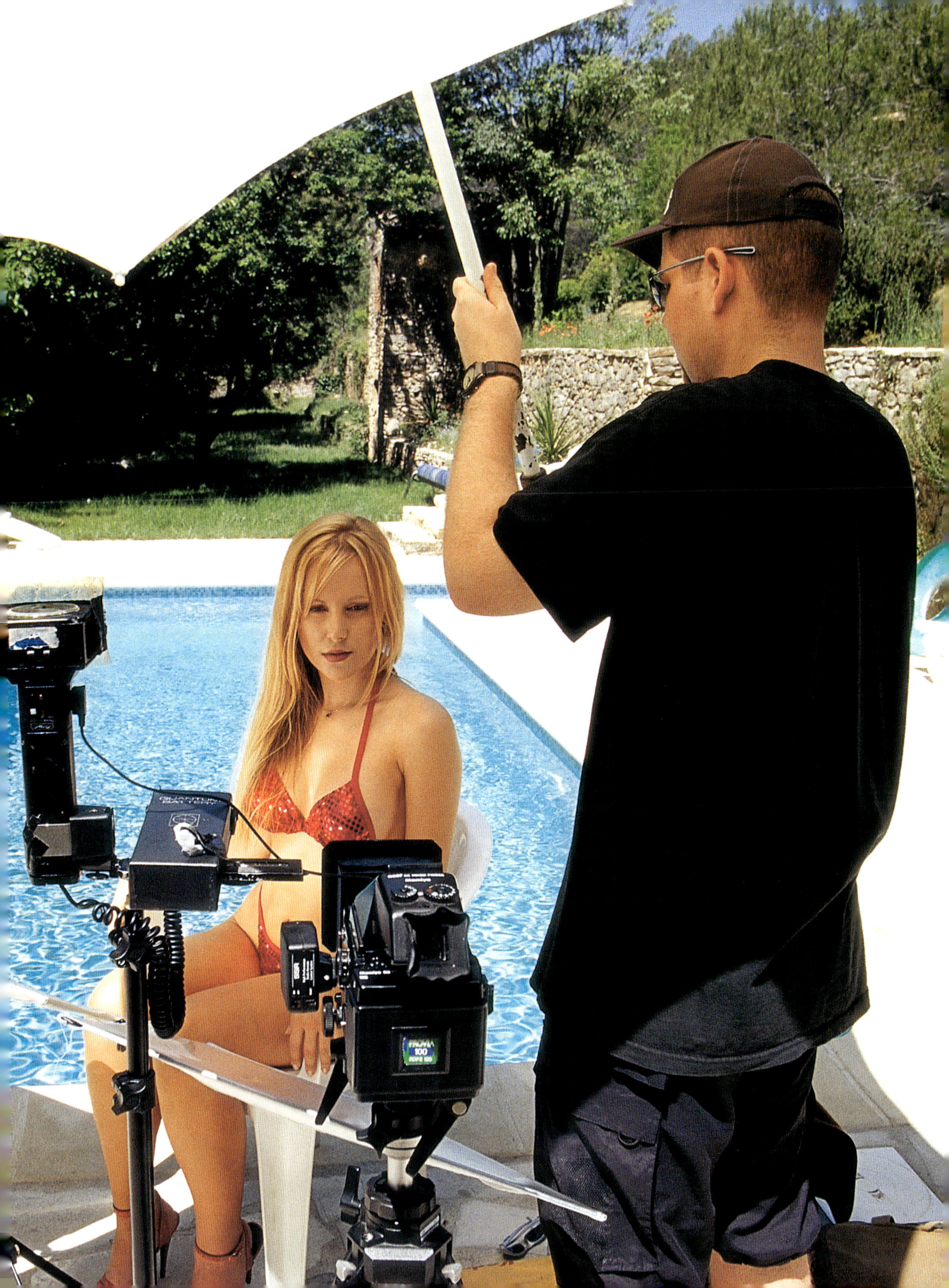
PROVIA
100

Cameras and formats

The choice of what camera to use is an important consideration for any photographer, whether amateur or professional. When I was starting out as a photographer, professional cameras such as the ones used by the likes of Terence Donovan and David Bailey were very expensive and completely out of my price range. I used to beg and borrow cameras from the photographers for whom I worked as an assistant until I could afford one of my own. Now cameras are more affordable, and the second-hand market is particularly competitive, partly because a lot of people are trading in their film cameras to switch over to digital.

Other factors to consider when choosing a camera are the cost and the quality of the lenses that go with that camera. Enthusiastic amateurs should be aware that you need to have a good range of lenses if, for example, you want to start experimenting with shooting exteriors.

35mm

Most amateur photographers start with a 35mm camera, which is a good choice for several reasons. 35mm cameras are cheaper than medium- and large-format cameras; they are easy to handle, portable and easy to manipulate. It is

OPPOSITE: This image was taken on a medium-format (6 x 7cm) camera. This format allows for good-quality enlargements – this image has been blown up 370 per cent without noticeable loss of quality or sharpness. **Mamiya RZ 6/7cm; 1/125 sec at f/16; 110mm lens; Fuji Provia 100**

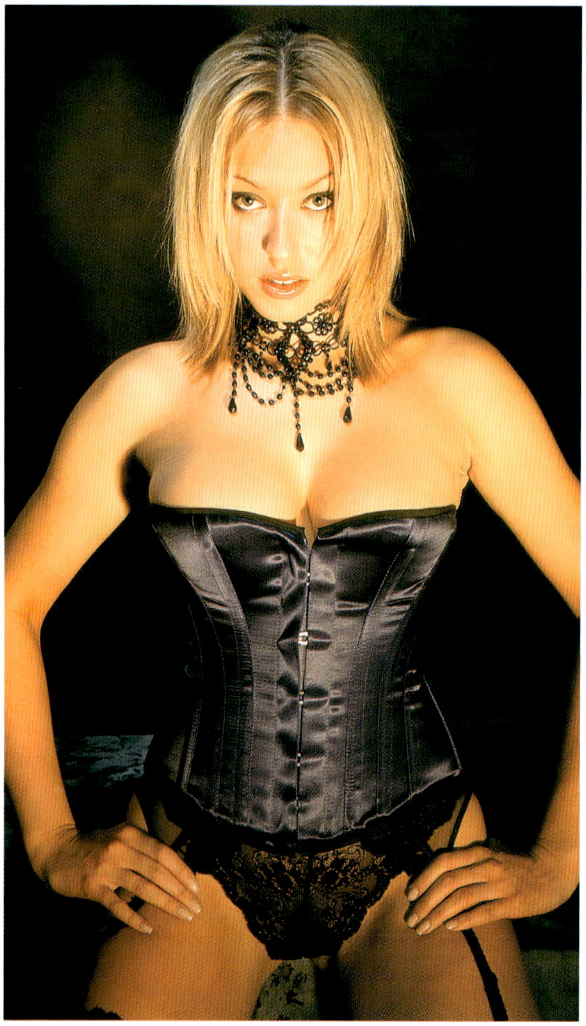

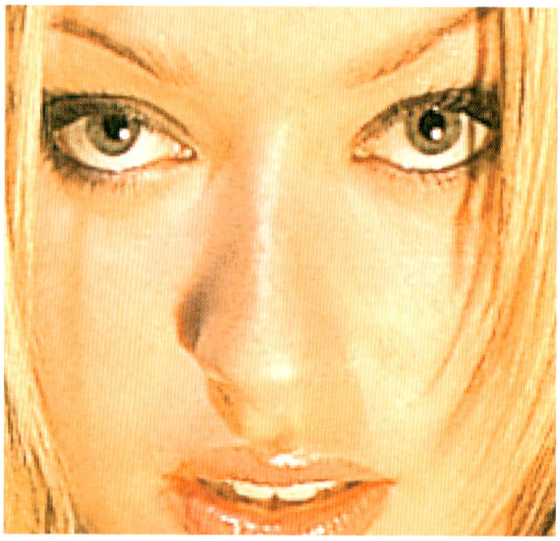

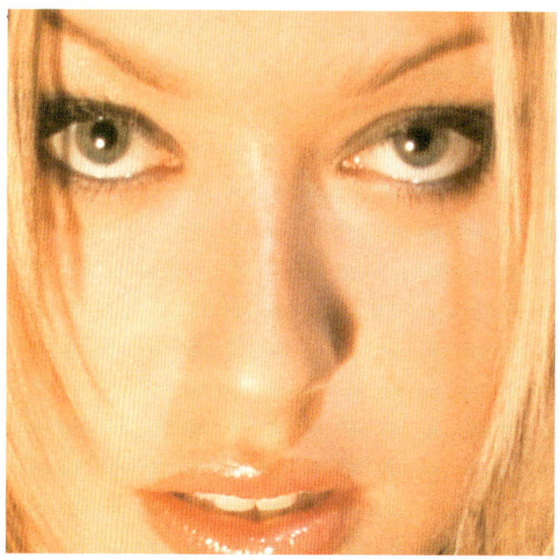

FAR LEFT: This shot was taken on 35mm and enlarged 370 per cent. **Canon EOS; 1/125 sec at f/16; 110mm lens; Fuji Provia 100**

LEFT: Using medium format (as seen in the lower picture) gives you more scope with picture editing. Although the grain structure is noticeable in the enlargement, the loss of quality is limited. Editing 35mm (shown in the upper picture) in the same way produces an unsatisfactory and grainy image. **Mamiya RZ 6/7cm; 1/125 sec at f/16; 110mm lens; Fuji Provia 100**

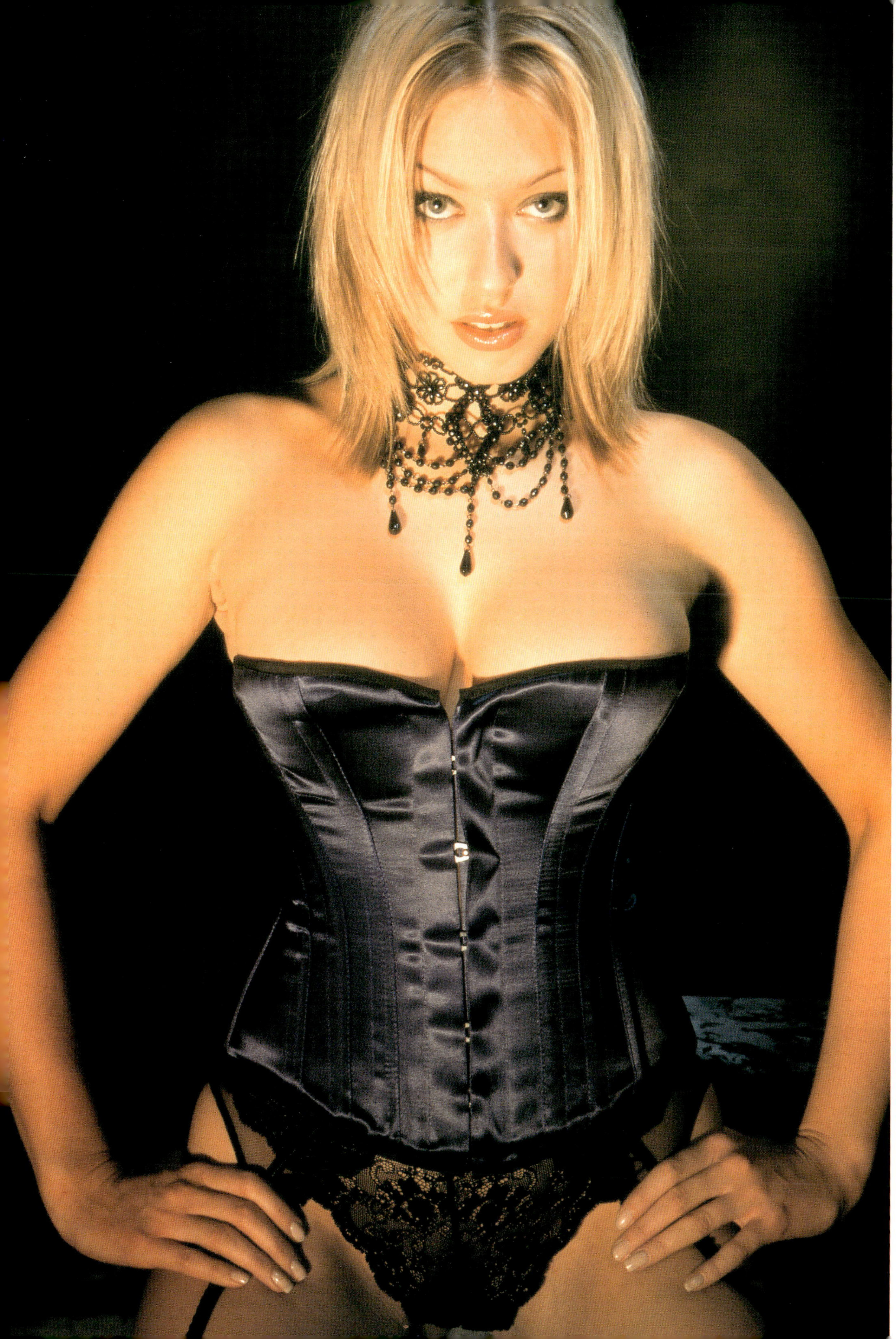

also possible to produce more animated images on 35mm because the cameras come with auto-focus, which is a huge advantage for action shots. Sports and high-fashion photographers (shooting catwalk shows, for example) use 35mm to great effect. Another advantage with this format is that you get more film in your camera and you can shoot around five frames per second.

One drawback of the 35mm format in the commercial context is that your options are limited when it comes to editing pictures. If you like a certain section of your image and want to blow it up, it will tend to look grainy.

Medium format

Medium-format cameras (6 x 4.5cm or 6 x 7cm) are the preferred option for professional photographers. For commercial purposes, the larger the format of camera that you use, the better the quality of image you will obtain at finished reproduction (that is, when the picture is reproduced in magazines, calendars, etc). Larger-format cameras produce larger negatives or transparencies, and pictures printed from these can be blown up to large sizes with little loss of sharpness of image detail.

Medium format is sometimes called the 'ideal format', because the size of negatives or transparencies used is in the proportion that fits most clients' requirements for vertical or horizontal rectangular images that can be comfortably blown up and reproduced on an A4 page, without loss of quality. Picture editing is also easier with medium format than with 35mm – because the film size is larger, it is easier to crop out parts and blow them up or manipulate them without notable loss of quality.

Another advantage for the professional photographer using medium-format cameras is that you can use a Polaroid adaptor with them. Taking Polaroid tests is a useful guideline to the lighting, exposure, camera angle and view of the subject before you take the real shot. It helps to prevent you making errors, and, if the client is on the shoot with you, he or she can see the test shot to give any feedback. It is possible to obtain Polaroid adaptors for 35mm cameras, but the adaptors are expensive and the resulting Polaroids are so small that they are not particularly useful in serious applications.

On the downside, medium-format cameras are, as one might expect, more expensive than smaller-format ones. They are also heavier and more cumbersome, and it is usually best to use them with a tripod to reduce camera shake, which makes it harder to take spontaneous shots.

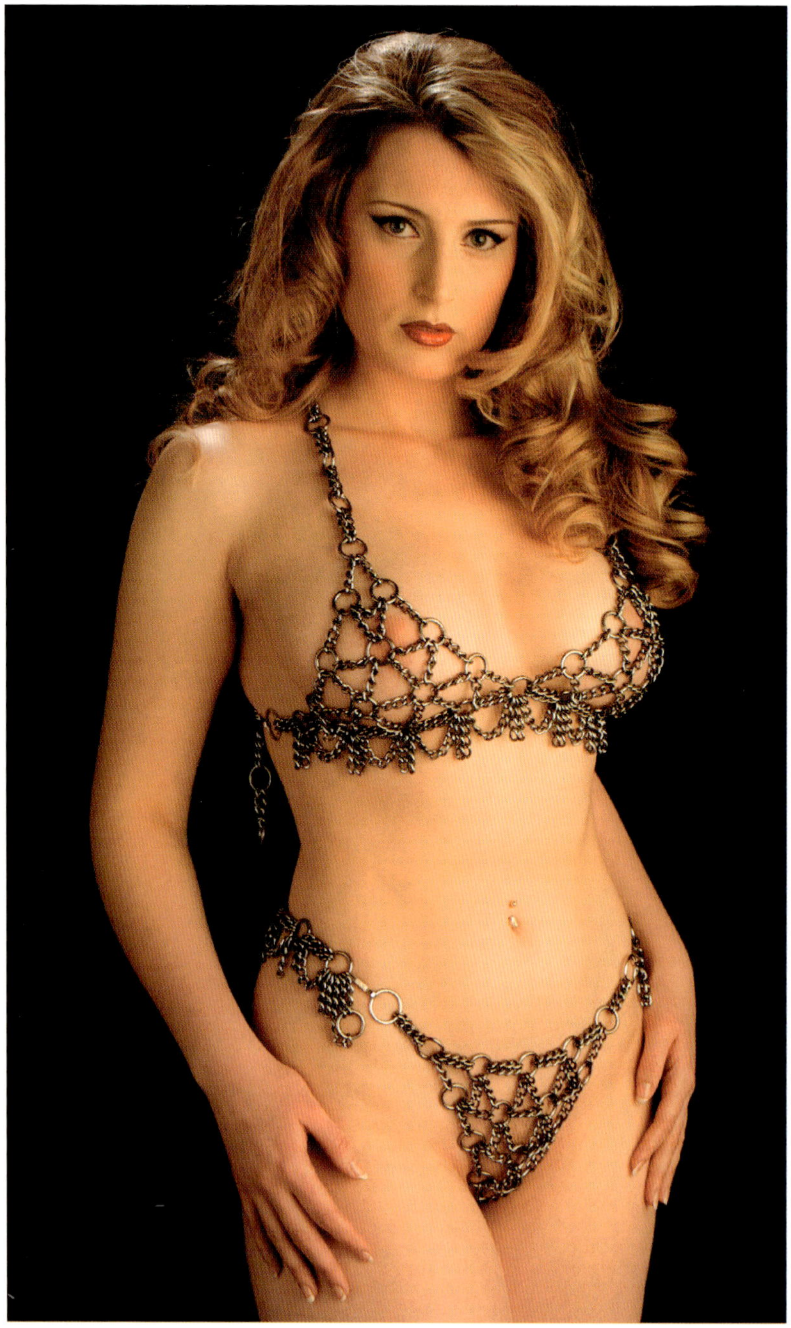

ABOVE AND OPPOSITE: Here, the subject has been shot on medium-format (opposite above) and digital 35mm (above) cameras. Below opposite, the digital image (right) pixellates when a detail is blown up, while medium-format film (far right) retains its quality.
ABOVE: Mamiya RZ 6/7cm; 1/125 sec at f/16; 110mm lens; Fuji Provia 100
OPPOSITE: Canon D30; 1/125 sec at f/16

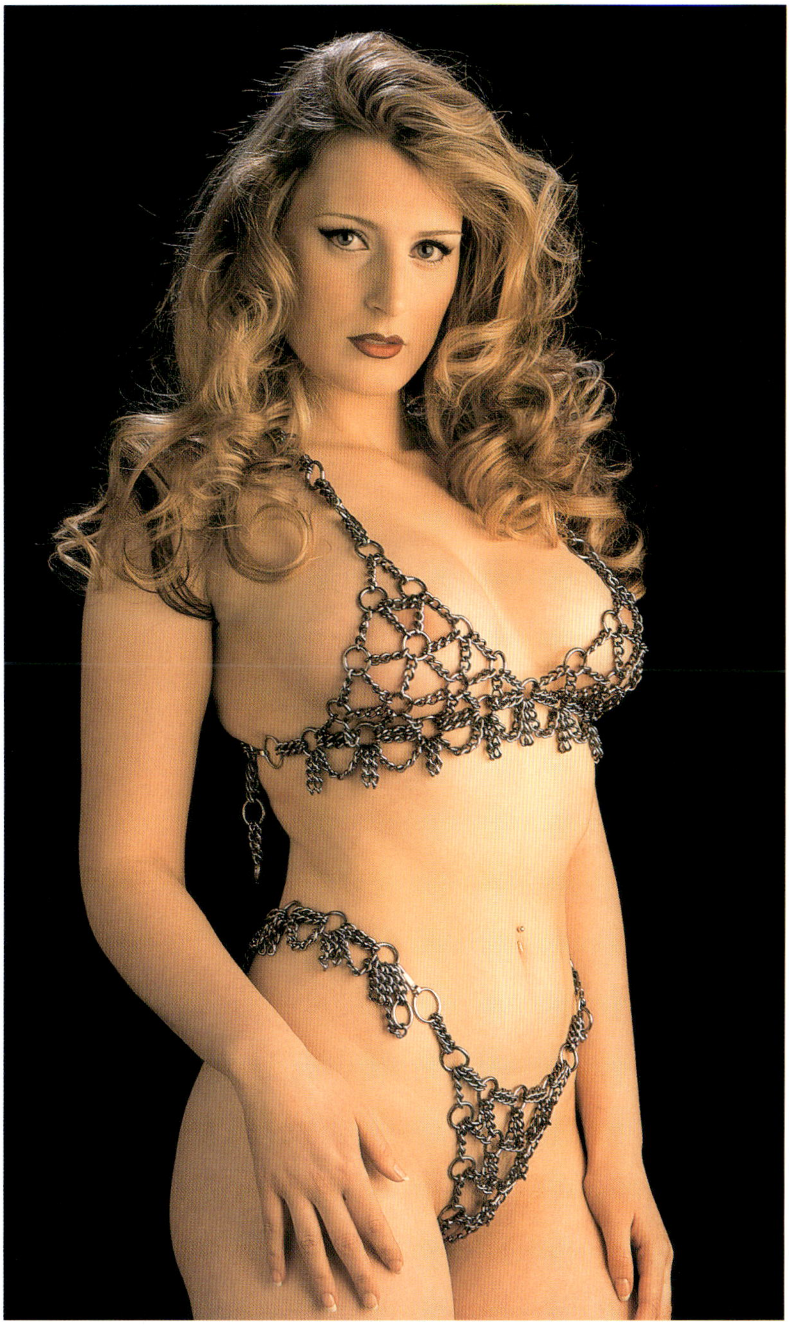

Large format

Large-format cameras are most commonly used for shooting products for top-end advertising clients. You need to use large format in these cases in order to correct the perspective of your image and keep everything in proportion (smaller-format cameras tend to have fixed film planes). If your camera angle is slightly higher or lower than the subject that you are shooting, the nearest point of the subject will appear larger than the furthest point, giving the impression that the image is distorted, a phenomenon known as converging verticals. Large-format cameras have manoeuvrable or swing lens and film planes that correct this distortion.

Using large format (negatives can be 4 x 5in) means that it is possible to blow images up to very large sizes – an important consideration for clients producing posters or billboards.

Large format is only occasionally used for glamour photography – the picture on page 122 is a rare exception. This image needed to be shot on large format because it was intended to be reproduced poster-size, and using medium format would not have produced an image of sufficient quality to be reproduced at this size.

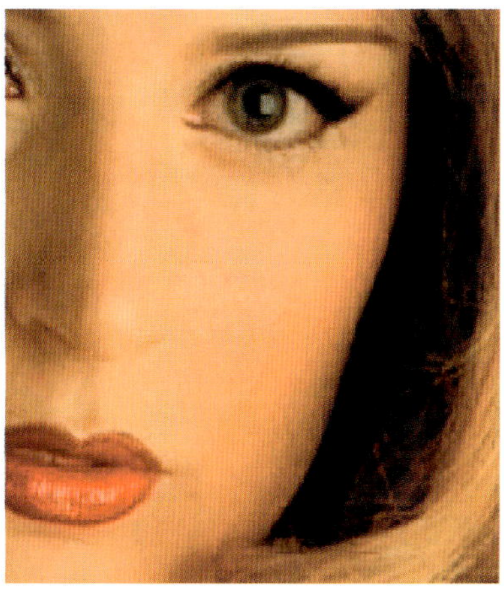

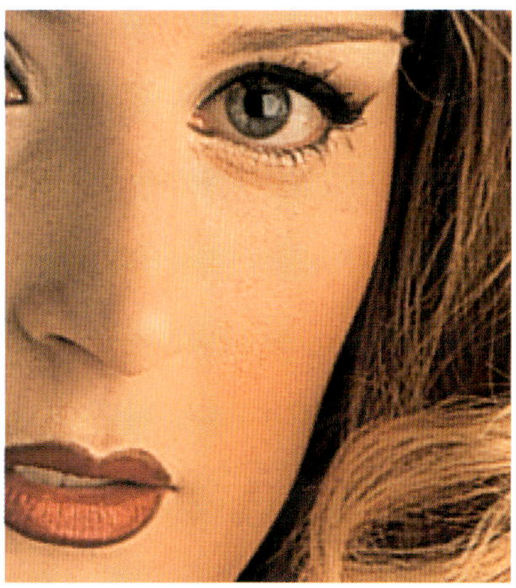

Digital

Digital cameras are here to stay; however, in my opinion they are in their infancy and have some way to go to match the quality of traditional film.

The professional glamour market is still dominated by photographers shooting on conventional film, since clients have not been totally convinced that digital photography is capable of delivering images of acceptable quality. At the same time, clients producing advertising and catalogues are using digital more and more often because of its convenience.

Digital offers many advantages to the amateur photographer, not least the fact that there are no film-processing costs. It is also easier to learn basic photographic skills on digital cameras because you have instant feedback: you can see your image immediately and reshoot if required.

Lenses and filters

Photographers use different lenses in different circumstances – photographing people requires using a different focal length lens than when photographing wildlife or landscapes, for example. The longer the focal length of a lens, the less depth of field; the shorter the focal length of lens, the more depth of field. This has important implications when you are shooting portraits – and glamour, beauty and fashion shots are all essentially aspects of portrait photography – you have to choose the appropriate lens to avoid distortion.

Wide-angle lenses

Wide-angle lenses include 24mm, 28mm and 35mm lenses: wider ones than these are obtainable, but they are moving into the range of fisheye lenses. Wide-angle lenses give a large depth of field and are primarily used for landscapes, interiors (where you want to photograph a whole room, for example) and large groups of people. Such lenses are not really suitable for taking portraits of individuals because they distort the features; the lens 'spreads' the image, making the subject's features appear wider.

50mm and 80mm lenses

The 50mm lens is often thought of as the standard lens, and is considered to give you what the eye sees. Beginners tend to start off with a 50mm lens because they are versatile: you can use it for landscapes and buildings, for example, as well as photographing people. 50mm lenses can also be used for full-length or three-quarter-length portraits, but if you come in any closer to the subject and attempt to do a head shot, then you will create some distortion in the features (although the distortion will not be as apparent as when using a wide-angle lens).

80mm lenses can also be used for portraits, particularly for three-quarter-length poses.

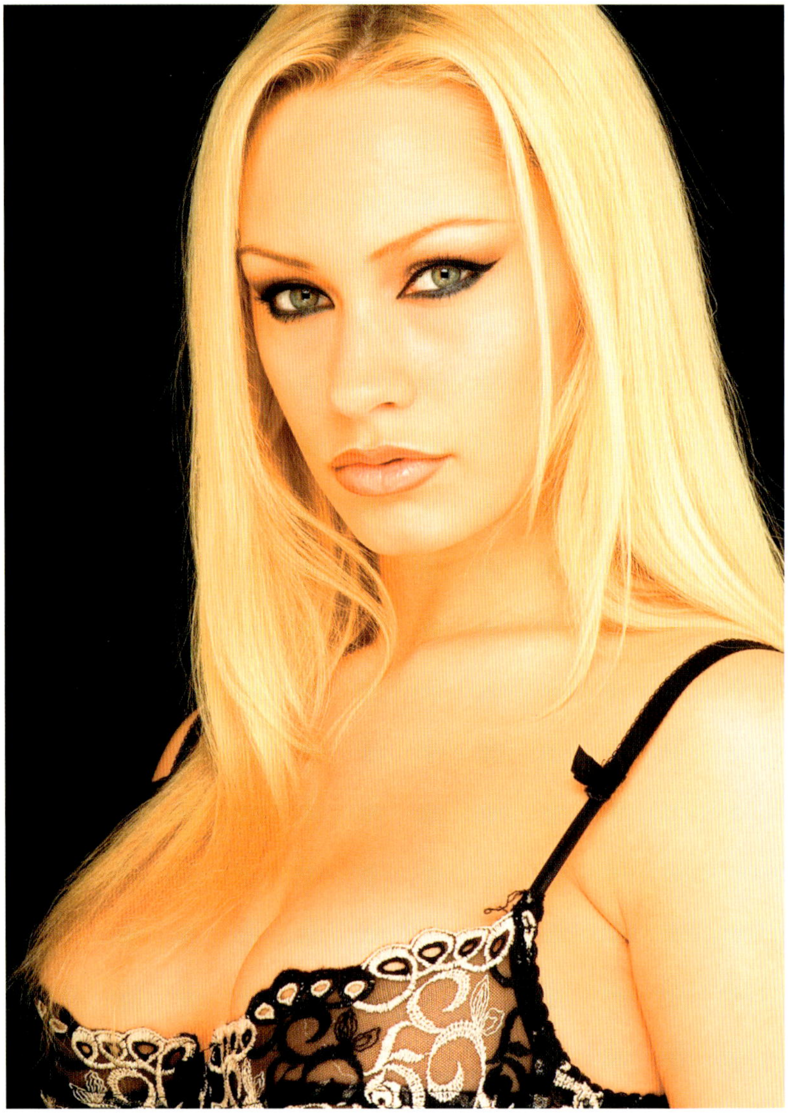

ABOVE: This image was taken with a softbox suspended on a boom above the model and a triflector positioned under her face to reflect light back on it. The use of a 100mm lens gives the correct proportions to the facial features. **Canon D30; 1/125 sec at f/11; 100mm lens**

Longer lenses

100mm lenses are the most commonly used fixed lenses for portraits and for three-quarter-length poses, because they give the correct proportions to the subject's facial features.

It is also possible to use longer lenses, but the camera needs to be sufficiently far from the subject to correct distortion. For location shoots I often use 150mm and 250mm lenses on my Mamiya RZ 6/7cm camera. These lenses are useful for capturing your subject against a background –

BELOW: The top image was taken with a 50mm lens, which creates a slight distortion: the model's forehead is widened. The bottom image was taken with a 35mm lens, and the distortion here is more apparent in the model's face and body.
Canon D30; 1/125 sec at f/11; TOP: 100mm lens; BOTTOM: 50mm lens

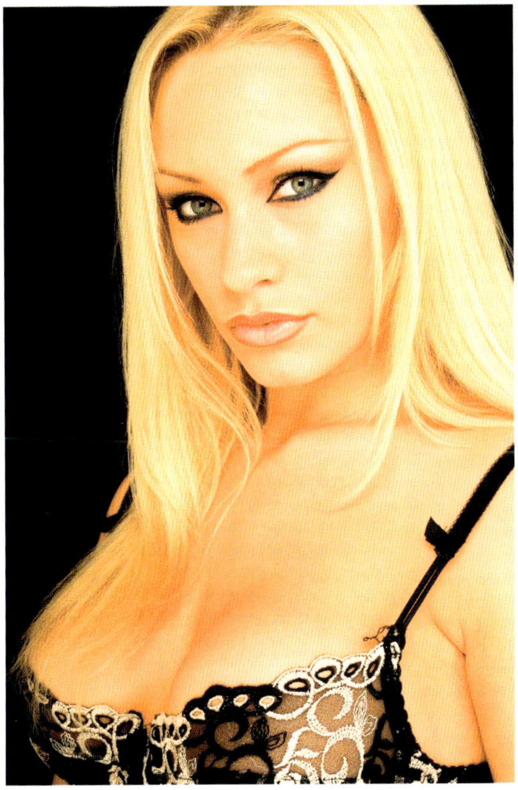

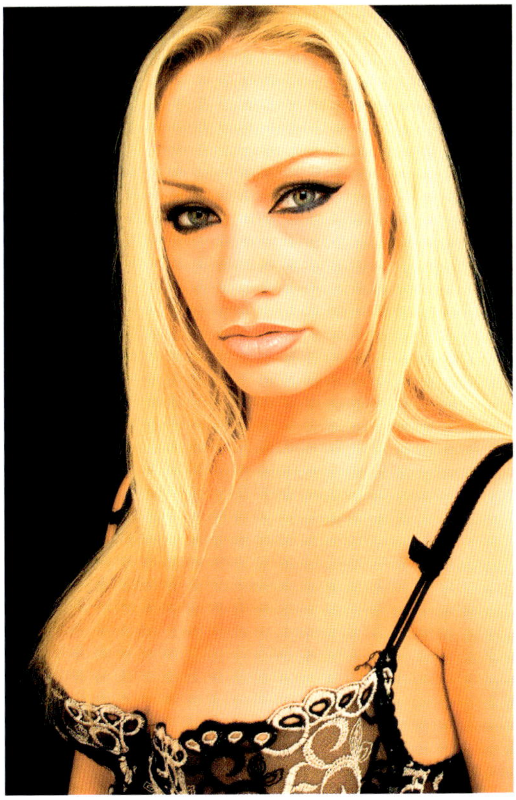

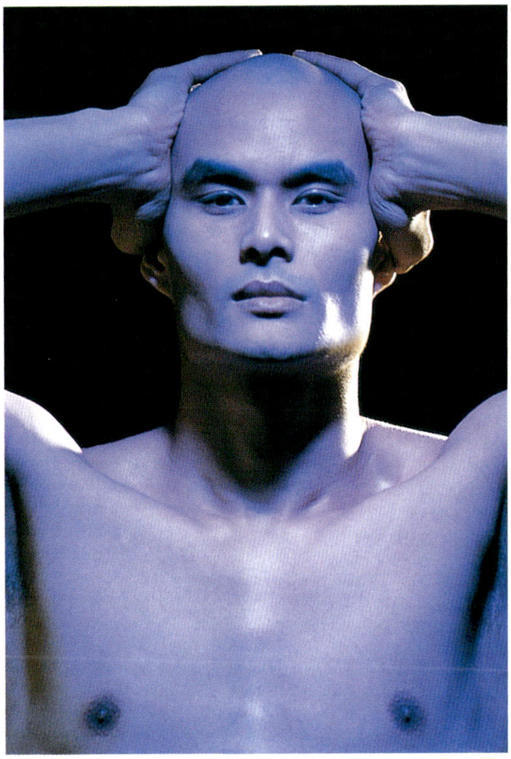

LEFT: I shot this image using a blue gel on a honeycomb attachment, which was suspended on a boom above the model. I used a salmon-pink gel on another honeycomb at an acute angle to the right of the model to create some highlights in the image.
Mamiya RZ 6/7cm; 1/125 sec at f/8; 150mm lens; Fuji Provia 100

the longer lenses have less depth of field and the background is therefore out of focus, throwing more attention onto the model.

Filters and gels

Coloured filters and gels are pieces of equipment that enable you to adjust the lighting effect on your subject to create more mood and atmosphere. Filters are attached to lenses, and gels to lights.

In glamour and beauty photography, warm-up filters are often used to warm up and improve a model's skin tones, particularly if a model has very pale skin. There are three strengths of filter – light, medium and strong – depending on how much the subject's skin tones need to be deepened.

Coloured gels can be used for different purposes. Using a warm pink filter, for example, can help to breathe some life into dark or black hair, which can otherwise look like a solid black mass. Blue gels help to enhance atmosphere and create a cool, moody or mysterious ambience.

A wide range of special-effects filters is available. I often use grad filters on location, as they are useful for brightening up skies. Other effects filters include multi-image and split-field filters.

Film

There are three main types of film: colour transparency (known as slide film), colour negative and black-and-white negative. It is possible to obtain black-and-white transparency film, but this is rarely used nowadays. Most of the film that I shoot is colour transparency, and it is accepted practice in commercial photography to use transparency film because of reproduction factors: reproducing from a tranny means that you are using a first-generation image, and you therefore optimize the quality of that image. However, amateur photographers tend to shoot negative film for prints rather than transparency film. It is cheaper to buy and cheaper to process – you can simply take it to a high-street processing lab.

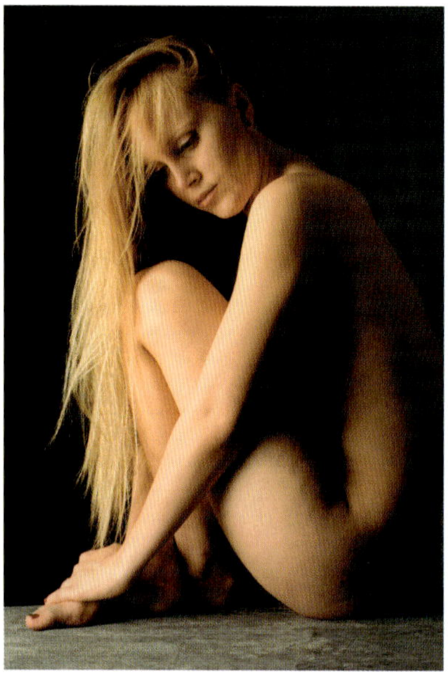

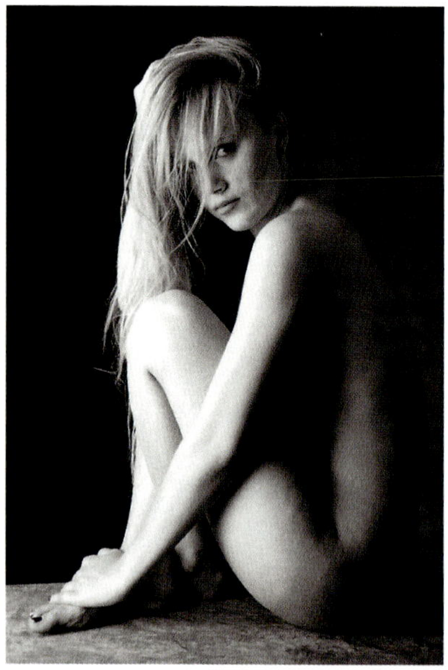

ABOVE: This shot works equally well in colour and in black and white. Successful black-and-white shots need to be contrasty and atmospheric.
Mamiya RZ 6/7cm; 1/125 sec at f/16; 110mm lens; LEFT: Fuji Provia 100 RIGHT: T-Max 100

ISO rating

Selecting the speed of your film is an important consideration. The lower the ISO of the film (that is, the slower the film), the better the quality of reproduction. Lower ISO films have a smaller, finer grain structure which means that you will obtain a sharper, more detailed image and a better quality of enlargement. Film speeds range from 25 ISO up to 6400 ISO. The higher-rated films are for use in lower-light conditions; for example, shooting a pop band on stage. You would need to use a higher ISO film in such a setting to get a reasonable shutter speed and aperture because the available light would be dim.

I usually employ 100 ISO film for beauty and glamour work, especially in a studio setting. I occasionally use higher-grain film for special effects: for example, the shot on page 119 was taken with 1000 ISO film because I wanted to create a more grainy, moody image.

Black-and-white film

Black-and-white photography is having a resurgence in glamour photography because its effects are more striking and more unusual than colour images, and some images have far more impact when shot in black and white than in colour. You also have the option to be more creative with your lighting when using black-and-white film; you can light more for mood and contrast. Black-and-white shots tend to be successful when they feature strong outlines, so experiment with the model's poses to create strong, graphic shapes.

Cross-processing

Cross-processing was developed in the 1970s – by accident – and involves processing colour transparency film in the C41 process originally designed for colour negative films. The technique results in the breakdown of the colour balance in the film emulsion, in the process creating green and magenta colour saturation.

This technique was embraced by the pop and fashion industries because of its striking and quirky results. The process is hard to control precisely, and the results are therefore somewhat unpredictable. It is worth experimenting with, however, because it can be highly unusual and effective.

OPPOSITE: The main image shows the striking results that can be obtained by cross-processing: the skin tones are bleached out and the colours are saturated. The inset picture shows the image processed normally.
Canon EOS 5; 1/125 sec at f/11; 100mm lens; Fuji Provia 100F

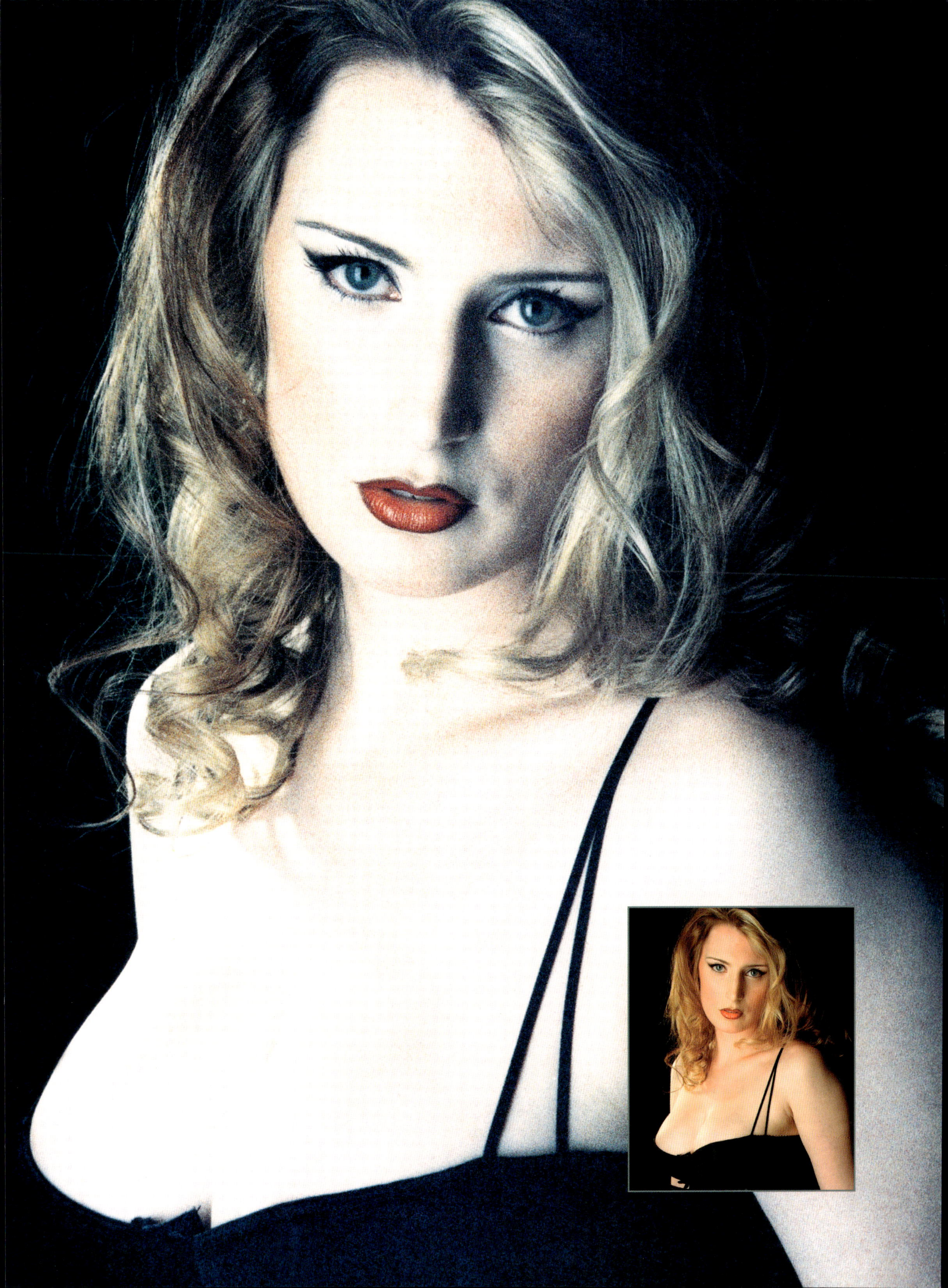

Lighting

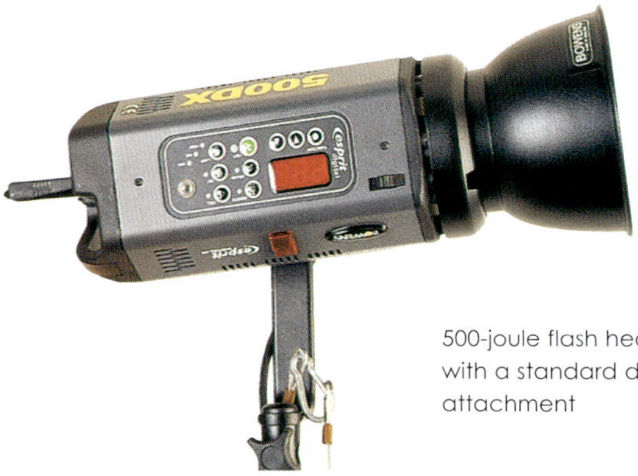

500-joule flash head with a standard dish attachment

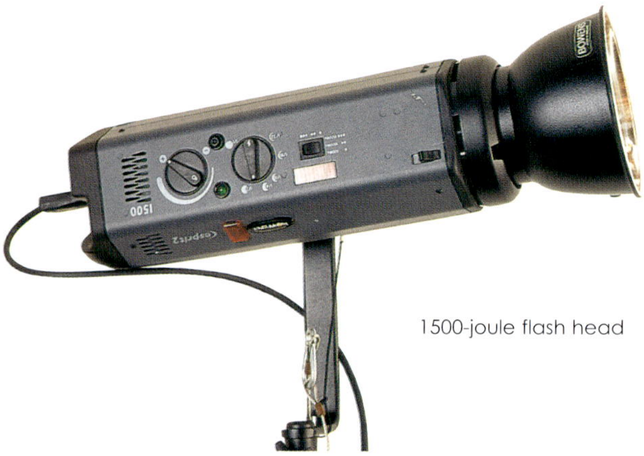

1500-joule flash head

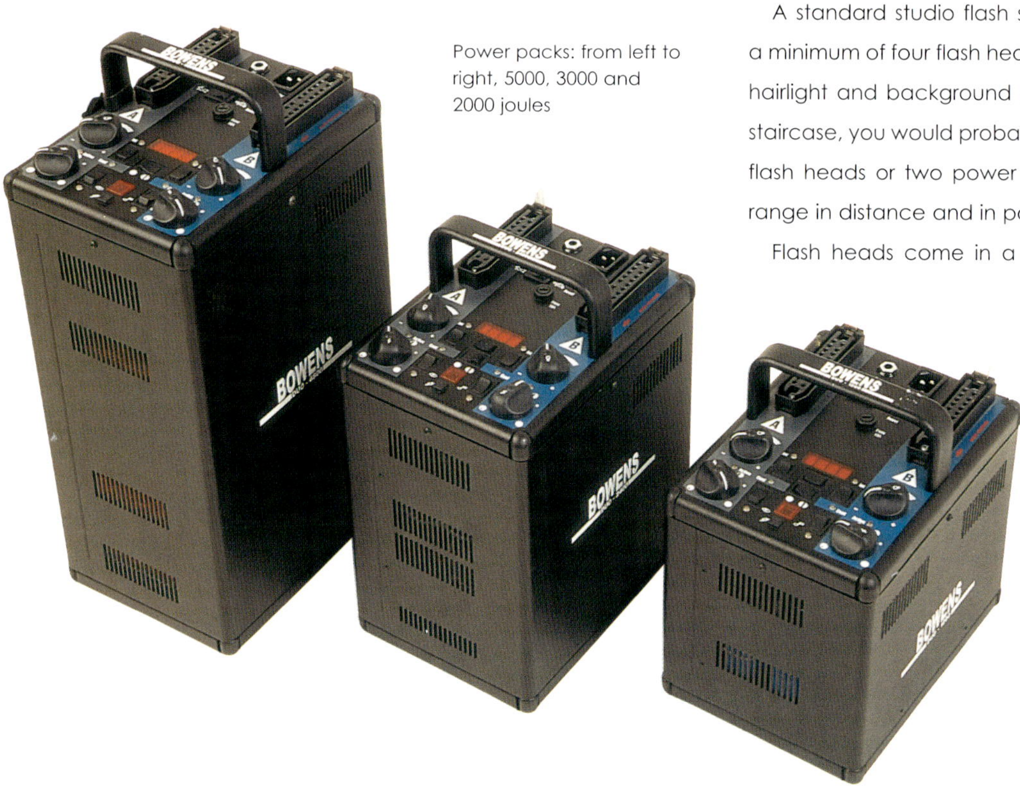

Power packs: from left to right, 5000, 3000 and 2000 joules

Lights are an expensive but essential part of the photographer's arsenal. The first thing you need are flash heads; you can then consider various attachments to create different lighting effects.

Flash heads

Flash heads are the basic studio light. You can buy either monoblocs or power packs. Monoblocs arc individually powered flash heads, where the power unit is contained within the head itself, while power packs allow you to run several flash heads from one power unit. Both run off mains electricity.

Both monoblocs and power packs have their advantages. For example, monoblocs offer more versatility when lighting wide areas – you can put one on each side of the room. You can't do this with a power pack because you are limited as to the length of the cable.

Power packs are initially more expensive to buy but give you the advantage of running several flash heads from the same unit. It is best to have more than one power pack, particularly if you are shooting on location. If you have only one power pack and it fails for any reason, then you will be stranded without any light source. If you use a monobloc system, then you will have alternatives should one fail.

A standard studio flash set-up for a portrait would comprise a minimum of four flash heads, working as a mainlight, fill-in light, hairlight and background light. To light an interior, say a large staircase, you would probably need a minimum of six monobloc flash heads or two power packs, because flash has a limited range in distance and in power.

Flash heads come in a variety of powers, most commonly

OPPOSITE: This image was taken with a softbox suspended on a boom above the model, a triflector underneath her and silver screens either side. This creates a soft, even and clean lighting with no real shadows.
Canon D30; 1/125 sec at f/11; 100mm lens

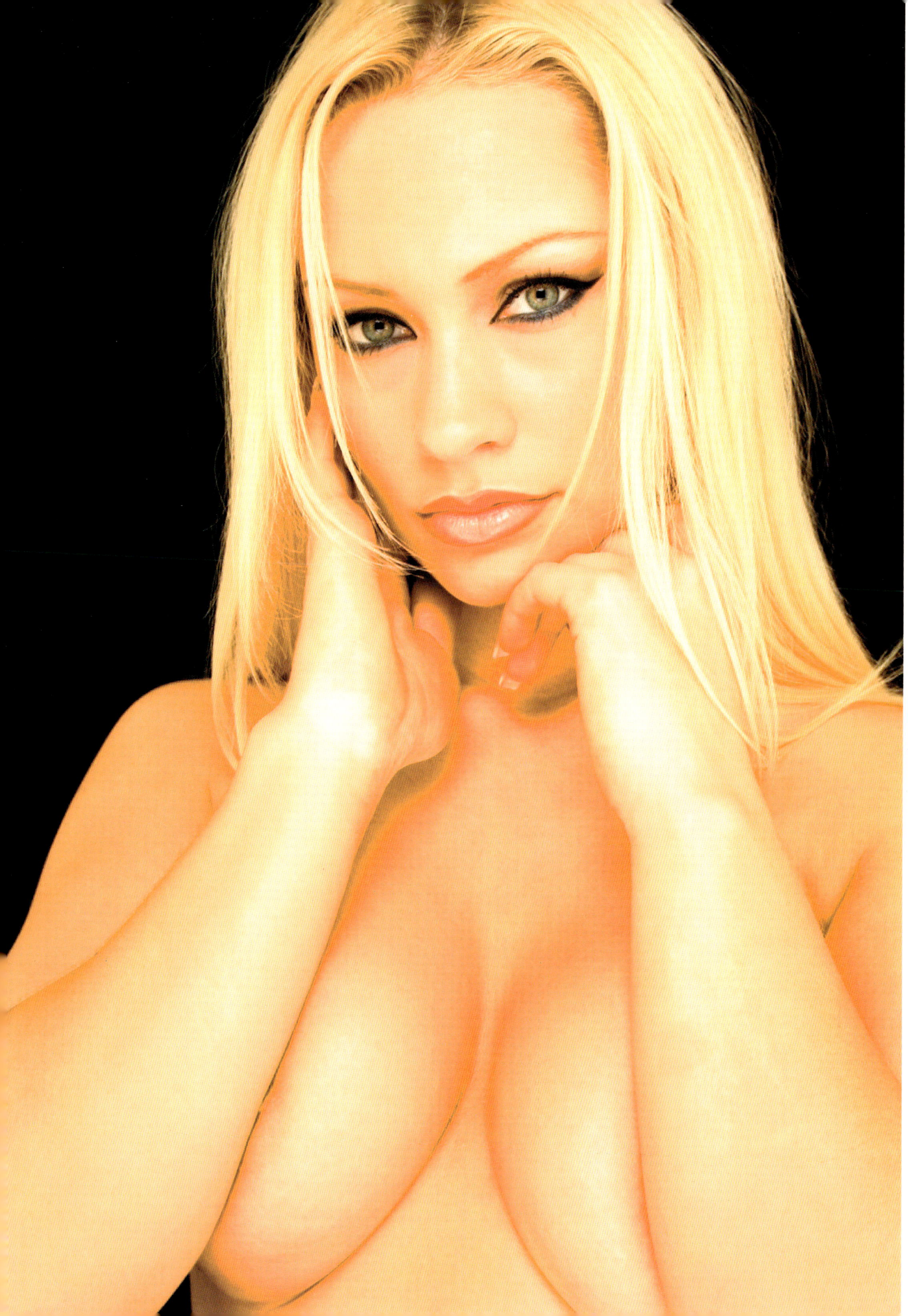

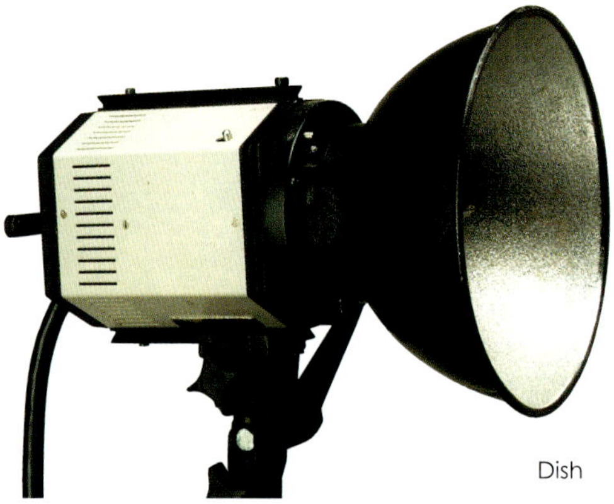

Dish

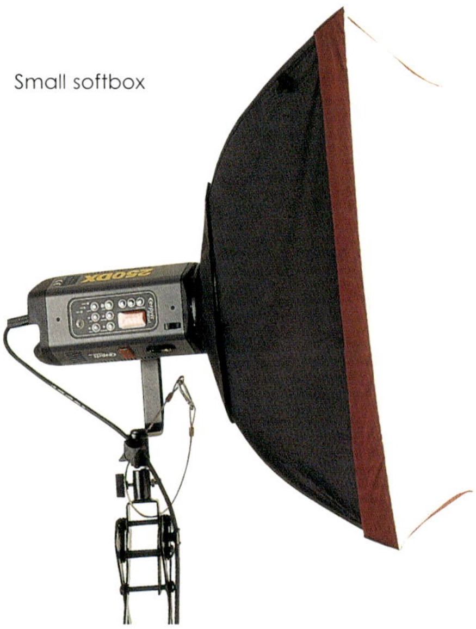

Small softbox

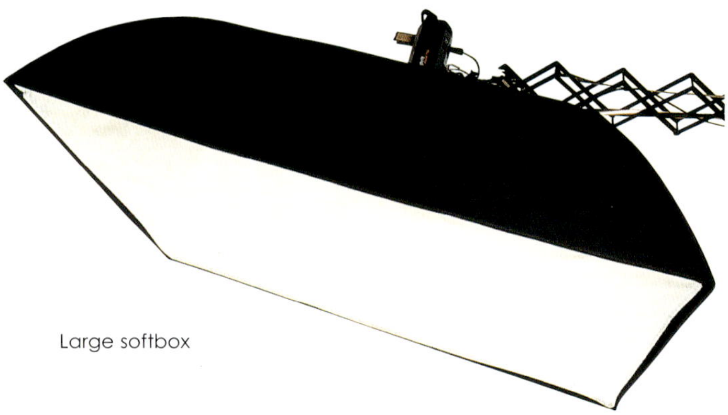

Large softbox

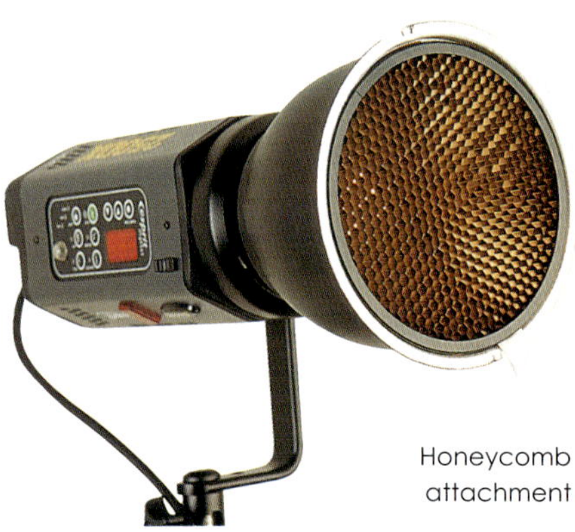

Honeycomb attachment

ranging from 500 joules up to 3000 joules. 500 joules is probably the minimum power unit for studio use, but using a flash of this capacity would restrict your options for diffusing or filtering the light source because using any attachments would cut down the light power. 1000-joule flash heads are probably more useful because you can add filters without losing too much power. This size of flash head is more expensive, but then 1000 joules offers you more scope.

There are numerous attachments that you can put on a flash head to obtain different creative lighting effects. The main ones are detailed below.

Standard dish

Standard dish attachments are used for illuminating backgrounds. You can also use them with umbrellas (see below): the dish guides the light into the umbrella.

Softbox

Softboxes are an essential part of any lighting kit. They come in a variety of sizes, from 60cm (24in) square to 2 x 1.3m (7 x 4ft). Softboxes are often used as the main light source for portraits, and you use a smaller softbox for a head shot and a larger one for a full-length shot. Softboxes are often used for beauty and glamour photography because they create a very soft, diffuse light that is warm, clean and flattering. Softboxes also offer the advantage of being versatile and easy to control when working in an enclosed environment. I often prefer to use a softbox rather than, say, an umbrella (see page 26) because with this you obtain more control of your light source.

Honeycomb

Honeycomb attachments can be used either to light a background or as a hairlight. They create quite a harsh, controlled light, and can be particularly useful when taking male portraits.

Snoot

Snoot attachments are very useful for creating light effects on a background; they can also be used as a hairlight. Snoots produce a very narrow, focused light source. You can exploit this

OPPOSITE: The main image here was lit with a honeycomb, a controlled light source that gives a lot of contrast to an image. The inset picture was lit with a snoot, a light source that directs light more narrowly than a honeycomb, and creates an even more dramatic effect.
Canon D30; 1/125 sec at f/11; 70mm lens

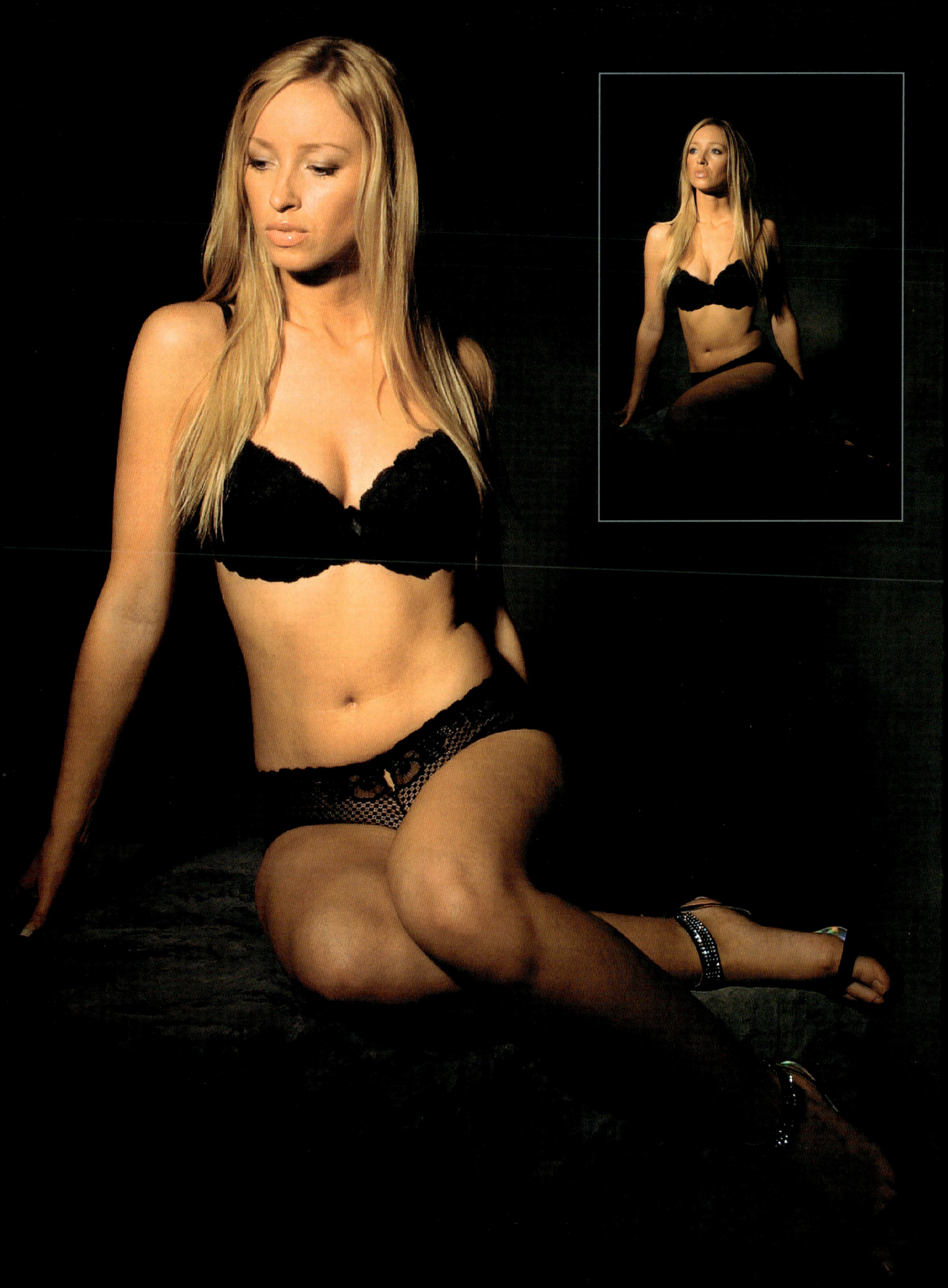

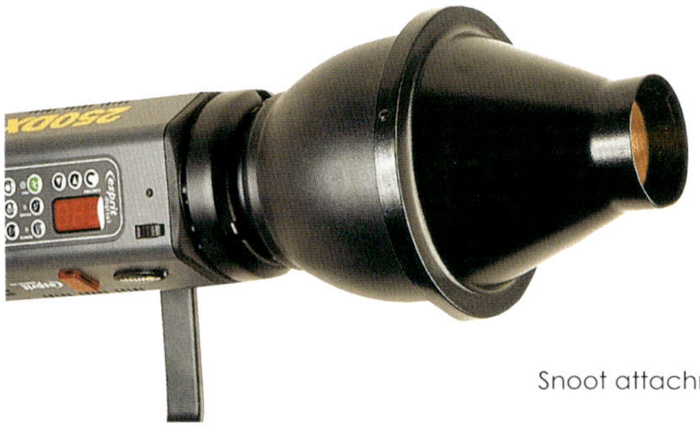

Snoot attachment

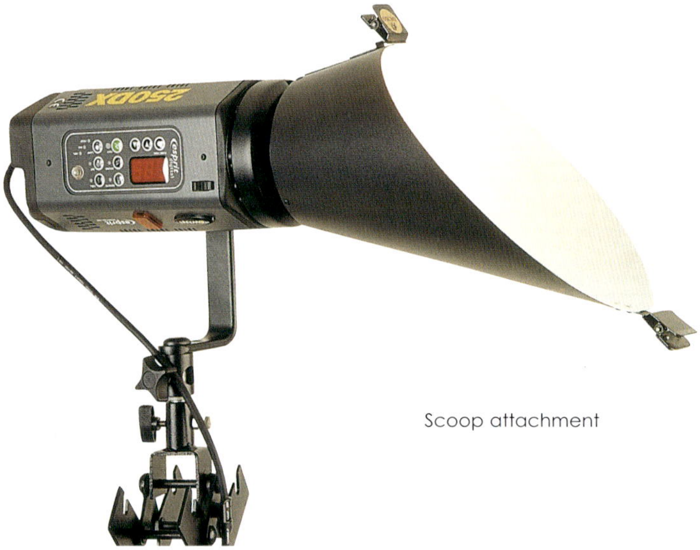

Scoop attachment

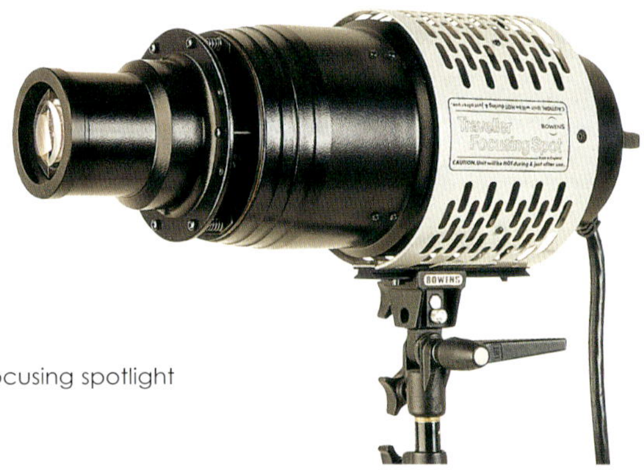

Focusing spotlight

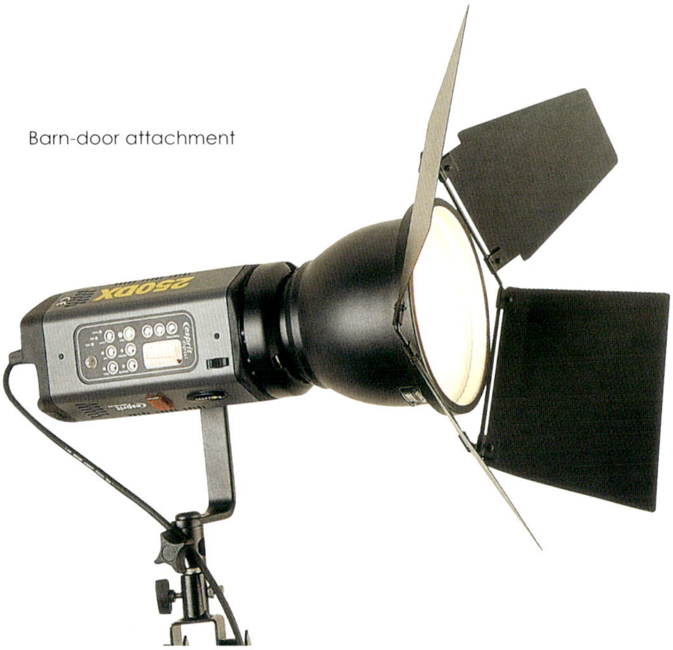

Barn-door attachment

characteristic for creative effect, for example by throwing focused highlights onto a small portion of a subject's face or to pick out a particular detail.

Scoop

Scoop attachments are primarily used for creating interesting ovoid shapes on backgrounds.

Focusing spotlight

The focusing spotlights used in photography developed from the spotlights used in theatres. These spotlights have a variety of uses: you can use them as a straight spotlight on your subject, or you can use them to light backgrounds in conjunction with various special-effect gobos, which create interesting backgrounds such as window effects or Venetian blinds. You can also use them with coloured filters. These effects can be a little gimmicky, but used with discretion they are very creative.

Barn doors

Barn-door attachments control the amount of light spillage and the direction of the light that you want thrown on your subject. They are useful for creating the impression of shafts of light falling on a background.

Reflectors

Reflectors are another essential item in studio lighting set-ups. They are used for reflecting light and controlling the amount of light that you have on your subject. Reflectors come in various sizes, most commonly from 60cm (24in) round to 2 x 1.3m (7 x 4ft). Smaller reflectors are used more for location work because they are portable. Larger reflectors are used more for studio work.

Reflectors come in a variety of colours, including white, silver, soft gold, gold and black, and the different colours produce different effects. White reflectors are useful if you want to create a soft fill-in light; silver reflectors create a harsher and more aggressive effect; soft gold reflectors are useful to warm an image up, for example, if your subject has pale skin; gold creates a stronger, warmer effect; and black reflectors are used as a shield to prevent light spilling onto a background. They are also useful for photographing people wearing glasses, as they cut out the light reflecting off the lenses of the spectacles.

OPPOSITE: This image was taken with a monospot, a type of spotlight that can be used to project special effects. In this case I used a gobo of a Venetian blind on the monospot to project the stripes of shadow onto the model.
Canon D30; 1/125 sec at f/8; 100mm lens

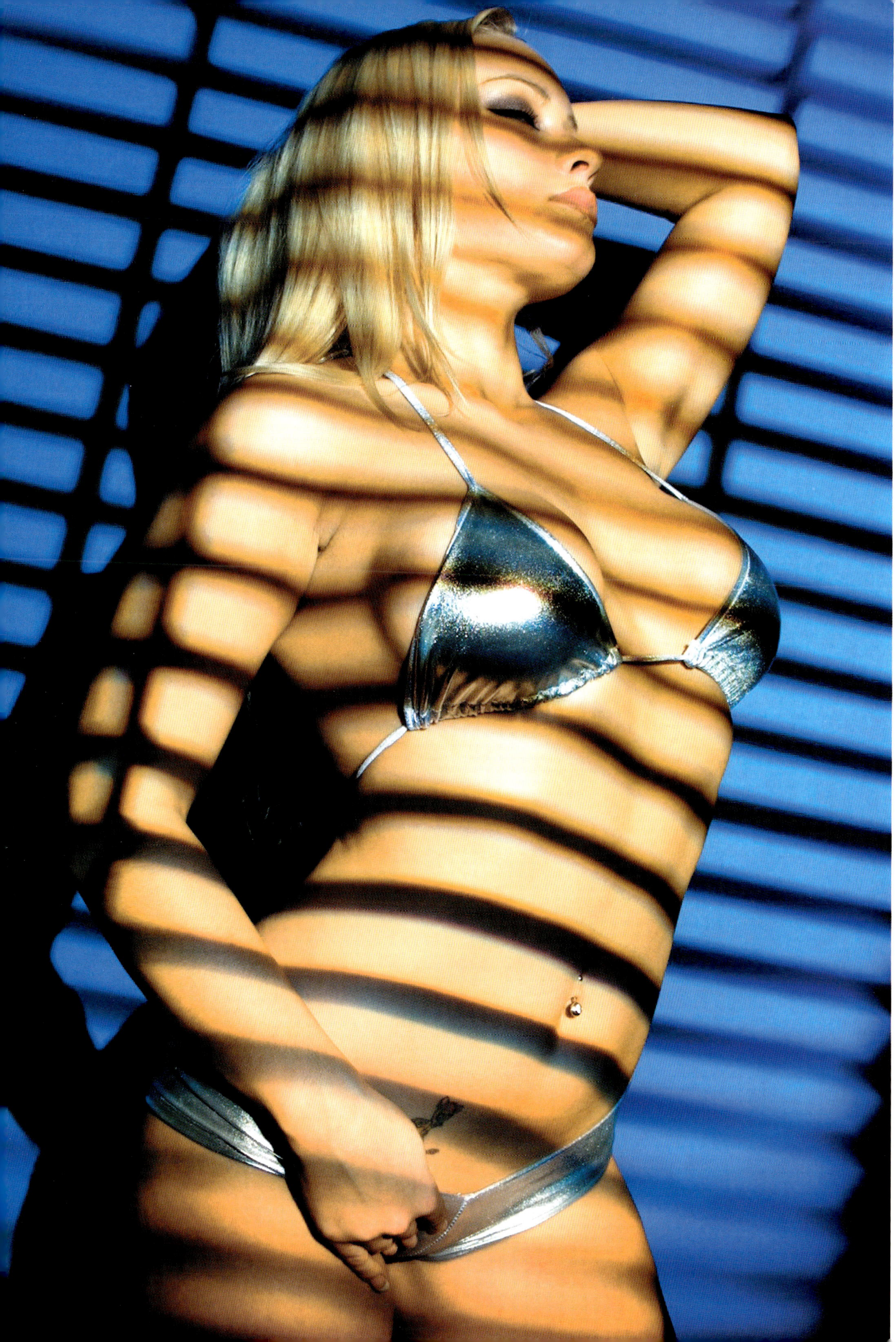

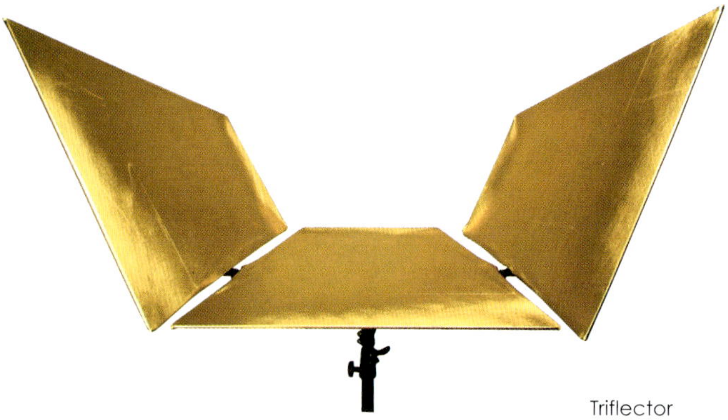

Triflector

Umbrella

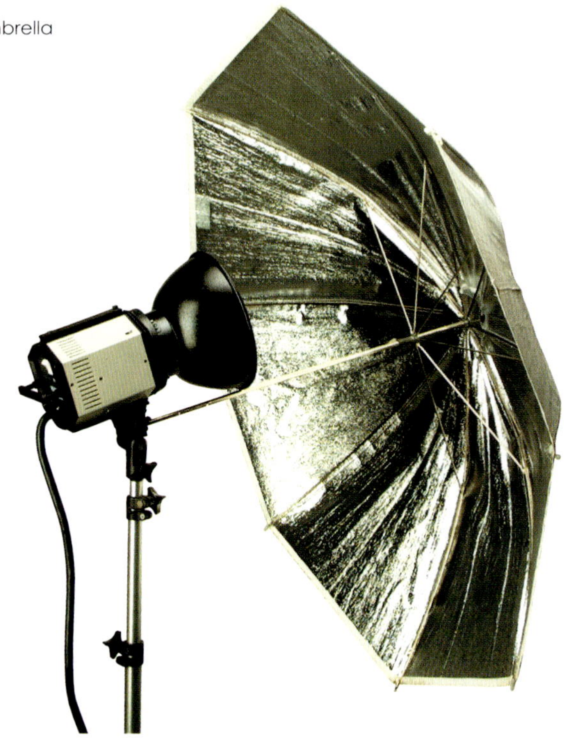

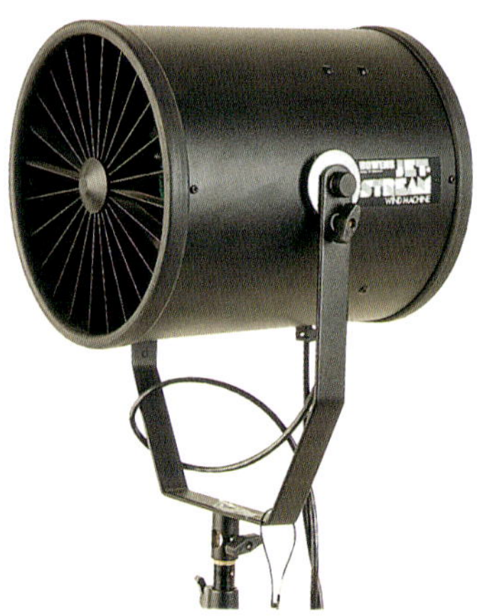

Wind machine

OPPOSITE: This image was taken with a softbox on either side of the model, another above her, and a gold reflector underneath her to strengthen the colour of the shot. I also used a wind machine to create movement in the model's hair making the shot more lively.
Canon D30; 1/125 sec at f/8; 100mm lens

Buying purpose-built reflectors can be very expensive, and a cheaper option is to construct your own out of polystyrene insulation boards. These come in white, but you can paint them black, using a water-based paint rather than an oil-based one.

You can also make an effective silver reflector by covering a piece of board with crinkled aluminium kitchen foil. To create a gold reflector, you could spraypaint one of these with metallic gold paint.

Triflectors

Triflectors are controllable reflectors consisting of three hinged panels: straight reflectors have just one rectangular panel. Triflectors are useful because they can be angled to bounce light onto a subject and control the amount of reflection. Again, purpose-built ones can be expensive to buy, but it is perfectly feasible to construct your own out of polystyrene boards.

Umbrellas

Umbrellas are used to create a very broad light source. I use them primarily for lighting large areas, particularly interiors that I want brightly lit. I tend not to use umbrellas in the studio, nor to use them as a main light source on location.

Umbrellas are cheaper than softboxes but are not so controllable. Because they are a broad light source, they tend to produce rather flat lighting.

Diffuser screens

Diffuser screens are the equivalent of the diffuser that you get on the top of a softbox, but are an independent screen. You can buy them ready-made, but they are expensive. It is possible to make your own from material made by Rosco Diffuser Flex, which is sold in rolls – just stretch the material over a frame.

Diffuser screens are useful if you need to diffuse your light source. You can also use them as silhouette screens where you light through the back and then shoot silhouettes against this.

Wind machines

Wind machines are, of course, not a piece of lighting equipment, but one can be a useful part of your studio set-up. They are particularly useful when shooting portraits where you want to create movement in the subject's hair or clothes. It is possible to adjust and control the direction and speed of the wind.

Wind machines are expensive, and it is usually more cost-effective to hire one for a day when you need one than to buy one. A cheaper alternative is simply to use a fan.

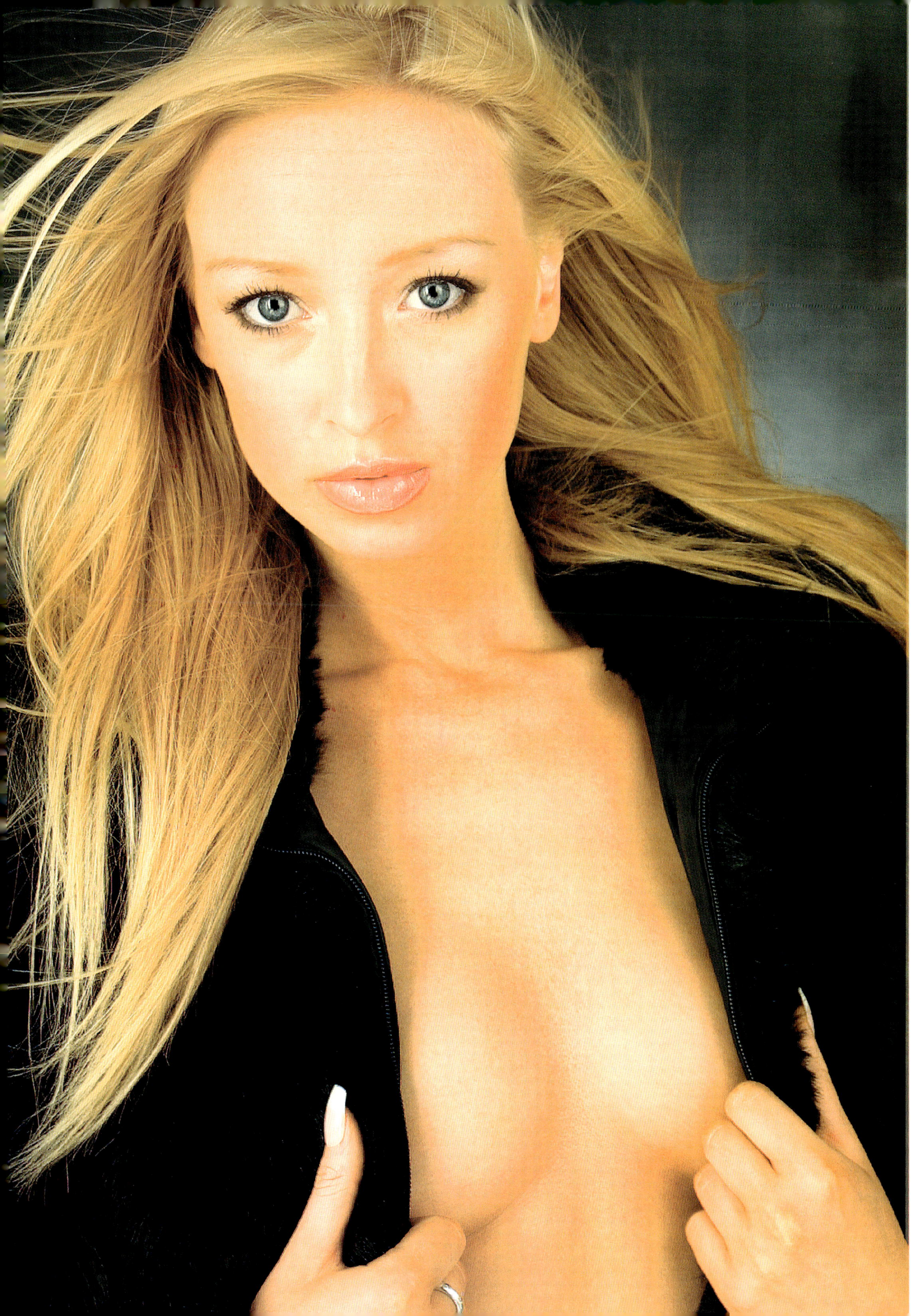

composition
and poses

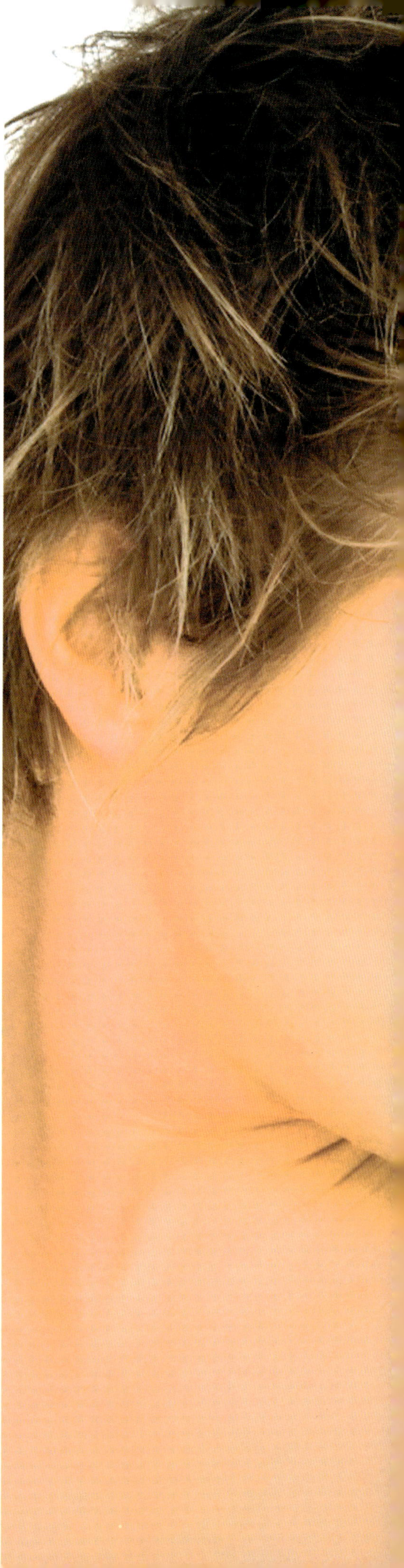

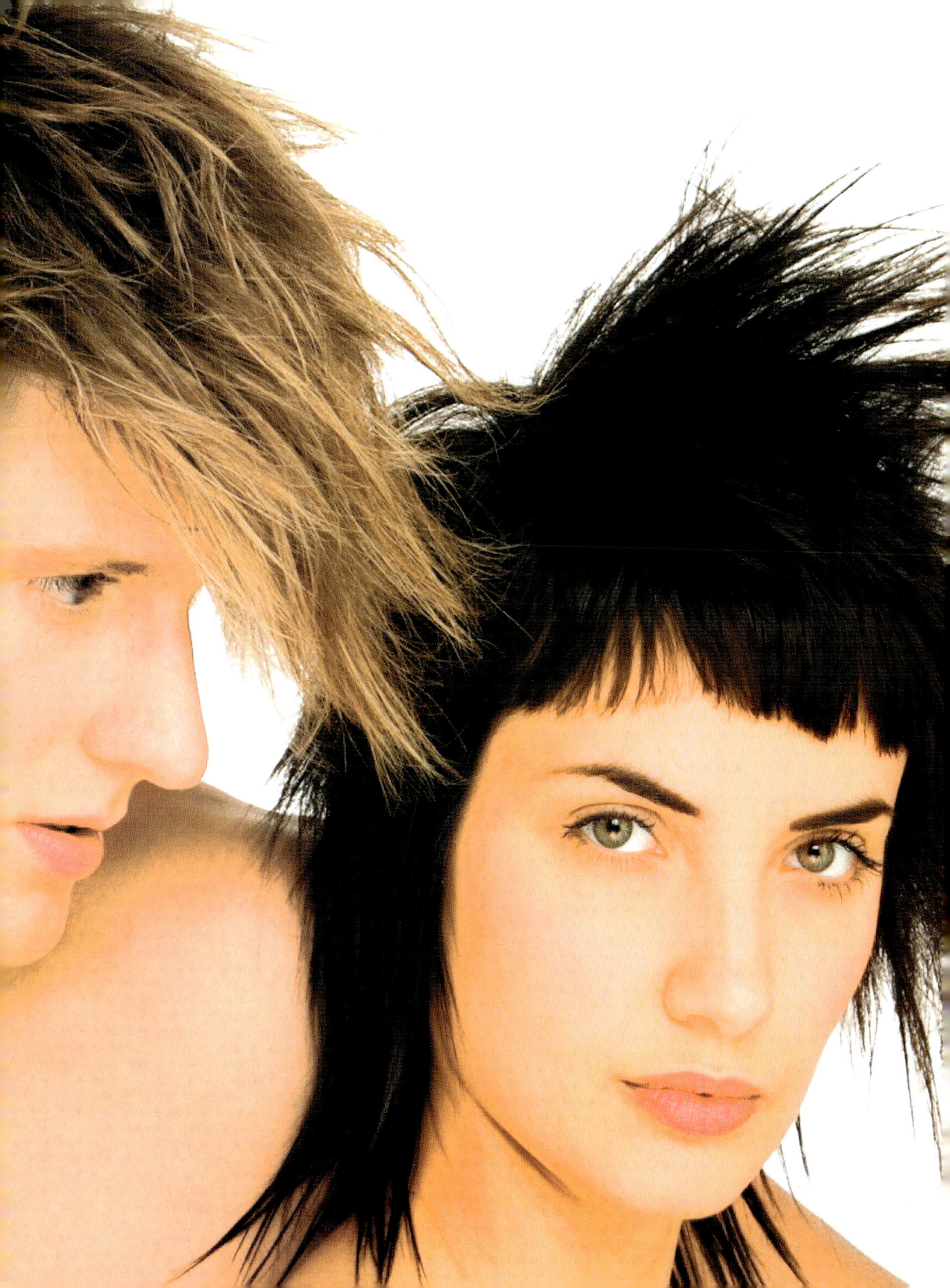

Working with models

Being able to work well with models is a fundamental part of glamour and beauty photography. You can be extremely skilled at setting up lighting and composing shots, but if you do not know how to establish effective communication with a model, than the shoot is unlikely to be successful.

Choosing models

For most commercial photography, the client and the photographer will work together to find the right model for the job. Different modelling agencies specialize in different types of models, such as fashion, beauty and glamour models. Although there can be some overlap between types, there are some fundamental differences. Fashion models, for example, have to be tall – at least 1.75m (6ft) – and very slim, while with glamour models height is less important, as their figure is the main concern. Beauty models tend to do mainly head shots – covers for magazines, for example – so they need to have strong facial features that are good for close-up work.

The first stage of casting a model is to ask the modelling agency for their models' composite cards. These cards have a series of images showing the model's range: the different looks and the variety of work that the model can do. After seeing the composite cards, a shortlist is drawn up and then casting is held. Casting calls are now almost always shot on video.

The professional attitude of the model is often as important a factor as how she or he looks. Many aspiring models assume that modelling is an easy life, but a lack of commitment and professionalism ensures that their career before the camera will be short. Good models are enthusiastic, confident in front of the camera, are prepared to work hard to achieve the right 'look', and most often have an instinctive feel for what will work to meet the client's requirements.

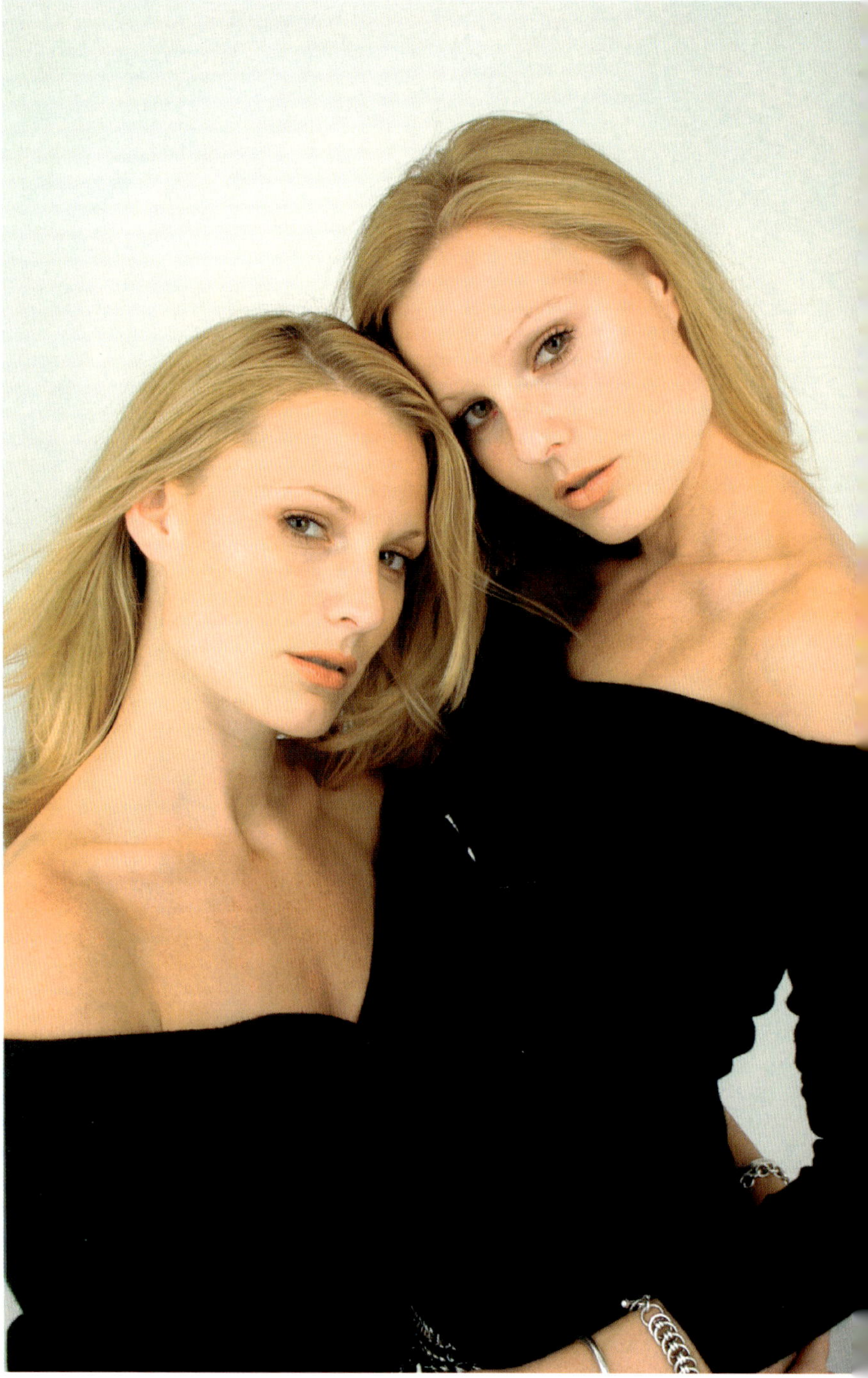

ABOVE: These twins work well as a modelling team, and here they position their heads closely together, with one slightly above the other, to create a relaxed and pleasing shot.
Canon D30; 1/125 sec at f/16; 100mm lens

Before the shoot

A lot of people, particularly when they are inexperienced at working with models, tend to assume that the model will just walk in to the studio and immediately start posing. This is not the case: you need to plan a session well in advance and have a good idea of what you want the model to do before he or she arrives.

You will also need to brief the model as to what sort of make-up and wardrobe are required for the shoot. Budgets tend to be limited, and specialist make-up artists are often used only for beauty shots. For glamour photography, it is the norm that the model does her own make-up. The model will also often supply her or his own clothes; in fact, this is often a consideration when casting. It is part of a glamour model's essential kit to have a good range of items such as shoes, jewellery, lingerie and swimwear.

Looking after the model

Clear communication and good rapport are essential when working with models. Bear in mind that during one hour in the studio you may only get 20 minutes' shooting time, so you have to use that time wisely. Explain to the model exactly what you want from him or her, and give them plenty of guidance and feedback while you are shooting so that they can adjust their poses according to what you have in mind.

This may seem an obvious point, but it is often overlooked by less experienced photographers: you need to remember that your models will become tired. When you are shooting head shots, it is best to shoot your subjects sitting down so they can rest their bodies. If you want your models to make any kind of eye contact with the camera, remember that they cannot just stare down the lens all the time – their eyes will soon become tired and lack sparkle, and this will show very clearly in the resulting photographs.

Let the models know when you are about to press the shutter so that they can prepare themselves to look fresh and animated. I tend to count a model into a shot (counting backwards from three, for example), so she or he knows exactly when I am going to take a shot and can prepare and arrange a pose accordingly.

Always treat your models with courtesy; ordering them around, losing your temper or shouting at them is not going to create a successful shot. You should also play to the model's strengths – some models look best when they are smiling and relaxed, while others show to their best advantage when they are apparently serious or mysterious. What works best on film is generally what the model feels most comfortable doing and most confident with, so take time to explore what that is.

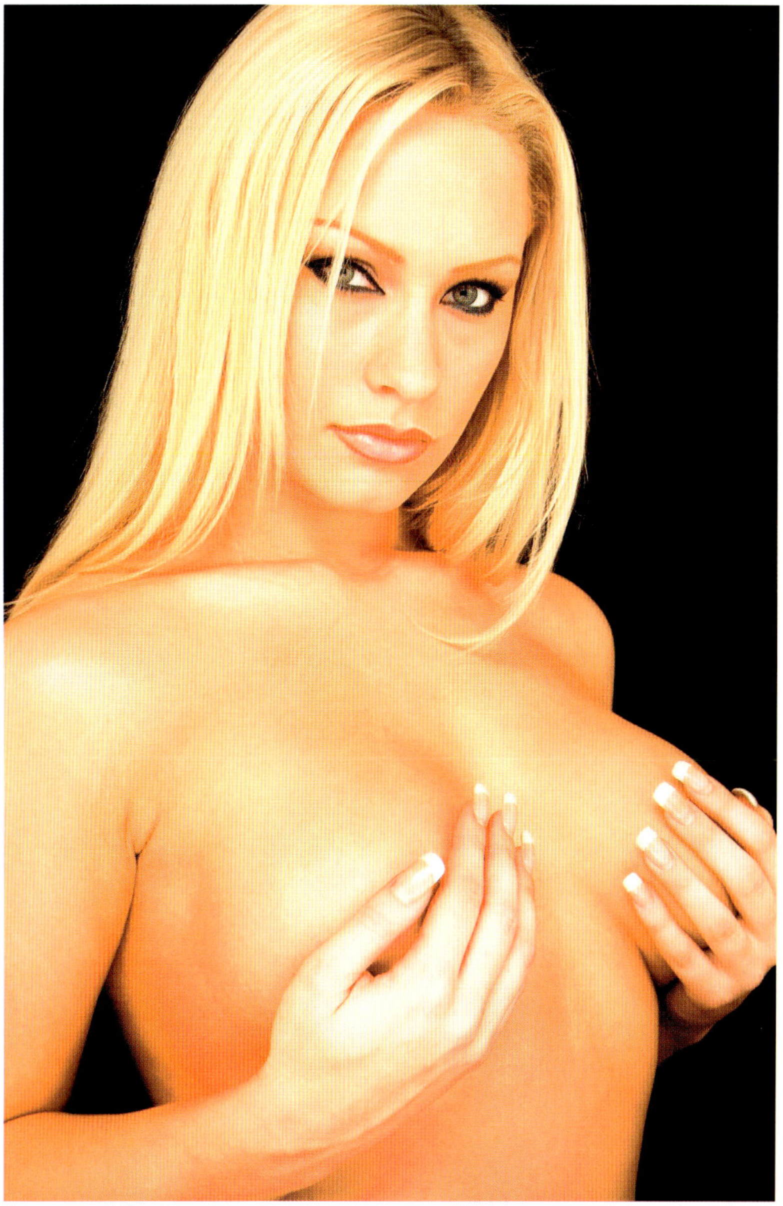

ABOVE: Confident eye contact, like that of the subject in this shot, distinguishes the experienced professional model. **Canon D30; 1/125 sec at f/11; 100mm lens**

Composition and format

The composition and format of your photographs will depend largely on what ultimate purpose each image is intended for. For commercial beauty and glamour photography, you need to bear in mind when composing a shot what format the image will ultimately be published in. For private or for more creative and artistic work, you can concentrate on composing an image that has most impact and best conveys the mood you want to impart.

Vertical images

A high proportion of glamour and beauty photography is destined for magazines and books, and a vertical A3/A4 format is standard. You therefore need to compose your shots with an eye to making sure that they will be in proportion to the page. It is also more common for models to be photographed sitting or standing up rather than lying down, and a vertical format is more appropriate for those poses, as you capture the detail and shape of the model without photographing large expanses of the background that you don't need in the final image.

Horizontal images

Most published images are vertical rather than horizontal: probably 75–80 per cent of the commercial images that I shoot are vertical rather than horizontal. There are exceptions, of course: advertising images and some images for glamour calendars occasionally use horizontal formats, particularly when the model is photographed in an exotic or unusual location and the background therefore becomes an important element for the atmosphere of the shot. The pictures on pages 74–75, 97 and 118–119 are strong examples of this. You have to be careful to strike the right balance when composing such shots so that you can still keep the necessary focus on the model.

Camera format

The camera format that you use will also affect how you compose a picture. If you are using 35mm, the transparencies that are produced are in different proportions from an A4 page – they are somewhat narrower – so the image will need to be cropped accordingly. If you get the proportions wrong, it can affect the overall impact of the image, particularly when it is blown up. This is why medium format, for example, 6 x 7cm, is often referred to as 'ideal format': it is exactly in proportion to the page format of most magazines and therefore little image editing is generally required. This is professionally known as being 'correct in pro' – the image is in the correct proportions so that it can be enlarged to fit the required space.

Picture editing

When composing shots for commercial purposes, you should try to fill as much of your format as possible, creating more impact and avoiding 'dead' space. However, if you go too close in on a subject you will not leave enough space for later editing. It's a tricky balance.

When shooting for magazines, you will also need to keep editorial requirements in mind. This is particularly the case for cover shots, where you need to leave space around the image for the magazine's name, straplines and text. If there isn't enough space, the client won't use the image.

Artistic images

When you are composing artistic and creative images, your principal concern will be about having the model create strong, graphic shapes with the poses that he or she assumes. You can experiment, for example, with producing semi-silhouette images with striking outlines, such as the shots shown on pages 60, 69 and 72–73.

OPPOSITE:
This composition works well because of the strong, simple, pyramidal outline of the subject. There is plenty of space in the image, but not dead space; it works to balance and strengthen the overall image. The way the model has crossed her legs and hands creates interesting and complex shapes that echo the overall shape created by the outline of her body.
Mamiya RZ 6/7cm; 1/125 sec at f/16; 110mm lens; Fuji Provia 100

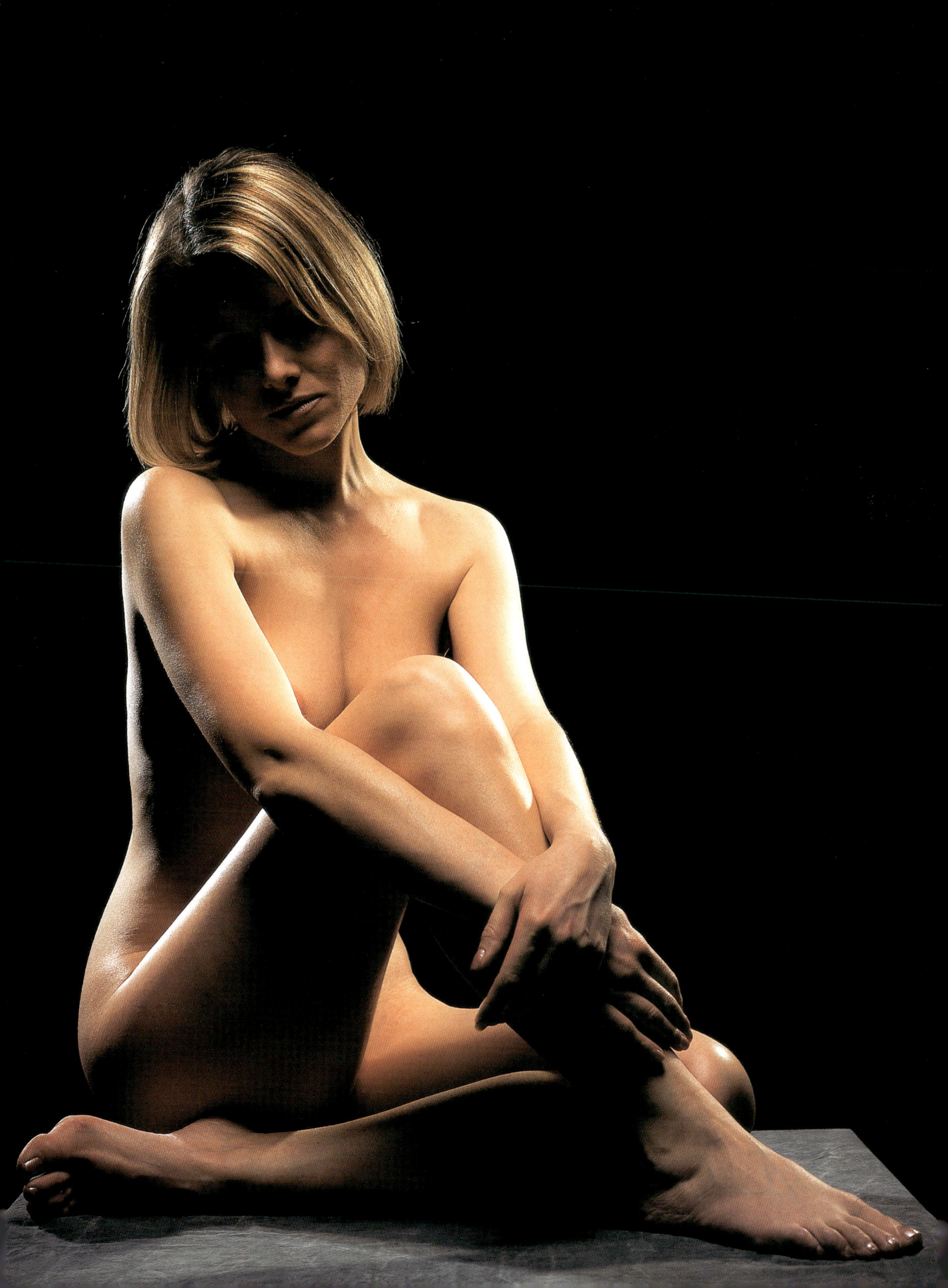

Head shots

In glamour and beauty photography, head shots are most commonly used for advertising beauty and hair products, and for magazine covers.

The most important element of composing head shots is to capture the eyes, as they are the most expressive part of a person's face. Portraits in which the subject looks directly into the camera, making eye contact, are often the most powerful because the viewer is drawn into the shot and connects directly with the subject.

An important part of composing head shots, therefore, is directing the model so that she or he can convey the expression or the emotion that is required. Experienced models tend to be relaxed and confident in front of the camera and have the versatility to assume different expressions convincingly. Inexperienced models often find making eye contact hard because it is very exposing, and the resulting shots tend to look weak. If the model is tense or nervous, this will be very apparent in the image. It's often best to leave such shots till later in a session, when the model is more relaxed.

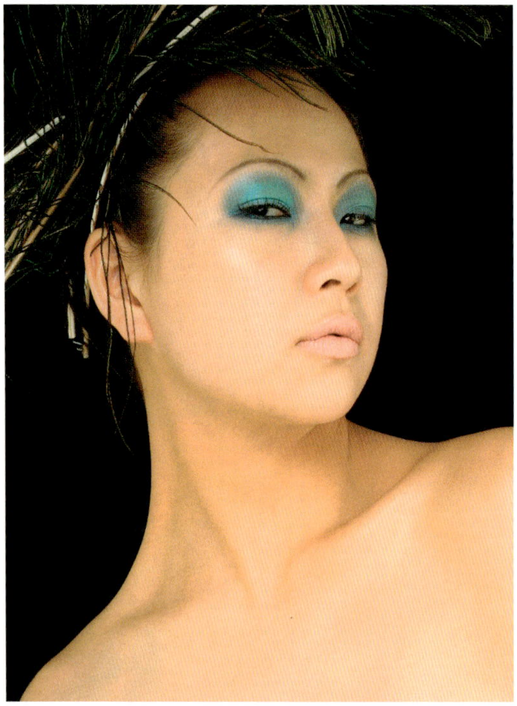

LEFT: I shot this hair and make-up image with the model's head positioned at an angle to the camera. This gave the final picture the dynamic feel that the clients were seeking.
Canon D30; 1/125 sec at f/11; 100mm lens

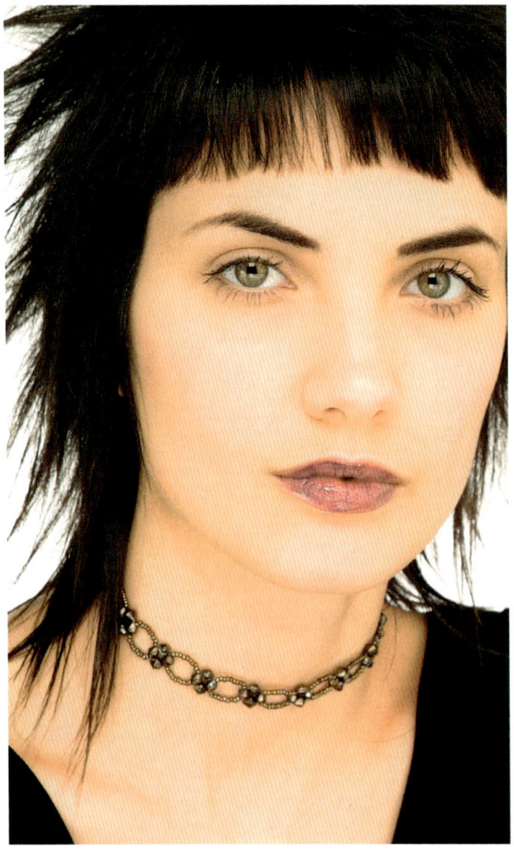

BELOW LEFT: This model has very good eye contact, and her eyes draw you in to the image. The shot was lit with a softbox above the model and a silver triflector underneath her.
Canon D30; 1/125 sec at f/11; 100mm lens

Proportion

Another consideration when taking head shots is the focal length of the camera lens. With a 35mm camera, the recommended focal length lens is 100mm; for a medium-format camera it is 150mm. Using these lenses will help you to capture an image where the subject's features are in the correct proportions, with little distortion.

You also need to be careful about how the model tilts her or his head, as this can sometimes throw the features out of proportion. If the model's head is tilted up, you tend to be shooting up the nose, which is not always photogenic, and the jaw will appear broader. Tilting the head down will make the jaw appear narrower.

BELOW AND OPPOSITE: This model was somewhat wary, and her reserve shows in the eye contact shot below. The main image, looking away from the camera, is more successful because she looks more relaxed: her expression is reflective and somewhat wistful, giving a pleasing softness to the overall image.
Mamiya RZ 6/7cm; 1/125 sec at f/16; 110mm lens; Fuji Provia 100

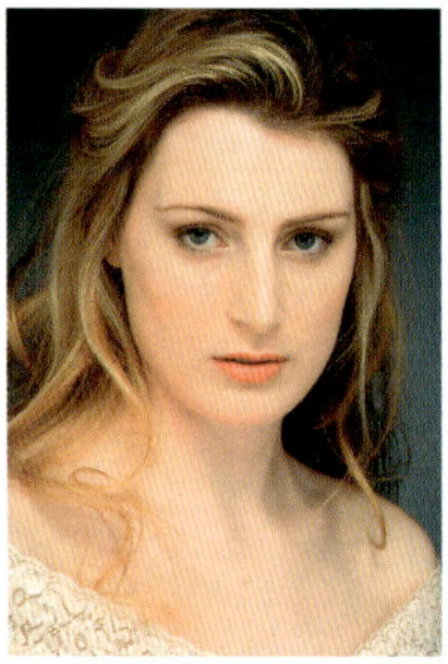

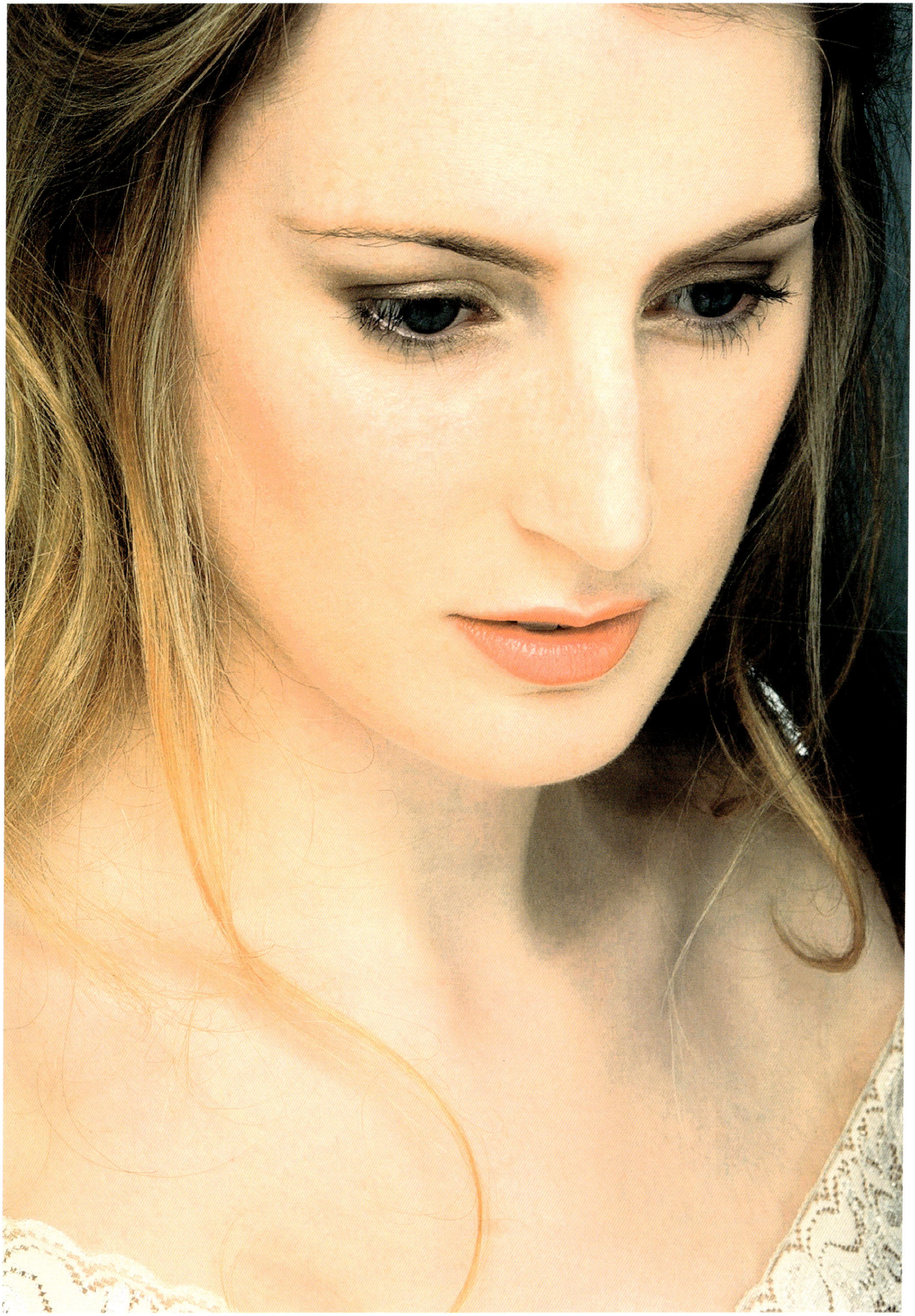

Head and shoulders

Head-and-shoulder shots are used in much the same way as head shots. When you are composing head-and-shoulder shots you will obviously have many of the same considerations as when composing head shots – however, a larger area of your model is being used, so you also have to bear in mind the neckline, shoulders, and possibly arms, elbows and hands.

The clothes that the model wears should complement the subject and not be too distracting – garish colours, for example, will battle against the model's skin tones. Necklines of clothes should be simple, as should jewellery. If you clutter the neckline with heavy jewellery you can distort the balance of the image and take the priority away from capturing the model's features.

Perspective

Your camera angle and position can affect the perspective of the model's features. If the model has a short neck, for example, it is better not to shoot from above, as the neck will appear even shorter; shooting from below can help to lengthen the neck and keep the features in proportion.

The breadth of the model's shoulders can also affect the overall proportions of the image. People with broad shoulders tend to look as if they have relatively small heads. This effect is exaggerated if they are facing straight on to the camera, so it is usually best if they turn slightly away from the camera. You then have to watch out for unsightly creases appearing in the model's neck as she or he turns away.

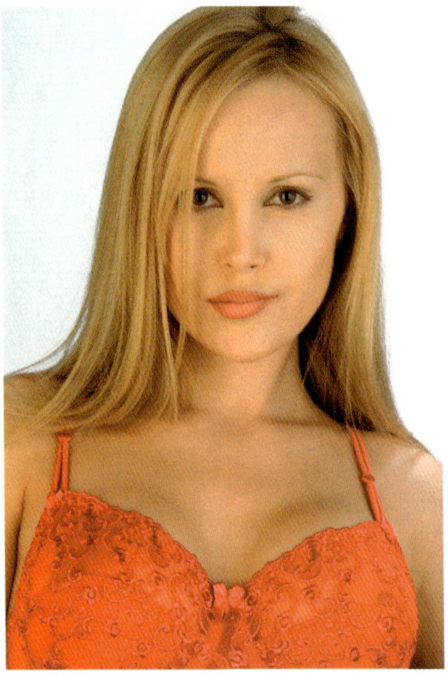

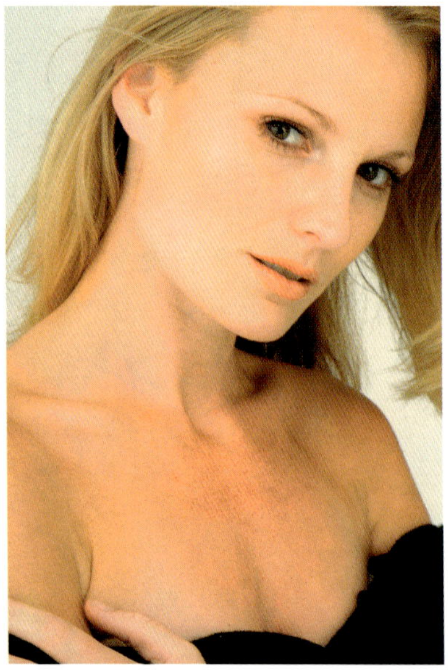

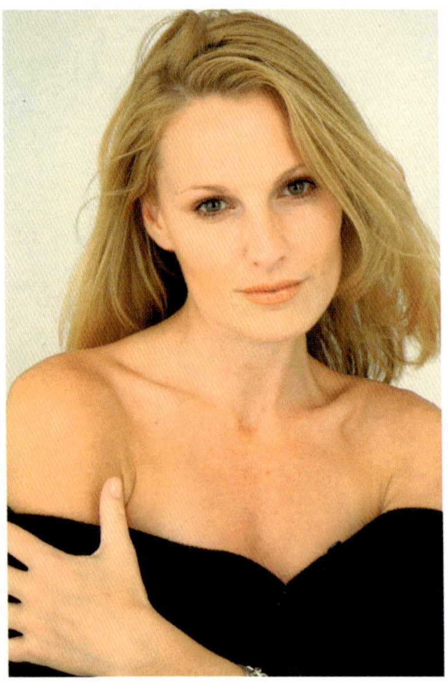

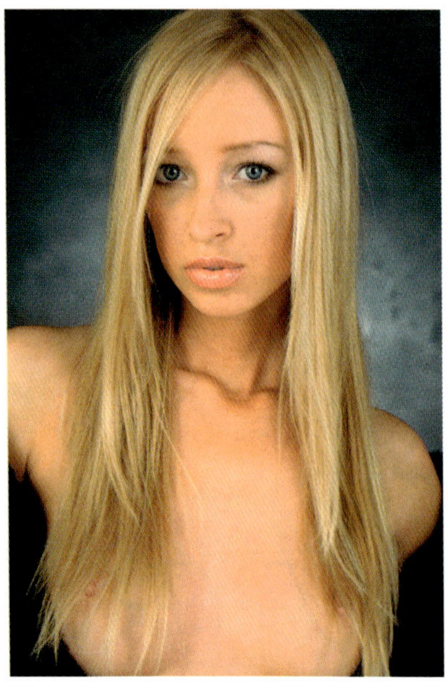

LEFT: The models in these pictures all look at the camera with confident eye contact. The images are enhanced by the simplicity of the necklines; there is just a subtle suggestion of a garment or a striking addition of colour.
TOP LEFT AND BOTTOM RIGHT: Canon D30; 1/125 sec at f/8; 100mm lens; TOP RIGHT AND BOTTOM LEFT: Canon D30; 1/125 sec at f/16; 100mm lens

OPPOSITE: This image is striking because of the model's almost hypnotic eye contact and the composition of the shot. The colours are strong and simple, with the model's dark hair, elegant necklace and dark top standing out against the white background.
Mamiya RZ 6/7cm; 1/125 sec at f/16; 110mm lens; Fuji Provia 100

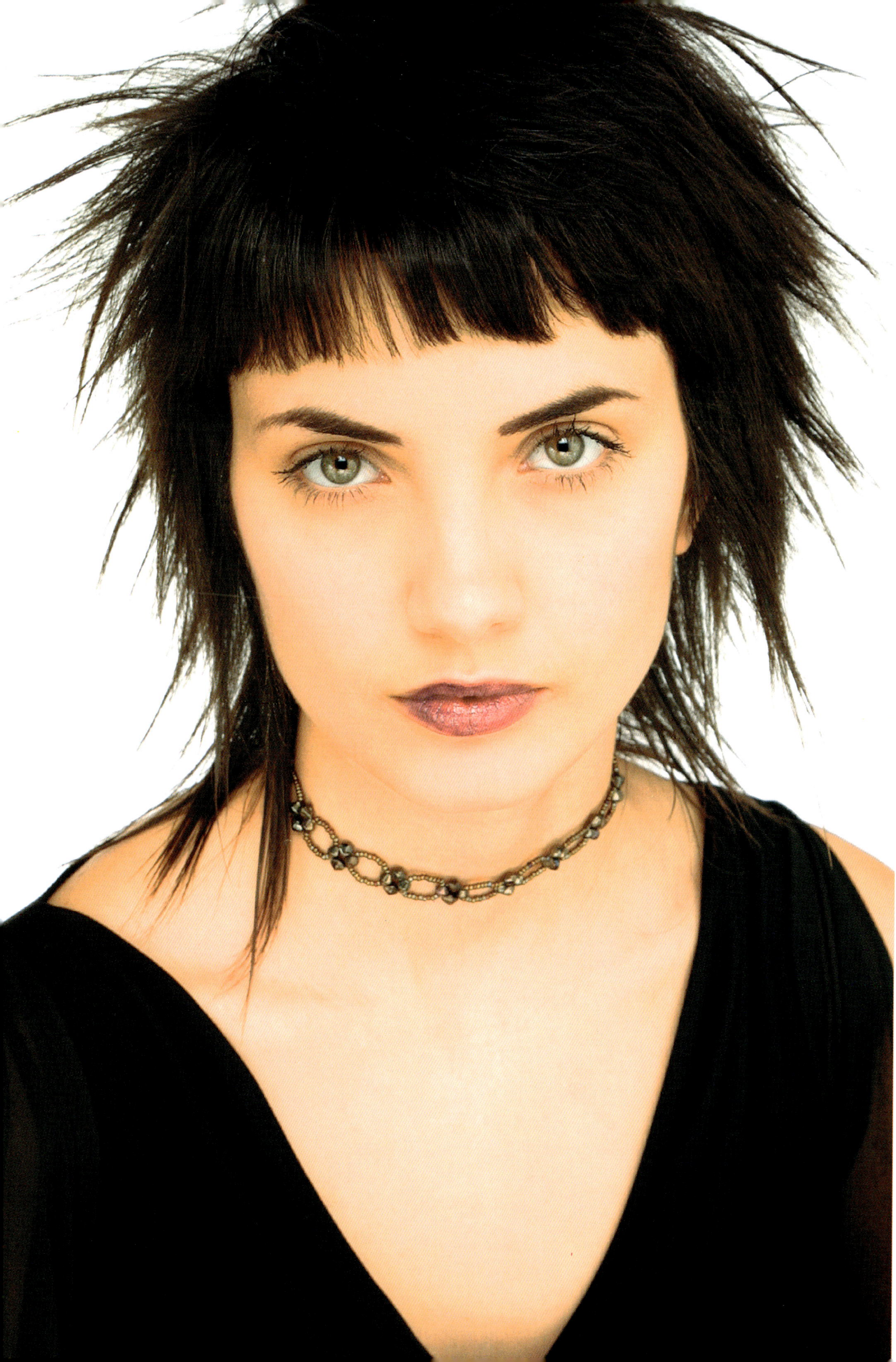

Hand positions

Including hands in glamour and fashion shots can help to introduce an interesting and dynamic element to the image, as hands can be very expressive. They are often underestimated, but effectively positioning a model's hands can help enhance the overall shape and mood of a shot, whether you are shooting head-and-shoulder shots, three-quarter-length or full-length images. You can use hands almost like a prop or an accessory: a model with her hands on her hips can look strong and sassy; a model with her hands in her hair can look sultry and seductive; while a model with her hands on her face can look contemplative and tranquil. In fashion shoots, the position of the model's hands can help to draw attention to a certain item of clothing.

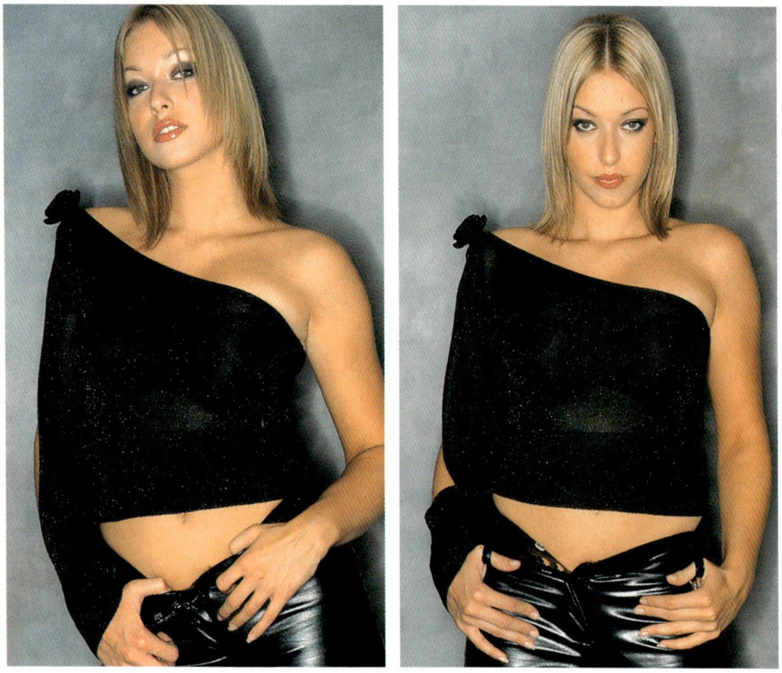

ABOVE: In the shot on the left, the model's hands look slightly claw-like because her thumbs are partially out of sight. The shot on the right works better: the hands look natural and are pleasingly arranged.
Mamiya RZ 6/7cm; 1/125 sec at f/16; 110mm lens; Fuji Provia 100

Problems

Hands are notoriously difficult to photograph so that they appear natural and aesthetically pleasing – all too often they can look clawlike or sausage-shaped. You have to have a very sharp eye for detail when arranging hands so that they make elegant and well-proportioned shapes that enhance the image. Hands in ugly, unnatural or stiff poses will only detract from the shot.

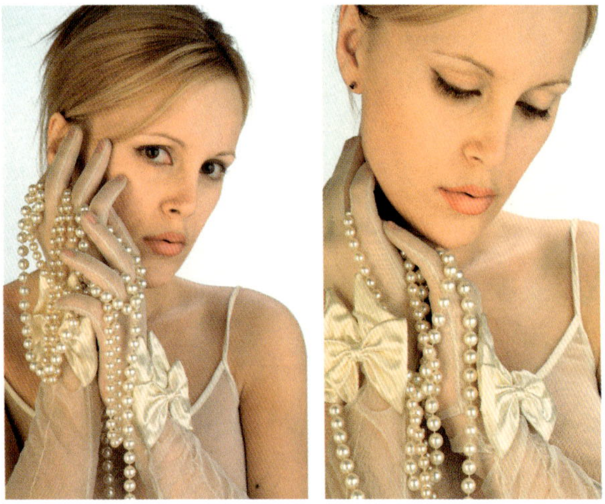

ABOVE: In the shot on the left, the position of the model's hands makes the image too busy and fussy: the fingers are splayed and cover the model's face. The shot on the right works better because it is simpler and the hands are more graceful. Having the model cup one hand in the other creates a neater and more fluid shape, and the hands make an elegant frame for the model's face.
Canon D30; 1/125 sec at f/16; 100mm lens

Checking hands

Of course, much depends on the condition of the model's hands, as even the most beautiful model won't necessarily have shapely and well-manicured hands. You should take as much care over the state of the model's hands as over the hair and make-up. The fingers should be evenly proportioned and the hands well-manicured, with no bitten or broken nails, no chipped nail varnish and no cuts or grazes.

There is always a way around such problems, however: I always keep a selection of gloves in my accessories cabinet should I be working with a model whose hands are less than perfect when I want to use them in a shot.

OPPOSITE: In this fashion shot, the position of the model's hands help to add interesting angles in the image that complement the angular shapes of the jacket.
Canon D30; 1/125 sec at f/5.6; 100mm lens

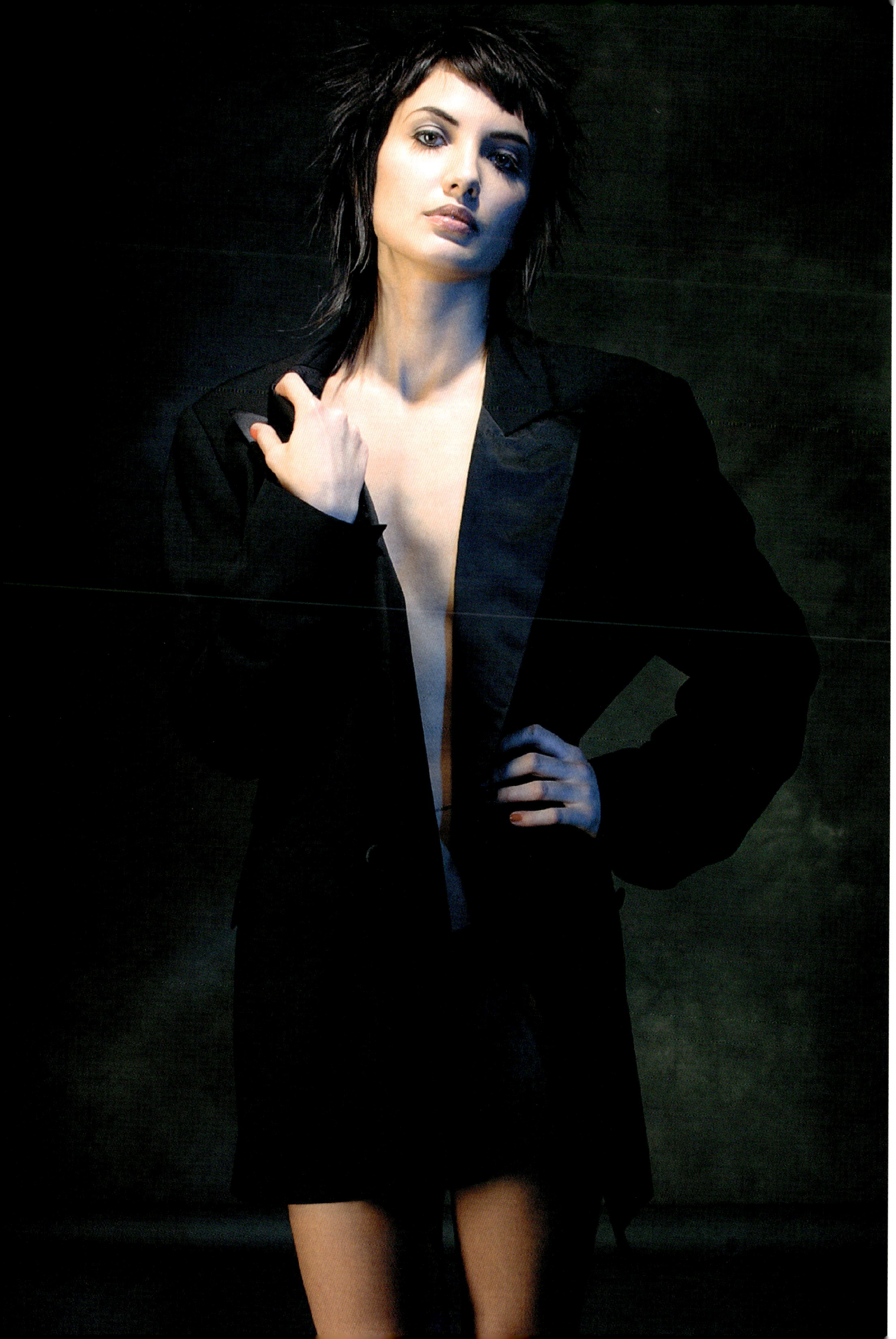

Three-quarter poses

Three-quarter poses are particularly popular in glamour and fashion photography, because they tend to be dynamic and have a lot of impact. They are rarely used for beauty photography, which tends to focus more on close-ups of the model's face. Three-quarter-length poses also present interesting creative challenges for the photographer: you still have to put the sort of emphasis on the model's face as if you were shooting a straightforward head shot, but you also need to capture the shape of the model's body, and keep both in balance to create an image that is striking and effective.

create an oddly proportioned image; besides, most knees are usually not so photogenic anyway.

Three-quarter poses are often used for magazine cover shots because they can be quite punchy and dynamic and are in the right proportion for the shape of the magazine page. Full-length images often have less of an impact because the subject appears small and narrow in proportion to the page. Three-quarter images are also useful from the editorial viewpoint; they fill enough space to make a strong impact, but there is sufficient space around them to put in the magazine's straplines and cover text.

OPPOSITE: In this shot, having the model pose with her hands in her hair adds a pleasing angularity to the composition that also helps to bring out the shape of her body.
Canon D30; 1/125 sec at f/5.6; 100mm lens

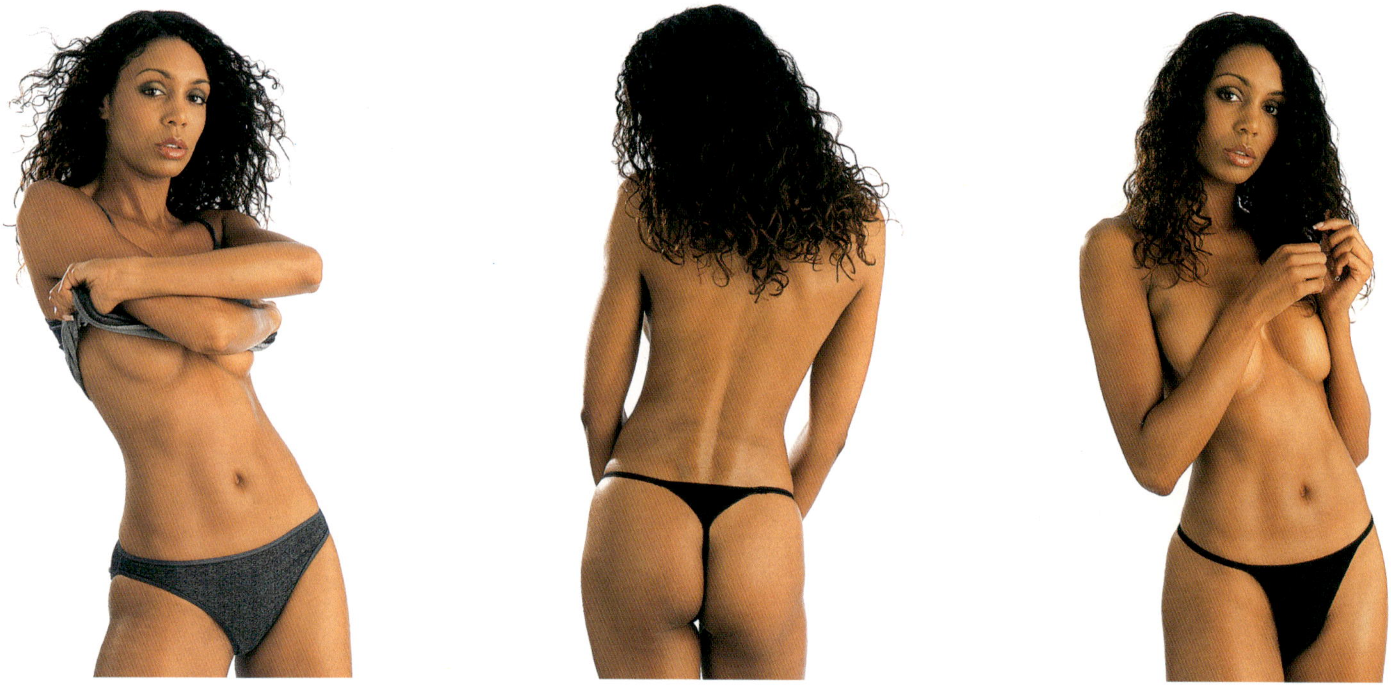

ABOVE: A wide range of poses and moods can be achieved with three-quarter poses, including simple back shots or more dynamic front shots with action and movement.
Canon EOS; 1/125 sec at f/11; 110mm lens; Fuji Provia 100

Glamour poses

Three-quarter poses are often used in glamour photography because you can capture most of the model's shape as well as her face, while keeping the overall image in good proportion. Cropping the picture across the model's thighs tends to create the most pleasing proportions. If you cropped at the knee, for example, you would

Fashion poses

Three-quarter poses are also a common feature of fashion photography. They allow the photographer to capture the important details of the garments that are being shown – obviously the main concern of the client – and also give the model scope to assume a wide variety of poses, whether animated, quirky, dramatic, alluring, cool or

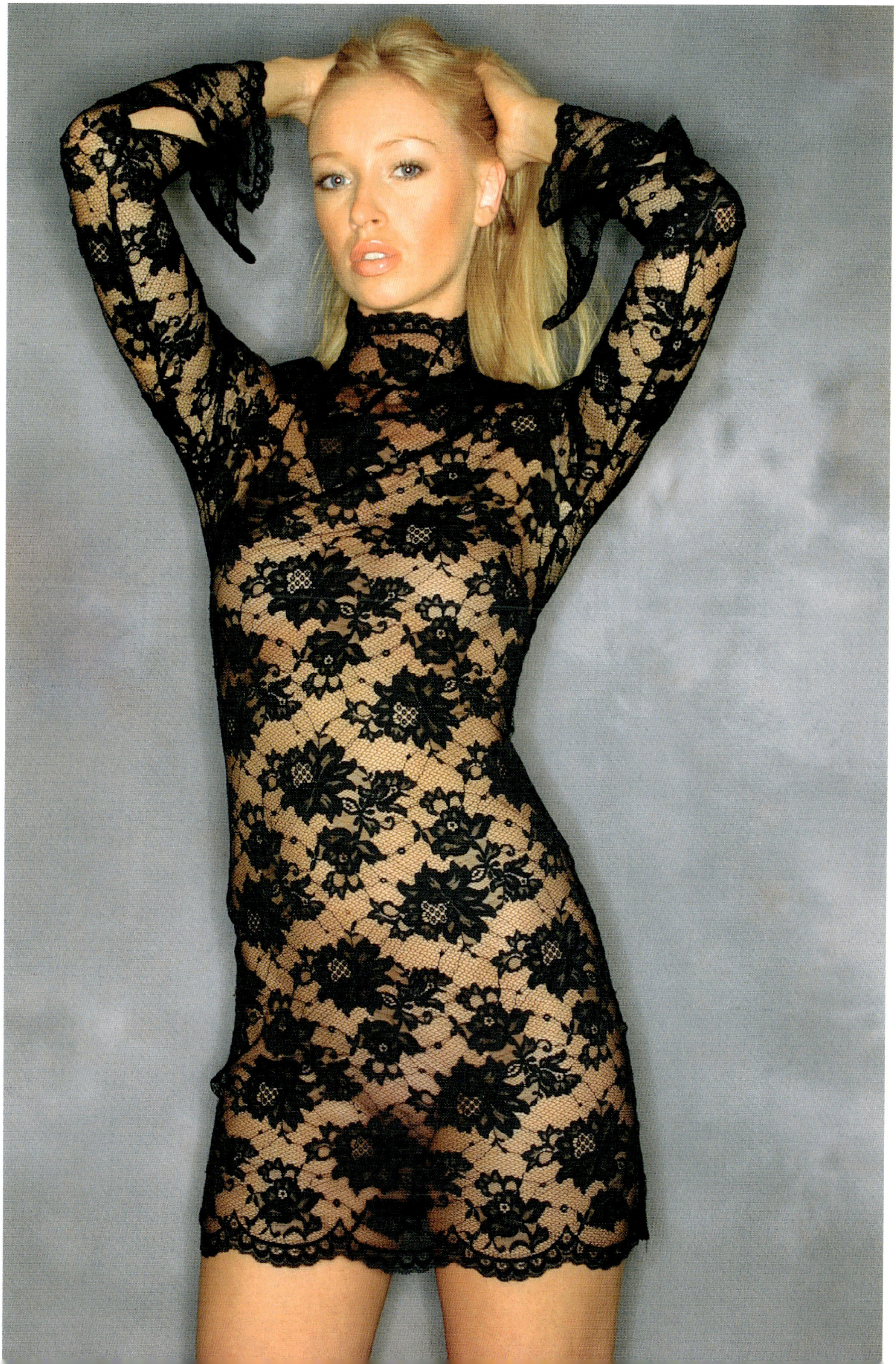

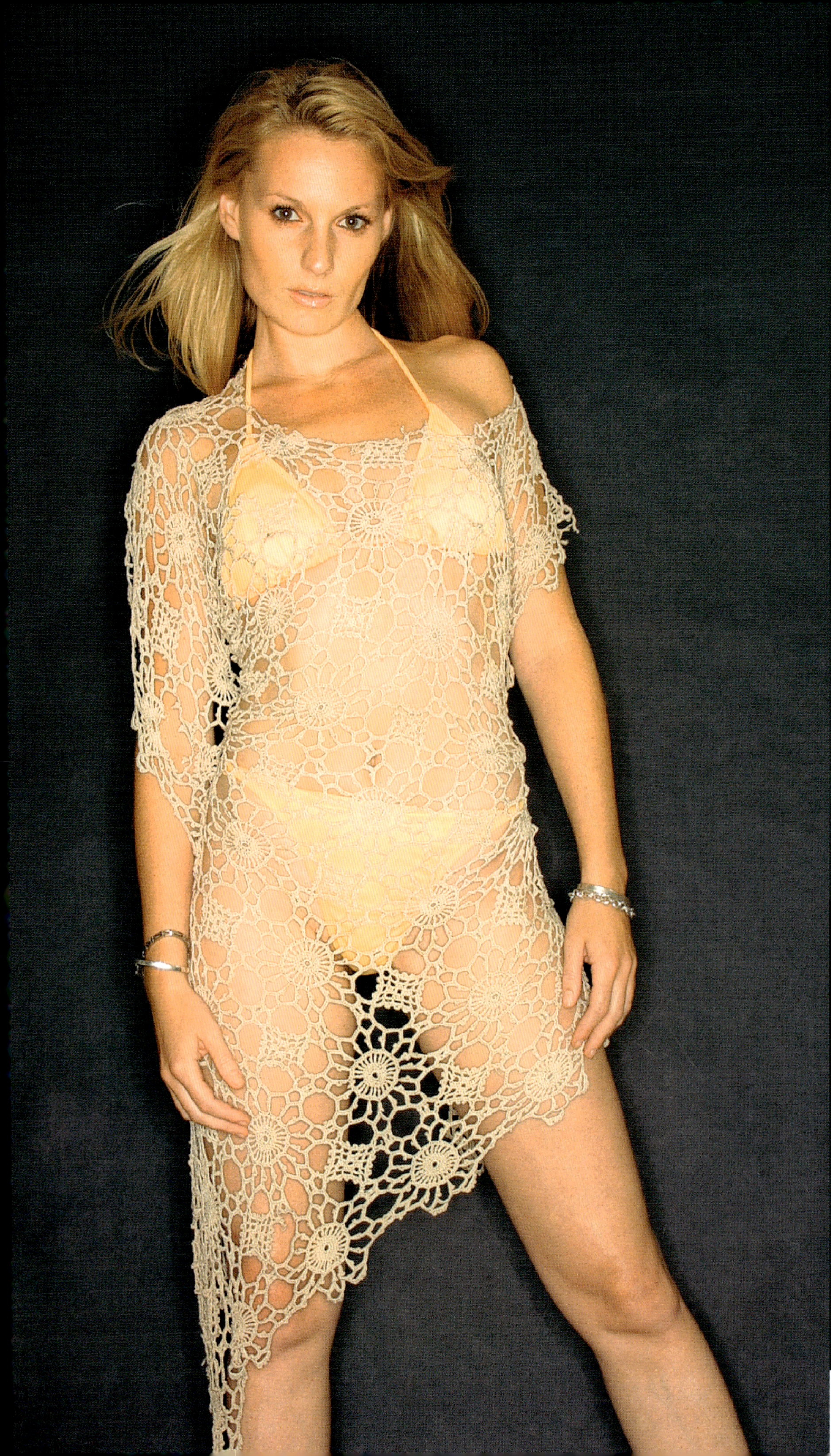
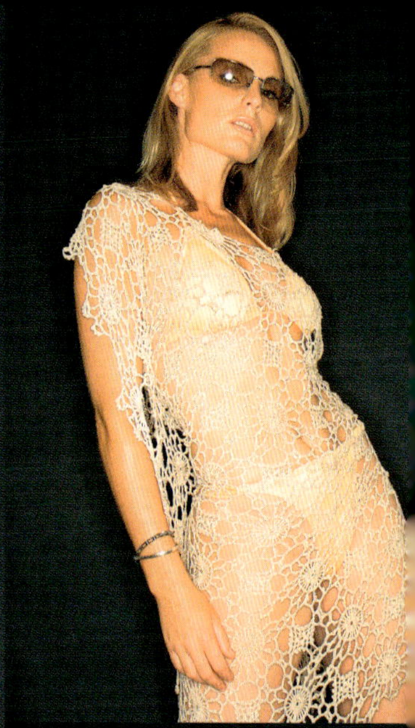
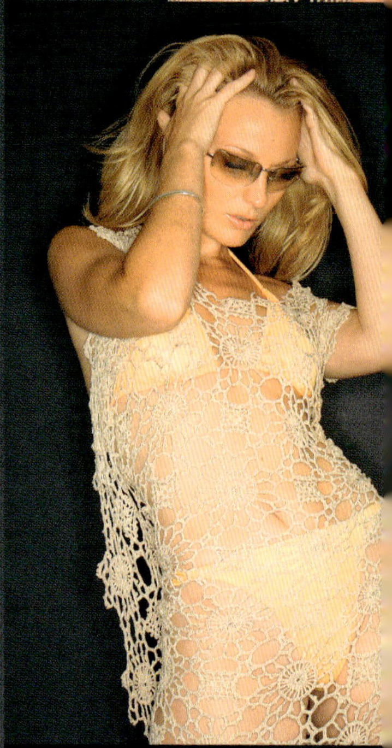
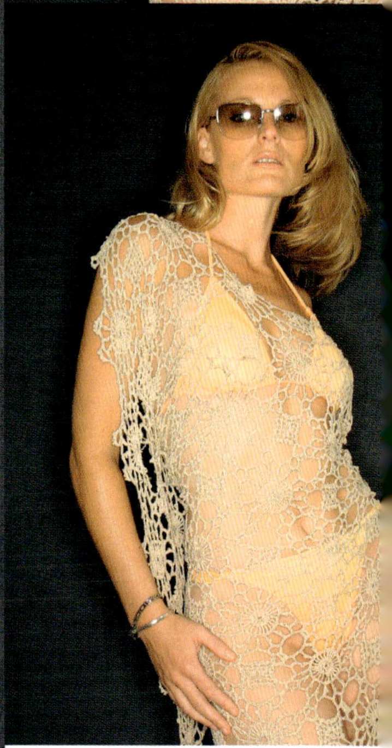

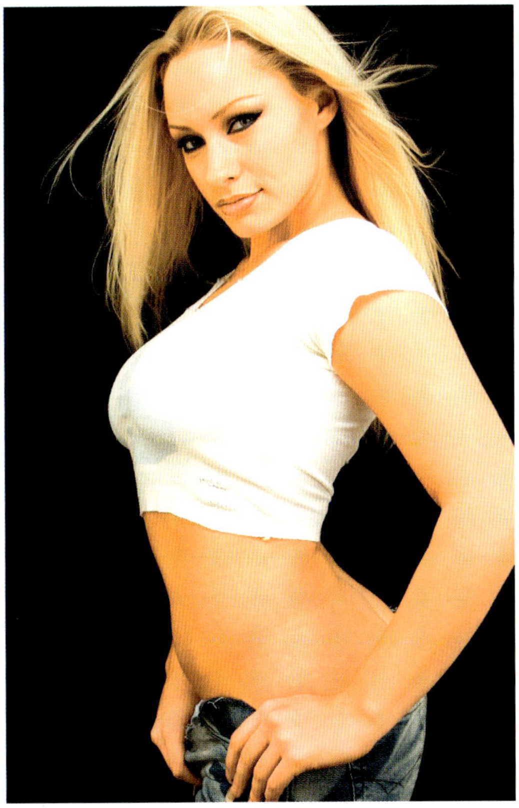

model needs to be well-proportioned: if someone has broad shoulders or a particularly narrow waist, their backs will tend to look out of proportion.

In general, you have more options as to what poses the model assumes and what interesting and expressive shapes these create. You can try strong, graphic shapes with the model front-on and experimenting with the positioning of her arms and hands. You can try dynamic, twisting poses with interesting movement in them. You can experiment with provocative semi-profile shots that show off the model's shape – all these types of shots can be successful and have a lot of impact.

LEFT: This is a standard glamour pose, with the model standing with her shoulders back and back arched to accentuate her shape. Posing the model against a black backdrop helps to lift her away from the background.
Canon D30; 1/125 sec at f/8; 100mm lens

thoughtful – whatever seems most appropriate to the style of the clothing and the mood that the client is trying to create in order to sell the product.

Versatility

Three-quarter-length poses offer a lot of scope and variety when composing shots. You can experiment with the model's position, shooting her straight-on, in profile, or taking back shots. These last shots, for example, often offer a pleasing simplicity and stillness to an image, although the

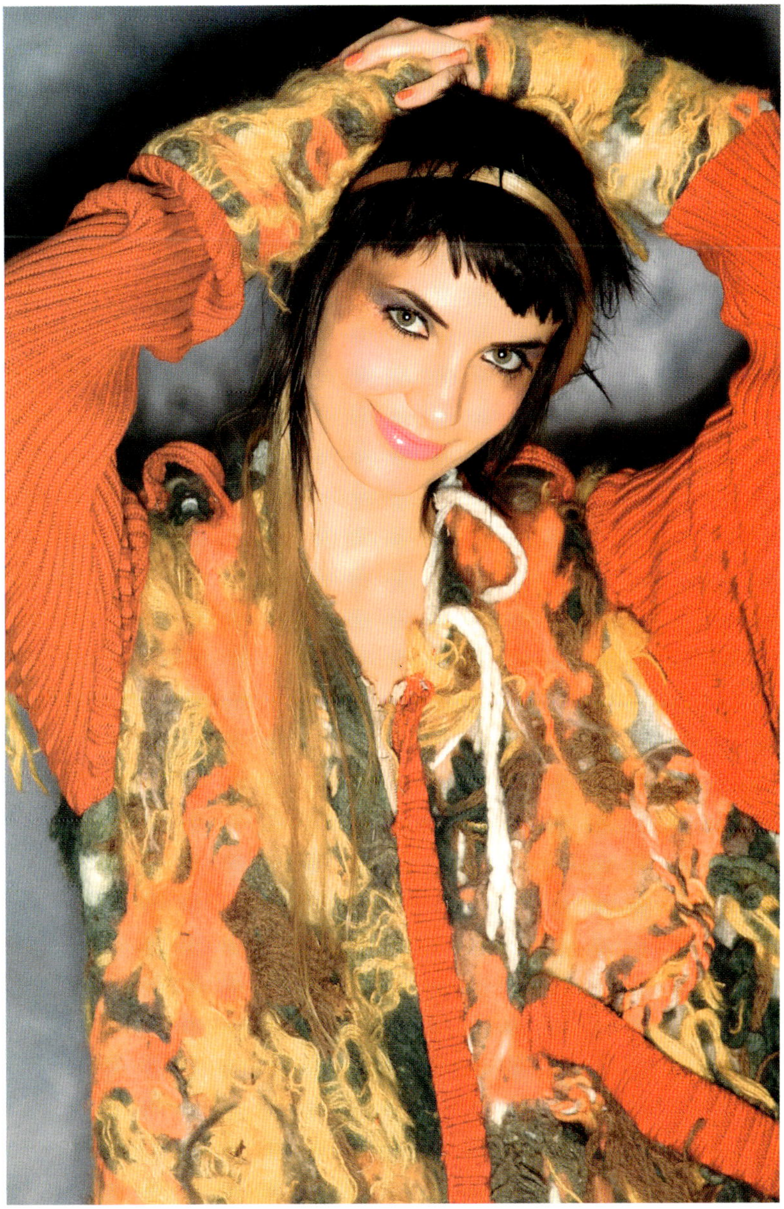

RIGHT: In this quirky fashion shot, the way that the model has posed her arms creates a pleasing frame for her face while showing off details of the clothes that she is wearing.
Canon D30; 1/125 sec at f/8; 100mm lens

OPPOSITE: This sequence shows how a model's pose can affect the success of a shot. The images on the right of the main shot don't have sufficient impact: the model's pose means that you cannot see the details of the garment that she is modelling. The way that these shots have been edited also means that the important detail of the asymmetric hem has been lost.
Mamiya RZ 6/7cm; 1/125 sec at f/16; 110mm lens; Fuji Provia 100

Full-length poses

BELOW: For this sultry glamour pose, the model nestles onto the back of a sofa. The provocative shapes of the model's arms and legs create relaxed and pleasing lines against the contours of the sofa.
Canon D30; 1/125 sec at f/8; 100mm lens

Full-length poses are used in both glamour and fashion photography, although there are often noticeable differences between images taken for the two genres. In glamour photography, the focus is on the model, while in fashion photography the focus is more on the clothes on the model.

Full-length poses are often quite tricky to compose successfully because you have so many elements to take into account. You have to concentrate on the model's facial expression and also on their body language and position, so there are more complicating factors.

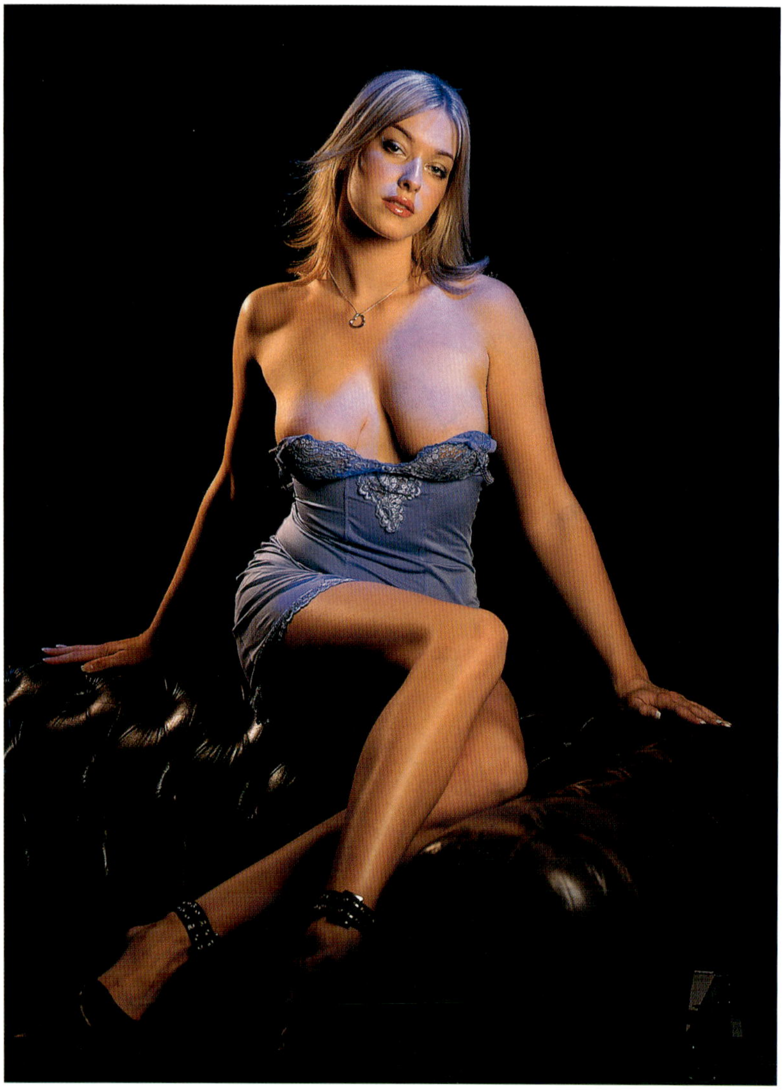

Camera position

The balance from the model's feet to the head has to give the impression of being in balance with the whole shot, or the overall image will look odd and out of proportion. Setting a lower camera angle can help – looking up at the model can create a better perspective and thus strengthens the image.

Posing the model

Having the model assume a position that looks natural and relaxed can be a challenge, but is essential to the success of the shoot. This is where experience tends to show. I wouldn't usually do full-length work with a less experienced model, who might find it very hard to pose naturally, and thus tend to look very stiff and wooden, with awkward, rigid body language. Experienced models tend to know what poses work best and manage to look natural and animated.

Full-length glamour poses often feature the model posing with props (see page 122) or standing against an interesting background (see page 95). The props or backdrops give something for the model to interact with and create more interest in the shot, but it is still the expression and pose that are the most important elements. The model needs to look relaxed and seductive.

In fashion photography, however, the clothes are the most important feature, and the pose has to work to show them off to their full impact. The model will often need to assume lively and animated poses, which also need to look natural.

OPPOSITE: It seemed appropriate for the model to assume a quirky and cheerful pose to show off the brash and colourful clothes in this fashion shot. The inset shot didn't quite work, as the model's pose looked somewhat wooden.
Canon D30; 1/125 sec at f/8; 80mm lens

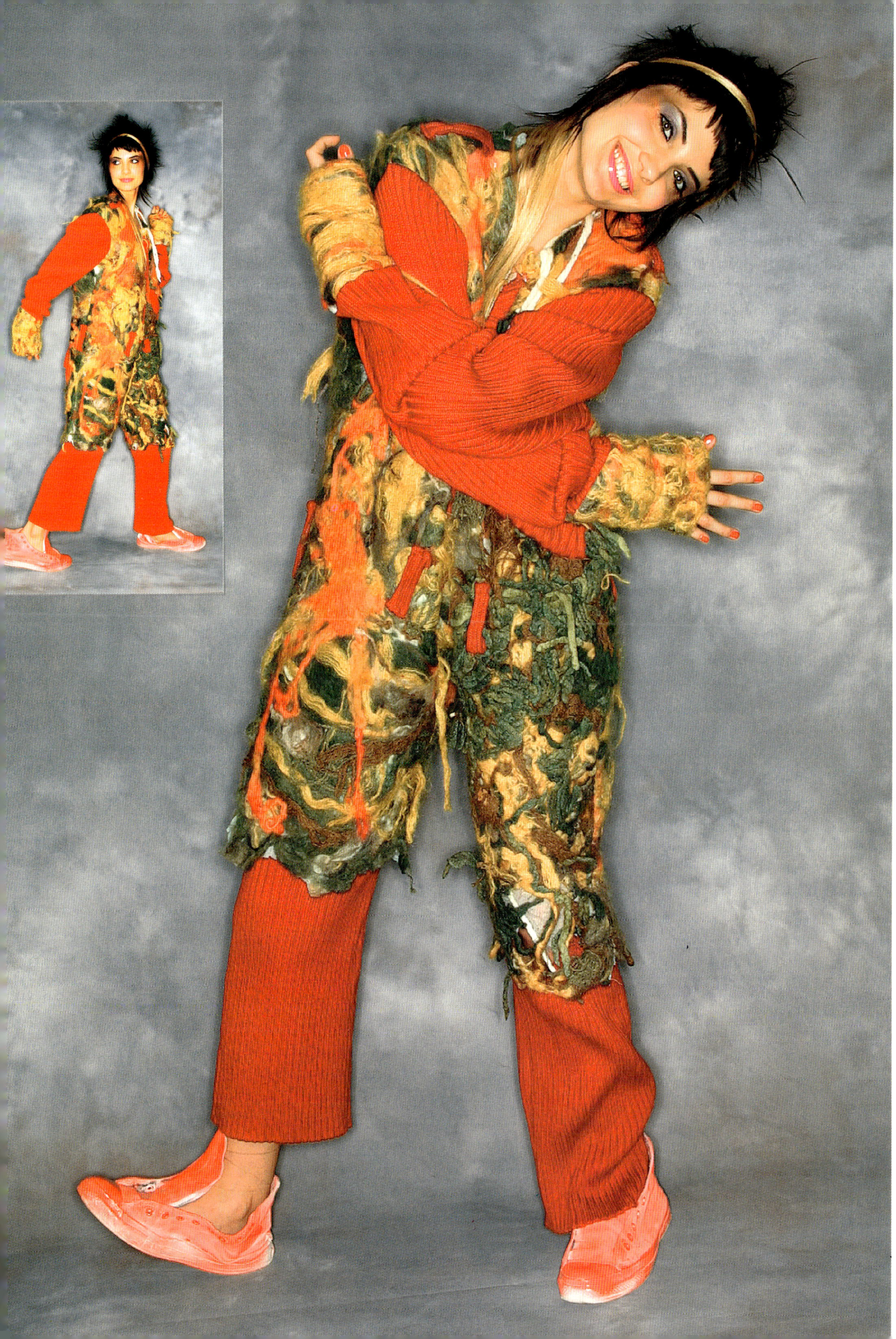

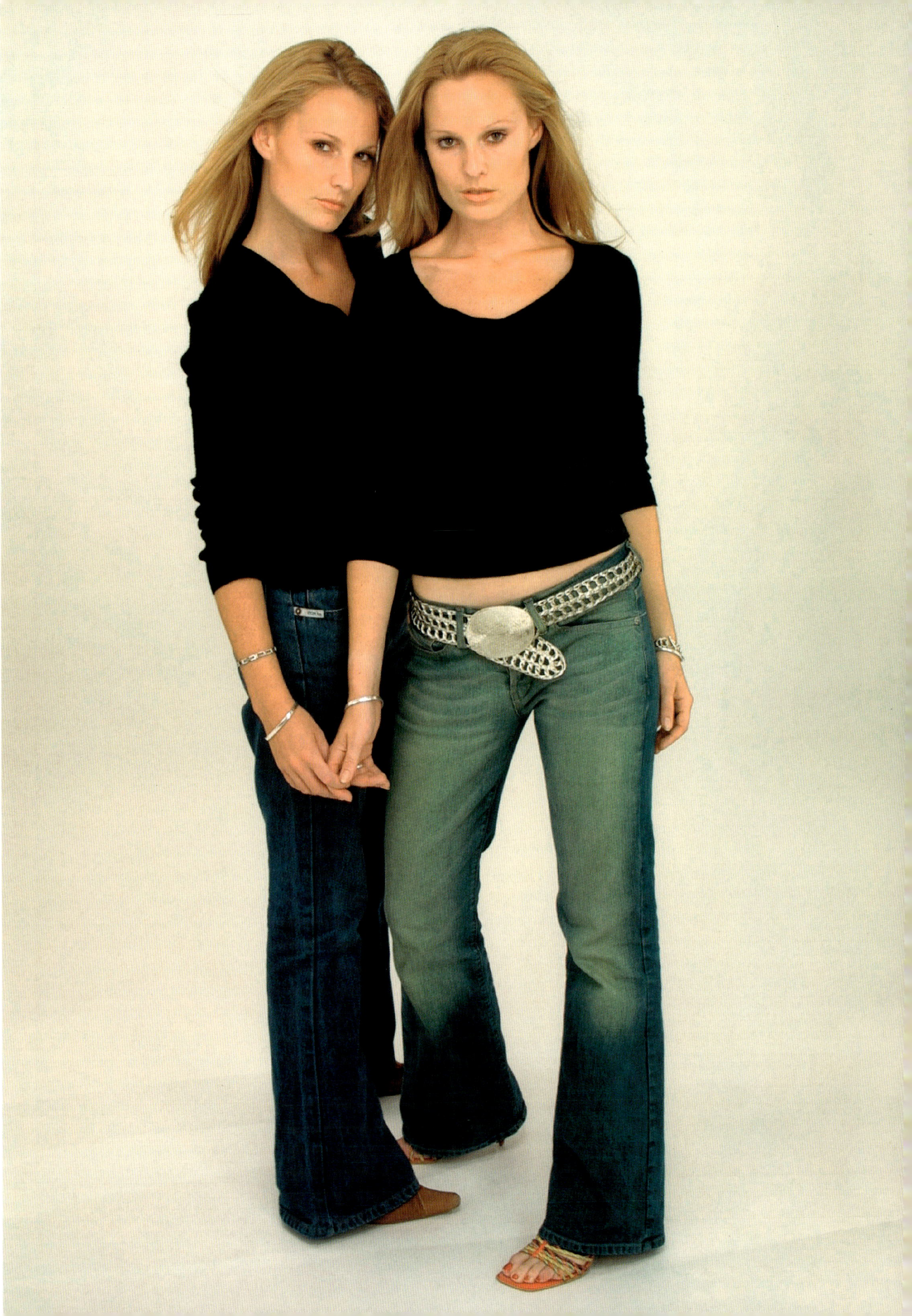

Full-length poses: two models

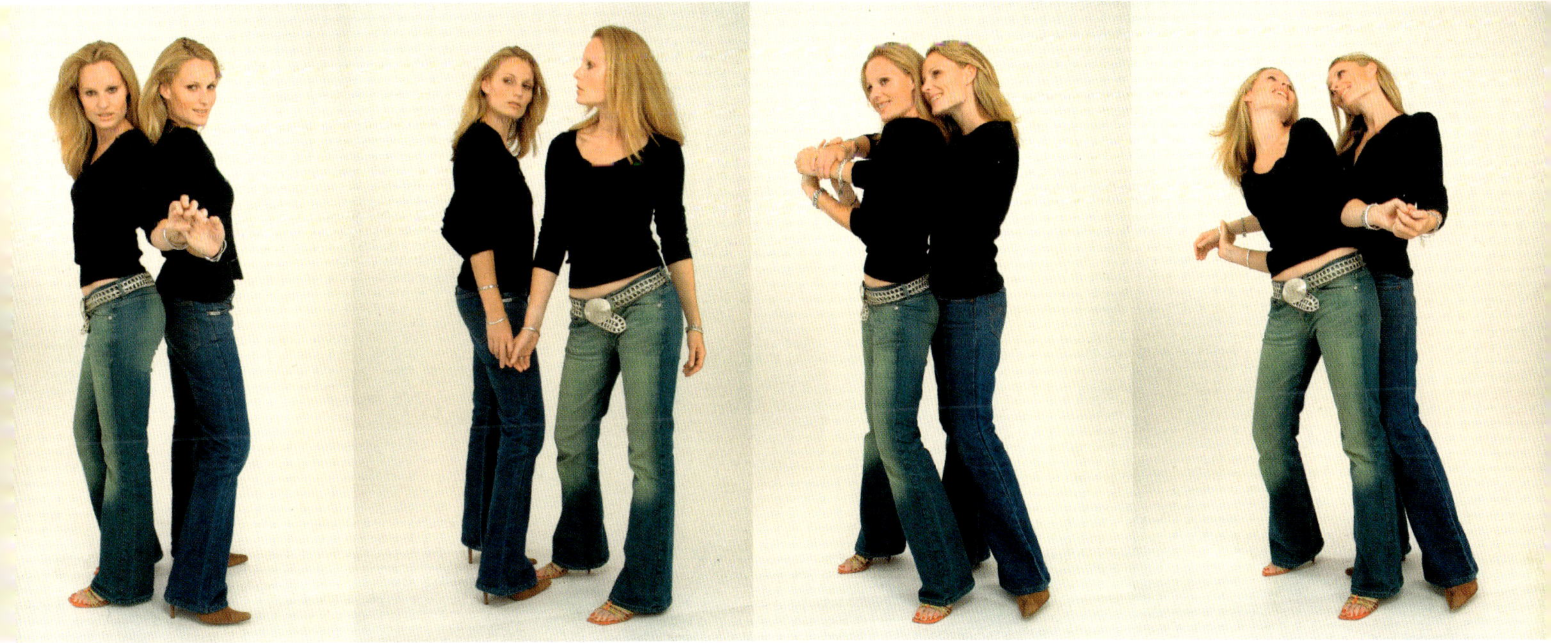

Full-length poses in glamour and fashion photography most commonly feature a man and a woman together and rely on the chemistry and interaction between them to create their impact (see pages 134–135).

Full-length poses featuring models of the same sex are rare in glamour, which relies most heavily on models on their own, but are more common in fashion photography; the models can wear outfits that complement each other and the shots therefore have more impact than showing one model on her own. In the shots shown here, for example, the fact that the models are identical twins who are wearing similar outfits adds a unique element to the pictures. The shots are dynamic because of the poses that the models are holding, but also have a pleasing symmetry and unity.

Working with two models

When you are using two models, you face the same problems as when shooting full-length portraits of a single model, added to which you have to consider how to compose the shot so that the interaction between the models creates an effective image. The rapport between the models is also an important consideration – they need to look relaxed and comfortable together and assume poses that makes their relationship look convincing. Obviously this wasn't a problem with the twins, but it can be a pitfall in other cases, particularly when shooting couples.

Problems in composition

Directing your models can be a complex business. Keeping the two models in proportion can be difficult; in the image second left above, for example, one model is standing slightly in front of the other and therefore looks bigger than her sister. It's also important to avoid cluttered shapes and awkward lines and angles. In the two images above right, the models' hands and feet are sticking out in a messy way. Keeping the pose simple and uncluttered is the best solution, as demonstrated in the main image opposite.

OPPOSITE AND ABOVE: When photographing two models, simple, dynamic poses tend to work best. There are lots of pitfalls to look out for, such as hands and feet sticking out at awkward angles and problems in perspective. The main image works well, with simple, flowing lines. The images above are less successful.
Canon D30; 1/250 sec at f/8; 50mm lens

Adding props

Using props and accessories can be an important part of a successful shot. They can add a finishing touch that lifts an image out of the ordinary, and also give the model something to interact with.

Collecting props

It is a good idea to have a general collection of props and accessories in your studio. This might include costume jewellery, hair accessories, lace gloves, sunglasses, hats and pieces of fabric to drape on the model. Such items can be found in markets, charity shops and boot fairs. I look out for items of local jewellery when shooting on location in places such as the Caribbean, as these can add an appropriately exotic touch to a location shot (see pages 100 and 102).

Using props

Using props and accessories can help to give more scope and variety to your compositions.

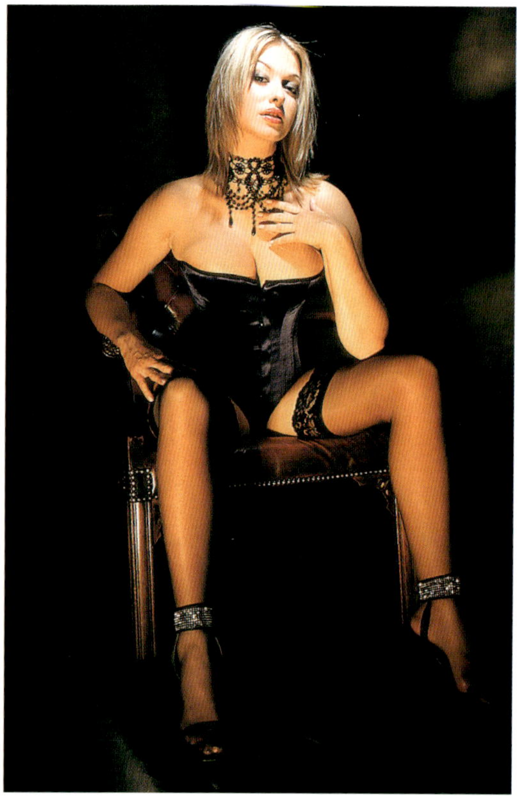

LEFT: Sitting on a chair allows the model to experiment with different expressions and poses.
Canon EOS; 1/125 sec at f/8; 100mm lens; Fuji Provia 100

OPPOSITE: The use of sunglasses adds an element of mystery to this image. It also gives the model something to do with her hands, adding another dynamic element to the picture.
Canon EOS; 1/125 sec at f/11; 100mm lens; Fuji Provia 100

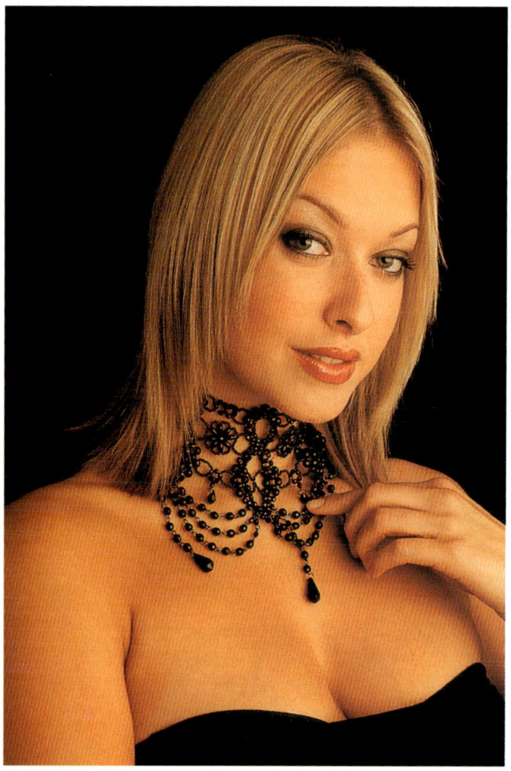

LEFT: The elaborate necklace enhances the sophisticated mood of this image.
Canon D30; 1/250 sec at f/8; 100mm lens

Something as simple as having your model sit down on a chair or stool opens up a whole new range of poses and expressions – the model has something to interact with, and you can create different shapes and moods.

Necklaces often make an effective accessory, adding an element of interest to a shot without overwhelming it. Necklaces can also often stand out well against the model's skin, creating an interesting contrast within the image (see pages 92 and 102).

Props such as necklaces and sunglasses also give the model something to do with her hands, which helps to create a more natural-looking and convincing image.

Working with models is an essential part of a glamour and beauty photographer's life. There is endless scope for posing models, and the good photographer is never afraid to experiment.

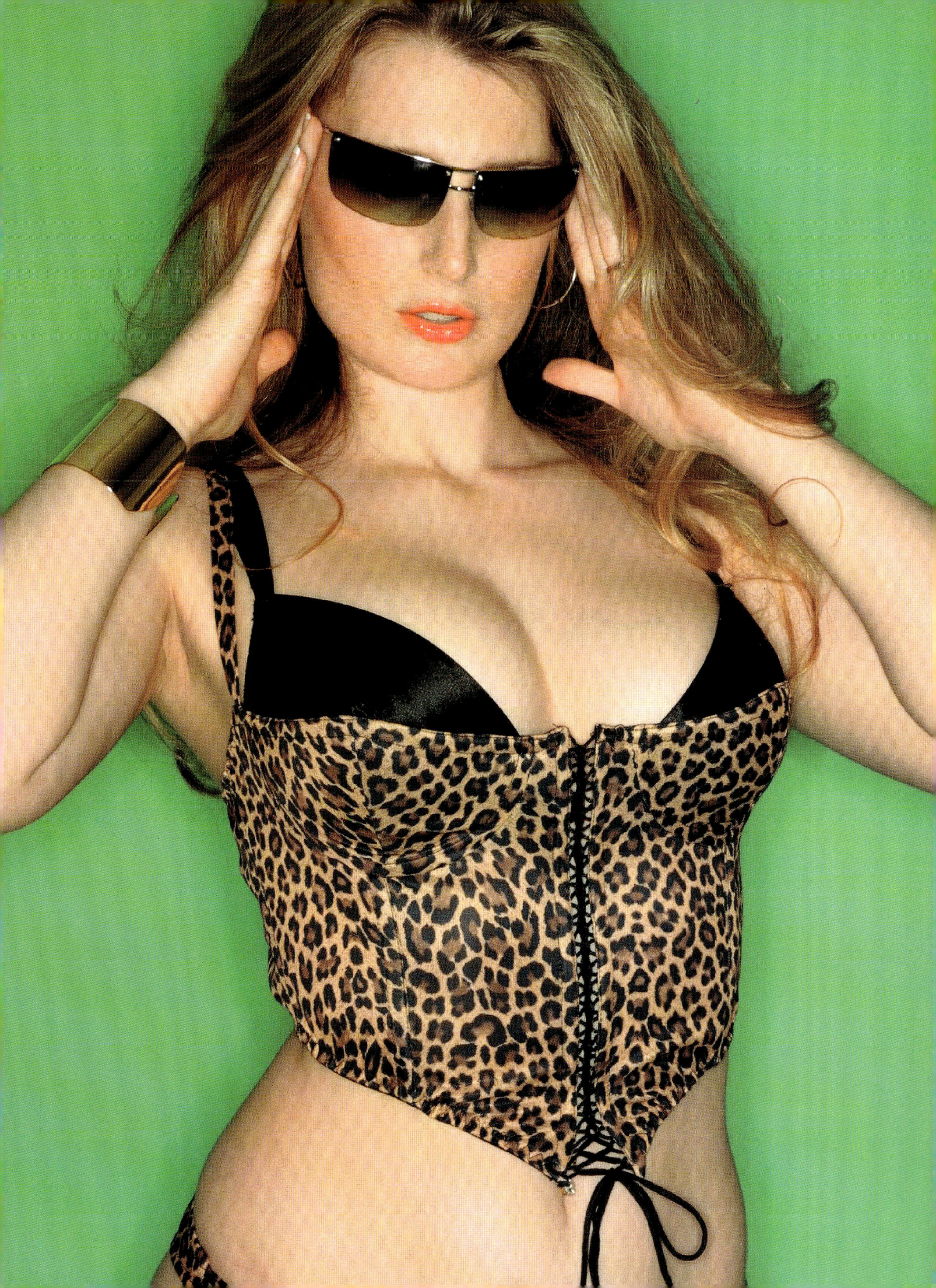

studio
glamour

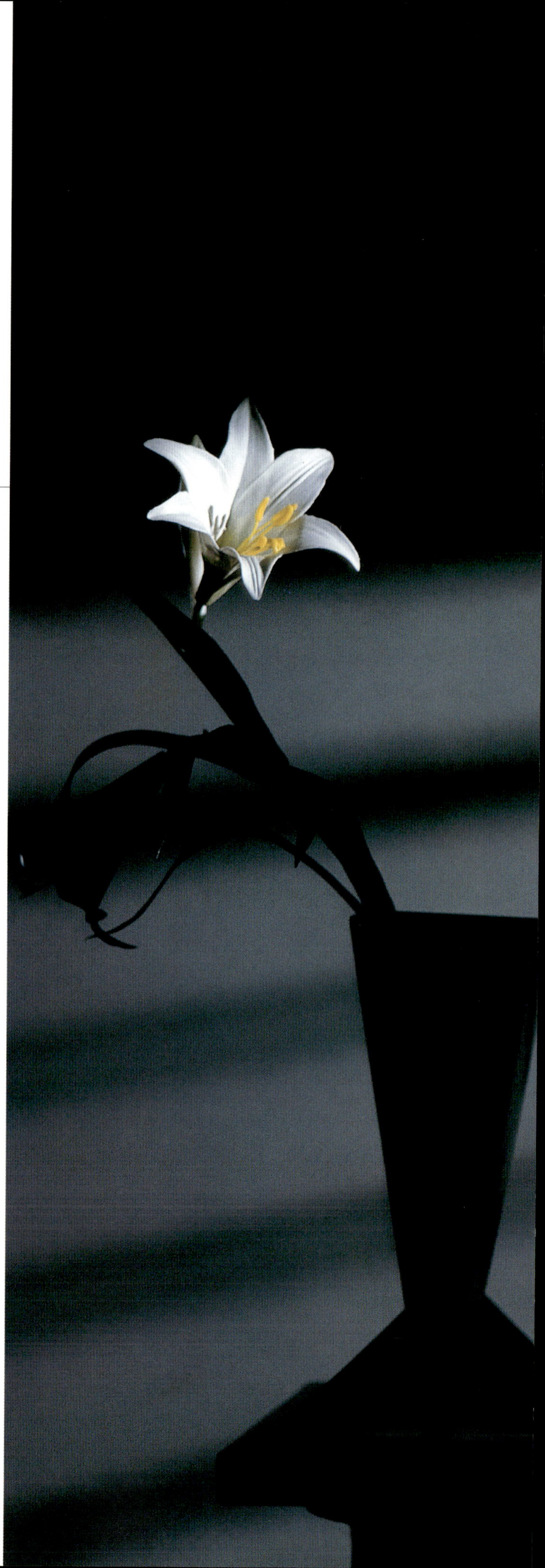

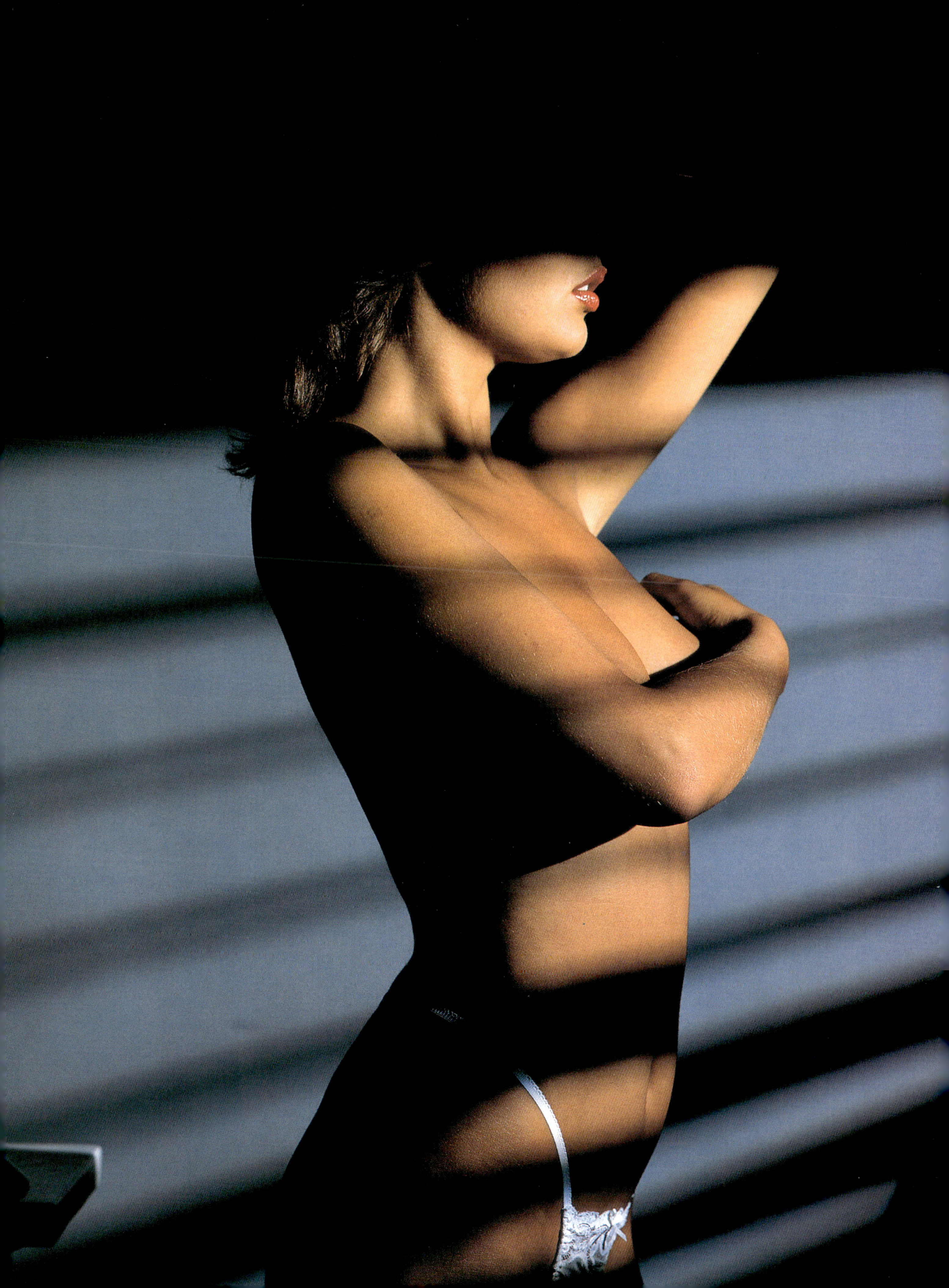

Basic studio set-up

The first consideration in setting up studio portraits is ensuring that you have enough room to work in. Enthusiastic amateur photographers often try to set up portrait shots in, say, their bedrooms or their living rooms, and the resulting shots are rarely particularly successful. Lack of space means that models are often forced to stand right up against a background, creating uncontrolled and unwanted shadows in the final image, while the photographer often struggles to position his or her light source at an adequate distance away from the subject.

The ideal studio

The minimum space you need in which to create a controlled environment appropriate for taking professional-looking photographs is a studio room that is about 8m (26ft) long, 4–5m (13–16ft) wide and with a ceiling that is at least 4–5m (13–16ft) high. High ceilings are necessary to enable you to install background drops; the further away the model is from the background, the more of the background will be seen in the resulting image.

Working in an adequate-sized space is also important to enable you to control your light source. If your workspace is too small, you will not have enough room to place your lights, and your images will tend to look flatly lit. You should be able to place your model 2–2.6m (7–9ft) away from the background, while the distance of your lights from your subject should be a minimum of 1.2–1.8m (4–6ft). The closer the subject is to the background, the harder it is to balance the light on the background and on the subject – the light becomes hard to control, and you will not create the sort of results that you are trying to achieve.

You also need to make sure that you can use a light purely to illuminate your subject and not your background; this helps to prevent the formation of unsightly and obtrusive shadows. Likewise, if you are using a light on the background, you can make sure that it only lights the background and doesn't spill over onto the subject.

Basic lighting set-up

The next consideration in setting up studio portraits is your lighting arrangement. You do not need a complex set-up to produce effective portraits. The basic lighting set-up that I used in the sequence of shots shown over the next few pages uses four lights (mainlight, fill-in light, background light and hairlight), but you can often get away with using only three lights: mainlight, fill-in light and background light – three lights, however, is probably the minimum requirement you need to create a good studio portrait.

I tend to avoid using umbrella lighting in the studio unless I am lighting a large group of people; it has a tendency to flatten the overall subject because of the broad, even spread of light that it produces. I prefer to use medium-sized softboxes as a mainlight because they offer a more controlled light source and create a softer lighting effect for portraits.

Tools for controlling light

Once you have your basic lighting set-up established, you can think about experimenting with controlling light sources. Screens and reflectors are useful methods of controlling, reflecting and diffusing your light source. A standard piece of 2 x 1.3m (7 x 4ft) polystyrene is perfectly adequate for this purpose if you don't want to go to the expense of buying one of the more expensive commercially available reflectors.

Triflectors, such as the one seen in the picture opposite, are useful for controlling light sources, as they reflect and bounce light under the model's chin and create highlights – known as catchlights – in the subject's eyes. This helps to create more

OPPOSITE: This shot reveals the basic set-up for the sequence of images shown over the next four pages. This is a pretty standard lighting arrangement for glamour portraits. The triflector in front of the model and the reflectors on either side help to control the amount of light on the model and on the background. **Mamiya RZ 6/7cm; 1/125 sec at f/16; 150mm lens; Fuji Provia 100**

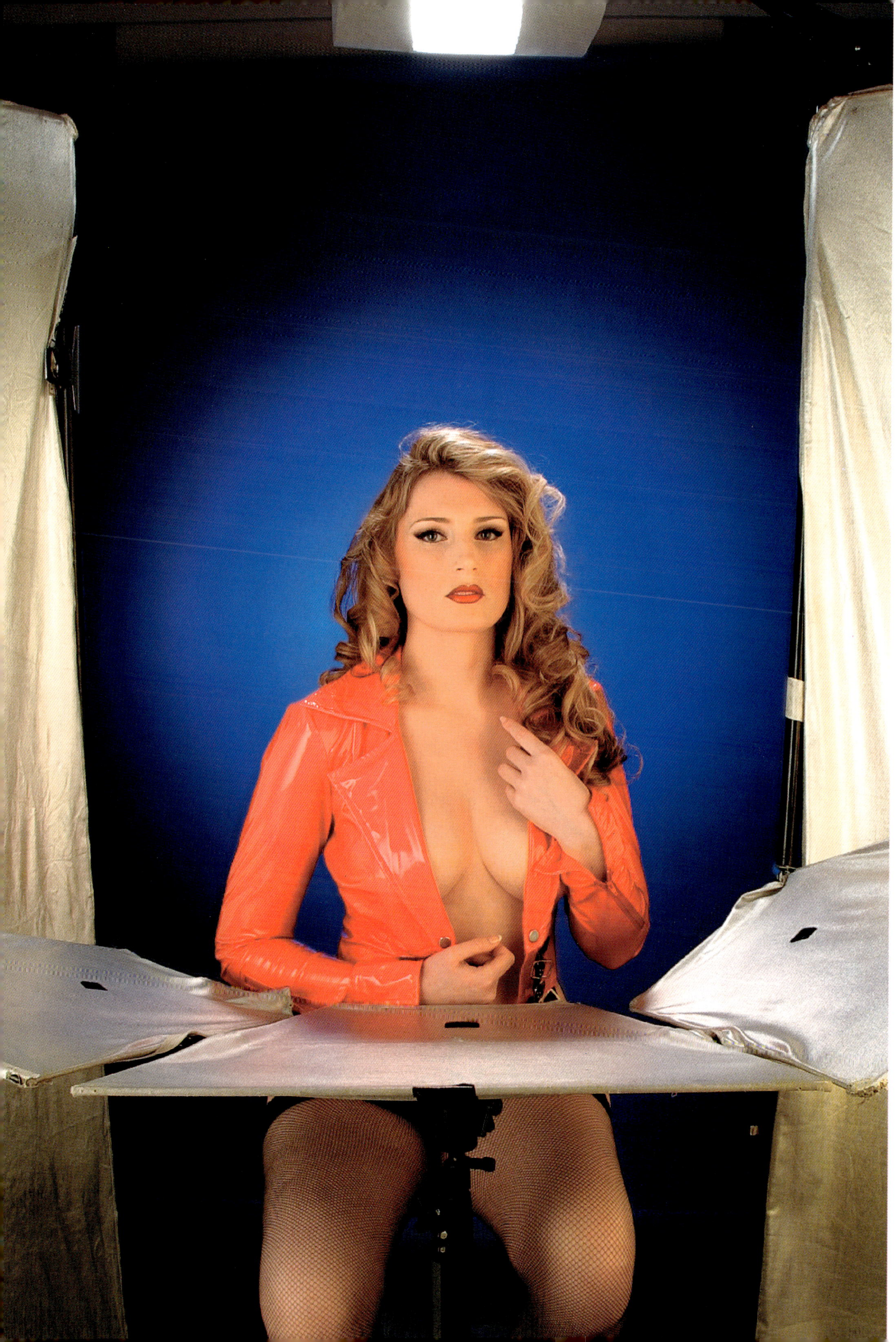

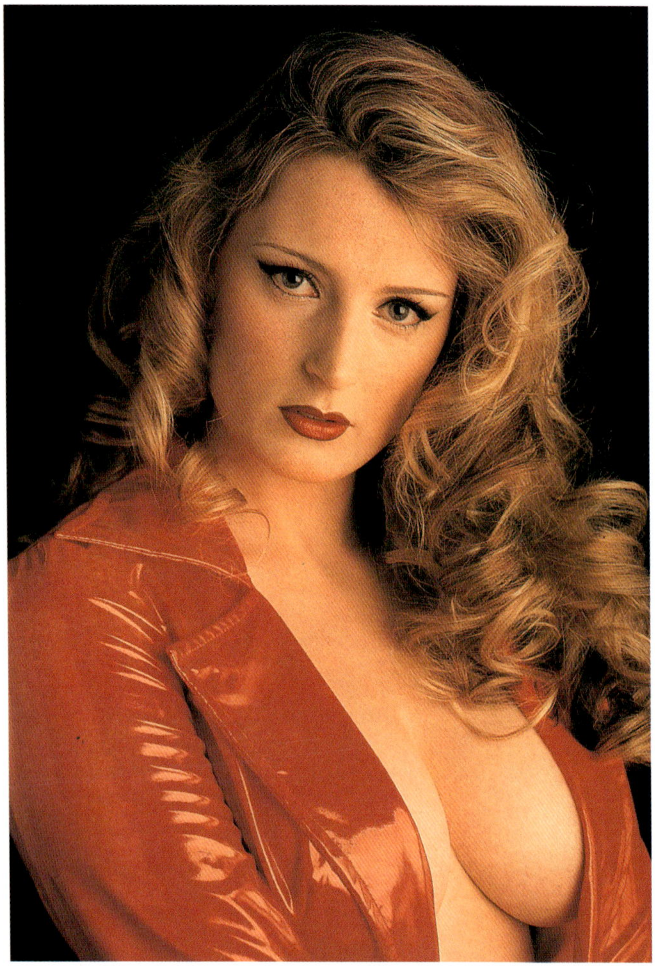

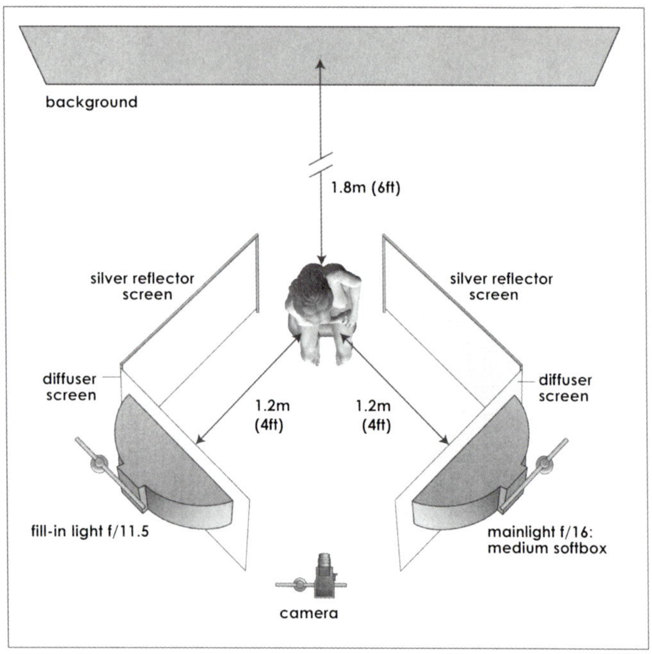

RIGHT: This shot was taken with the mainlight plus a fill-in light, which was placed on the left-hand side of the model to fill in details of the left side of her face, hair and body.

LEFT: This shot shows the use of mainlight only. The light source, a medium-sized softbox, was placed at a 45-degree angle to the model on camera right. This light creates good modelling on the right-hand side of the model.

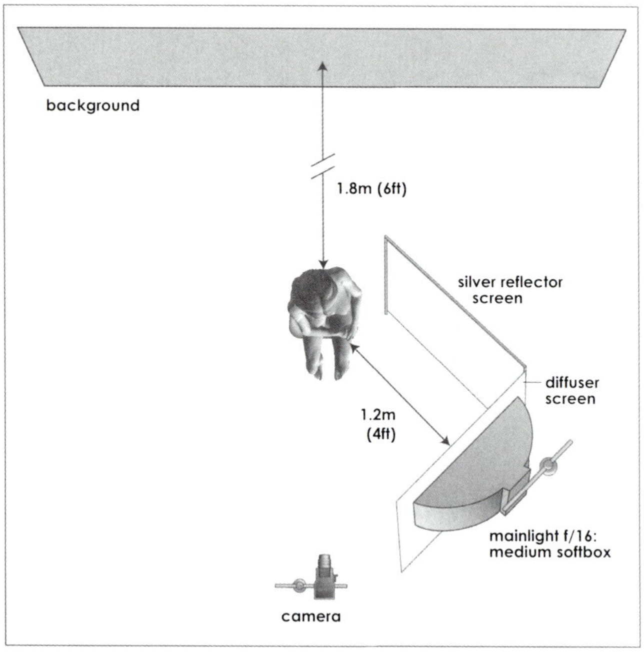

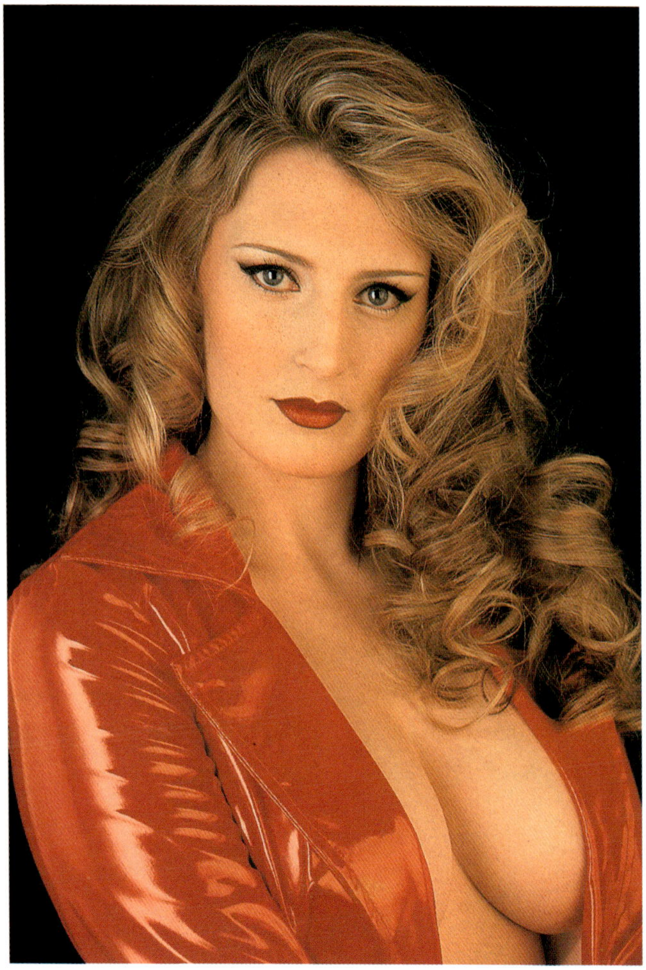

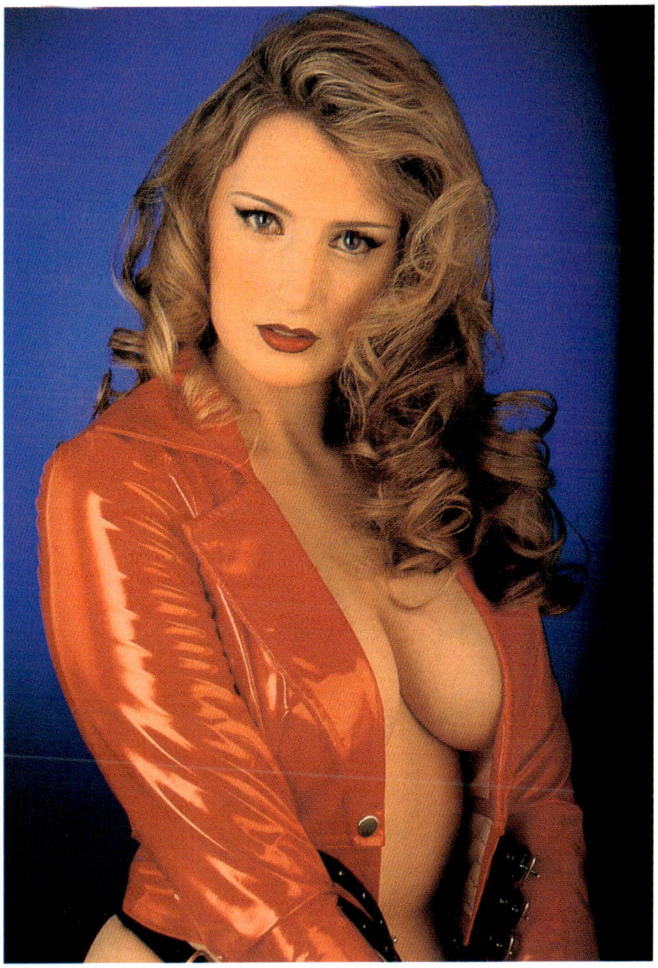

LEFT: This shot was taken with the mainlight, fill-in light and a background light. I used a honeycomb attachment behind the model to create the 'halo' effect on the background and the model. Using a light blue filter on the background light helped to increase the intensity of the blue backdrop.

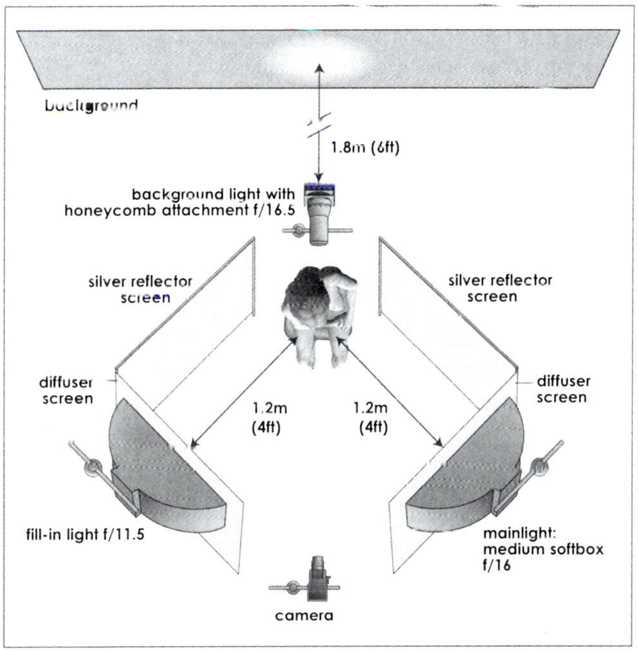

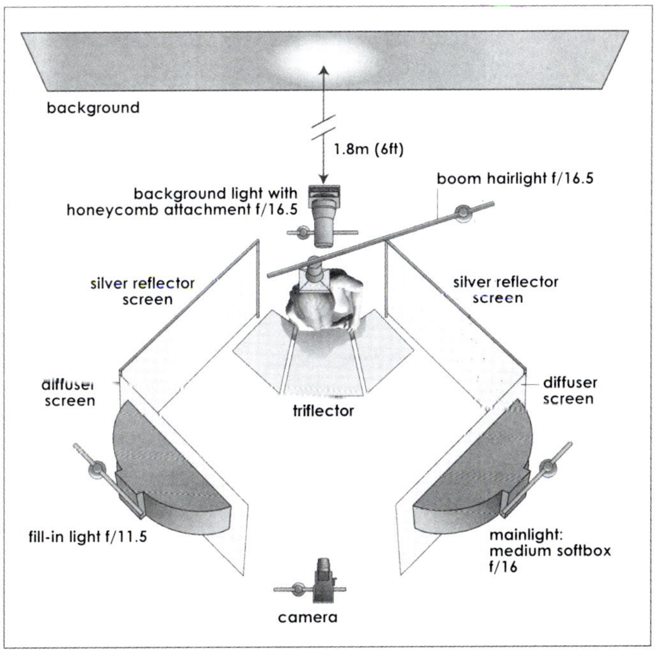

RIGHT: Here I used the three lights as before and brought in a hairlight as well. This was placed on a boom stand above and behind the model's head. The hairlight creates highlights in the model's hair, bringing more life into the image. Some light has also spilled onto the top of her jacket, creating further detail.

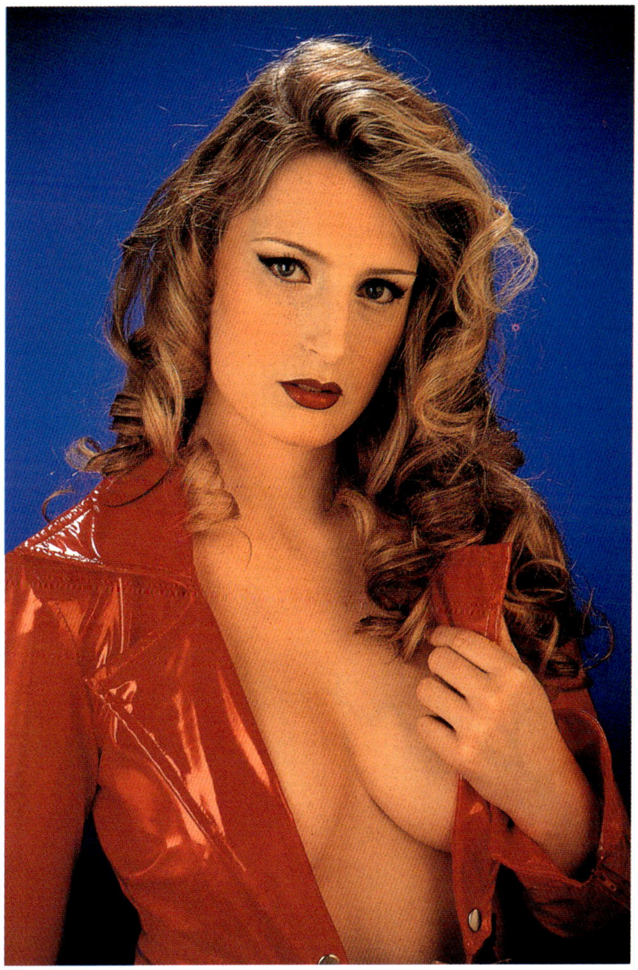

OPPOSITE: This shot uses the standard set-up of mainlight, fill-in light, background light and hairlight, as described on the previous page. **Mamiya RZ 6/7cm; 1/125 sec at f/16; 150mm lens; Fuji Provia 100**

BELOW: I also shot the model with ringflash, which creates a very different effect. The lighting is flatter, more intense, contrasty and aggressive. **Mamiya RZ 6/7cm; 1/125 sec at f/8; 150mm lens; Fuji Provia 100**

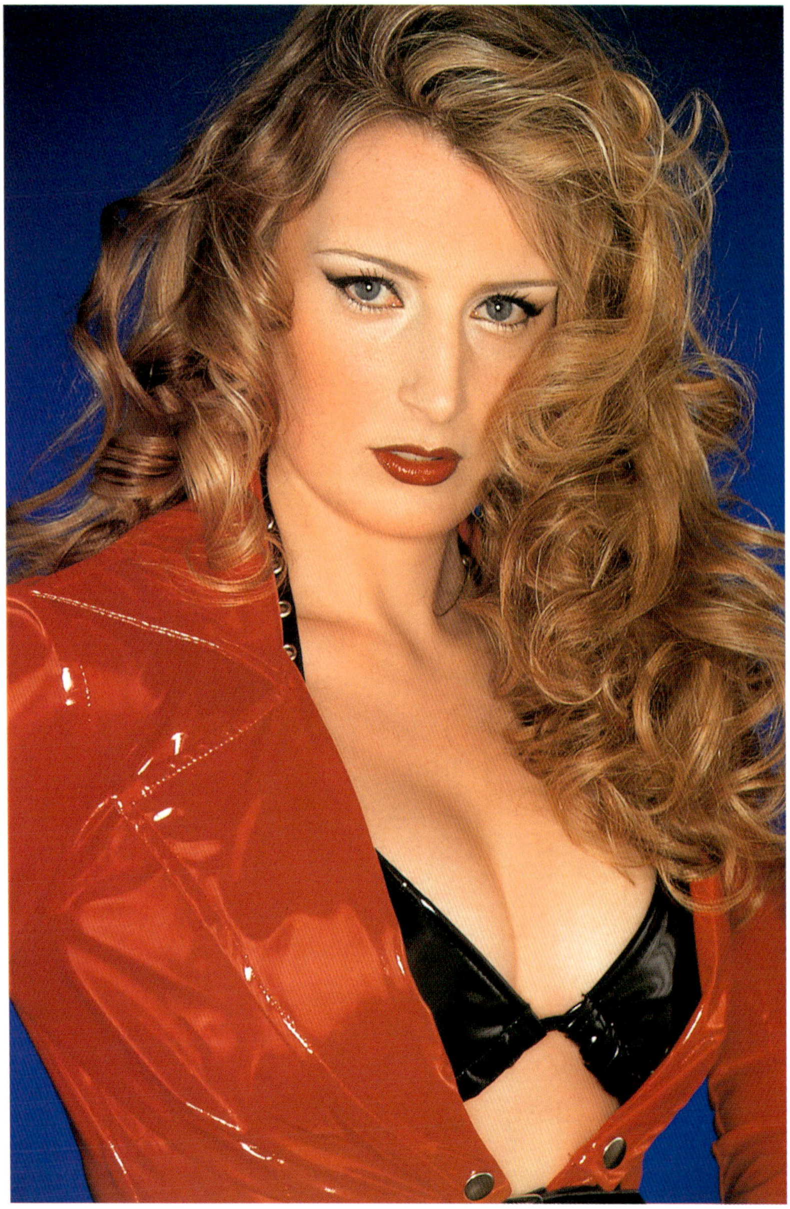

dynamic and lively-looking portraits because the eyes have a little extra sparkle and expression.

Backgrounds

Your choice of background is another important consideration when setting up studio portraits. A lot of photographers use coloured paper back-grounds, which are often known by their trade name, Colorama. These are useful, but be aware that they can tend to create a rather flat-looking image, particularly if you light with flat lighting rather than controlled lighting: flat lighting tends to make the colour of the background look weak and washed out.

I often use backgrounds of painted canvas rather than flat paper, and find that this creates a richer and more textured effect in the image, with pleasing variations in colour and tone. This effect is enhanced if you use a mottled backdrop, which you can create by spray-painting the canvas. A textured backdrop often enhances strong compositions (see pages 66 and 70).

Simple white-and-black backdrops are always useful to keep in the studio. Mid-grey is also very versatile – you can create different colour backgrounds by using coloured gels on your background lights, and mid-grey is ideal because it absorbs these different colours.

On strong colours such as blues and reds, you can use additional lighting gels to enhance the intensity of the colour, as in the image opposite. This also helps to create a better contrast in the shot; in this picture, for example, there is a pleasing punchiness to the contrast between the strong red of the model's jacket and the vivid blue of the backdrop.

Other useful items

Boom stands and lights (like the one shown in the set-up on page 53) are very useful because they allow you to light your subject from above. You can use boom stands to support a hairlight, or for lighting backgrounds from an acute angle, and these lights are also useful for shooting still lifes.

Items of furniture, such as stools and leather armchairs, are useful when shooting portraits, as they will give you a greater number of options for posing a portrait subject.

You should also have a gadget case in your studio for essential items such as bulldog clips, gaffer tape and double-sided tape. You can use bulldog clips for supporting backgrounds, or for clipping up model's clothes to get them to sit right if they are a little too large. Double bulldog clips are very useful for attaching filters to lights. Gaffer tape is extremely strong and can be used to tape backgrounds down. Double-sided tape can be used to tape down collars or belts and the like that won't lie flat.

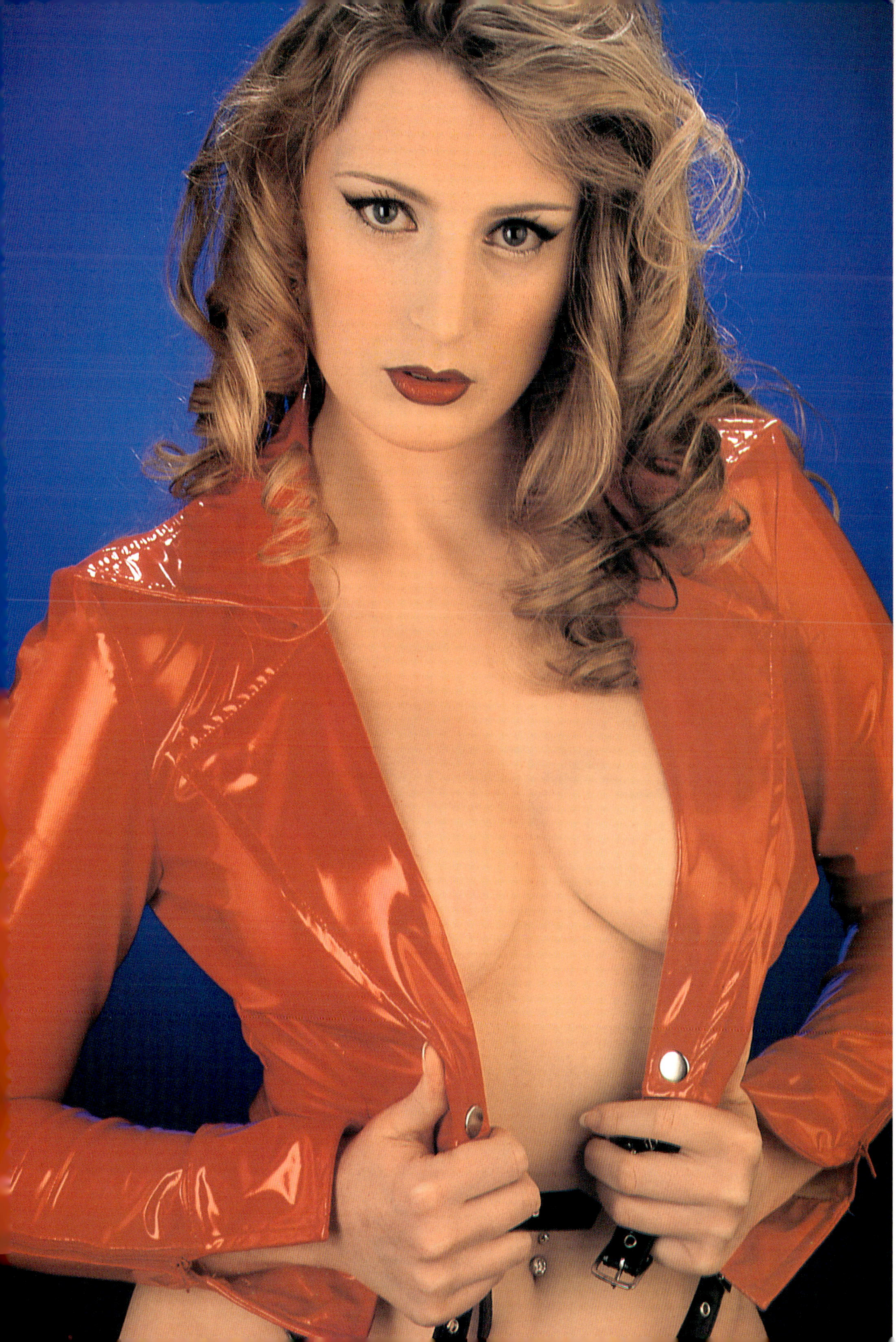

Studio glamour techniques

It is important to master the basic techniques of beauty and glamour studio portraits before you advance to more creative and experimental techniques – you need to be a completely competent technician and be able to understand the structure and balance of your lighting set-up.

You need to fully understand, for example, how to work out the ratios on your basic lighting set-up before trying out more innovative ways of working. For basic studio work, if your mainlight (which is your exposure light) is f/11, then your fill-in light should be half a stop less at f/8.5.

The hairlight has to be set to balance the rest of the lights. The exact setting will depend on the colour and density of the model's hair: the light for blonde hair can usually be set at f/11.5, while the light for black hair, which soaks up a lot of light, needs to be around f/16.

The setting for the background light depends on the density of the colour of the backdrop. It usually needs to be half a stop more powerful than the mainlight, but a deep blue background, for example, will need to be more powerful still. Be aware that your eyes are far more sensitive than film will ever be, and until you are experienced, you will tend to underestimate the amount of light that dark subjects, which absorb more light, will need on them to capture sufficient detail.

Once you have grasped the basics of technical knowledge, you can start to experiment with more innovative lighting, special effects and even processing techniques.

Ringflash lighting

Ringflash lighting is a technique that originated from macro and medical photography. If you are photographing a very small object, it is usually a struggle to get a light source close enough to illuminate it. Using ringflash bypasses this problem because you can put your camera lens through

BELOW: The shot on the left shows the basic set-up for a simple beauty portrait. The mainlight is a small softbox above and to the front of the model. The use of the triflector underneath the model's face and the reflectors on either side direct the light to create an overall clean and even light that is soft and flattering.
Mamiya RZ 6/7cm; 1/125 sec at f/11; 150mm lens; Fuji Provia 100

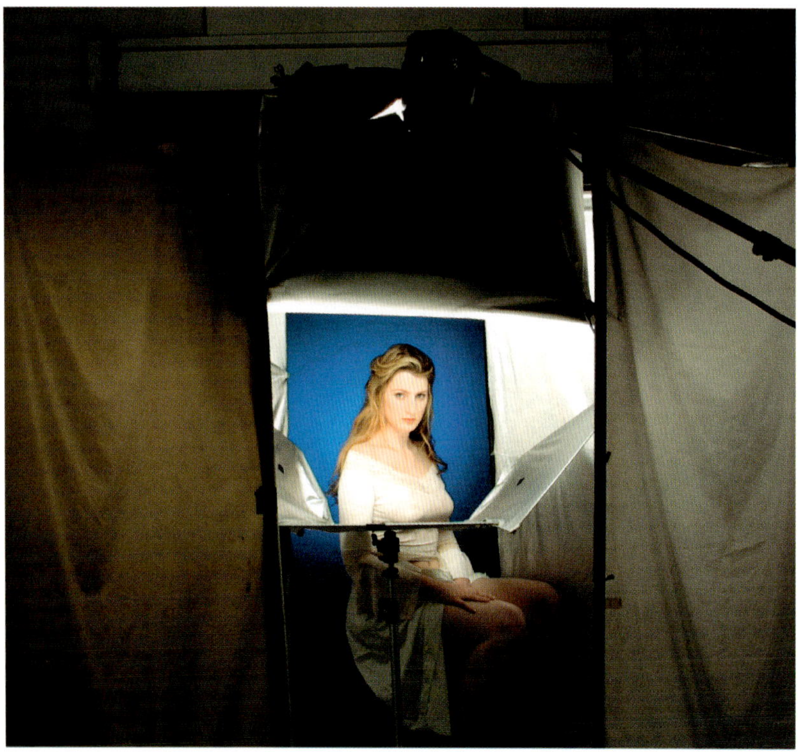

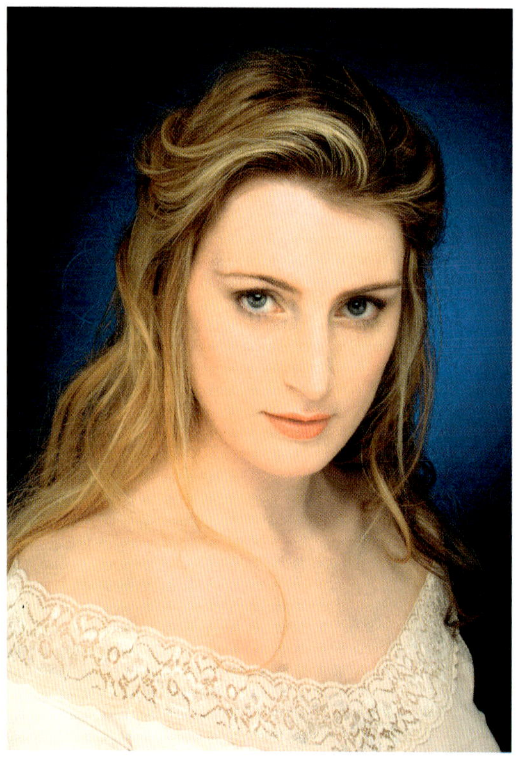

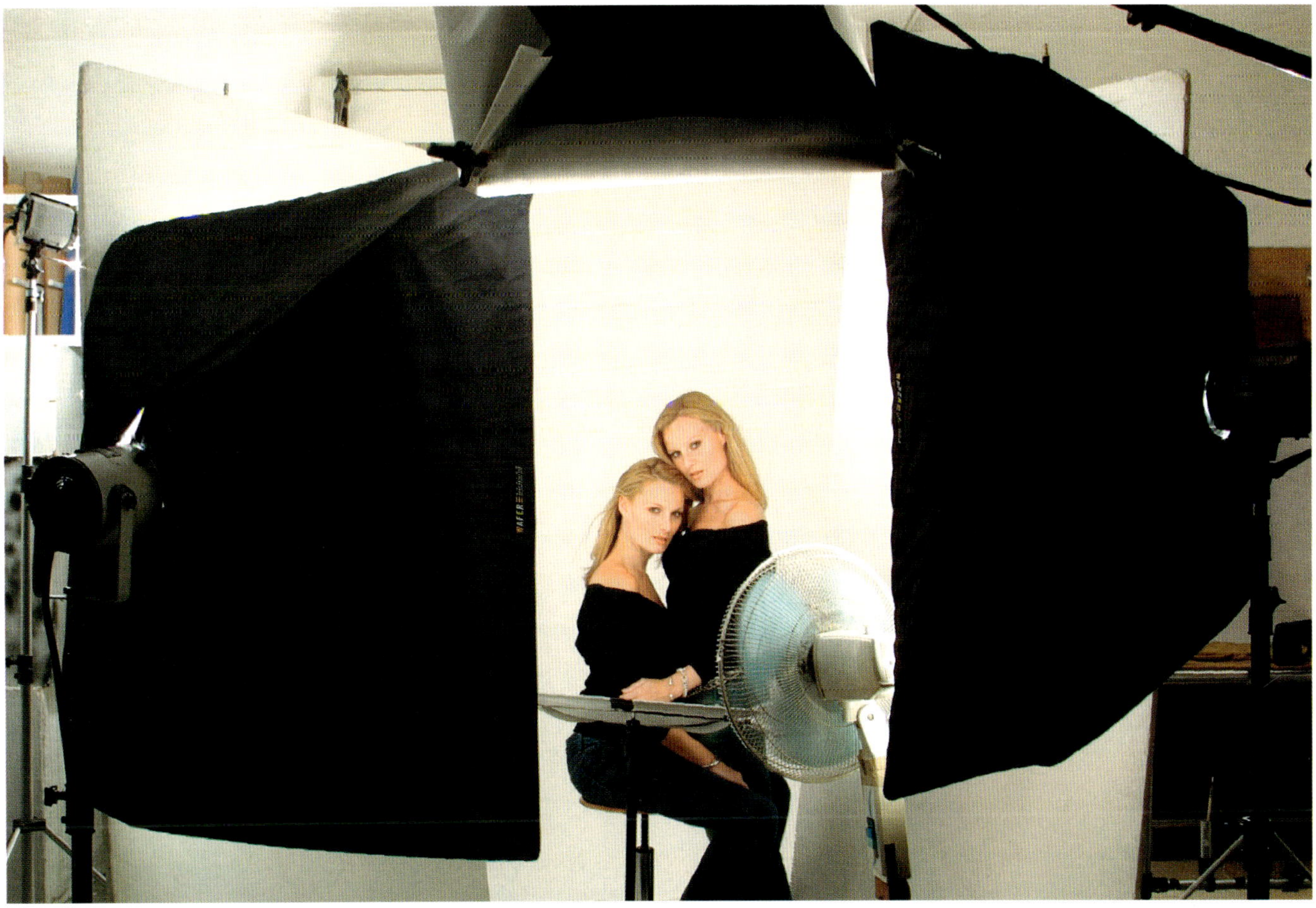

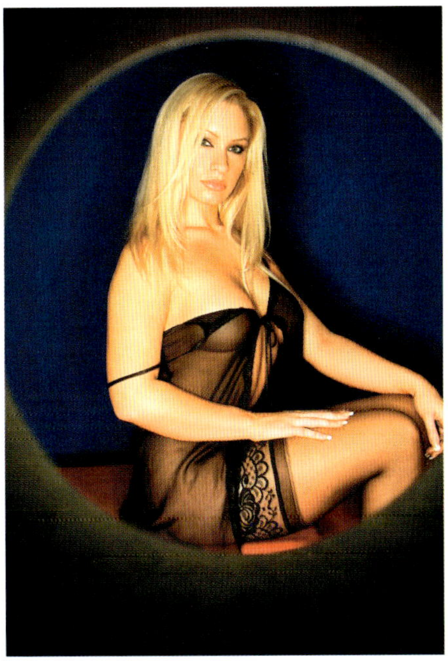

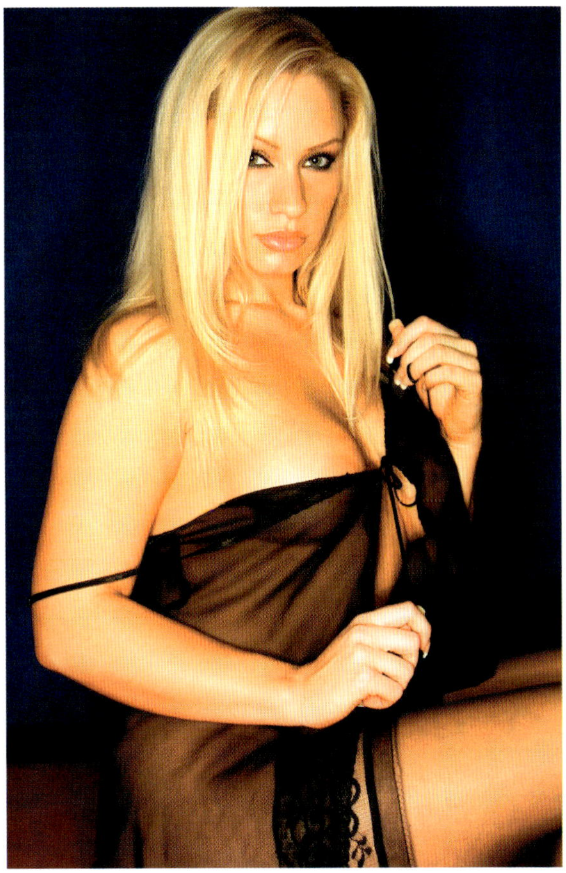

ABOVE: The image above shows another basic beauty portrait lighting set-up. There is a medium-sized softbox on either side of the models, and a small softbox above, to create a tent lighting system – each light was set to the same f-stop. Additional screens were used to the back and sides of the models to impart more softness to the shot. The resulting image is warmly and evenly lit, and very flattering to the models' skin tones.
Mamiya RZ 6/7cm; 1/125 sec at f/16; 150mm lens; Fuji Provia 100

LEFT: These images were taken with ringflash: the image on the far left shows the view through the lens, and the shot on the left shows the final picture. Ringflash produces intense colours and rich skin tones.
Canon D30; 1/125 sec at f/8; 100mm lens

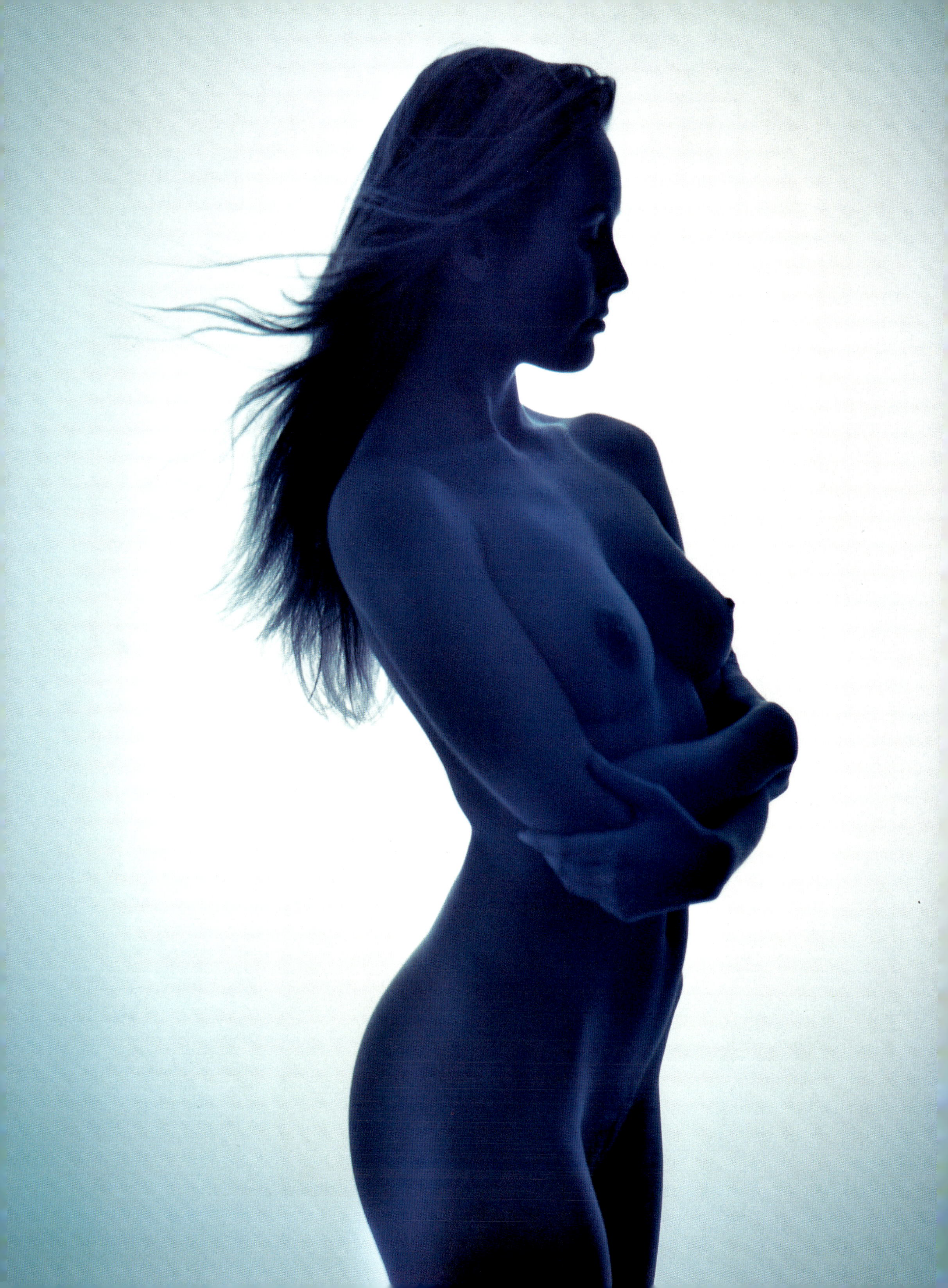

the centre of the flash. In the 1960s, this technique was adopted for use in fashion photography, and is still very popular today.

Ringflash is not the sort of lighting to use for a traditional beauty or glamour portrait, as it is a very harsh and aggressive light that gives a rather 'false' effect. It really flattens out detail and skin tones and tends to create red-eye because the flash light reflects back off the model's retina – an effect that some clients like because it is somewhat surreal. Ringflash does, however, create very stylish and punchy images, with strong, saturated and somewhat unnatural colours and a general surreal and fantastical feel, which is why it is still a popular technique for fashion and style photography.

If you want to experiment with this technique, you need to take particular care with your model's make-up; everyday make-up is nowhere near strong enough for studio photography in general and ringflash photography in particular, because the flash lights will just wash it away. Eye colour, blusher and lipstick all need to be very strong or they simply will not be picked up in the final image.

Silhouette lighting

Silhouette lighting is an interesting technique to experiment with if you want to try something artistic and creative: it is a way of capturing the shape of the model's form without the detail, so you can concentrate on creating strong, clean and powerful graphic images (see pages 72–73) Using coloured gels on your lenses adds another interesting element to a silhouette image (see opposite). This technique can also be taken a step further by placing reflectors in front of the model to bounce light back on the subject, creating soft detail in the subject while still retaining the overall silhouette effect.

OPPOSITE: I created this silhouette image by lighting the model from behind with a large softbox through a diffuser screen. I used a blue gel on the flash head to obtain the overall blue cast to the image.
Mamiya RZ 6/7cm; 1/125 sec at f/8; 150mm lens; Fuji Provia 100

Rimlighting

Rimlighting is a technique that I call 'painting with light'. It is a creative technique that is good for figure work, as it highlights body shape and form and picks up details.

To create rimlighting, the light source is placed behind and to the side of the model at an acute angle. You need a direct light source with a honeycomb, snoot or barn-door attachment. These different attachments guide the light source in a very controlled and precise way onto the areas of the body that you want to highlight, so you can be very specific about where you want the light to fall on your model's body.

BELOW: This image shows rimlighting. The model is lit at an acute angle with two honeycombs set behind her to light the edge of her body. This lighting is most effective with a dark or black background.
Mamiya RZ 6/7cm; 1/125 sec at f/8; 150mm lens; Fuji Provia 100

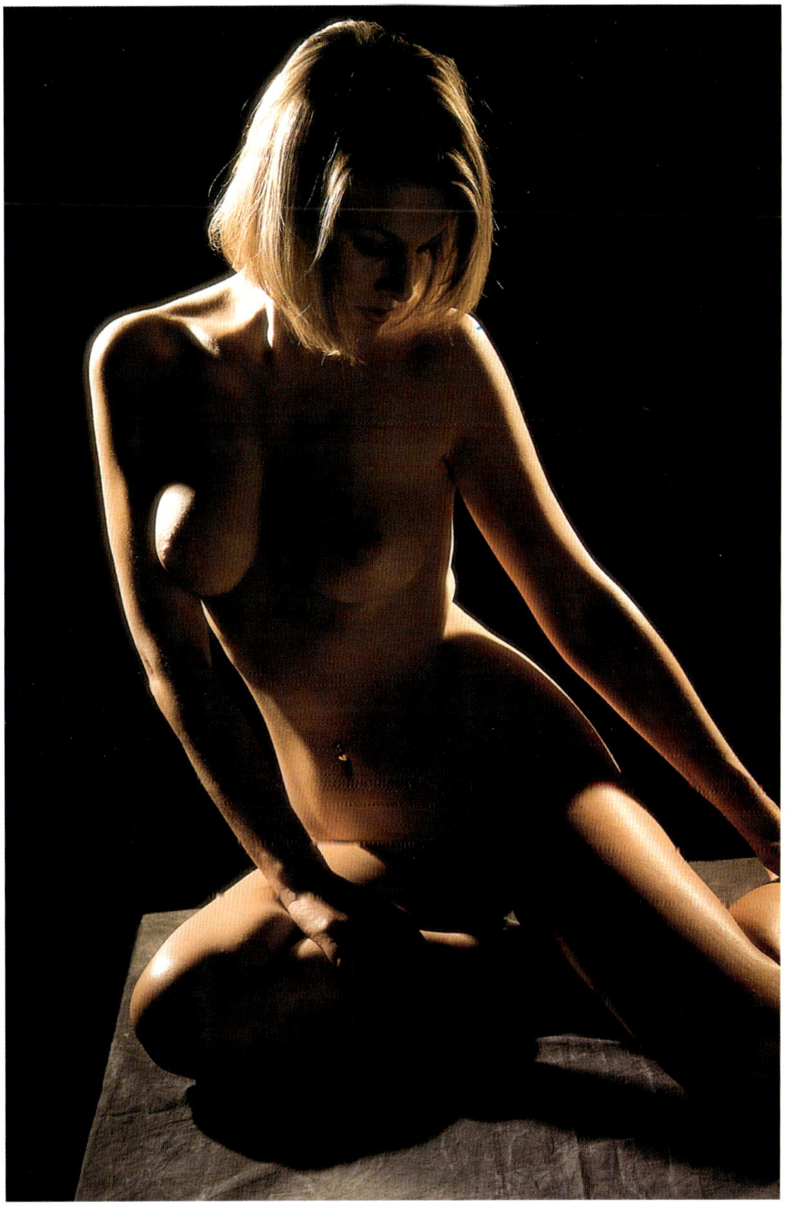

Rimlighting can be used effectively in conjunction with other forms of lighting such as toplighting, where you highlight the edge of the subject's body and fill in some of the details of their form as well. This is a particularly good creative technique with which to shoot the angular shapes and musculature of male models (see page 140).

Toplighting

Toplighting creates a similar effect to rimlighting, but here the light source is placed to the back of, and above the model. Again, you need to be able to precisely control the light, so you need to use a honeycomb or barn-door attachment on the flash head. The most important aspect of this creative technique is to have complete control of your lighting so that you can illuminate exactly the areas of your model's body that you want to be emphasized.

Filters

Using filters on lights can help to create innovative effects and impart different atmospheres to your images. Combinations of red and blue filters can be used to striking effect – place a red filter on one light and a blue filter on another, and you can get quite a surreal effect where they merge. Blue filters on their own are particularly good for creating mood – they create quite an otherworldly and mysterious effect (see page 60) – and red filters create quite a sexy atmosphere used on their own.

Trying out what different effects you can get with filters is a good experimental exercise and gives you a chance to see the whole scope of what is available. These effects can be successful, or they can be gimmicky and over-the-top – you just have to try them and see what works.

Gobos

Gobos are special effects that are projected from a monospot light. They are expensive to buy, but can be hired by the day if necessary. They are very useful if you are trying to simulate a specific effect – there are hundreds of different types commercially available that simulate, for example, Venetian blinds, New York skylines, window shutters and church windows.

Gobos are useful when you are trying to create a sense of location, whether this is realistic or fantasy. If you want to create an effect of someone sitting in the light from a window, for example, this can be fairly easily achieved by using a gobo to give the suggestion of a window frame and simulate the feeling of light being projected through a window. This way, you don't necessarily have to go through the routine of building a whole elaborate set in order to obtain an effective image (see right).

Image processing

Using different processing techniques is also a way of extending your creative repertoire. Cross-processing, for example, produces some very interesting effects, as it creates green highlights and magenta shadows. This unusual effect can enhance the impact of an image (see page 19).

Another innovative technique to experiment with is solarization (see right). There are various ways of creating this effect, depending on whether you work on a print, a transparency or a negative. If you are using a transparency, solarization occurs when a small flash gun is fired in the darkroom as the film is being developed, causing part of the film to turn from positive to negative. The results can occasionally look gimmicky, but they can be very effective when used on the right image.

Using sets

I have sometimes been required to construct a fairly complicated studio set. For the image on

RIGHT: I created the New York skyline effect in this image by using a special-effect gobo and projecting it through a Venetian blind. I lit the model with a blue filter, highlighting her face with a snoot. To add further interest, the shot was partially solarized to create the distortion in colours.
Mamiya RZ 6/7cm; 1/125 sec at f/11; 110mm lens; Fuji Provia 100

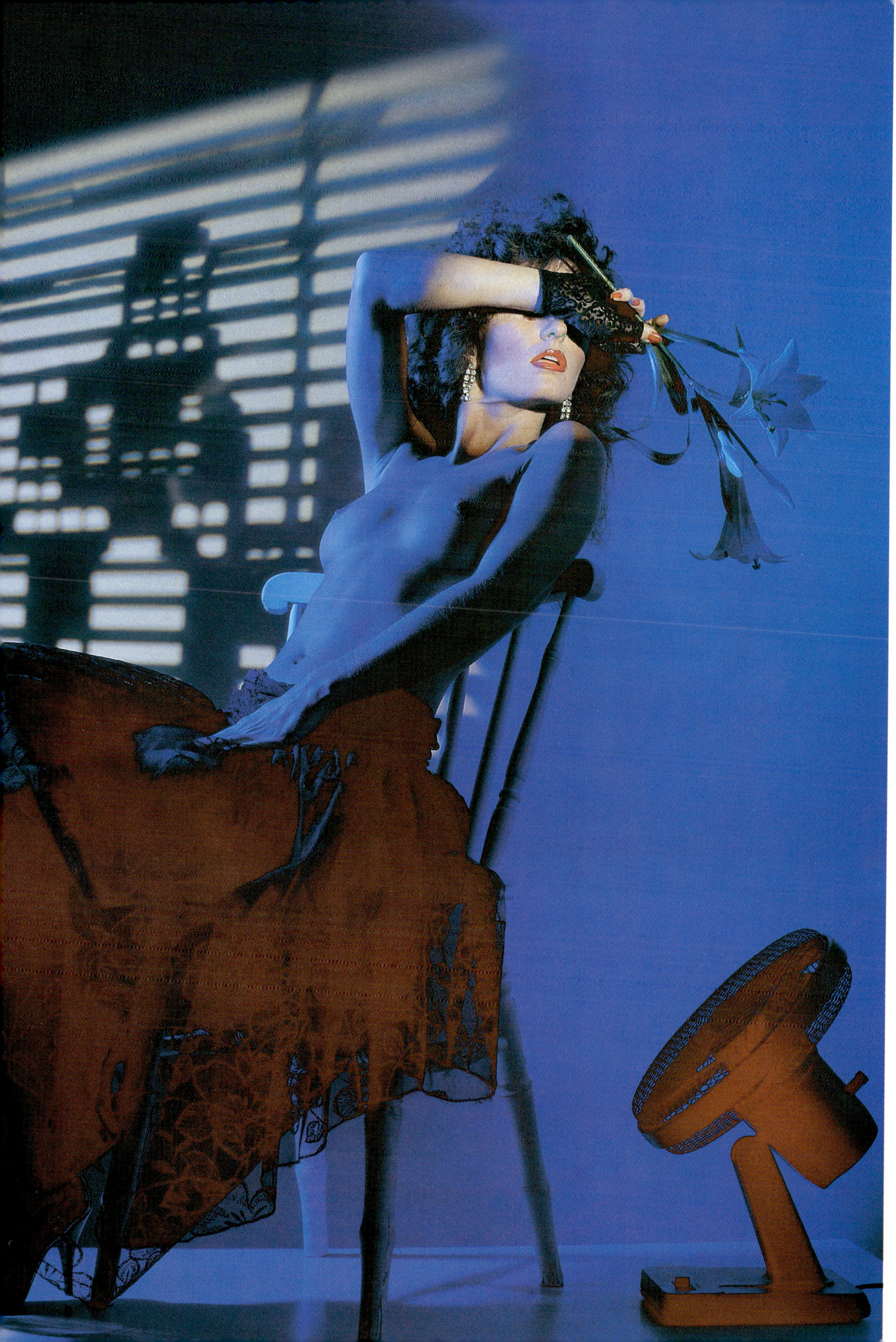

page 65, for example, I needed to create the box-like set from butted-together tiled boards, which was quite time-consuming. It is possible, however, to give a flavour of a location or atmosphere without having to build a whole set – using a few simple props and accessories, such as exotic plants or intricate Oriental screens and furniture, can give an effective impression of a realistic location.

Shutter speed

Another method to achieve interesting results is experimenting with shutter speeds to capture movement. In the picture below I used a shutter speed of 1/30 sec in order to capture the movement of the water droplets while keeping the model sharp – about the slowest I could go. If you use a longer exposure, the model may move, and you will capture her movement too.

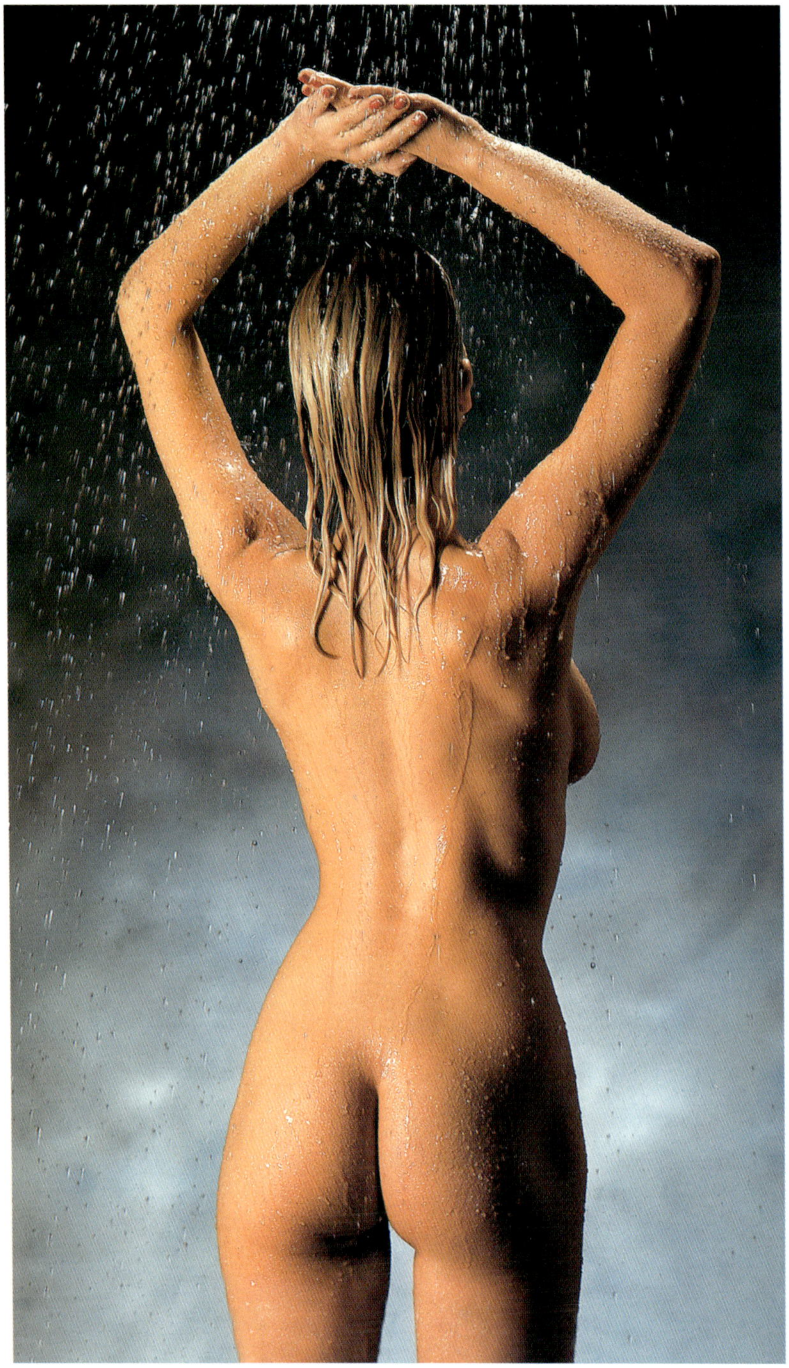

OPPOSITE: I constructed a studio set out of tiled boards to create this striking image. The most difficult part of creating a full-length top shot of someone lying down is to be able to get directly above the subject. You can't just climb up a ladder; you need to build some form of overhead gantry. I lit the shot fairly evenly from above, using a medium-sized softbox to light the model and a honeycomb spotlight to highlight the model's hands and arms. **Mamiya RZ 6/7cm; 1/125 sec at f/11; 110mm lens; Fuji Provia 100**

LEFT: In this image, I placed a softbox to the left of the model and a honeycomb to pick up the detail of the water droplets. I used a long shutter speed to convey the feeling of the water drops falling. **Mamiya RZ 6/7cm; 1/30 sec at f/11; 110mm lens; Fuji Provia 100**

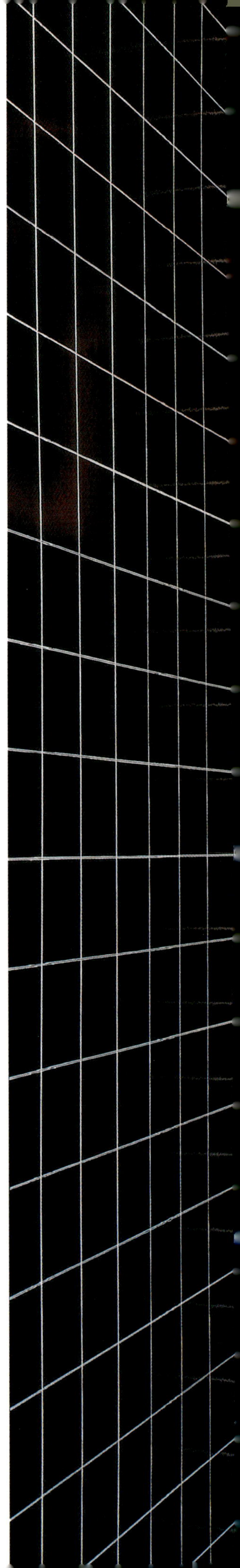

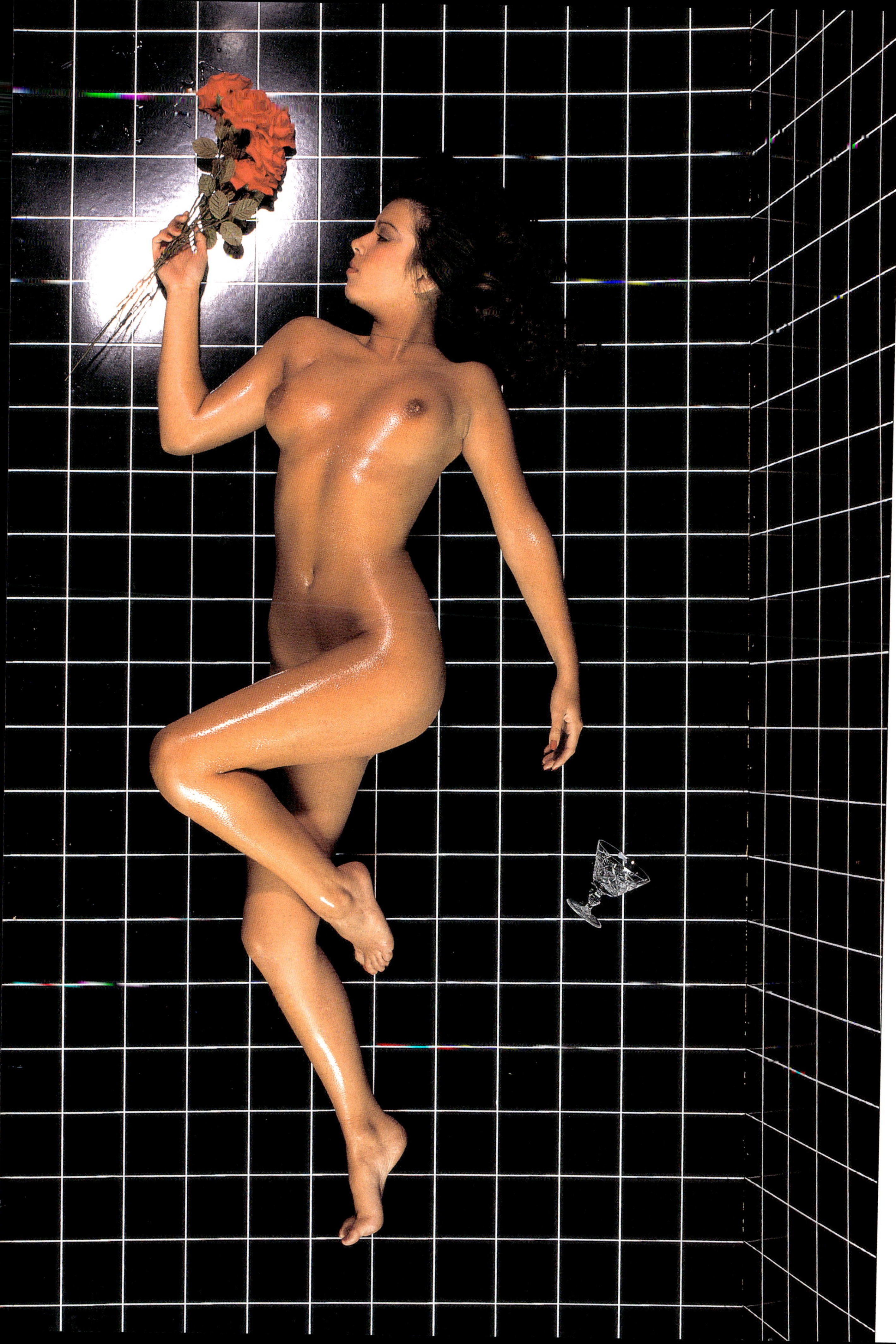

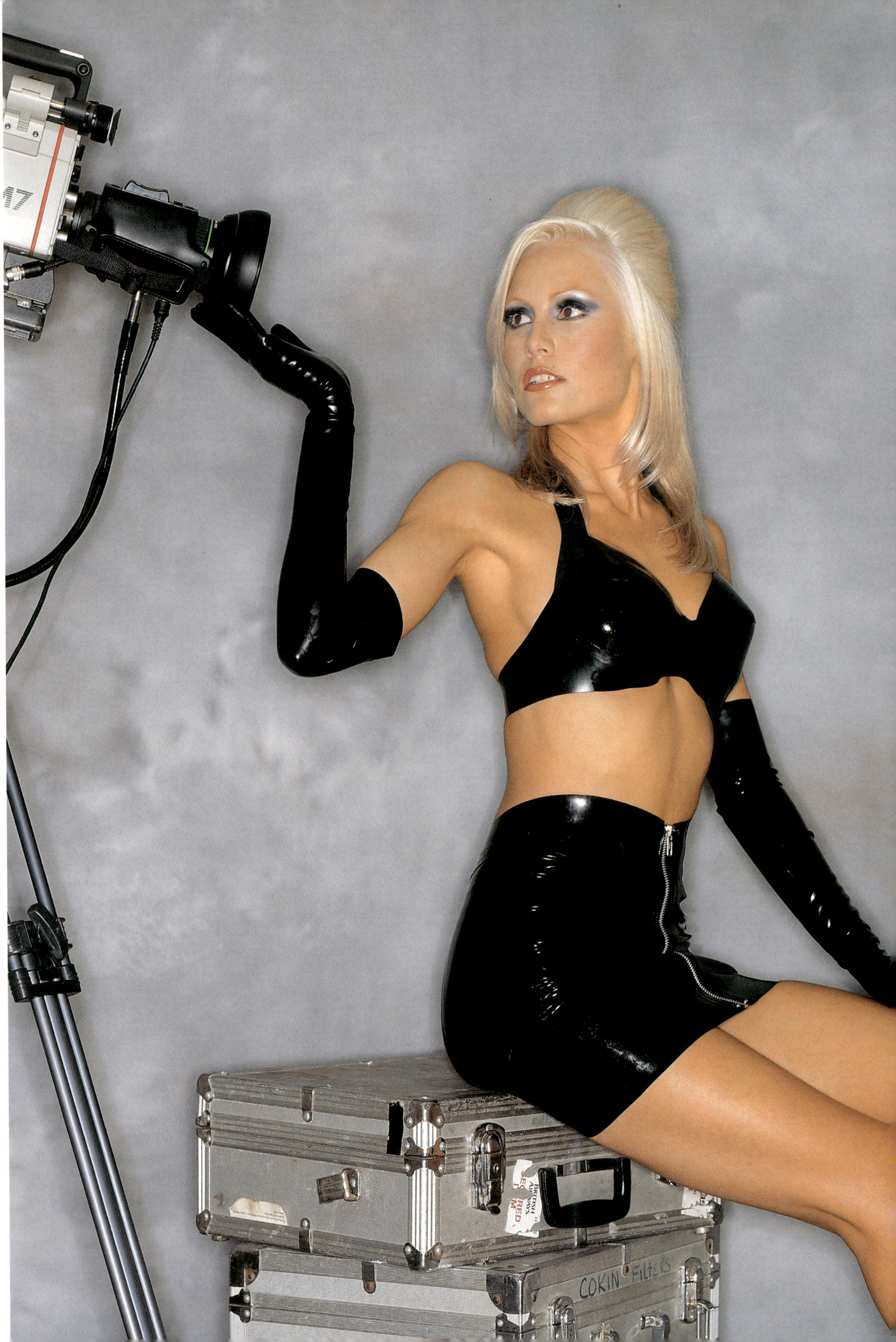
COKIN

Portfolio

OPPOSITE: This image was shot using ringflash, which helped to create the self-conscious hyperreality of the image. The light makes the black PVC costume look very glossy and intense. The unusual props also add to the ironic image, with the model sitting on camera cases and posing herself in the lens of a video camera.
Mamiya RZ 6/7cm; 1/125 sec at f/16; 110mm lens; Fuji Provia 100

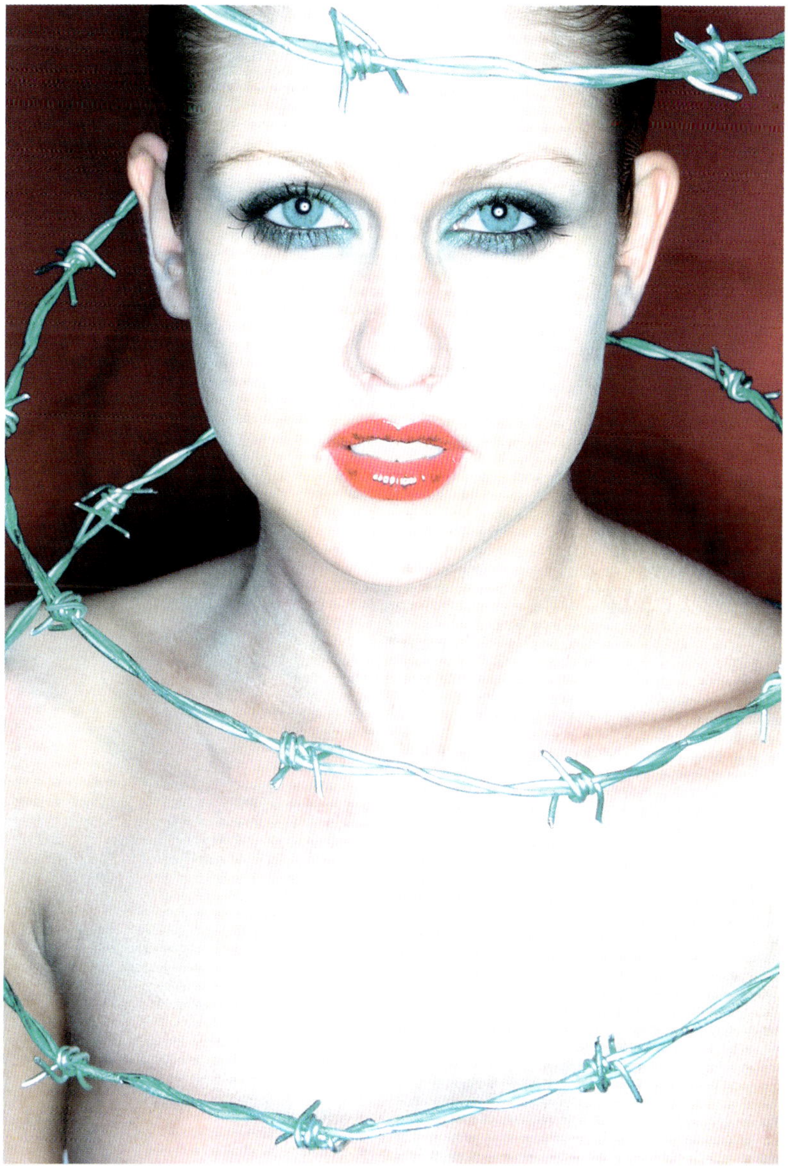

RIGHT: I created this image using ringflash, which is a very strong, direct light source. The potency of the light source helps to create the impact of the picture – the model's eyes look bigger and the colours come out more strongly, with the dark red background making a striking contrast with the blue barbed wire.
Mamiya RZ 6/7cm; 1/125 sec at f/11; 180mm lens; Fuji Provia 100

PAGE 68: This image was shot with ringflash, which makes the skin tones of the model very rich. The colours of the maroon canvas background and the red of the model's costume also have a lot of impact.
Mamiya RZ 6/7cm; 1/125 sec at f/16; 110mm lens; Fuji Provia 100

PAGE 69: I created this semi-silhouette image by placing a softbox behind the model. I draped the white cotton material, which went translucent when wet, over the model to create interesting graphic shapes.
Mamiya RZ 6/7cm; 1/125 sec at f/16; 110mm lens; Fuji Provia 100

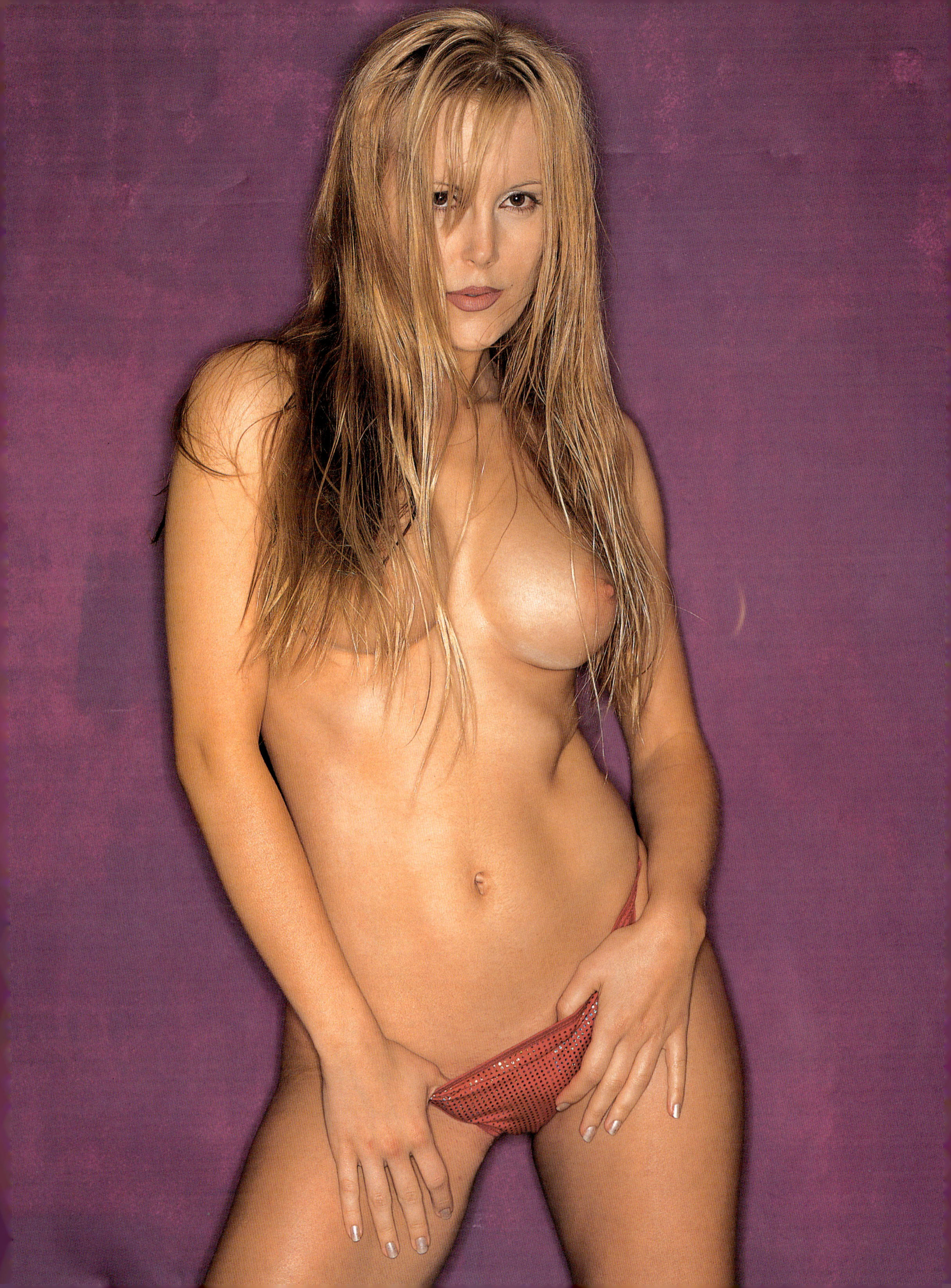

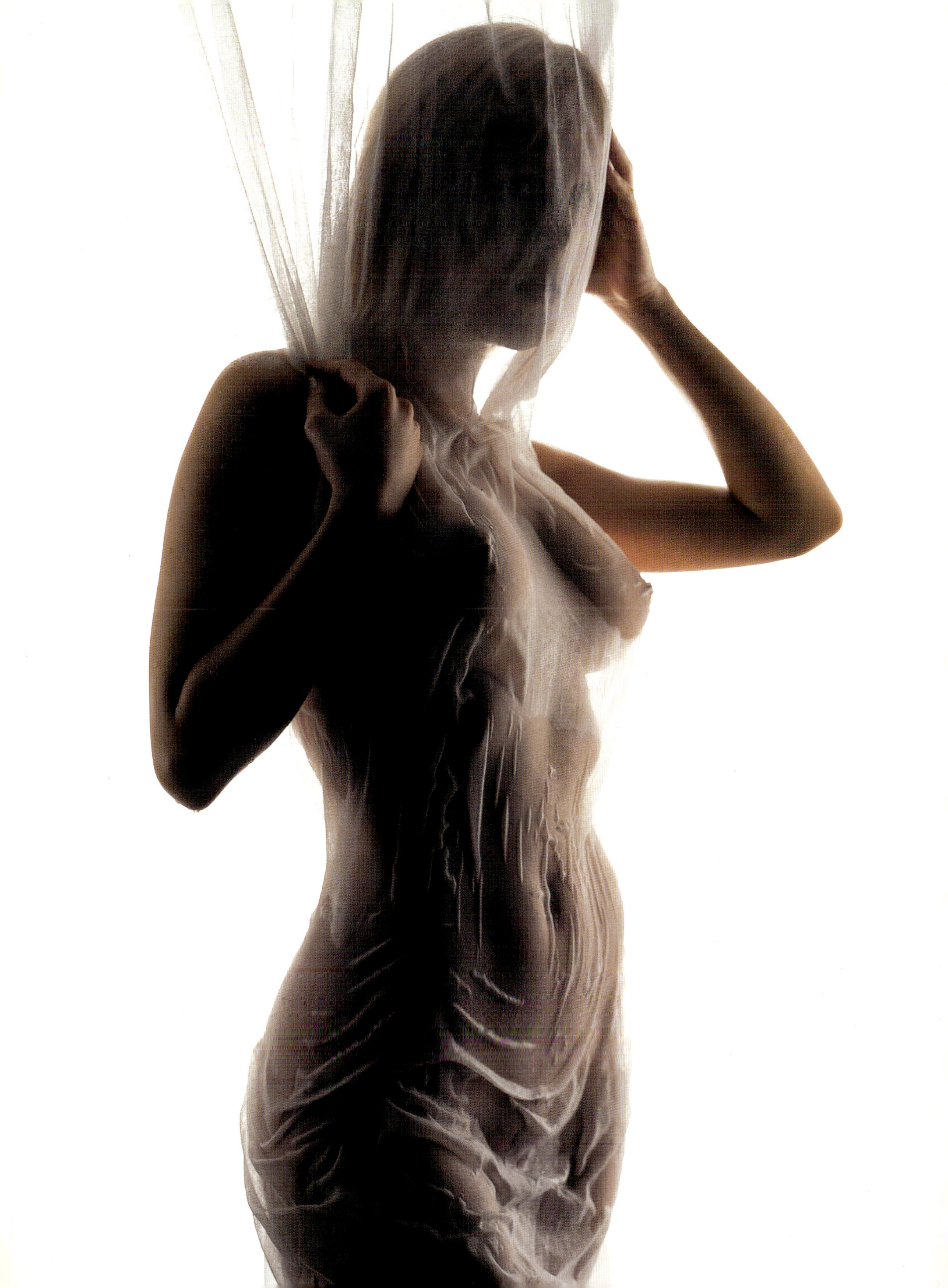

BELOW: This artistic figure shot was lit with one softbox to the left and a reflector to the right of the model, while the background was lit with a honeycomb attachment. To create the background I used a white canvas backdrop, which gave a pleasing texture to the overall image. The soft lighting and subdued colours combine to create a subtle and harmonious image.
Mamiya RZ 6/7cm; 1/125 sec at f/8; 150mm lens; Fuji Provia 100

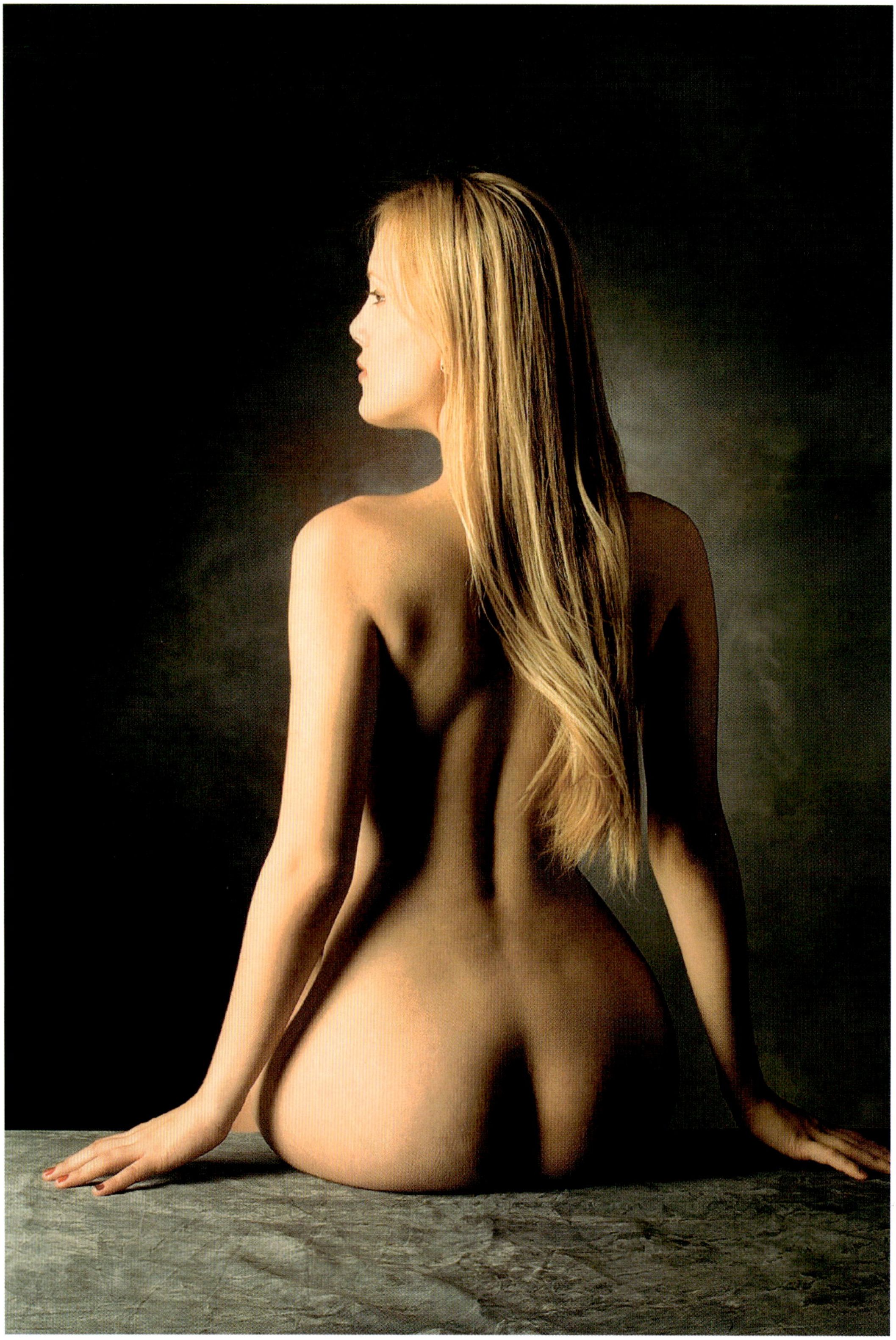

OPPOSITE: I shot this picture as a promotional image for the manufacturers of special-effect filter, who wanted me to demonstrate how such a filter could be used to create movement in an image. Such effects can be rather gimmicky in a portrait, because they tend to detract attention from the person you are photographing. That is why I used the mask as a prop – it creates an interesting effect, while the main focus is still kept on the model. I used a basic portrait lighting set-up: mainlight, fill-in light and hairlight. The black and silver of the props and the costume work well with the model's platinum blonde hair to create a sophisticated look to the image.
Mamiya RZ 6/7cm; 1/125 sec at f/16; 150mm lens; Fuji Provia 100

PAGES 72–73: In this shot I was aiming to get a strong graphic image, with the silhouetted outline of the model's body standing out against the sharp, horizontal lines of the blind. I lit the model from behind with one softbox through a diffusing screen.
Mamiya RZ 6/7cm; 1/125 sec at f/16; 110mm lens; Fuji Provia 100

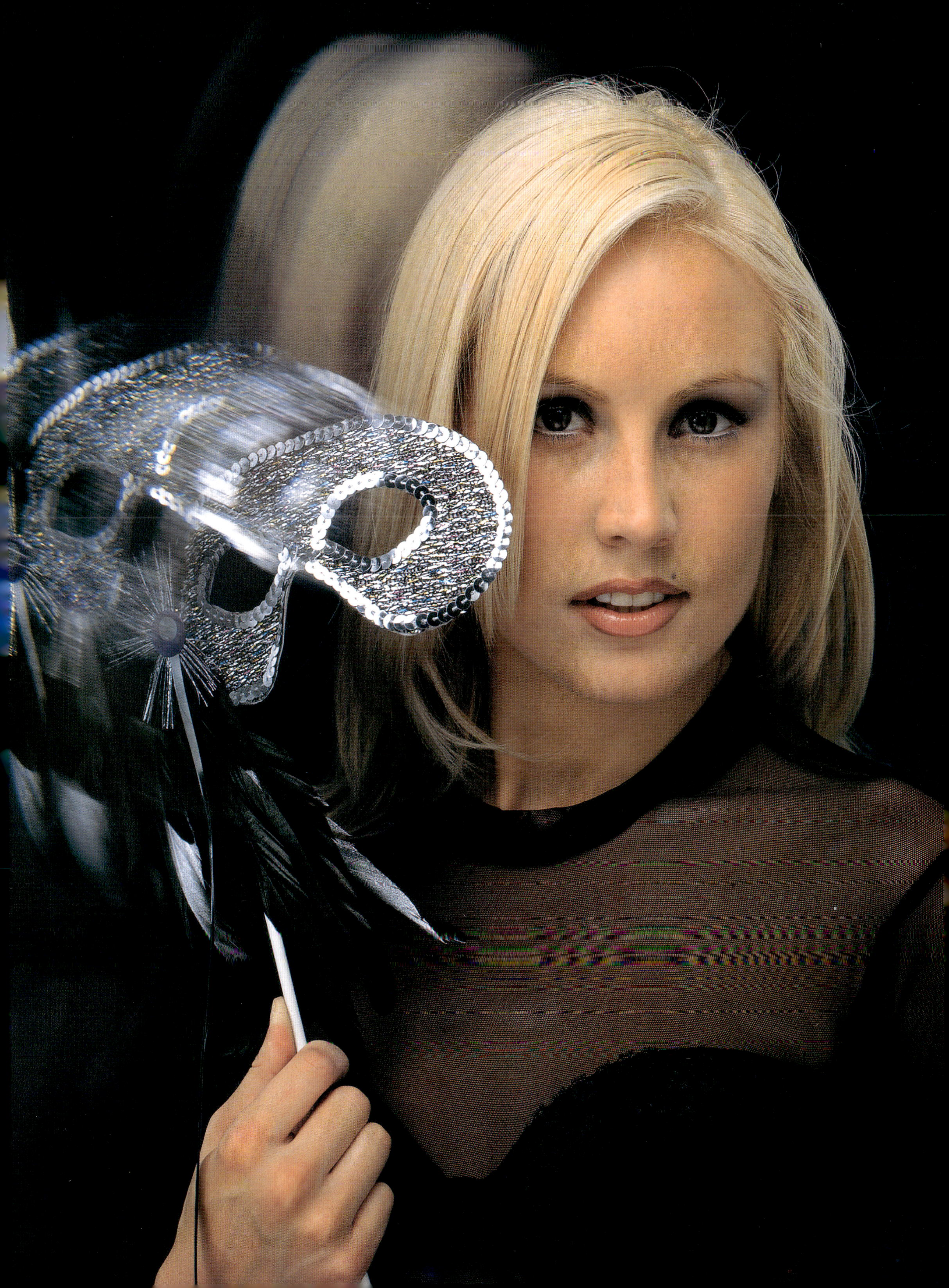

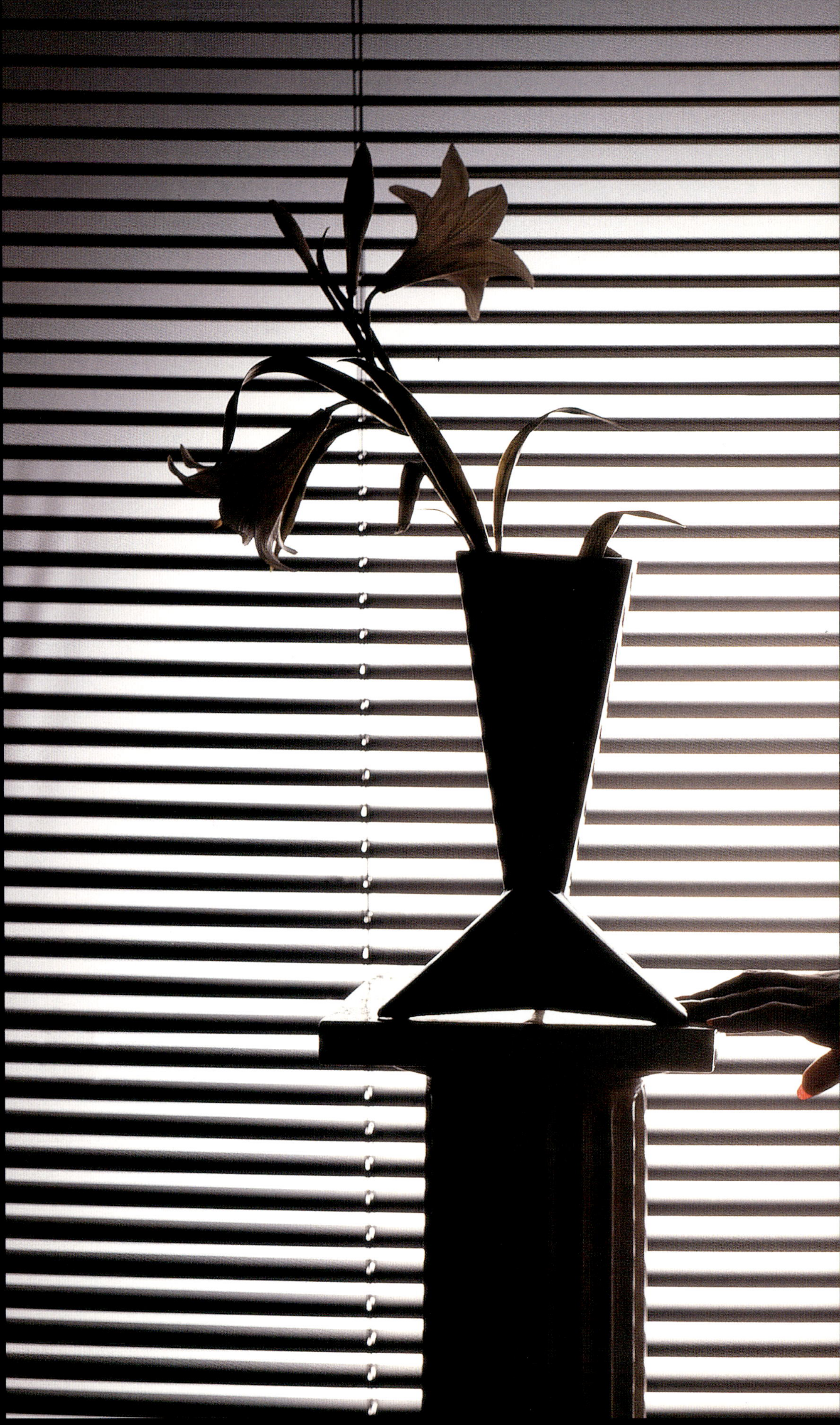

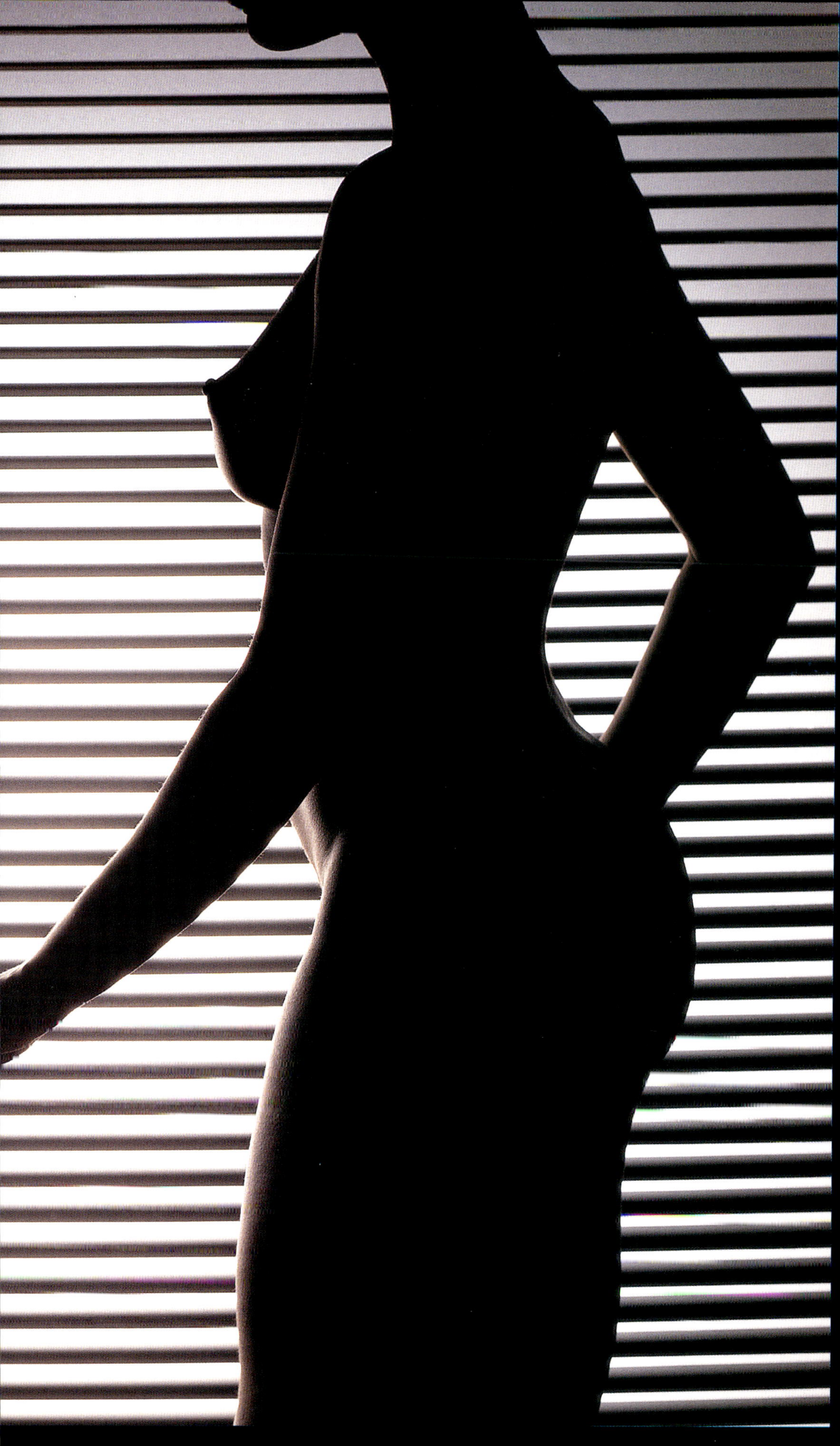

exterior locations

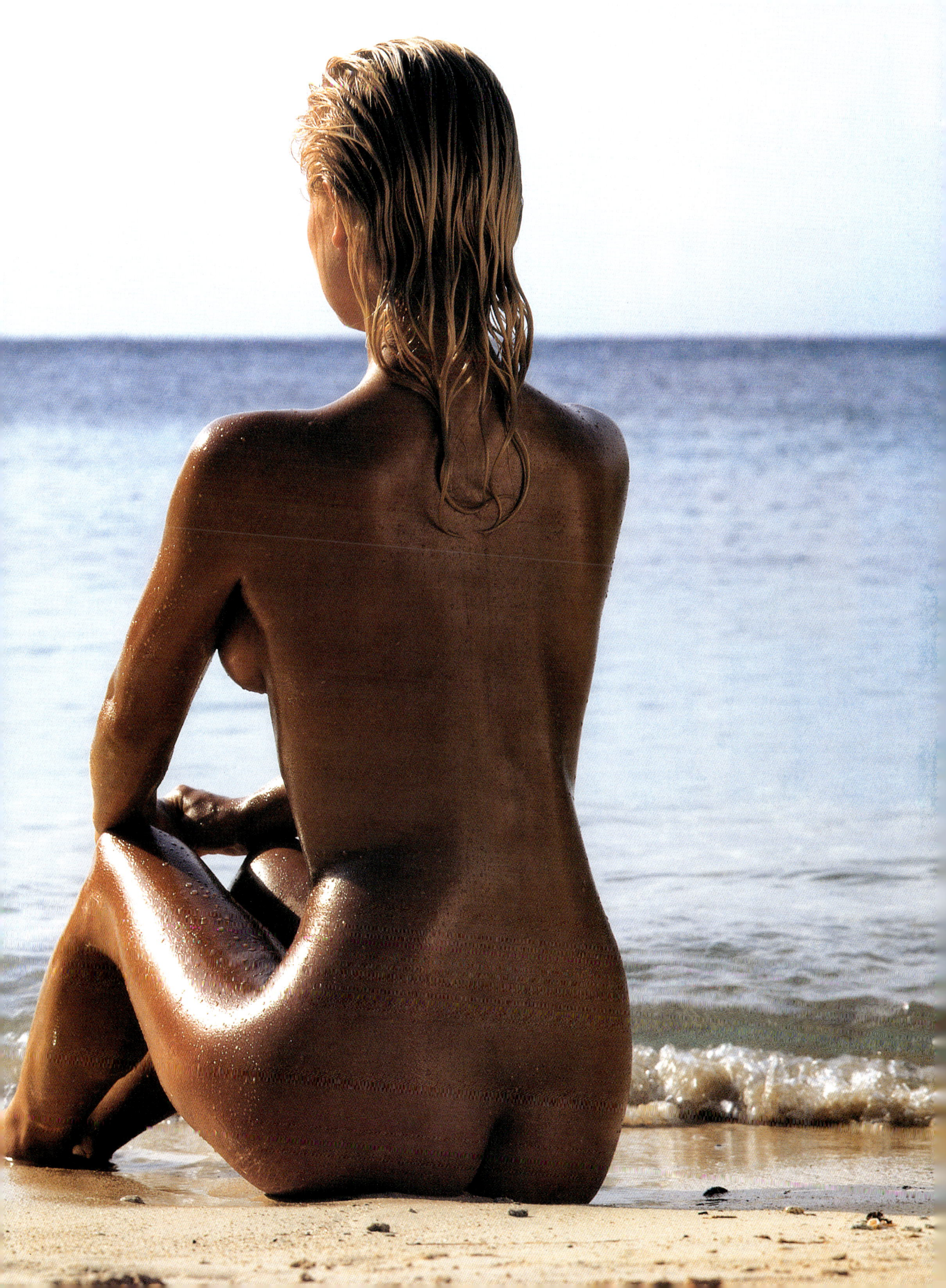

Finding and using locations

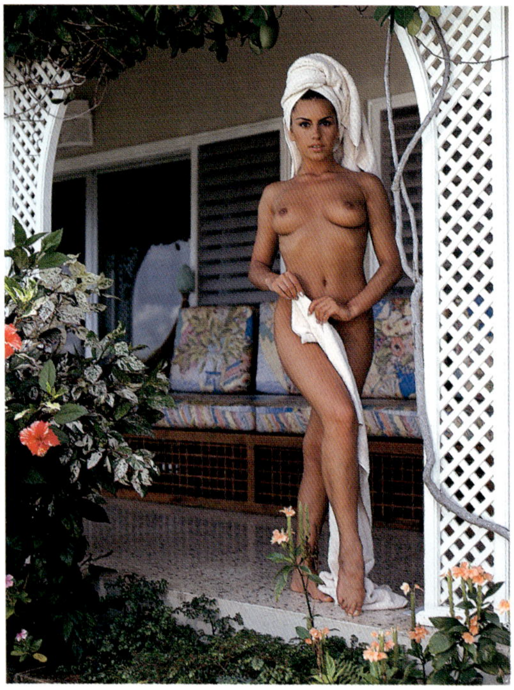

LEFT: This shot was taken at a villa in Jamaica for a calendar. The location was chosen for its decorative balustrade and attractive plant life. When using a colourful and exotic location it is best to keep props and styling simple, as I have here with the use of the white towels. This helps draw attention to the model without overloading the picture with colour and detail.
Mamiya RZ 6/7cm; 1/60 sec at f/8; flash on background at f/5.6; 110mm lens; Fuji Provia 100F

For the amateur photographer, working in exotic overseas locations may seem like the ultimate aspiration. But even if you can only dream of shooting in the Caribbean or other such places, there are certain photographic principles – such as the methods for working in different exterior lighting conditions – that you can just as well apply when shooting in more modest surroundings.

Popular glamour locations

Exotic exteriors are a standard feature of glamour photography. Lush locations help to captivate the glossiness and fantasy aspect of glamour, far removed from the mundanity of everyday life. Exotic locations also give the photographer unparalleled aesthetic potential. For example, beaches are a perennial favourite for glamour shoots, offering expanses of white sand, green palms and turquoise water – flattering colours that combine effectively. Beaches also provide a variety of backdrops against which to place models: in the sea itself, by the shore or against rocks. You can experiment with strong, vibrant colours and effective colour contrasts (see pages 101 and 103). Deserts are another evocative location (see page 97), as they usually have a superb quality of light that changes dramatically throughout the day. They contain fantastic landscapes with wide-open spaces, striking rock formations and interesting plant life. They also afford privacy, an important factor when choosing a glamour location.

Other popular glamour locations include swimming pools, lagoons, waterfalls and jungles. Swimming pools give you wide scope when posing models – you can shoot them by the pool, in the water itself, or emerging from the pool, and you can exploit the pleasing colours of the water and the effects of movement in water (see page 105). Lagoons, waterfalls and jungles offer interesting settings with exotic foliage to experiment with as a backdrop. Because these places tend to be shady, you can achieve pleasing effects, for example, with dappled light and shade.

Preparing for location shoots

Location shoots need a lot of planning: you can't just turn up in a foreign country with your models and your equipment. Finding suitable locations can take a lot of initial time and research. It is possible to use a location-finding company, although such firms tend to charge a steep fee for their services, which you or your client will have to pay on top of the location hire fee. A cheaper option is to look through glossy magazines or Sunday supplements that feature fashion and travel spreads, as these usually credit the location used and include contact details.

You often need permission from local authorities to shoot in certain places. You may also experience hassle from Customs officers when trying to take equipment into or out of a country, so you need to sort out the necessary permits and

OPPOSITE: This shot was used by a postcard company, and was taken on a beach in Jamaica in the midday sun. The model's face is out of view because she had just removed her make-up! I thought that the red material draped over the model's body would make a stunning colour contrast against the turquoise sea. To strengthen the colour, I used a polarizing filter to increase contrast and make the sea and sky look bluer. In such cases, you have to allow for the strength of the filter, and you need to set a one-stop exposure compensation.
Mamiya RZ 6/7cm; polarizing filter one stop compensation; 1/250 sec at f/11 (without filter); final exposure 1/250 at f/8; 110mm lens; Fuji Provia 100

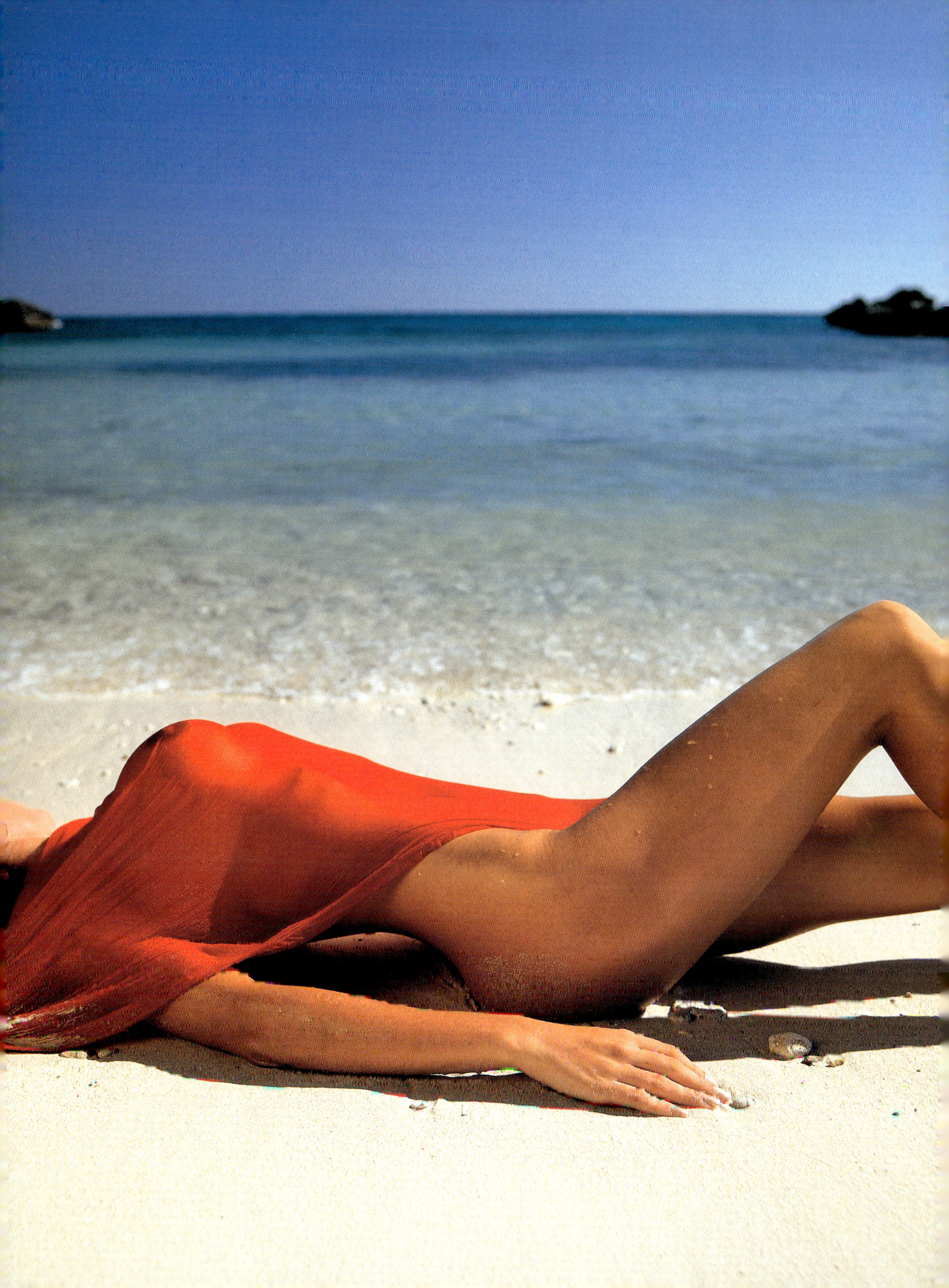

Customs documentation before you leave. I make a duplicate list of my camera equipment with serial numbers, together with a list of camera bodies and lenses, and have this list stamped by Customs at the departure airport. This offers some protection against Customs on the return journey suggesting that I bought the equipment abroad and am thus liable to VAT and tax. This would also be useful should any of your equipment be stolen while on location – you may come under the suspicion that you have sold it while abroad.

Checking out locations

Doing a reconnoitre of locations before you set up a shoot there is absolutely vital. You need to take a compass with you and check the position of the sun and work out the best time of day to shoot. If you are planning an evening or sunset shoot, then look to the west for hills, cliffs or ranges of tall trees, as the sun will disappear behind them. Look out for features such as cables, telegraph poles and wire fences or ugly buildings, as these will make an unsightly backdrop and will have to be avoided.

OPPOSITE: This picture was commissioned by a photo library as a beauty stock shot. The location was Dunns River Falls in Ocho Rios, Jamaica. I made sure do a reconnaissance trip first to check the best time for shooting – this image was taken at 7a.m., when warm, dappled light was coming through the trees in the background and the model was still lying in shadow. I had to work quickly, as the light would have been too high by 7.30a.m. and the mood and atmosphere that I wanted to capture would have been lost. Also the water was very cold so I couldn't let the model lie there for very long. **Mamiya RZ 6/7cm; 1/15 sec at f/5.6; 150mm lens; Fuji Provia 100F**

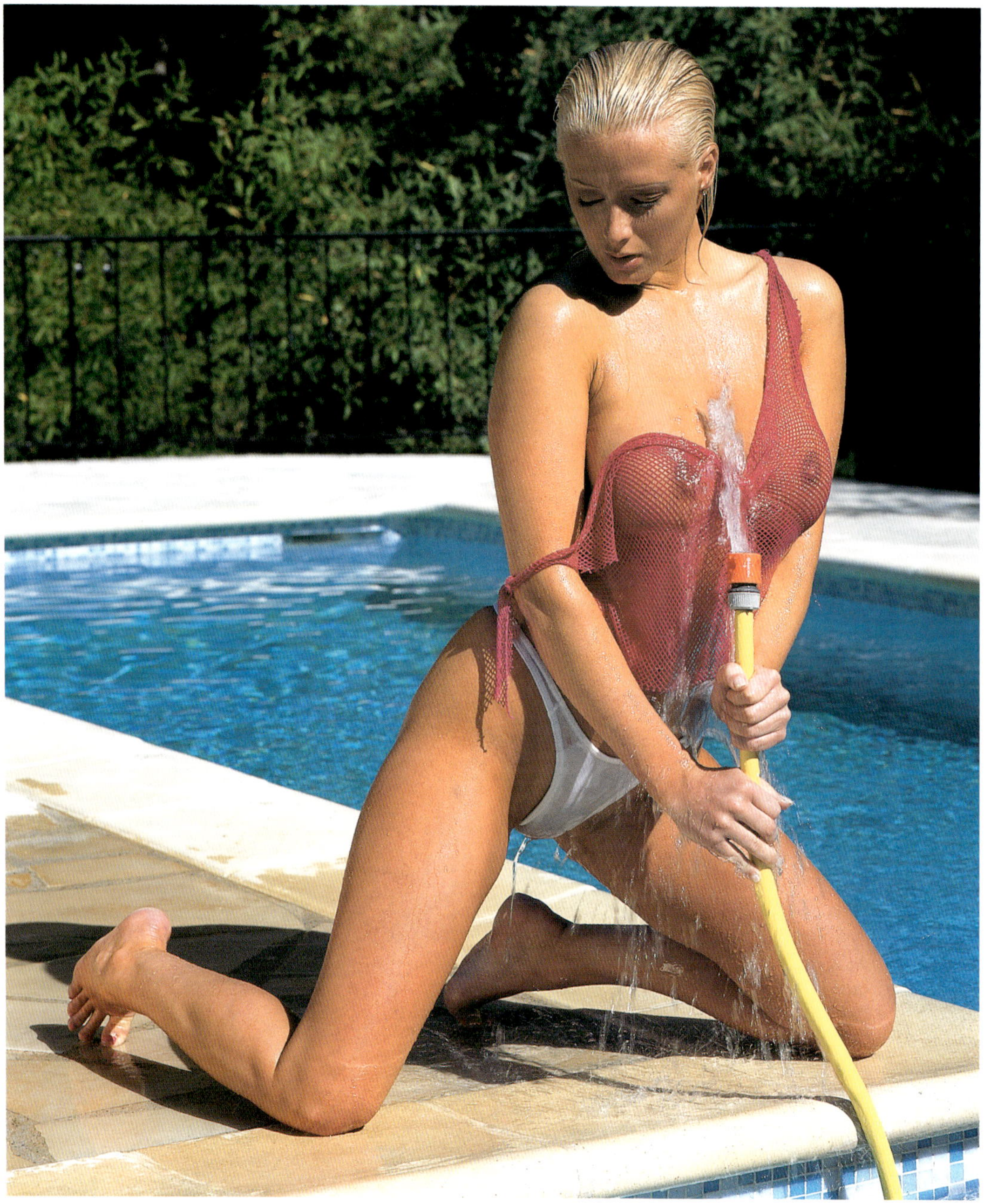

LEFT: Usually when shooting at swimming pools you have to check when members of the public are likely to be around. However, I was able to hire this pool, and so did not face the problem of public intrusion. I chose the pool because it was a good shape and the foliage offered an interesting background. This shot was taken at 5p.m., when the light was warm and the shadows were starting to lengthen. I used a 150mm lens to slightly soften the background, and a silver reflector to fill in the left-side shadows on the model. **Mamiya 645; 1/250 sec at f/11; 150mm lens; Fuji Provia 100F**

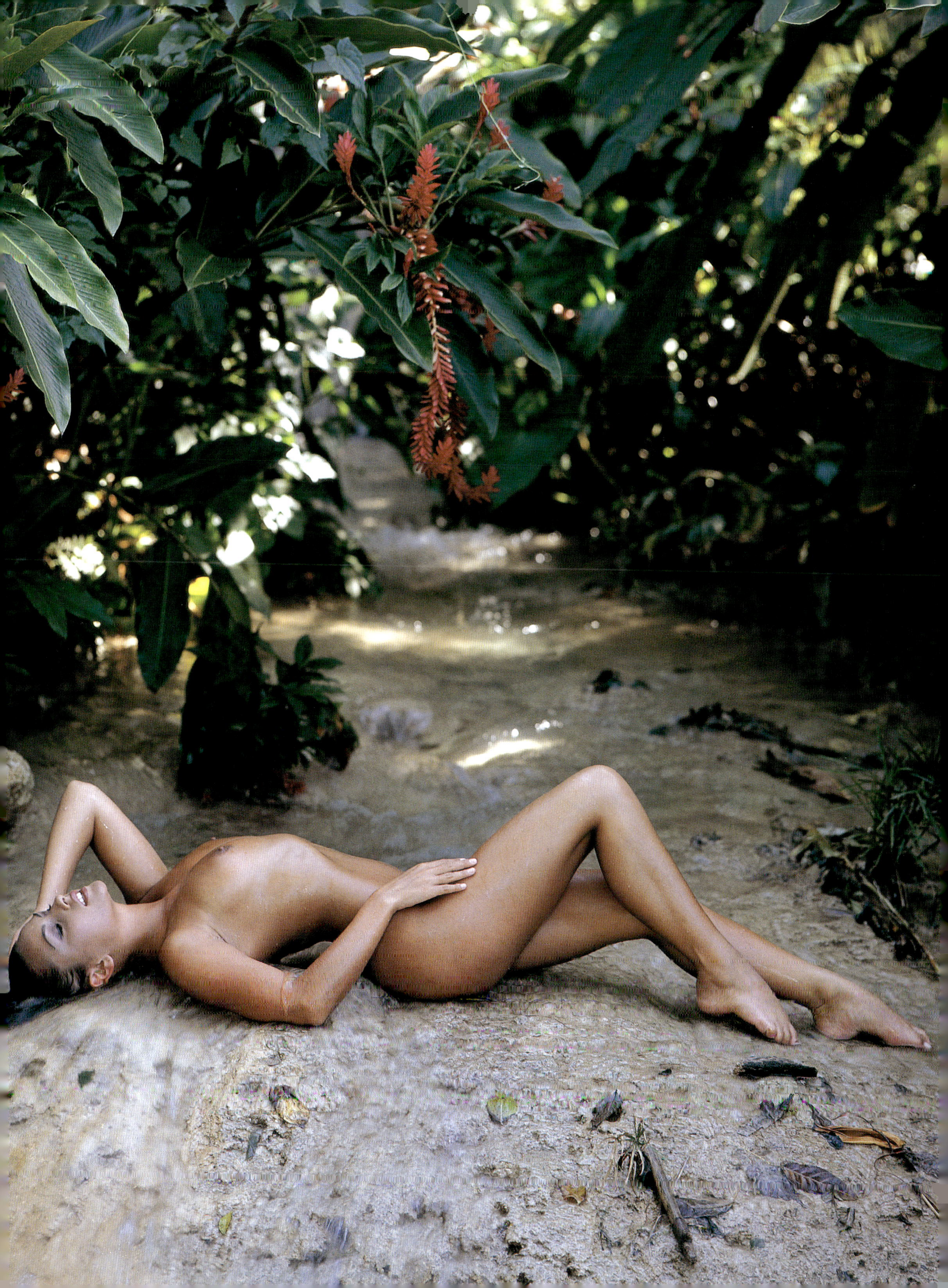

BELOW: This image was taken in southern France as a stock calendar shot. I thought that the pile of logs and the wall gave a pleasing rustic feel to the shot that complemented the model's Wild West-style outfit.
Mamiya RZ 6/7cm;1/125 sec at f/16; 110mm lens; Fuji Provia 100

You should also keep an eye out for features in the landscape that you could include in the shoot, such as trees with interesting bark or foliage, weatherworn walls, piles of wood or boulders.

Privacy and seclusion are extremely important factors. Bear in mind if you are using popular beauty spots that such places are likely to attract lots of visitors, which is also the case with public places such as beaches and swimming pools. You do not want to expose your models to unwanted scrutiny, and equally you do not want to offend anyone with public nudity, so either shoot at times of the day when passers-by are less likely to be around, or take your models to a secluded location. Such a location should also be accessible, however – I once did a shoot in St Lucia that involved trekking up a mountain for four hours. By the time we got there, the crew and models were exhausted and the day was wasted.

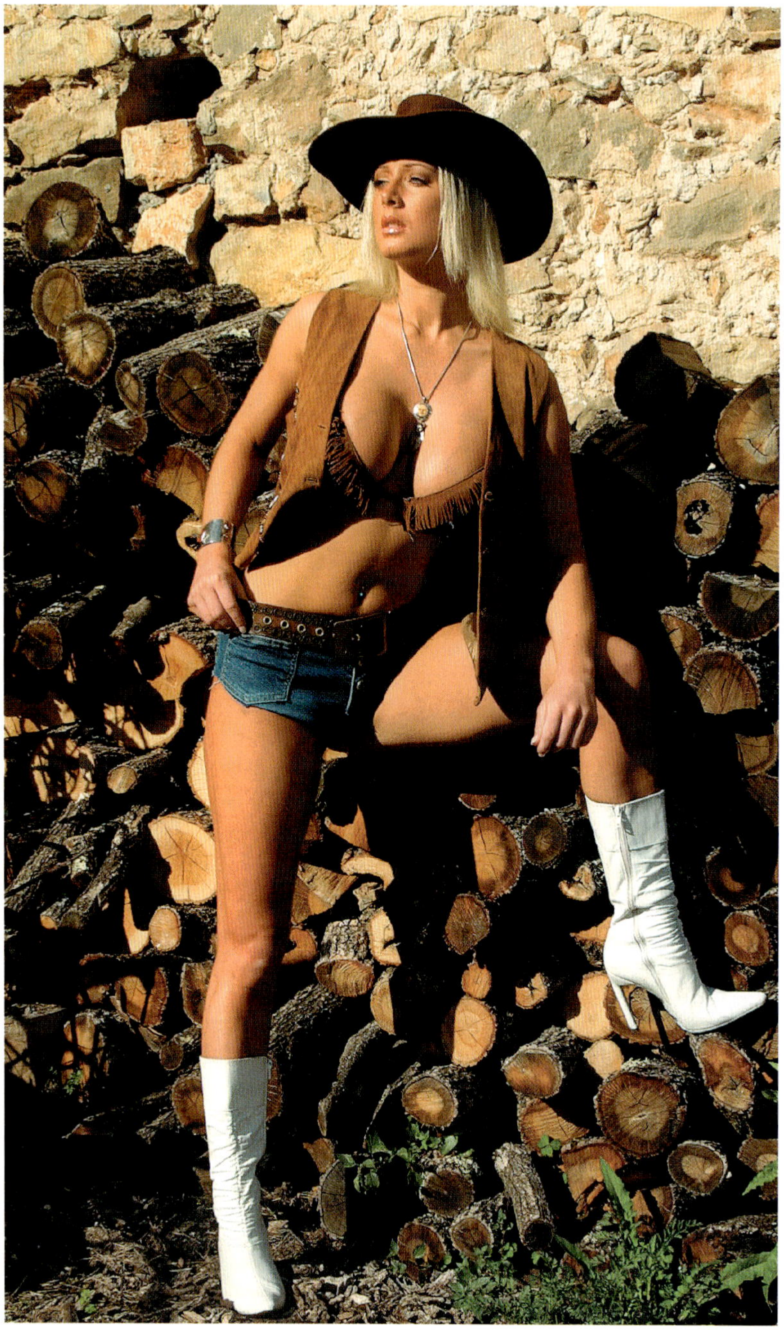

Practical considerations

Shooting on location presents a number of practical difficulties: glare from the sun and from water can cause flare in the lens, so it is best to use a lens hood. Film needs to be kept out of the heat and direct sunlight, so you should keep your film in a cooler bag for protection. Load and unload your film in a cool or shady area, and keep all exposed film together and clearly marked as 'exposed' – it is easy to lose film on location, or to accidentally reload exposed film.

Shooting by water, whether the sea or waterfalls, creates the problems of trying to keep all your equipment dry. I use a black plastic bag over my camera and a clear plastic bag taped over my flashgun. I also keep a soft lens cloth to hand to wipe any spray off the lens.

Shooting on beaches presents the additional problem of protecting your equipment from sand. Put all your equipment cases onto a plastic groundsheet, and where possible keep them in the shade. Keep cameras and lenses in large self-sealing plastic bags, which will also protect your equipment in case of sudden showers.

You also need to consider the models – they should wear sunblock, and if you are shooting in water, they should wear waterproof make-up.

OPPOSITE: These images were shot at midday. The small image at far right above was taken with available light only. I found this effect overlit and harsh, so I used an umbrella and a reflector (shown far right below) to diffuse the light, with the more pleasing result shown in the main image. The umbrella also served the practical purpose of preventing the model from squinting in the bright sunlight.
Mamiya RZ 6/7cm; 1/125 sec at f/8; 150mm lens; Fuji Provia 100F

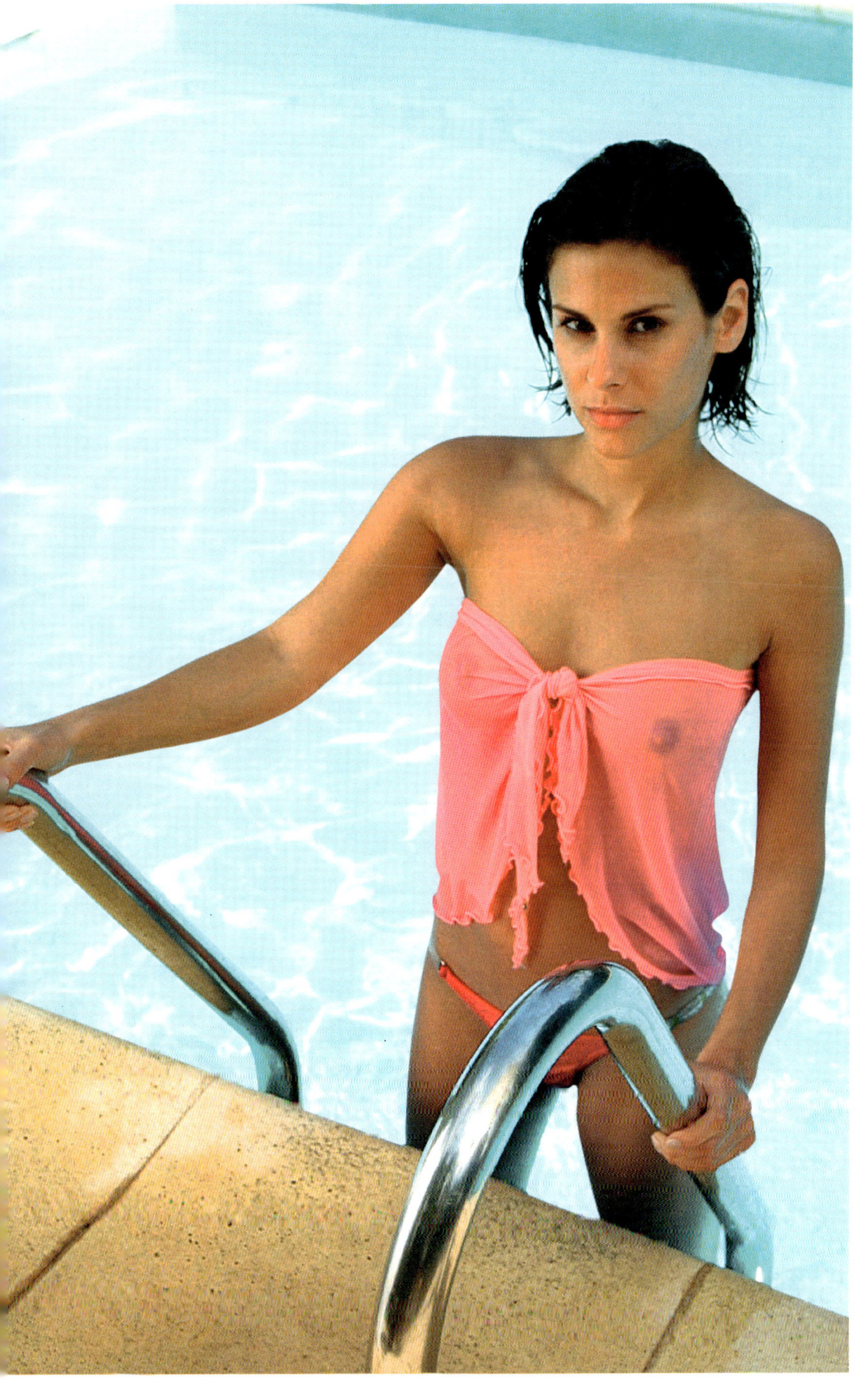

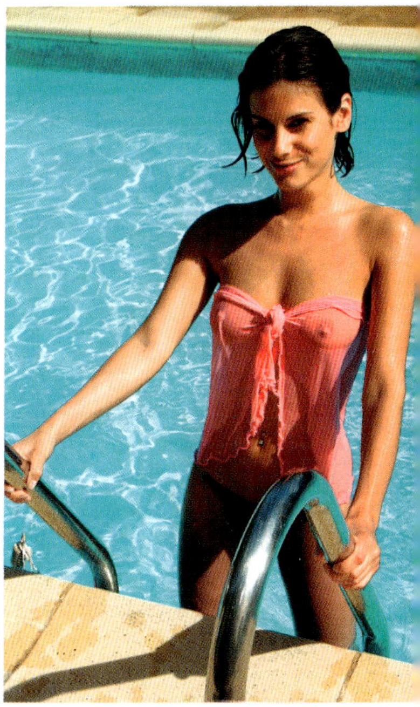

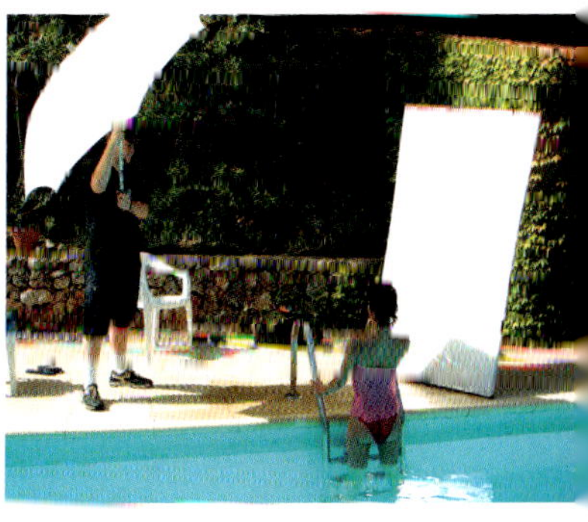

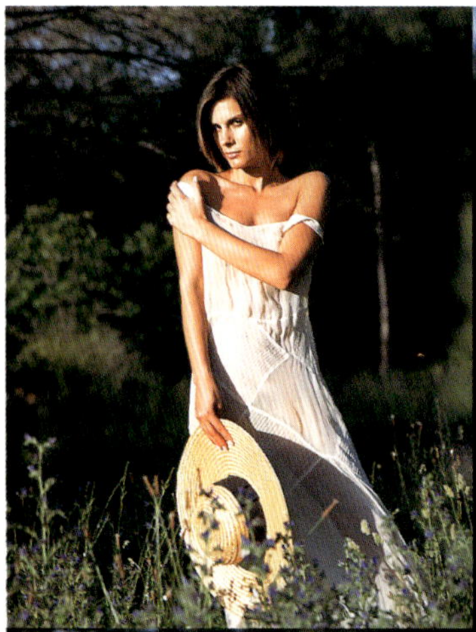

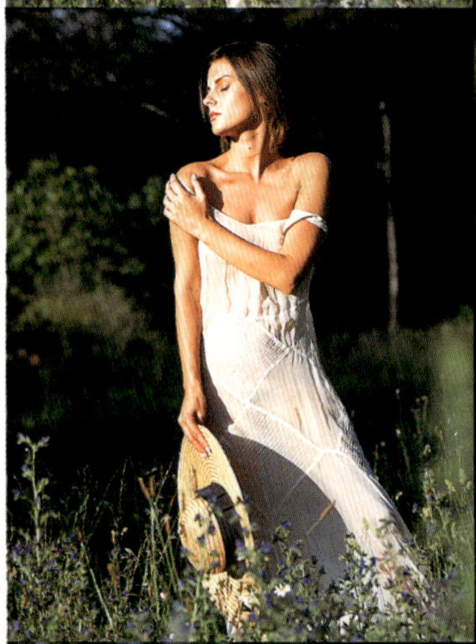

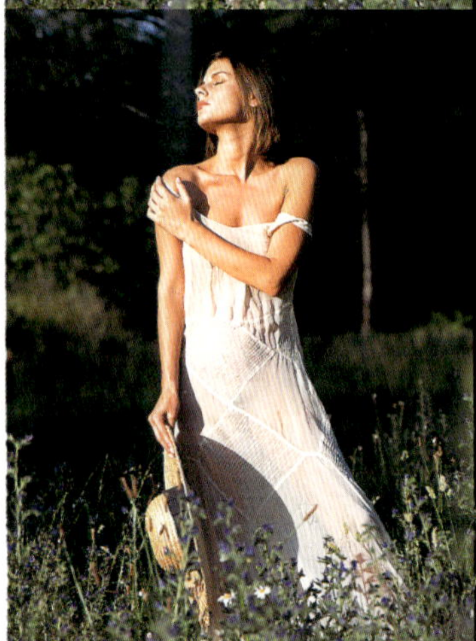

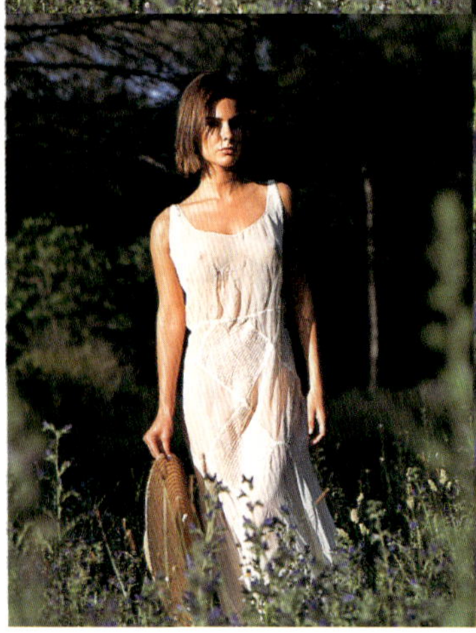

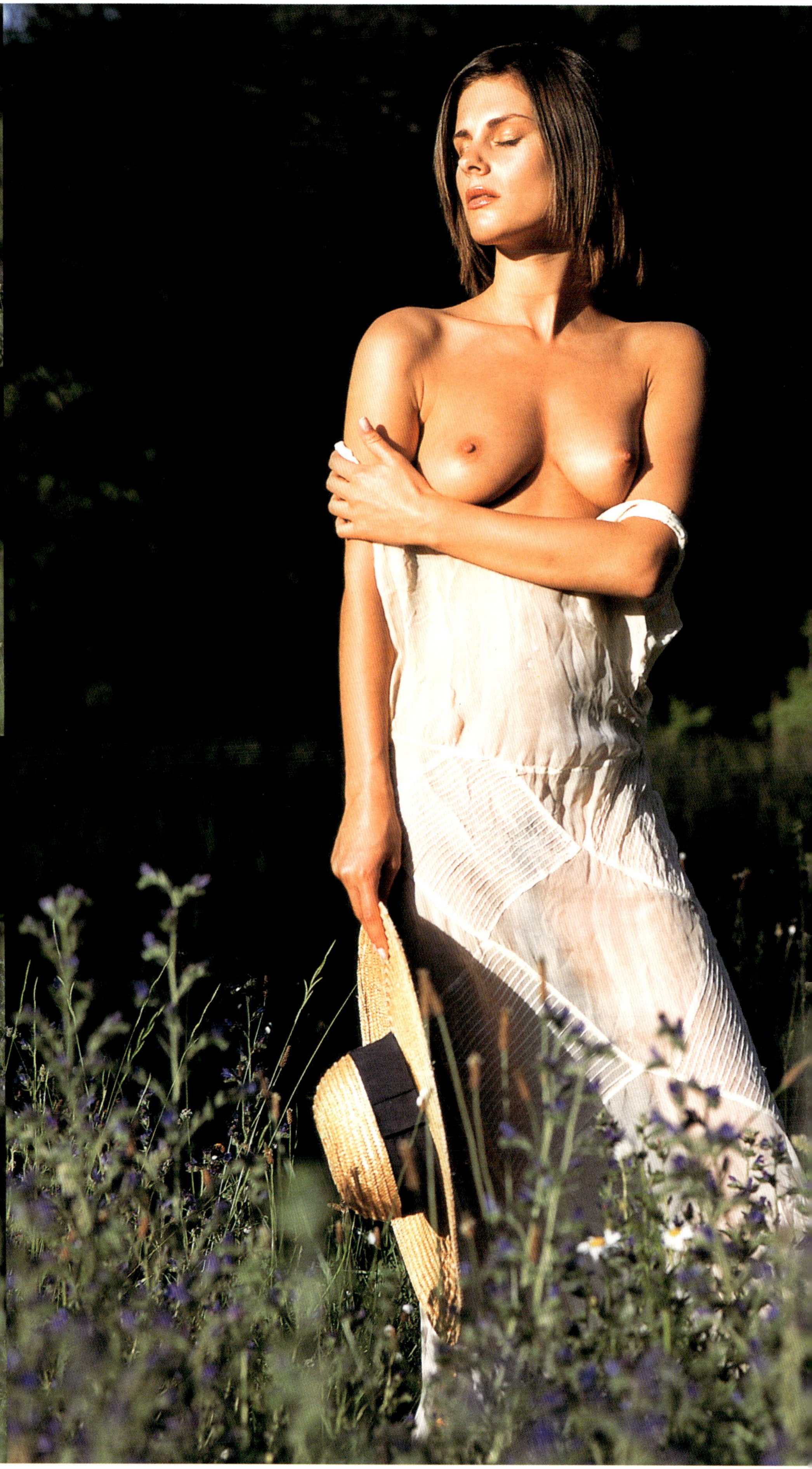

Lighting conditions

RIGHT: This picture was taken at 6.30a.m. The model is bathed in a soft warm light, while the background is subdued.
Mamiya RZ 6/7cm; 1/250 sec at f/11; 150mm lens; Fuji Provia 100F

FAR RIGHT: This shot was taken in the shadow of a tree when the sun was high. Shooting in shadow can allow you to capture pleasing skin tones; it is also good for capturing location detail as the background is lit more strongly than the model.
Mamiya RZ 6/7cm; 1/60 sec at f/5.6; flash at f/4; 150mm lens; Fuji Provia 100F

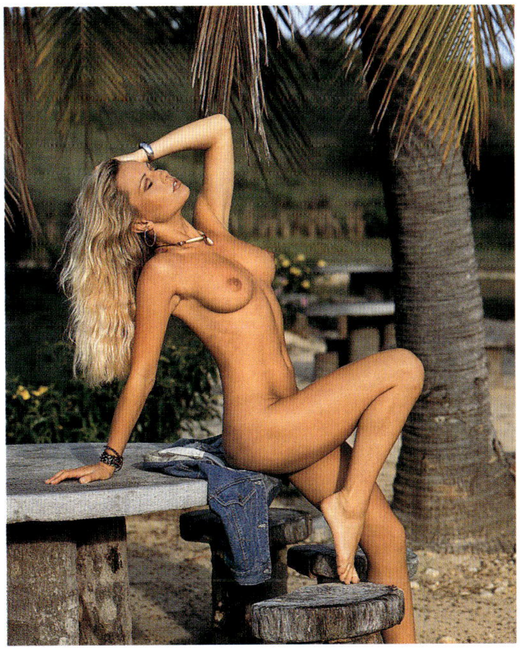

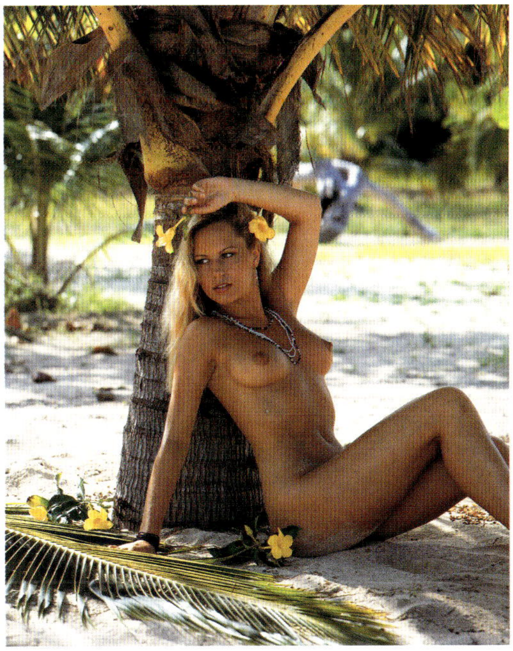

Morning light

Using morning light can be very effective for glamour and beauty photography because of the special quality of the light at that time – it is at its softest and most pleasing, and gives everything a delicate glow. However, this beautiful light is very brief, at its peak it might only last for half an hour to an hour. The best time to work is early, between 5a.m. and 8a.m., as after that time, the light starts to get harsher and colder as the sun gets higher. At the peak of morning light, you can work with available light only, as it is so warm and soft, but when the sun gets higher, you may have to start using very soft filters to warm the image up. You have to be careful to do this subtly, however, or you are liable to kill the mood.

Preparing for a morning shoot is far more stressful and pressured than preparing for an afternoon or evening shoot because of the time constraints and logistical difficulties involved. You have to be strict with your team to make sure that they all get up on time and are ready to work hard, and you need to get to the location at least an hour before you start shooting, to set up the equipment and to allow the model time to prepare. You often arrive in semi-darkness and the sun comes up suddenly, so you have to be ready for it.

You also have to work quickly. Morning shoots seem to be particularly prone to setbacks – on one occasion my assistant even forgot to bring the camera with him! In addition, no matter how early you arrive at a location, there may be people there before you: I once got to what I thought would be a deserted beach in Jamaica at 5.30a.m. to find a group of fishermen already there.

The midday sun

Ideally I would not recommend anyone to shoot in the midday sun, but sometimes there is no choice. Photographing on location is an expensive business, and you should try to use your time wisely, which may mean shooting in less than ideal light and finding methods of overcoming it.

When faced with harsh direct overhead sunlight, I tend to use the umbrella method. This technique is very useful for creating soft lighting for heads and

OPPOSITE: This series of shots was taken in morning light, as you can tell from the acute angle of the shadows and the warm glow on the model's face. We experimented with the model trying different poses, turning her head away from the sun or closing her eyes.
Mamiya 645; 1/250 sec at f/8; 150mm lens; Fuji Provia 100F

half-length shots, and avoids harsh shadows, squinty 'panda eyes' (see below) and burnt-out highlights. First I use a 2.6m (9ft) white translucent umbrella, held over and above the model, shielding her from the direct sunlight and creating an overall soft effect. I then add a silver triflector, which reflects light back on to the model and prevents the image from becoming too flat. Next, I use a Metz flash gun, placed by the camera and set at one stop under my main exposure, to add a little sparkle to the model's eyes – for example, if my daylight exposure under the umbrella is 1/125 at f/11, I set the power of my flash to f/8.

You can also be creative with the positioning of models to overcome the problems of working in harsh midday sun. Having the model stand up or lie down helps with the problem of harsh shadows, while having the model close her eyes or wear sunglasses prevents her from squinting into the sun.

One positive aspect about photographing in the midday sun is that colours become very vivid and intense at that time. Use this to your advantage when trying to capture strong colours – using a polarizing filter can assist you to enhance colour contrast, and can also help to make a model stand out against a darker background, as in the picture opposite.

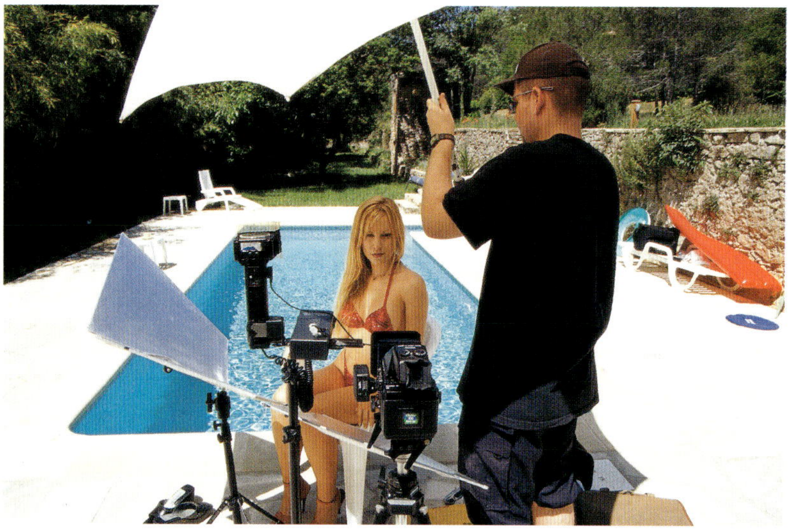

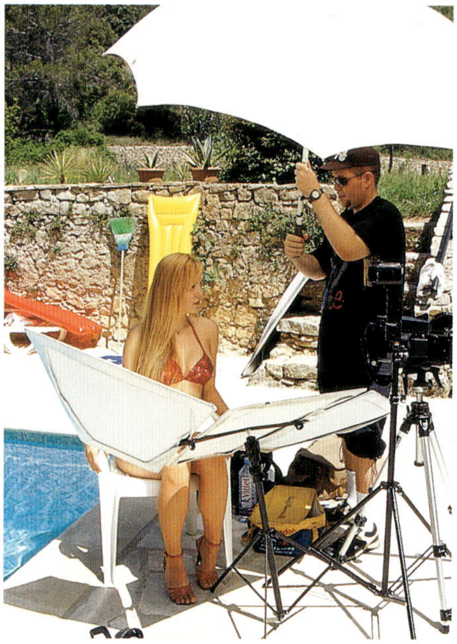

ABOVE AND LEFT: Setting up the umbrella, triflector and flash gun.

OPPOSITE: This image was taken in the midday sun. I used fill-in flash and reflector to put the model's face in shadow, as if her face had been in full light it would have created harsh, unflattering shadows. I used a polarizing filter to cut down on the amount of highlights created by the midday sun, which also increased the contrast of the shot, helping the model stand out against the very dark background. The use of white props also strengthened the shot, as the colours are strong and clear.
Mamiya RZ 6/7cm; 1/60 sec at f/8; 150mm lens; Metz 45 flash set at f/5.6; Fuji Provia 100F

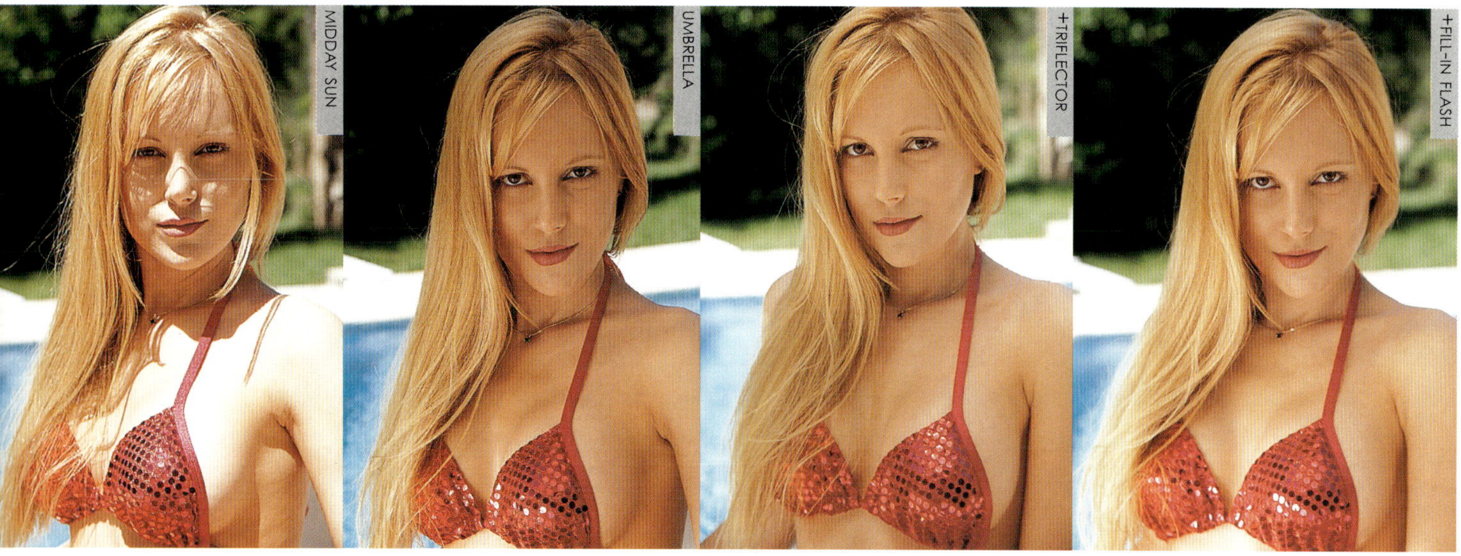

ABOVE LEFT TO RIGHT: The midday sun creates harsh shadows and squinty 'panda eyes'. The addition of the umbrella softens the light; the triflector throws light back onto the model's face; and the fill-in flash adds the final sparkle.
Mamiya RZ 6/7cm; 1/125 sec at f/11; 150mm lens; Fuji Provia 100

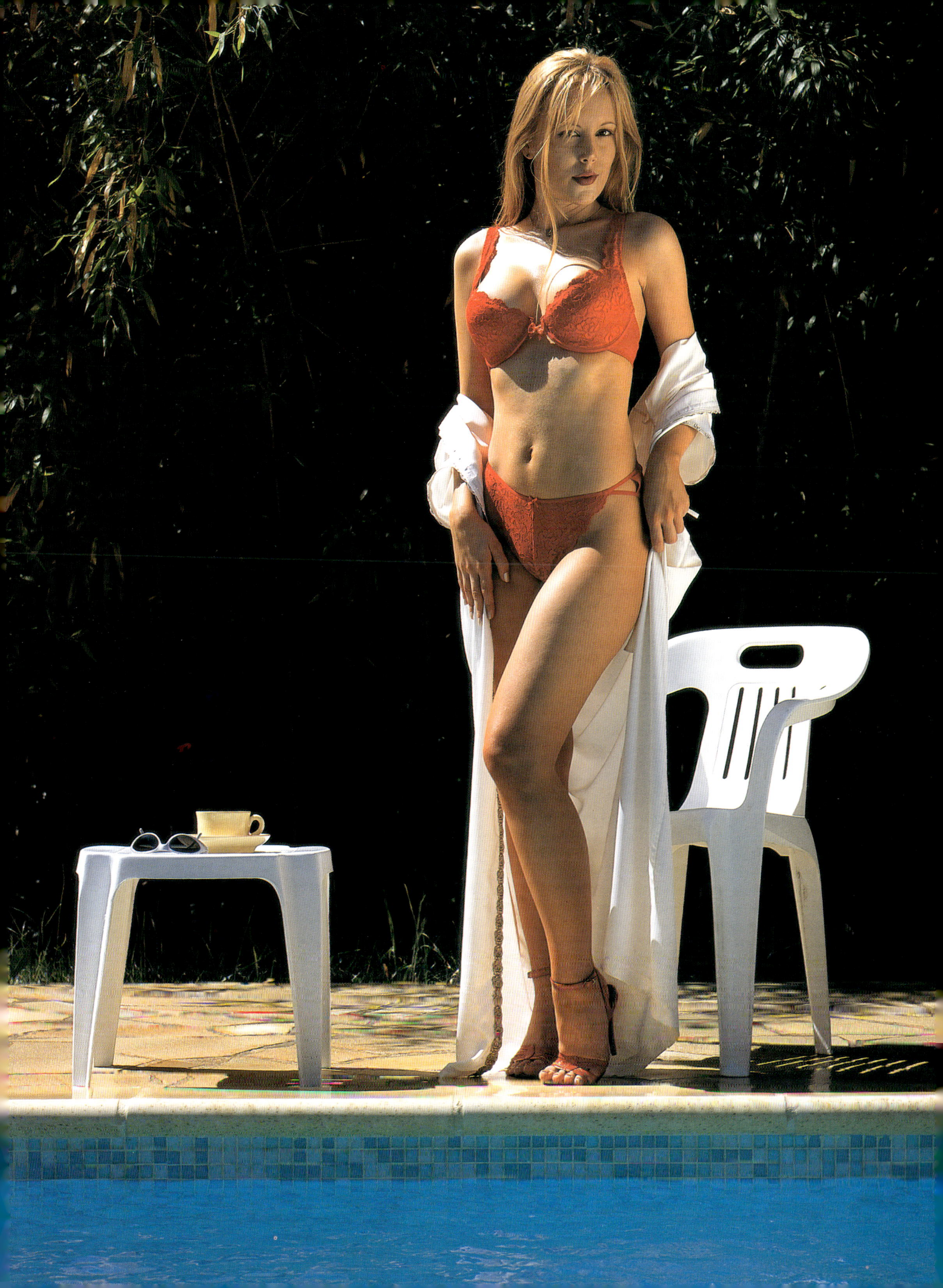

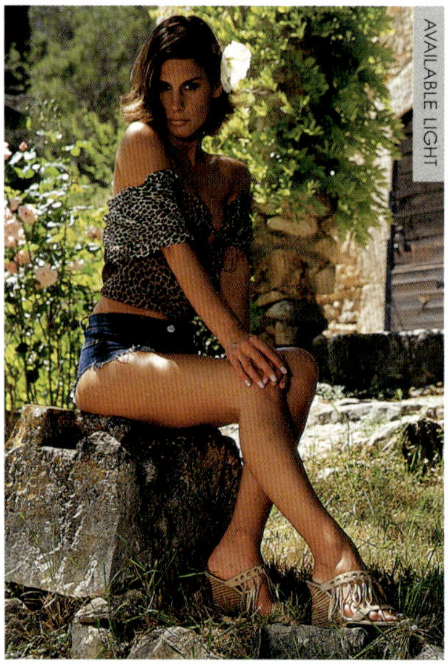

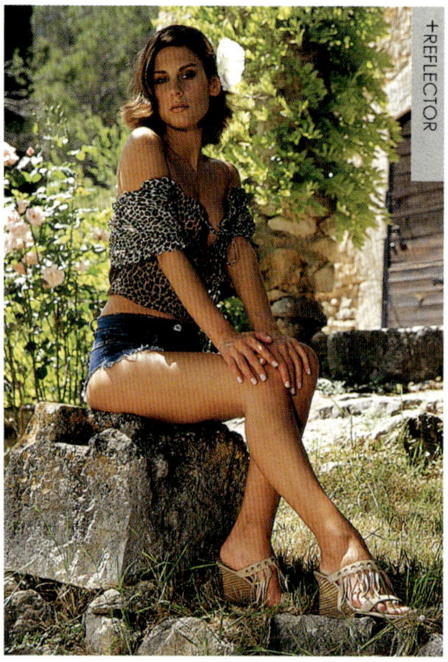

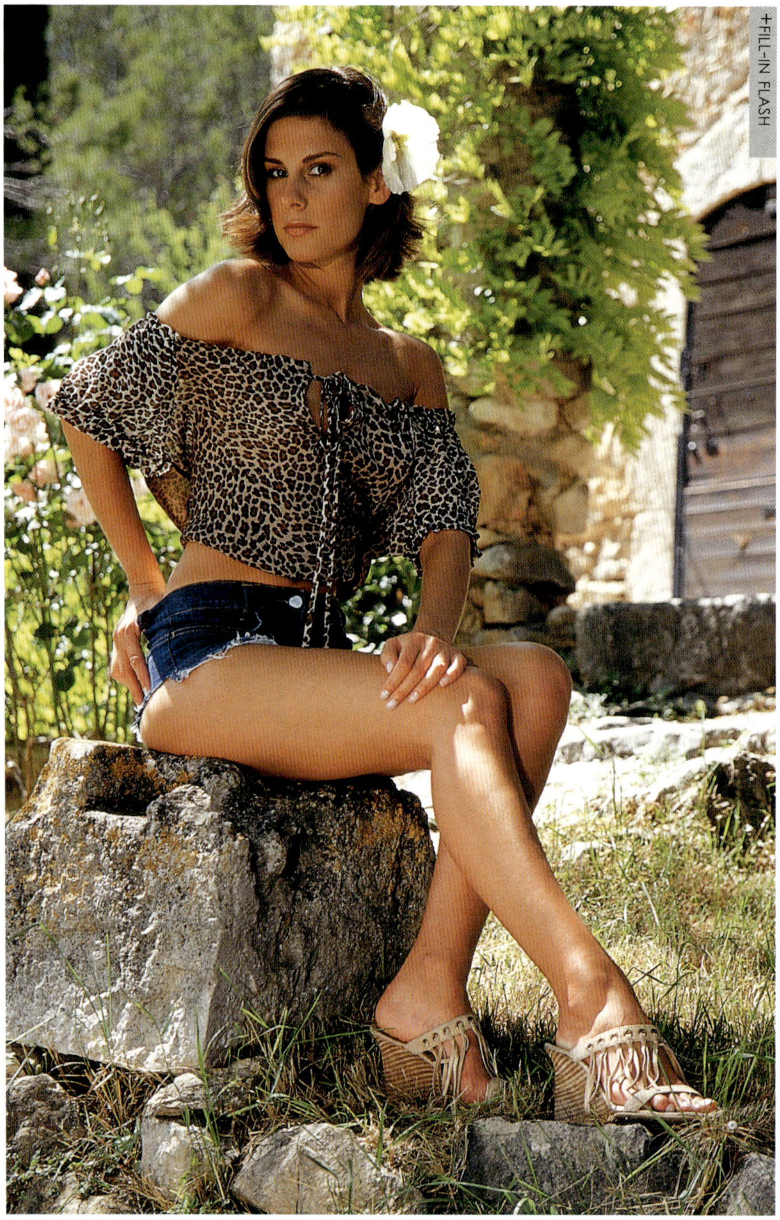

Shooting in shadow

When the sun is high you also have the option to shoot in shadow, which gives some creative opportunities to capture different moods of light streaming through leaves of trees and to create interesting shadows on the model (see page 93). I tend to use a large (2 x 1.3m/7 x 4ft)) silver reflector to reflect some light back onto the subject. This has to be used carefully, however, or you can overdo it and kill the mood of the shot.

Another technique is to use fill-in flash. Set the flash to one stop less than the camera exposure – if the exposure under the tree is 1/60 at f/8, set the flash power reading to f/5.6, which helps to fill in the shadows. You need to control the balance between subject and background so you don't lose the subject against the backdrop.

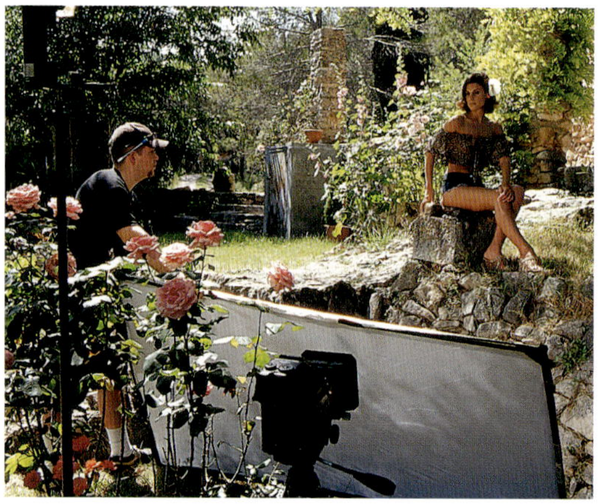

LEFT AND ABOVE: These shots were taken at midday with the model in shadow. The final image, using a reflector and fill-in flash (set-up shown above) produces a nice clean image with a good contrast between the subject and the background.
Mamiya RZ 6/7cm; 1/125 sec at f/8; flash set at f/5.6; 150mm lens; Fuji Provia 100F

OPPOSITE: This image was shot under the shadow of a tree at midday. As you can see, the sun is brighter on the background, but the model is evenly lit. This was achieved by using fill-in flash with a warm filter attached to it (flash power set at f/5.6) and a soft gold reflector to enhance the warm effect. To make the model stand out, I overexposed the daylight in the background by reducing my shutter speed from 1/125 at f/8 to 1/60 at f/8, and overexposed the background by one stop.
Mamiya RZ 6/7cm; 1/60 sec at f/8; 150mm lens; Metz 45 flash set at f/5.6; Fuji Provia 100F

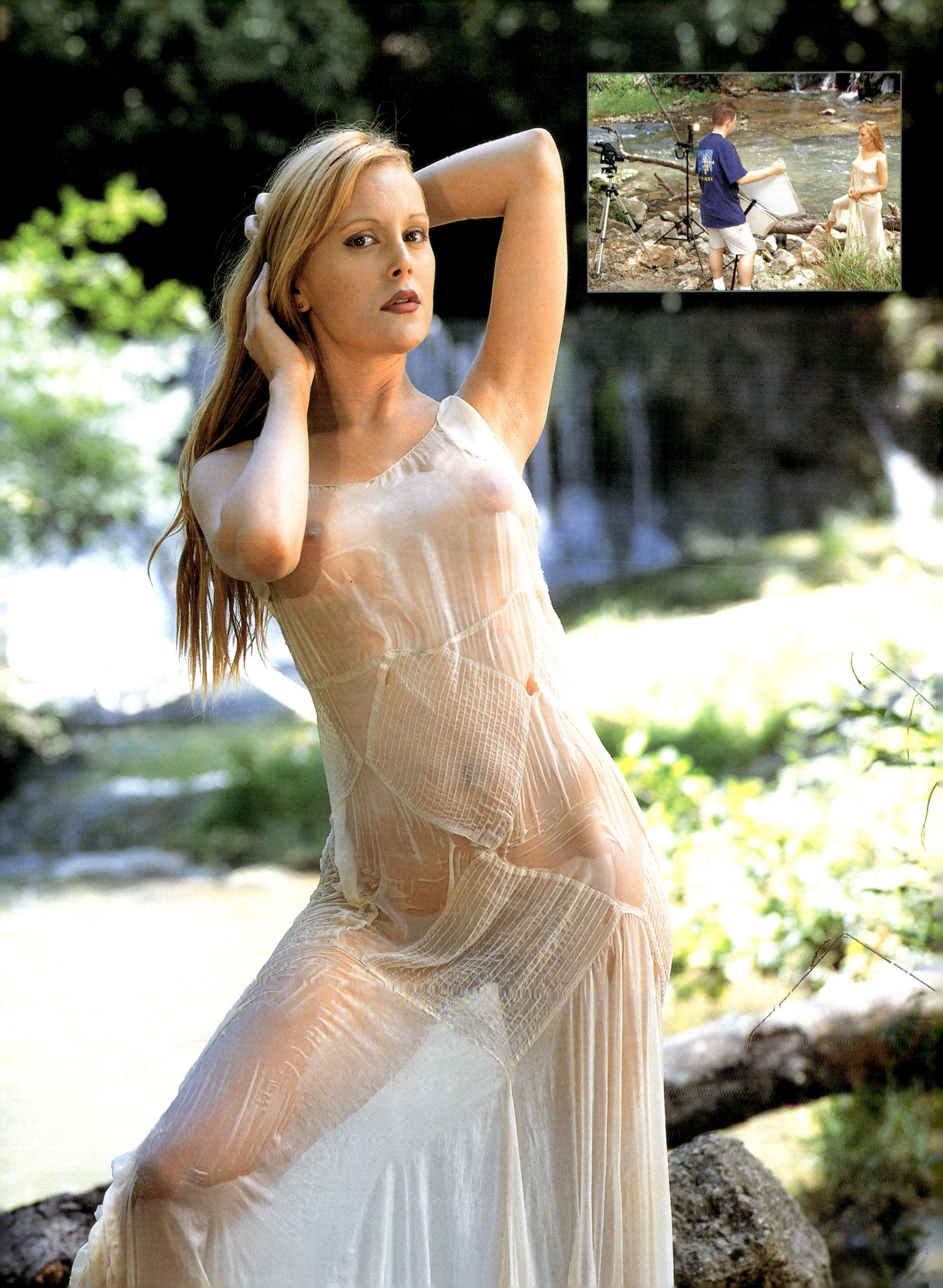

Evening light

This is my favourite time of the day for shooting exteriors, especially on deserts, beaches and anywhere where there is a broad expanse of landscape. From about 4p.m. on in summer, the light seems to take on a new mood, slowly warming up as the afternoon progresses to evening, creating soft shadows and making the subject glow.

When shooting in this light I tend to keep my techniques very simple, as the lighting can usually take care of itself at this time of day. I keep the subject lit from one side, using a soft, warm reflector to fill in the shadows on the opposite side of the model.

The distance the reflector is placed away from the subject determines how much mood you can create. When the reflector is closer, the result is less contrasty. You can experiment to decide what sort of mood you prefer – more subtle or more harsh.

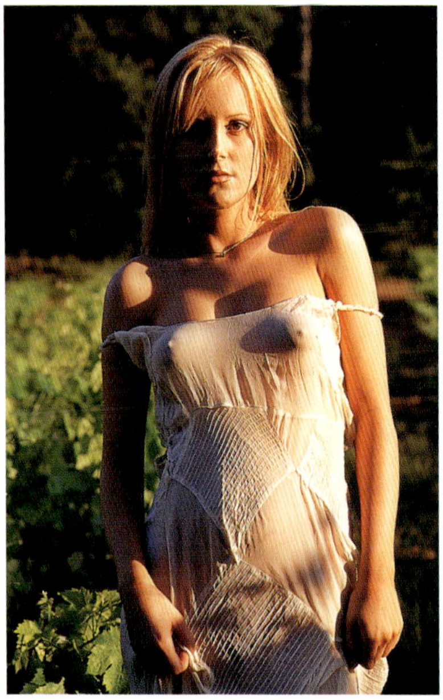

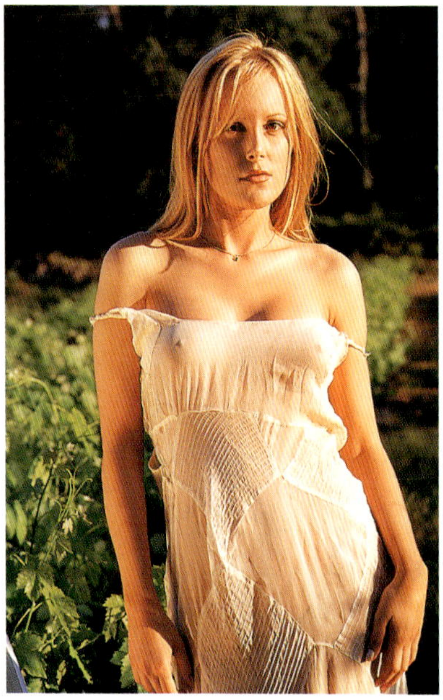

ABOVE AND BELOW: These images were taken in evening light. The picture above left was taken with available light only, which was falling at an acute angle on the right, creating strong shadows. The quality of light was pleasing, but I wanted to put more light on the model, so I used a reflector (below).
Mamiya RZ 6/7cm; 1/60 sec at f/8; Metz 45 flash set at f/5.6; 150mm lens; Fuji Provia 100F

Sunset

Sunset is also a very evocative time of day to shoot, but, like morning light, is very brief. It is best to use the light of the setting sun in a flat, wide expanse of landscape. If there are rolling hills, they will block out the sunset. You can often obtain interesting semi-silhouette images at this time, but you need strong and dynamic poses to make this work. In the image opposite, for example, the position of the model's arms creates visual interest along with the complex shape of the motorcycle.

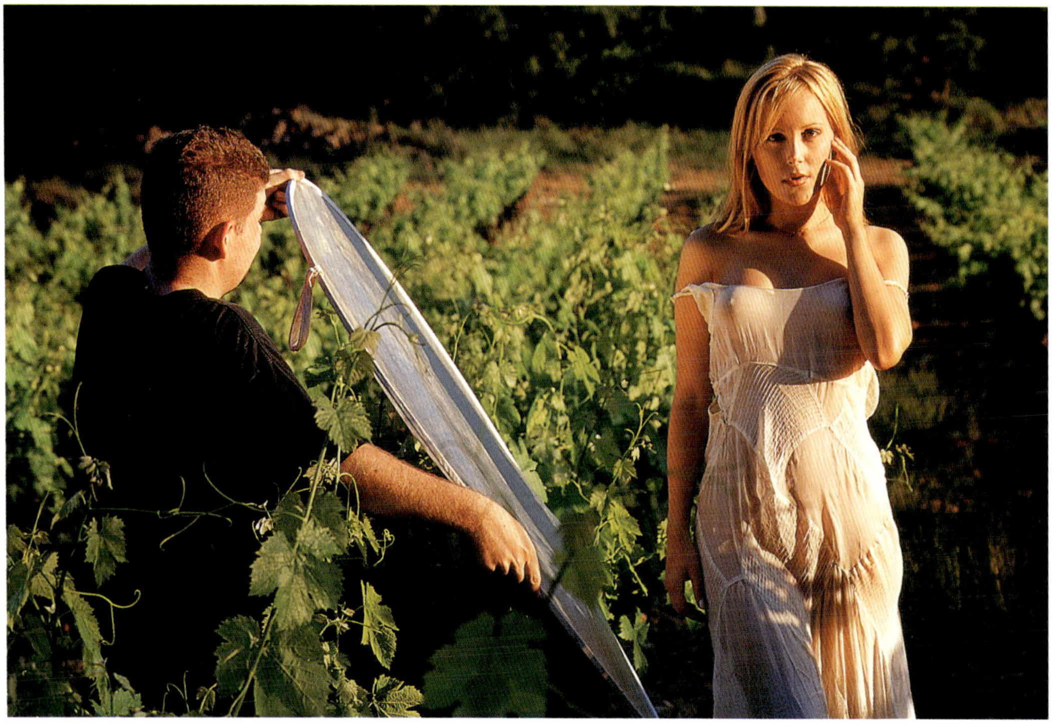

OPPOSITE: This image was taken at sunset, which creates semi-silhouette lighting. Your model needs to assume a strong pose for such shots to work; here, an interesting line is created by the model putting her hands in her hair. The colours are rich and warm, and the sea enhances the depth of colour created by the sun. I strengthened the image by using a Cokin soft orange filter to add a little more warmth and depth to the colours. You should use filters subtly or you can overdo the effect.
Mamiya RZ 6/7cm; 1/30 sec at f/5.6; flash set at f/4; 110mm lens with Cokin warm filter; Fuji Provia 100F

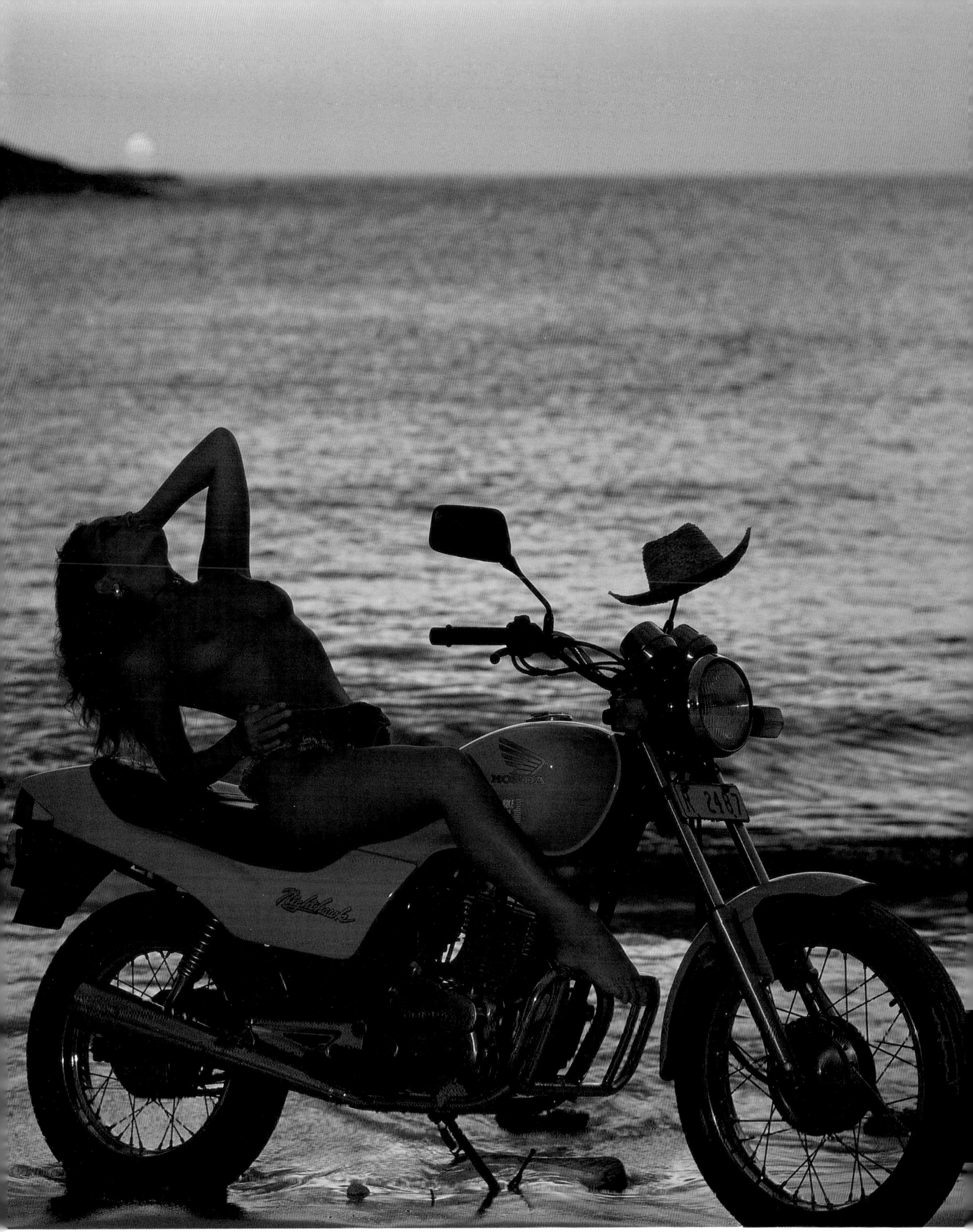
HONDA
R 2487

Lighting exterior to interior

Another common lighting technique used in location glamour photography is lighting exterior to interior. This is when your subject is standing outside – in a doorway, for example – and the interior is used as a backdrop. You can approach lighting such shots in several ways: one is to use a simple reflector to illuminate the model and a flash to light the interior, as in the image shown at the bottom of the page. This produces an image in which subtle details of the interior create an interesting backdrop to the main subject.

The other approach is a method that I call 'Playboy-style' lighting. This results in quite an over-the-top, artificial effect, which tends to give the location the overlit feel of a studio set. It is not to everyone's taste – some people find that it gives the model a plastic look – but it is a popular style in some sectors of the glamour market. The images shown here, for example, were commissioned as stock calendar shots.

To achieve this look, you light the model with a reflector and light the interior background with a flashlight. You then add an effect light, such as a honeycomb attachment, to create a concentrated and intense light that illuminates both the model's hair and the interior background. It is this light that is the key to creating the harsh, studio-set atmosphere of this technique.

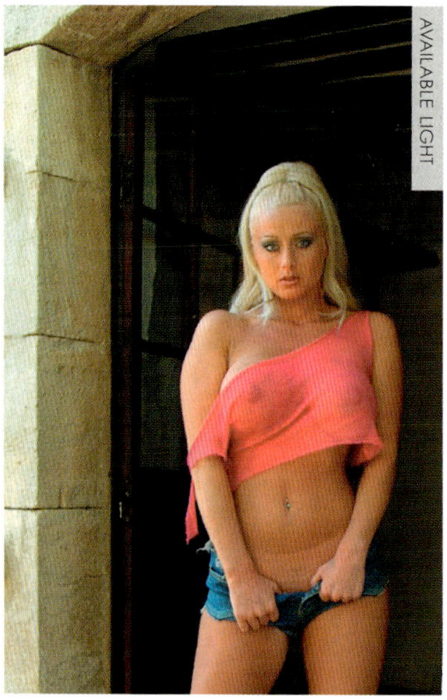

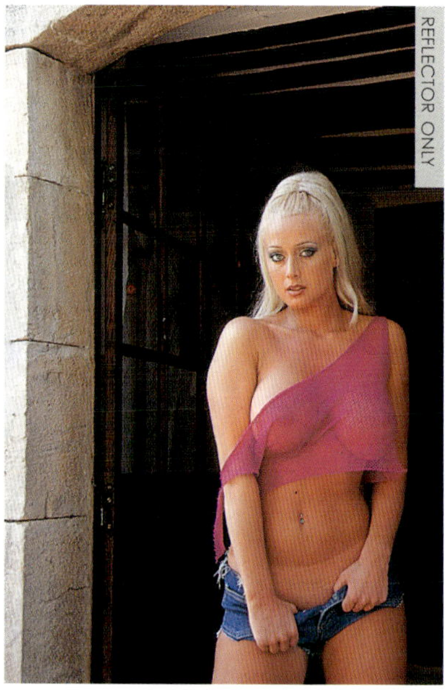

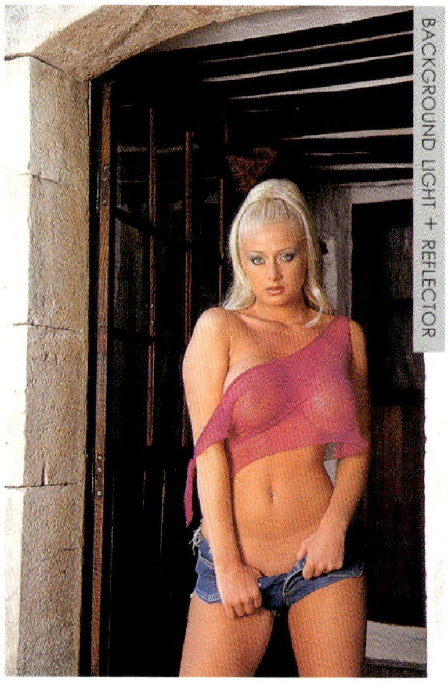

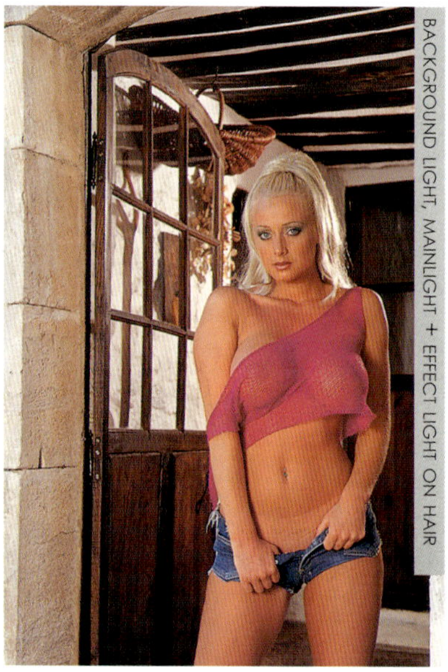

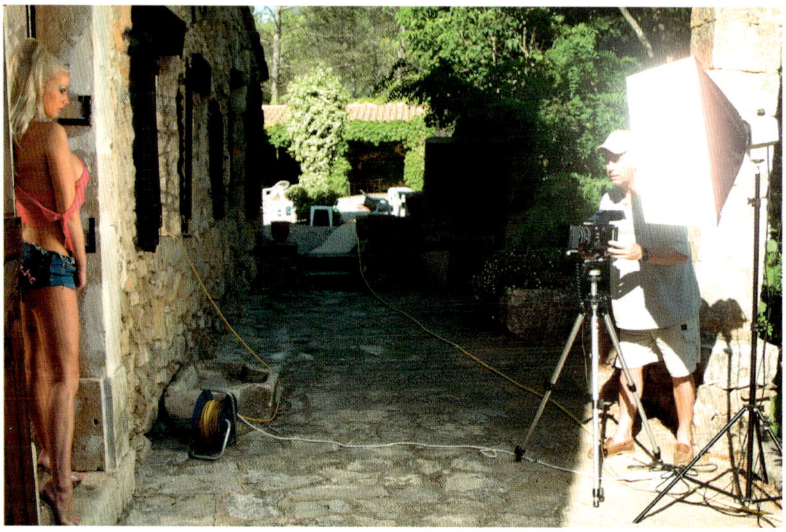

RIGHT AND OPPOSITE: Using the doorway creates a strong frame in which to place the model. The first picture (top left) was shot in available light. I then added a reflector to light the model from the front (top right). In the third picture I added a flashlight to light the background (centre left). Iln the final set-up, I added an effect light behind the model to light her hair, which also lit the background and the door. I deliberately 'overlit' the background in order to create an artificial, studio-set feel to the image (centre right). We experimented with the model trying a variety of three-quarter and full-length poses. In my opinion, the three-quarter poses were more successful, as the full-length ones were a little too busy. Cropping in closer on the model created more impact (opposite).
Mamiya RZ 6/7cm; main light 1/125 sec at f/8; background light f/11; hairlight f/8.5; 110mm lens; Fuji Provia 100F

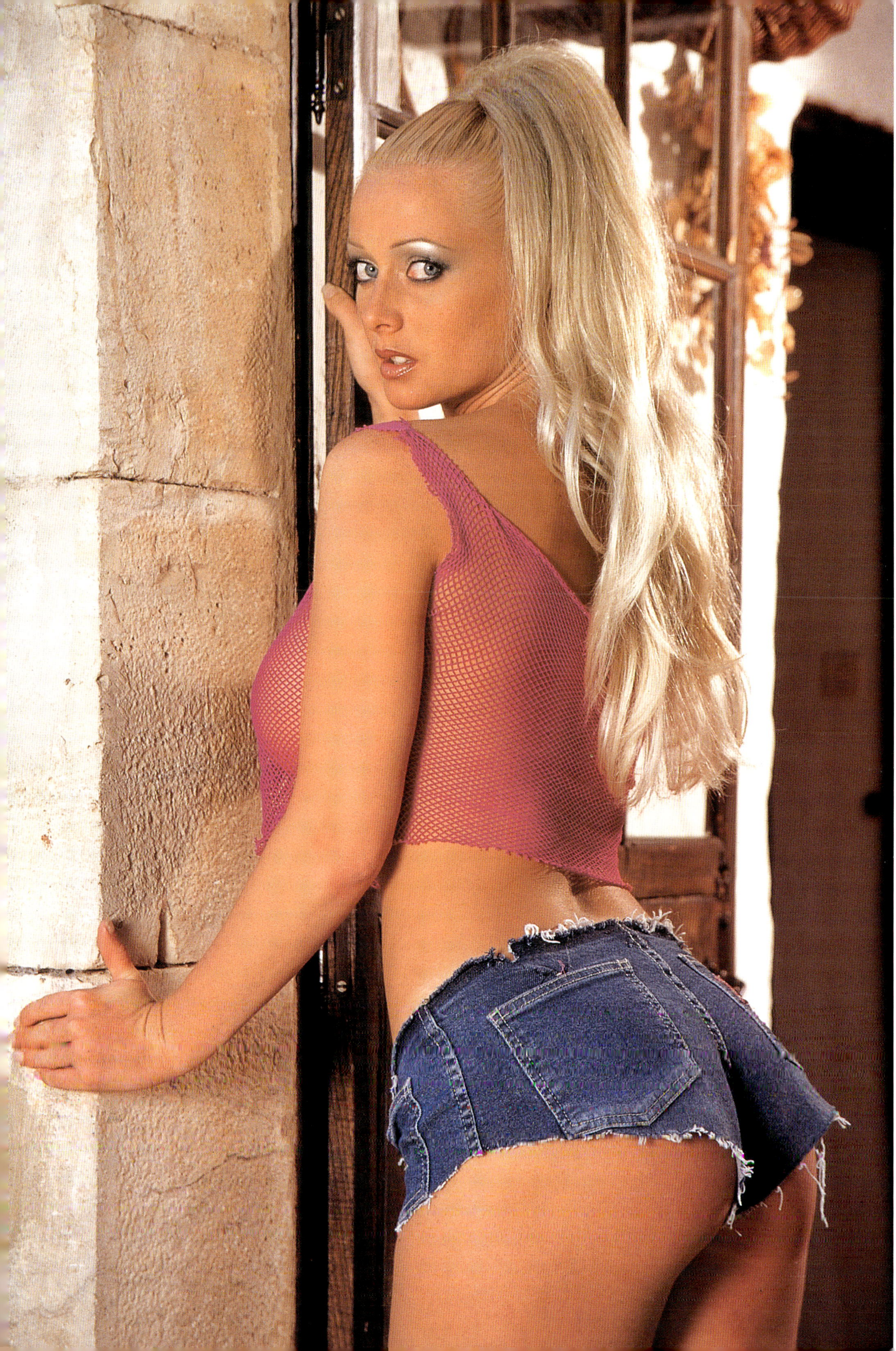

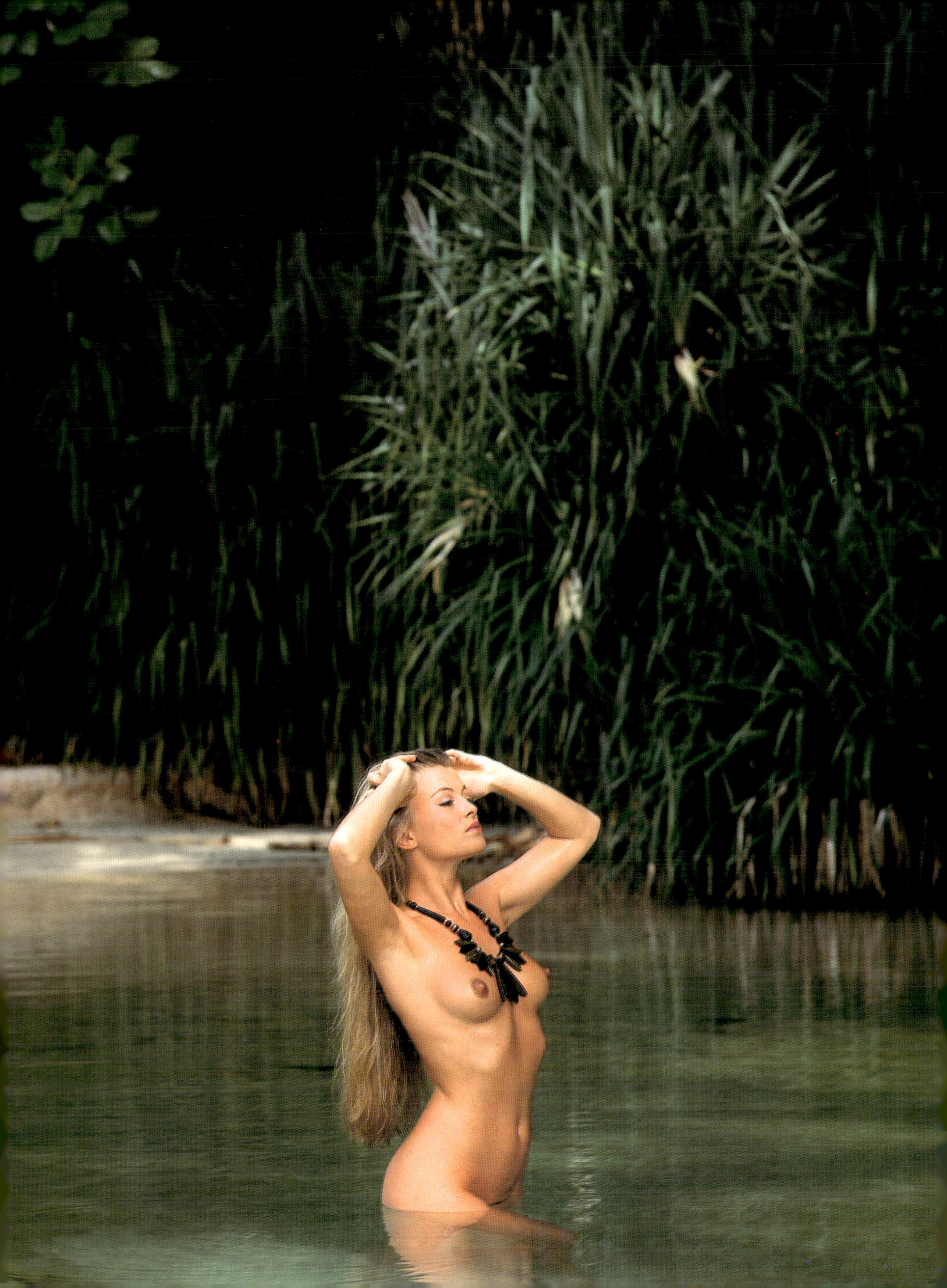

Portfolio

RIGHT: Taken on a beach in Jamaica, this is an example of when you can shoot in the midday sun, using the palm to throw interesting shadows on to the model's body. I also used a gold reflector to help fill in some of the shadows on the side of the model's body. **Mamiya RZ 6/7cm; 1/125 sec at f/16; 110mm lens; Fuji Provia 100**

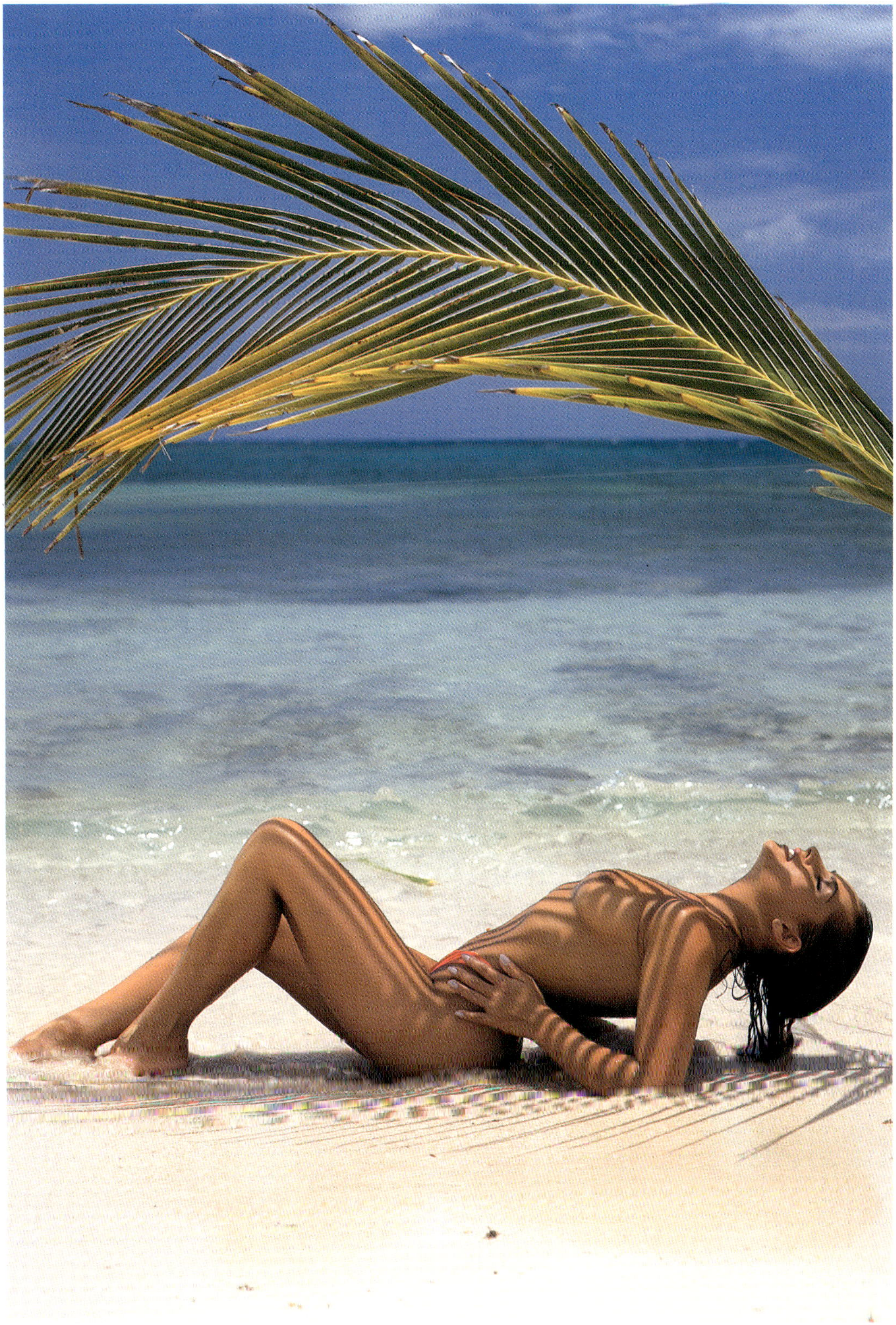

OPPOSITE: The location for this image was Frenchman's Cove in Jamaica. The shot was taken in a lagoon at 5a.m., when the early dawn light was soft and warm. The light catching the trees in the background helped to add atmosphere to the shot and gave it more depth of colour. The light is so soft at this time of day that you generally don't need any reflectors or fill-in flash – but you have to work quickly, as the quality of light does not last for long. **Mamiya RZ 6/7cm; 1/60 sec at f/5.6; 250mm lens; Fuji Provia 100**

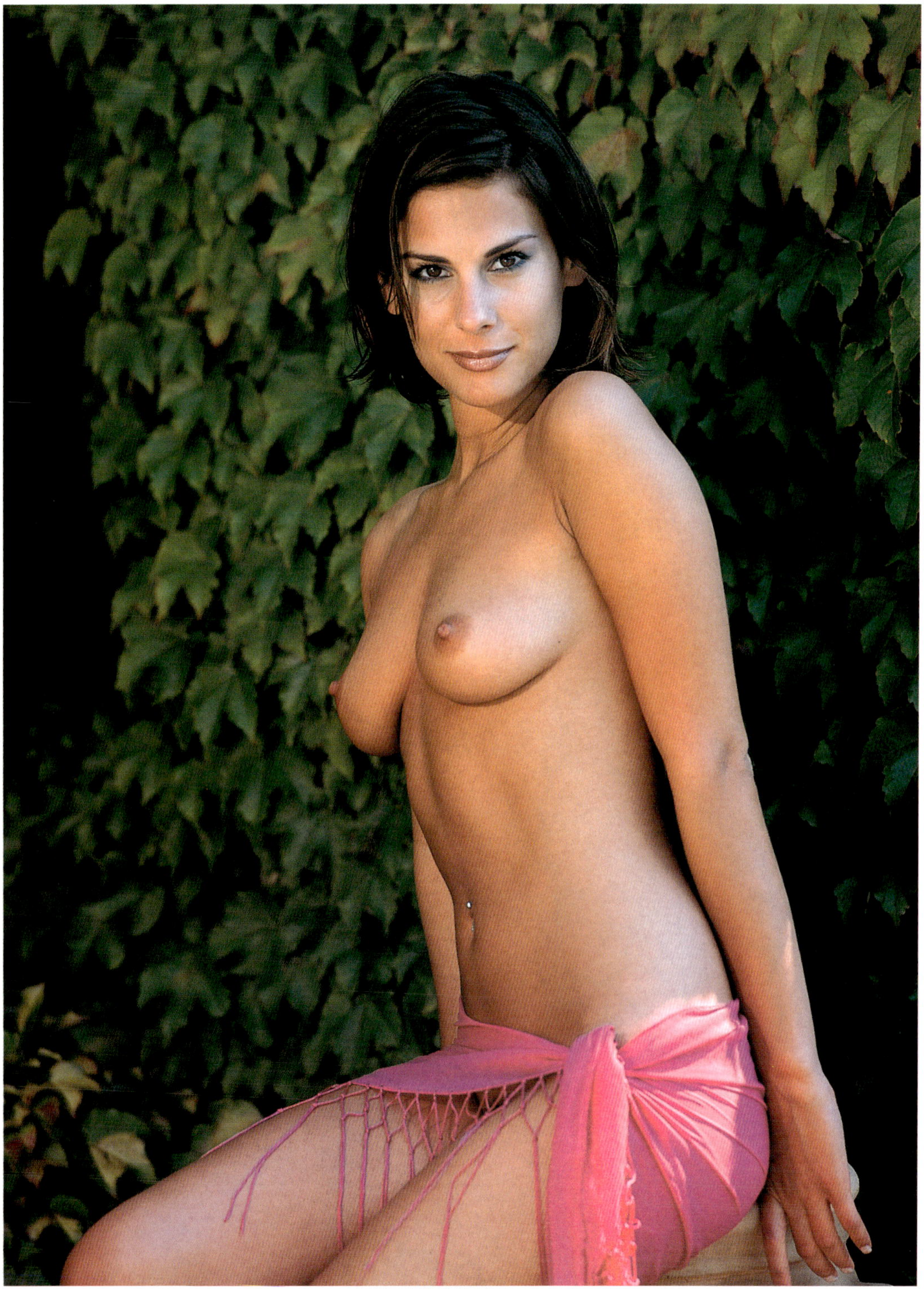

LEFT: The vines in this shot created a simple, textured background, almost like a painted canvas. The tones are subdued because the picture was taken in shadow. I used a warm gold reflector on the model to make her skin tones stand out against the dark background. The addition of the vibrant colour of the sarong helps to draw in the eye without unbalancing the overall simplicity of the shot. **Mamiya RZ 6/7cm; 1/60 sec at f/5.6; 150mm lens; Fuji Provia 100**

OPPOSITE: This image was taken in Provence in low light, in the shadow of the tree. I used a gold reflector to kick a little more light into the shot. The dappled light in the foreground and around the model's feet creates an interesting painterly effect. This shot works well because of the textural contrast between the rough, fissured quality of the tree bark and the smoothness of the skin of the model leaning against it. The model's pose is simple and naturalistic. **Mamiya RZ 6/7cm; 1/125 sec at f/16; 110mm lens; Fuji Provia 100**

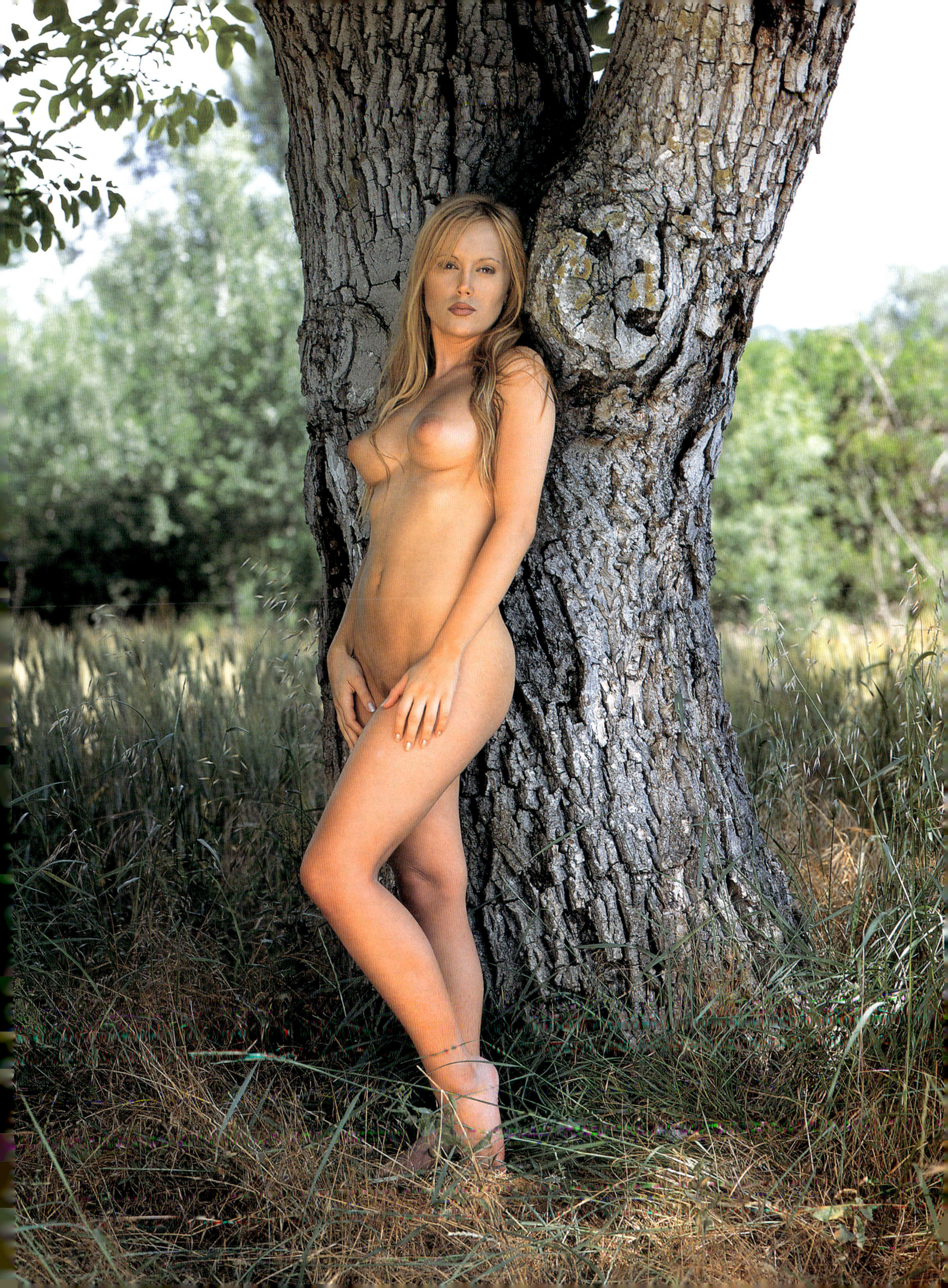

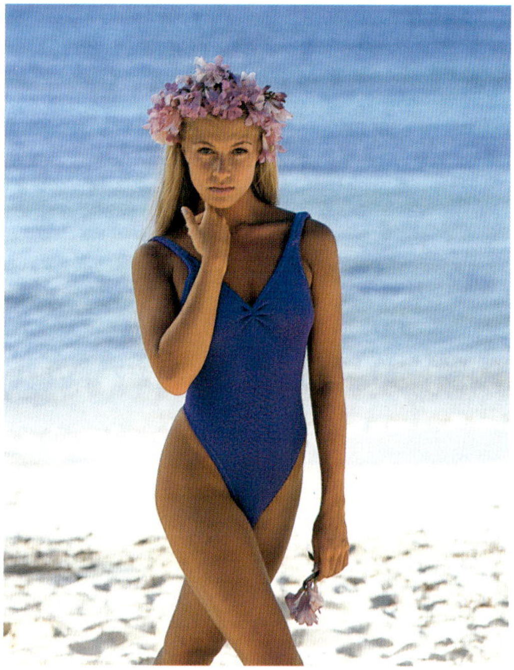

ABOVE: This shot was taken at midday using umbrellas. The colours are punchy and strong, and the overall effect of the shot is enhanced by the vivid colours of the model's swimsuit and flowers, which contrast well with the blue of the sea. The strong, simple lines created by the pose also contribute to the effectiveness of the shot.
Mamiya RZ 6/7cm; 1/250 sec at f/8; flash set at f/5.6; 150mm lens; Fuji Provia 100F

RIGHT: This image was taken in Arizona for a calendar with a Native American theme, hence the props of the bow and arrow. The cacti and the unusual rock formations of the desert location made a superb backdrop for the image, which was taken in the warm glow of late-afternoon sunlight.
Mamiya RZ 6/7cm; 1/250 sec at f/11; 110mm lens; Fuji Provia 100F

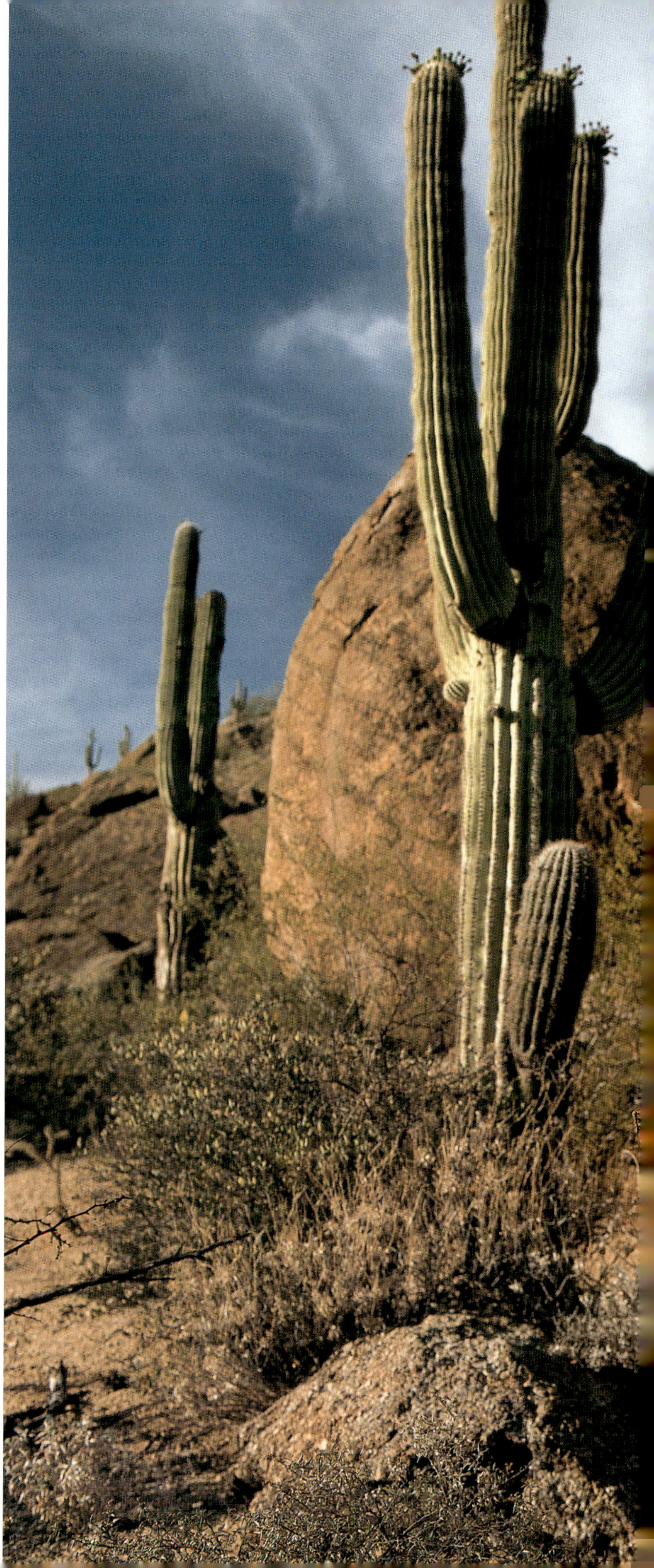

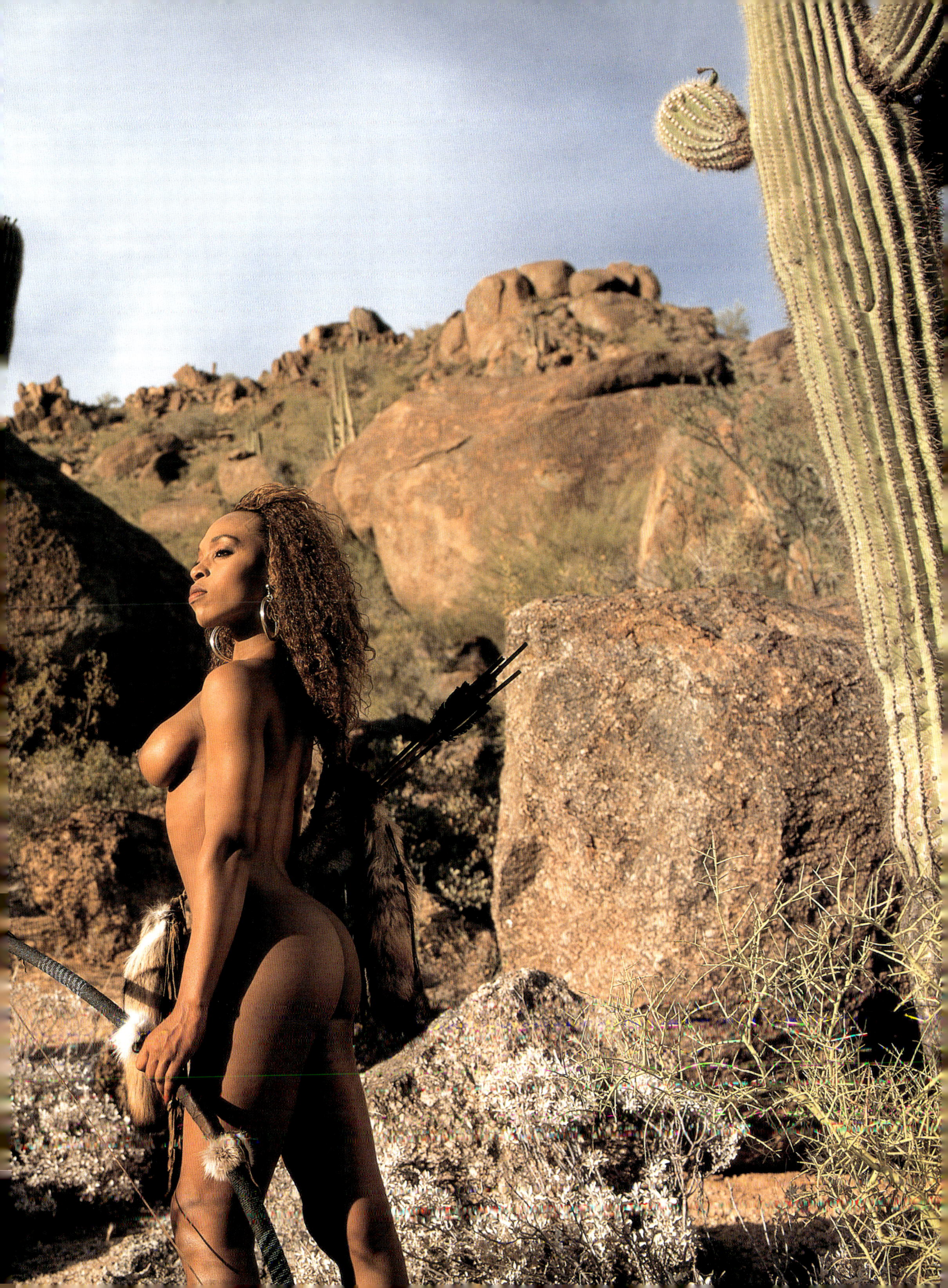

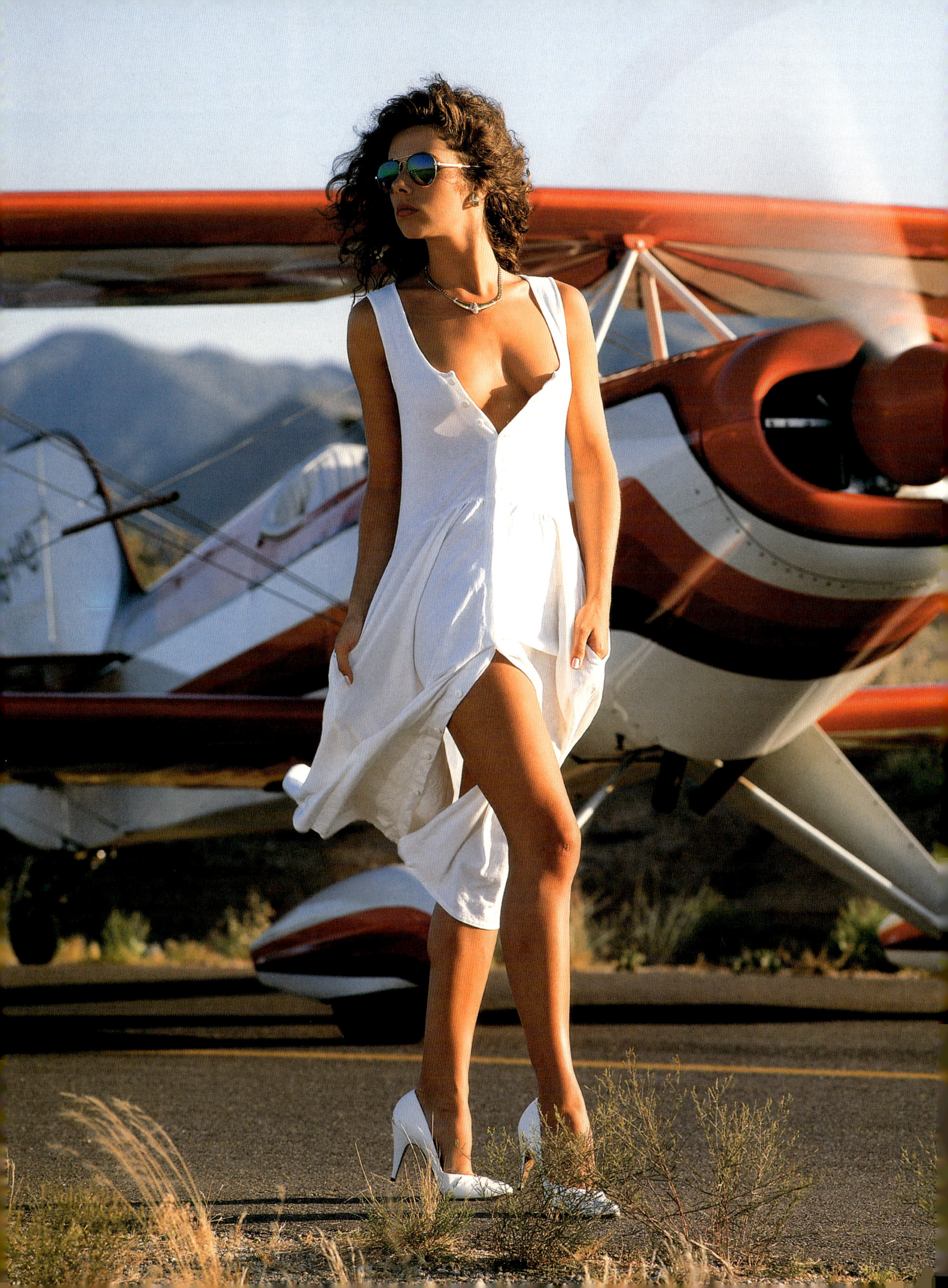

OPPOSITE: This image was taken on an airfield in Arizona. The pilot of the biplane set the engine running in order to create the effect of wind blowing the model's hair and dress. The image was shot at 5p.m., and I used just a little fill-in flash to bring some more light into the picture.
Mamiya 645AF; 1/250 sec at f/11; fill-in flash set at f/8; 150mm lens; Fuji Provia 100F

BELOW: This was shot at midday with the model under a white canvas hoarding, which created a soft light on her. Allowing your background to go slightly brighter than your subject helps to create more emphasis on the model. Using the stools helped produce an interesting composition.
Mamiya 645; 1/60 sec at f/8; flash set at f/5.6; 150mm lens; Fuji Provia 100F

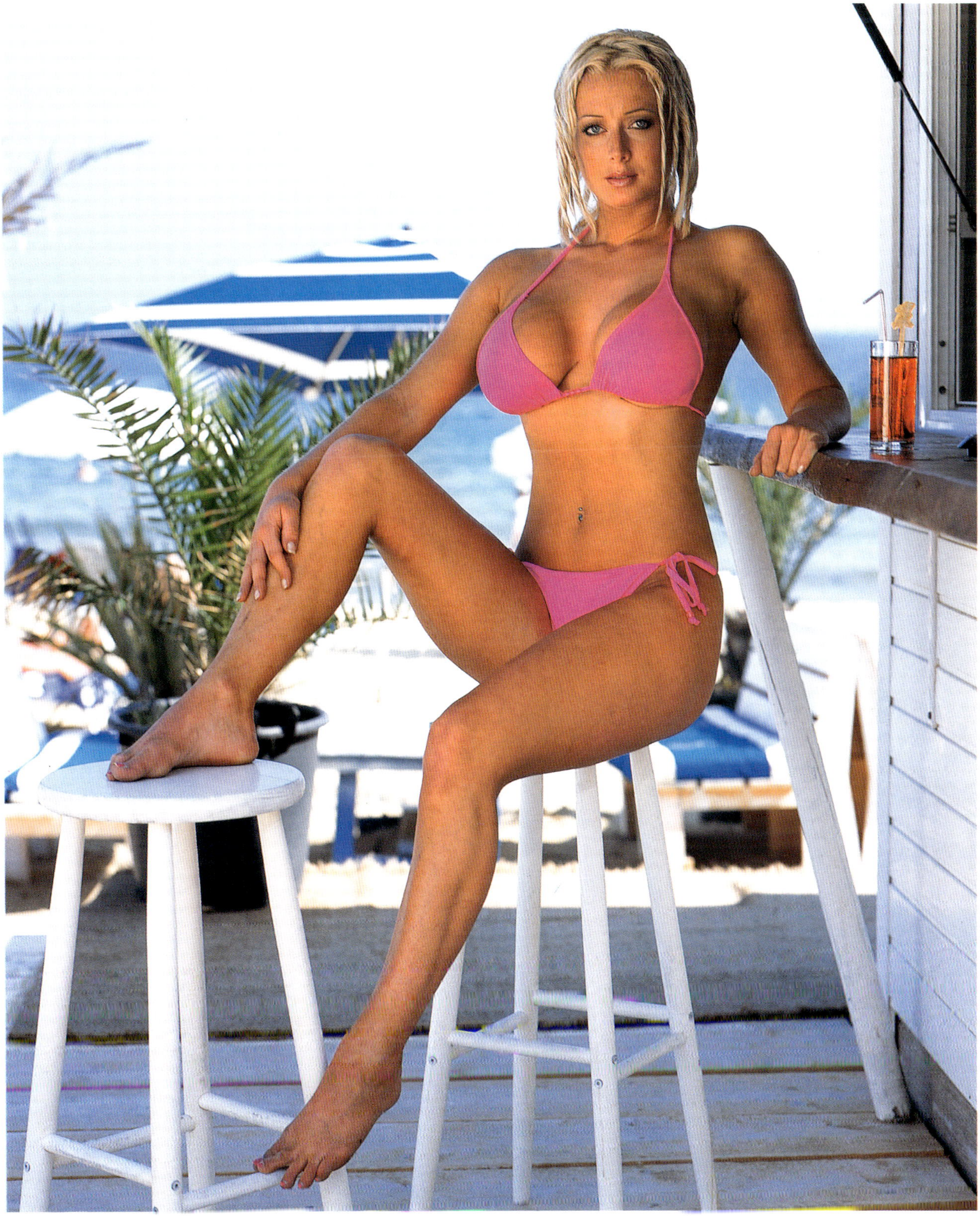

BELOW: This was shot in mid-afternoon when the sun was still quite high. I used a slow shutter speed (1/30 sec at f/22) to capture the movement of the water, and used a reflector and a small amount of flash to help freeze some of the water droplets. The model's simple but dynamic pose adds to the effectiveness of this image.
Mamiya RZ 6/7cm; 1/125 sec at f/16; flash set at f/11; 110mm lens; Fuji Provia 100

OPPOSITE: This shot was taken for an underwear catalogue. The image was taken at midday, when the strong light helped bring out the intensity of the colours of the umbrella, the bikini bottoms and the sea. Two gold reflectors were used to bring more light into the picture, and I used a polarizing filter to enhance the colour contrast.
Mamiya RZ 6/7cm; 1/125 sec at f/16; 110mm lens; Fuji Provia 100

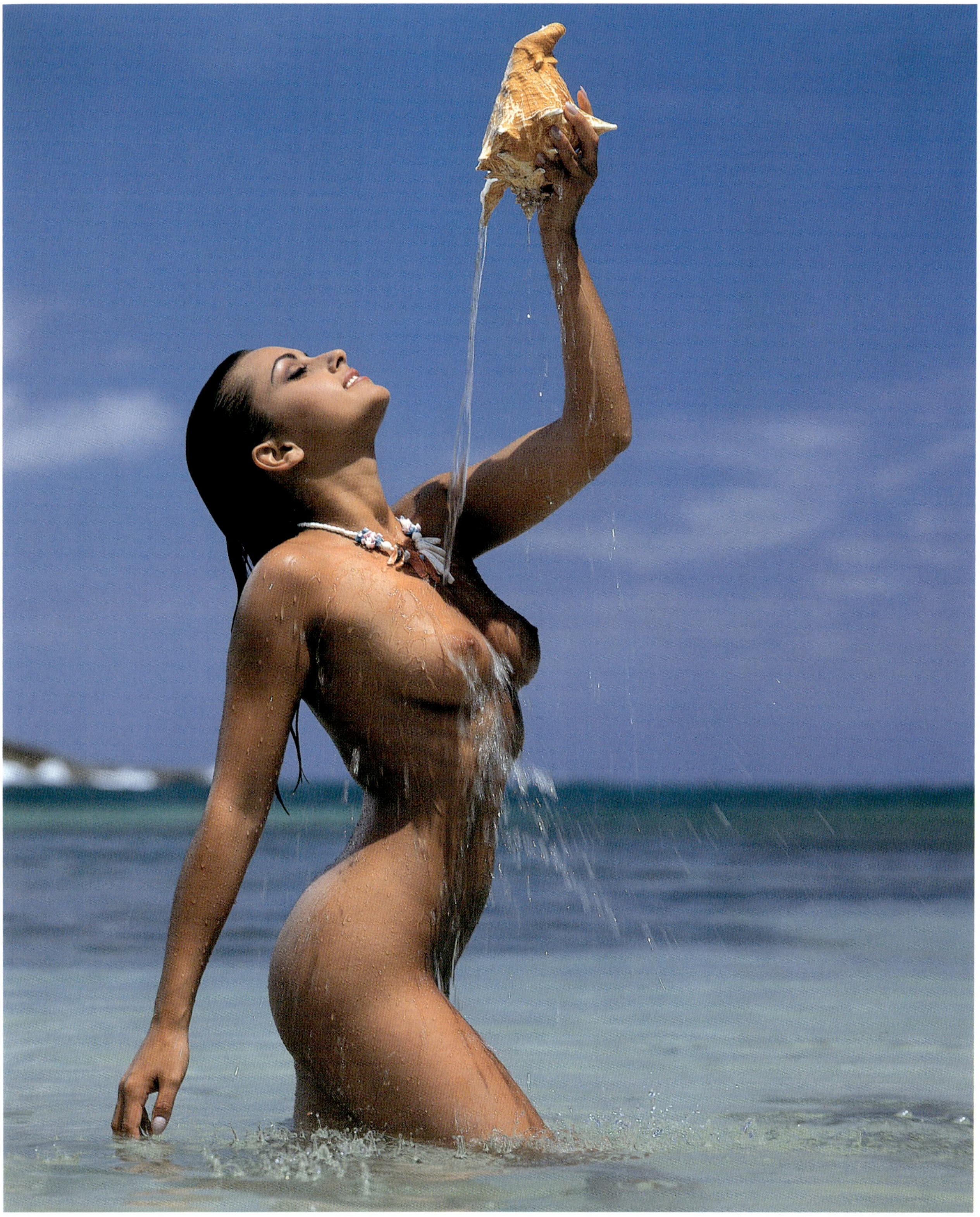

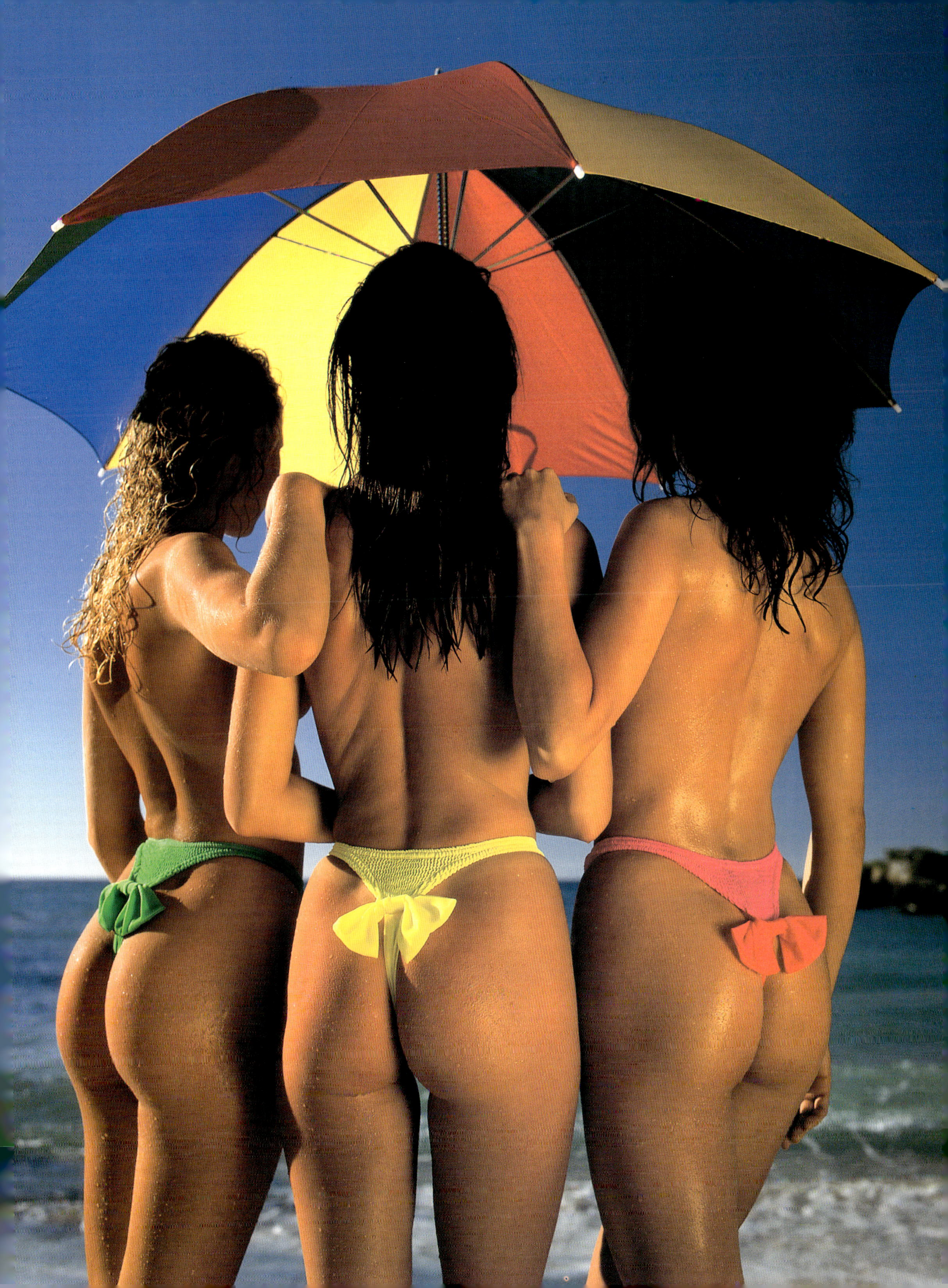

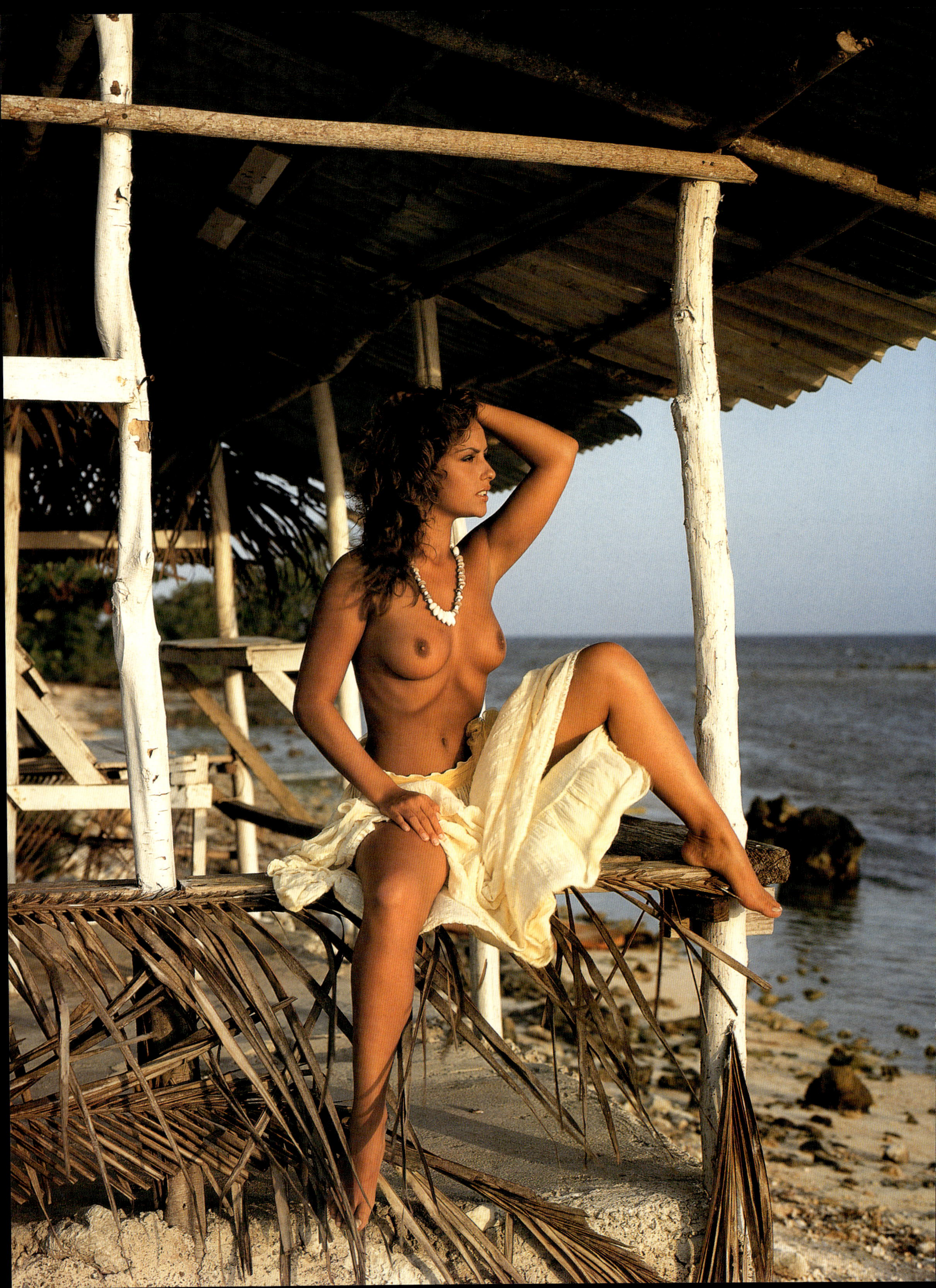

OPPOSITE: This was taken in the late afternoon, which creates a soft, pleasing light. The composition works well, with the model framed by the struts of the hut. Her skirt and shell necklace harmonize with the white wood, while contrasting with her skin and the dark roof and foreground.
Mamiya RZ 6/7cm; 1/60 sec at f/5.6; 150mm lens; Fuji Provia 100

BELOW: This was taken at midday, but the model's horizontal position overcomes the problem of the harsh shadows that you would usually encounter when shooting at this time. The red airbed stands out well against the blue sea, and I used a polarizing filter to further enhance the contrast.
Mamiya RZ 6/7cm; 1/125 sec at f/11; 110mm lens, Fuji Provia 100

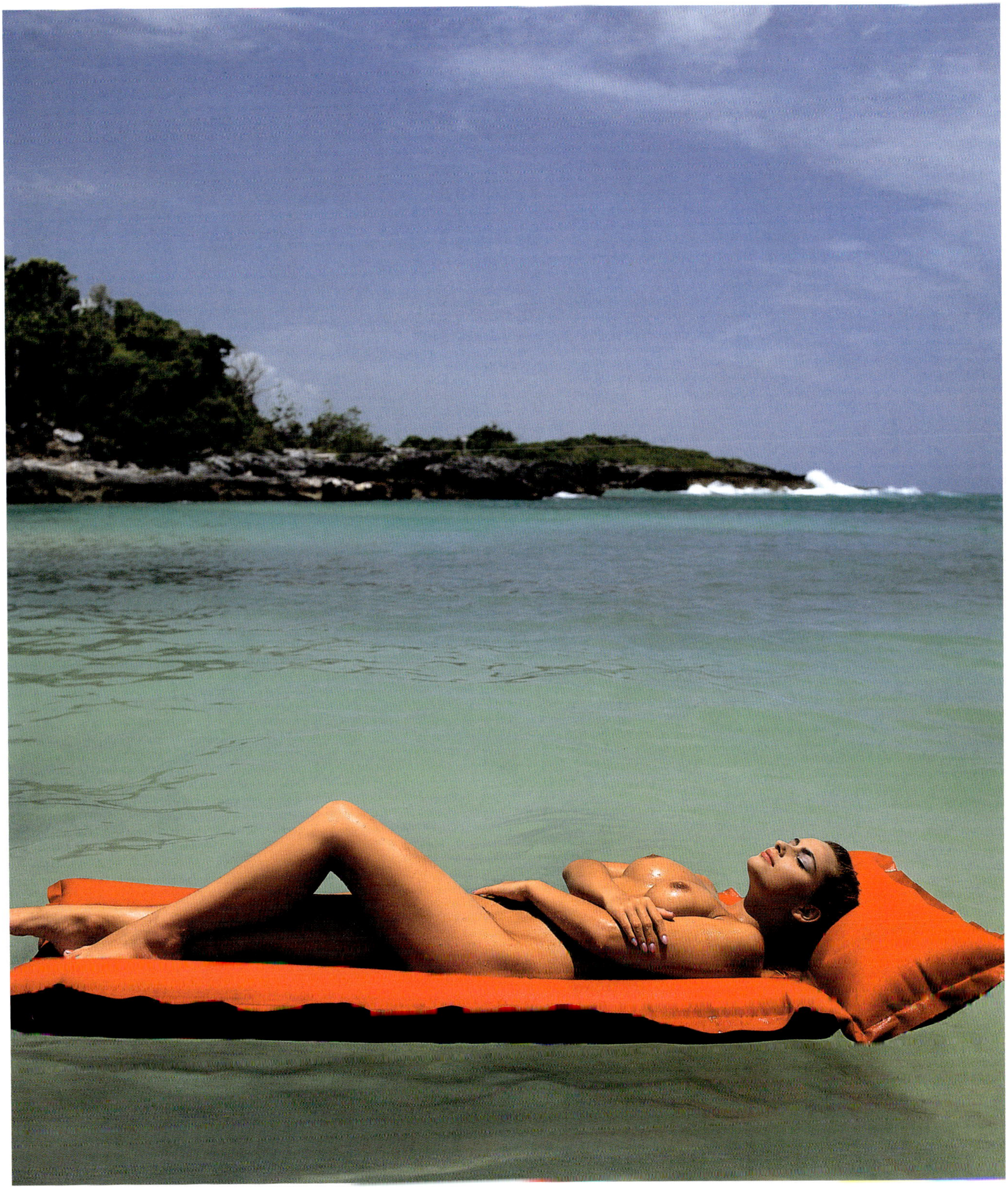

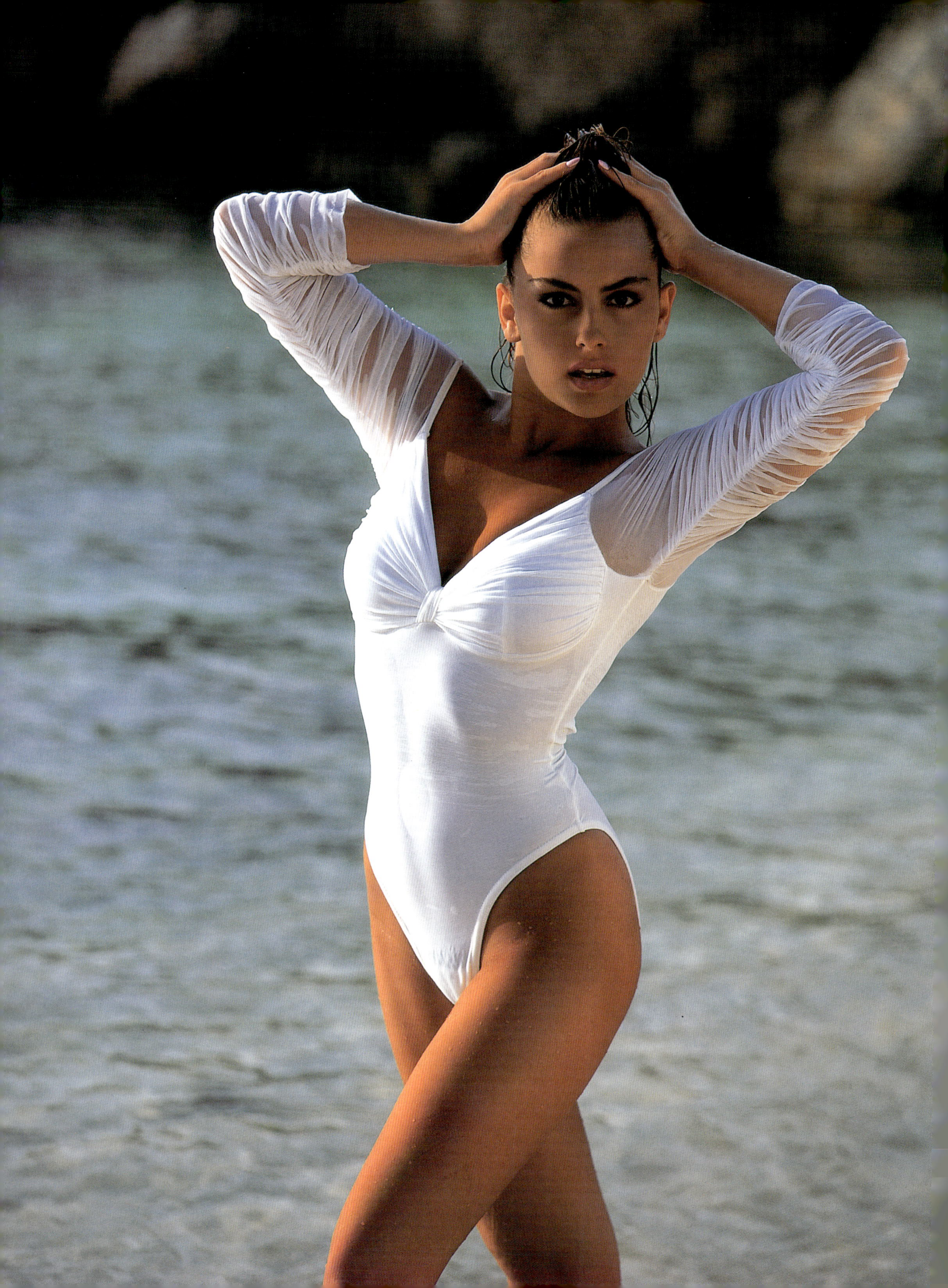

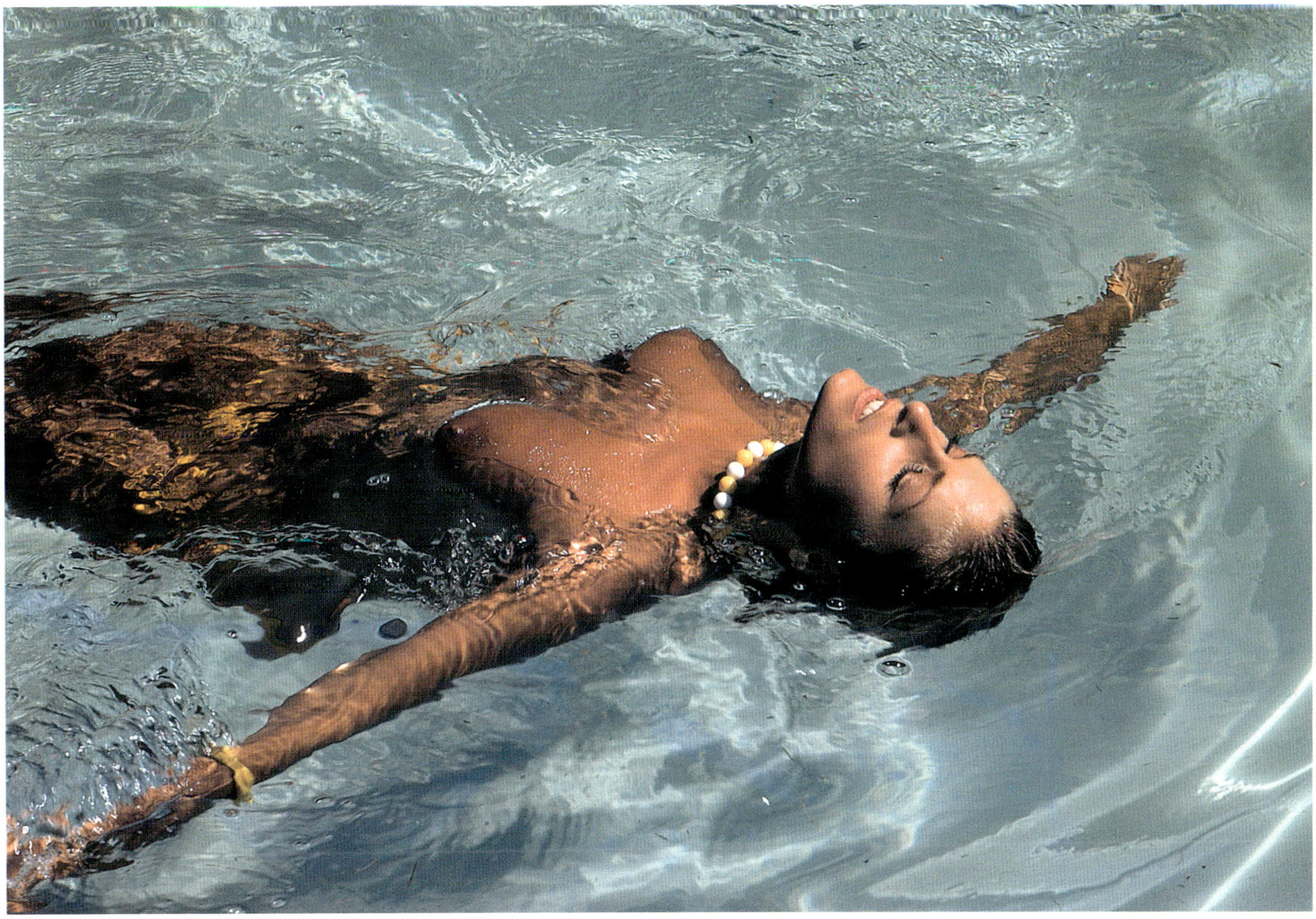

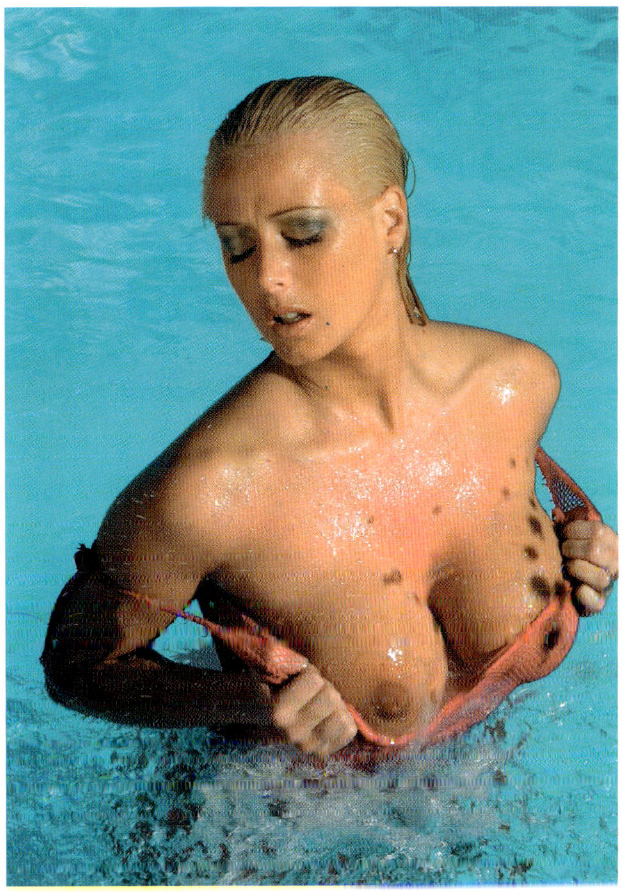

ABOVE: This shot was taken at midday; having the model lie on her back and close her eyes overcomes the problem of harsh shadow and the 'panda-eye' effect. The movement of the water created interesting patterns, and I used a slow shutter speed (1/30 sec at f/16) to capture this effect.
Canon EOS 5; 1/250 sec at f/8; 150mm lens; Kodak Ektachrome 100S

RIGHT: This was shot in the late afternoon. Again, I used a slow shutter speed to capture the movement of the water, where the shadow creates an interesting dappled effect. I used a fill-in flash to fill out the shadows.
Mamiya RZ 6/7cm; 1/125 sec at f/16; 110mm lens; Fuji Provia 100

OPPOSITE: This picture was taken in evening light, when the colours of the background become warm and subdued. These muted tones help to emphasize the lighting on the model and the white of her costume. I used a simple gold reflector to bring light back onto the model's face and body.
Mamiya RZ 6/7cm; 1/125 sec at f/8; 250mm lens; Fuji Provia 100F

interior locations

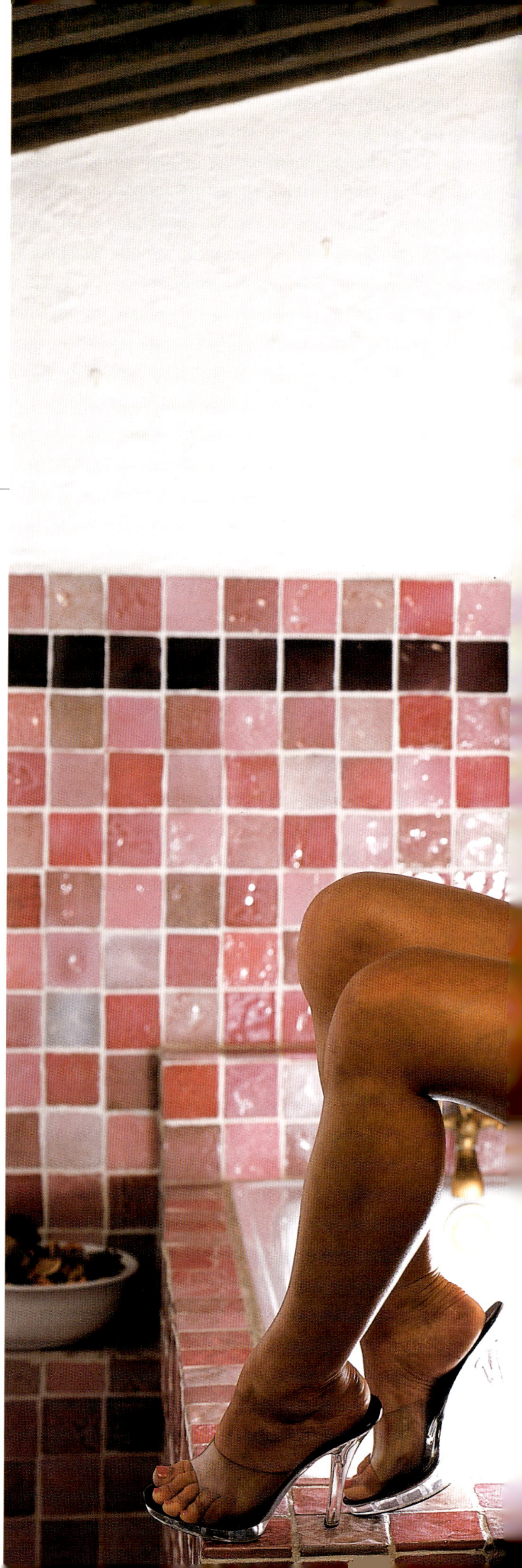

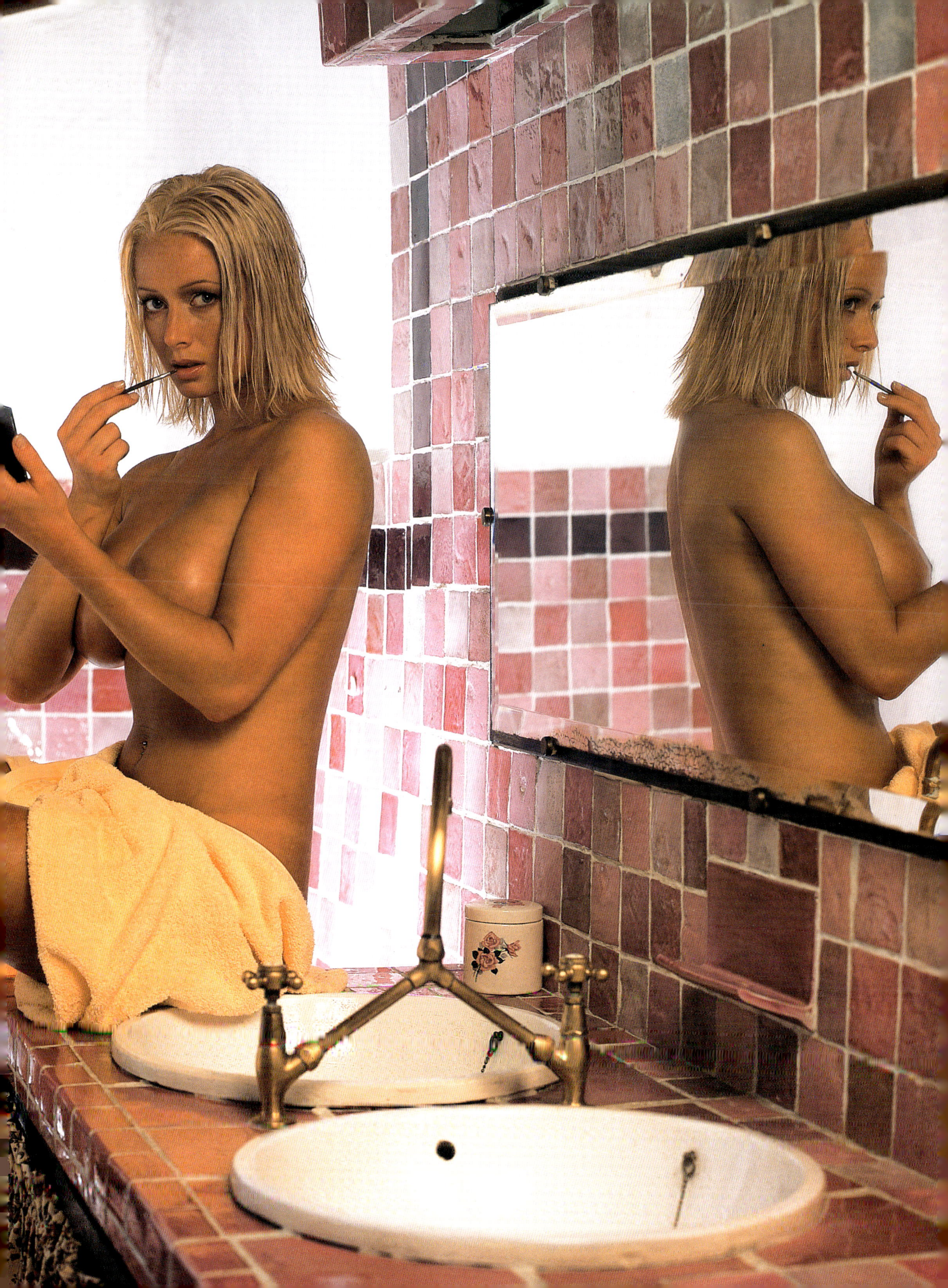

Using locations

The atmosphere of an interior location adds something to a shoot that just can't be manufactured in a studio setting. It is often more creatively satisfying to use a location, because you can take a good variety of shots and experiment with different angles, lighting and so on, while retaining the overall mood of the place. Your whole shoot will have a pleasing aesthetic and stylistic unity. You can use a location's characterful features – such as interesting windows, fireplaces or staircases – to set the model against. It is also often possible to use props and accessories found at the location to great effect.

Finding an appropriate location is much more cost-effective than mocking up a set in a studio. It also makes the logistics of a shoot much easier: something as simple as hiring a couch for a day can be expensive, and, of course, gives you very little scope in terms of how you can set up a shot and how the model can interact with the prop. In any case, your requirements may be far more extensive than just using a couch. You might want to use a sleek, modern setting, such as a chic, minimalist apartment with white walls, stripped-down wooden floors and sparse furnishings, or you might want an opulent interior filled with extravagant furniture and rich colours.

From a commercial viewpoint, clients, whether for fashion, beauty or glamour photography, often request that a shoot be done in an interior location, not just because it is cheaper: it is usually the case that the client has a specific 'story' that they want to tell or a certain product that they want to promote – whether that product is a catalogue, a glamour calendar, a line of clothing or a consumer item. The location has to be appropriate to that product and has to enhance its image to the consumer.

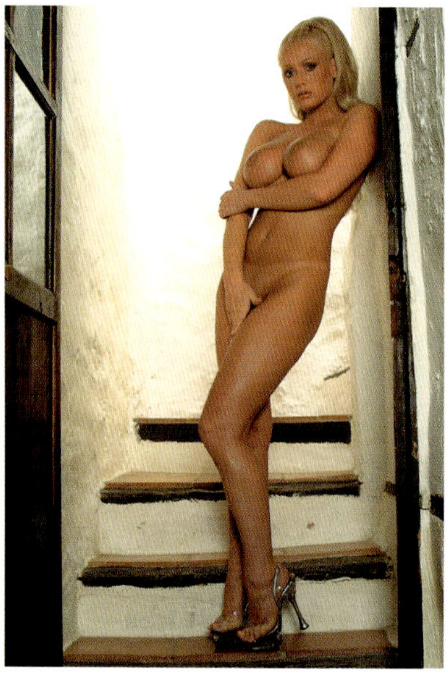
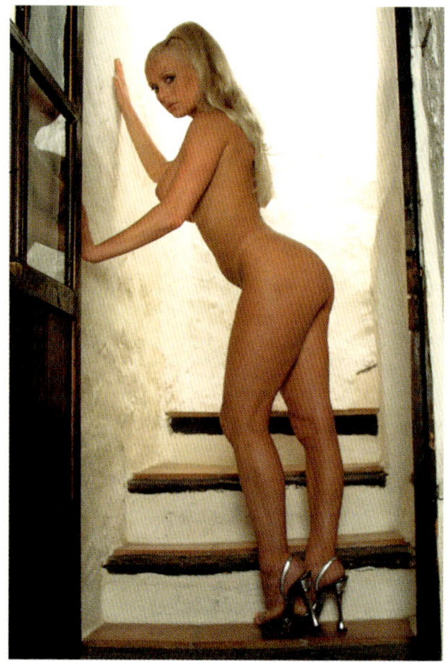
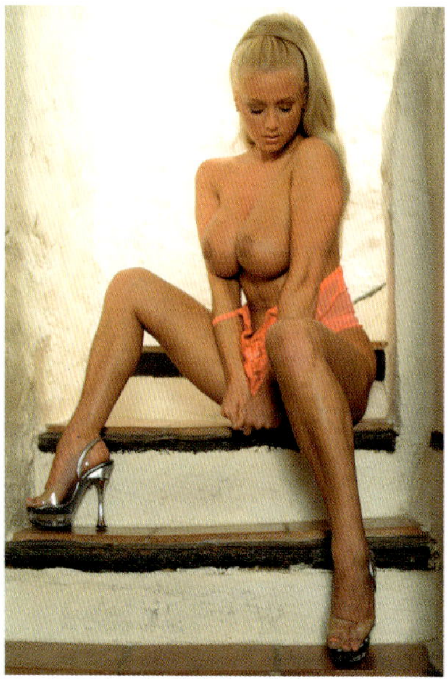
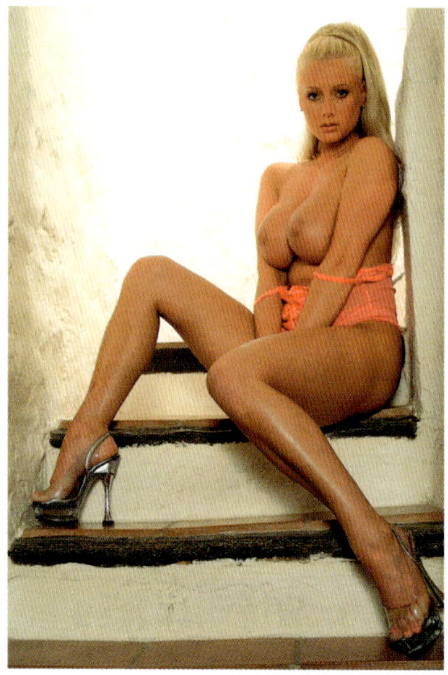

ABOVE AND OPPOSITE: This rustic staircase offered a versatile setting – its narrow, linear shape made an effective frame in which the model could try a variety of dynamic poses. The creamy walls and dark wooden steps made a backdrop that was simple and unfussy yet atmospheric. The lighting set-up was quite simple: there was a small softbox to illuminate the model, and a backlight at the top of the stairs to illuminate the wall and give the impression of light cascading down the stairs. The top of the wall was deliberately burned out to highlight the figure. I kept the camera position low in order to accentuate the length of the legs and body. **Mamiya RZ 6/7cm; 1/125 sec at f/8; 110mm lens; Fuji Provia 100F**

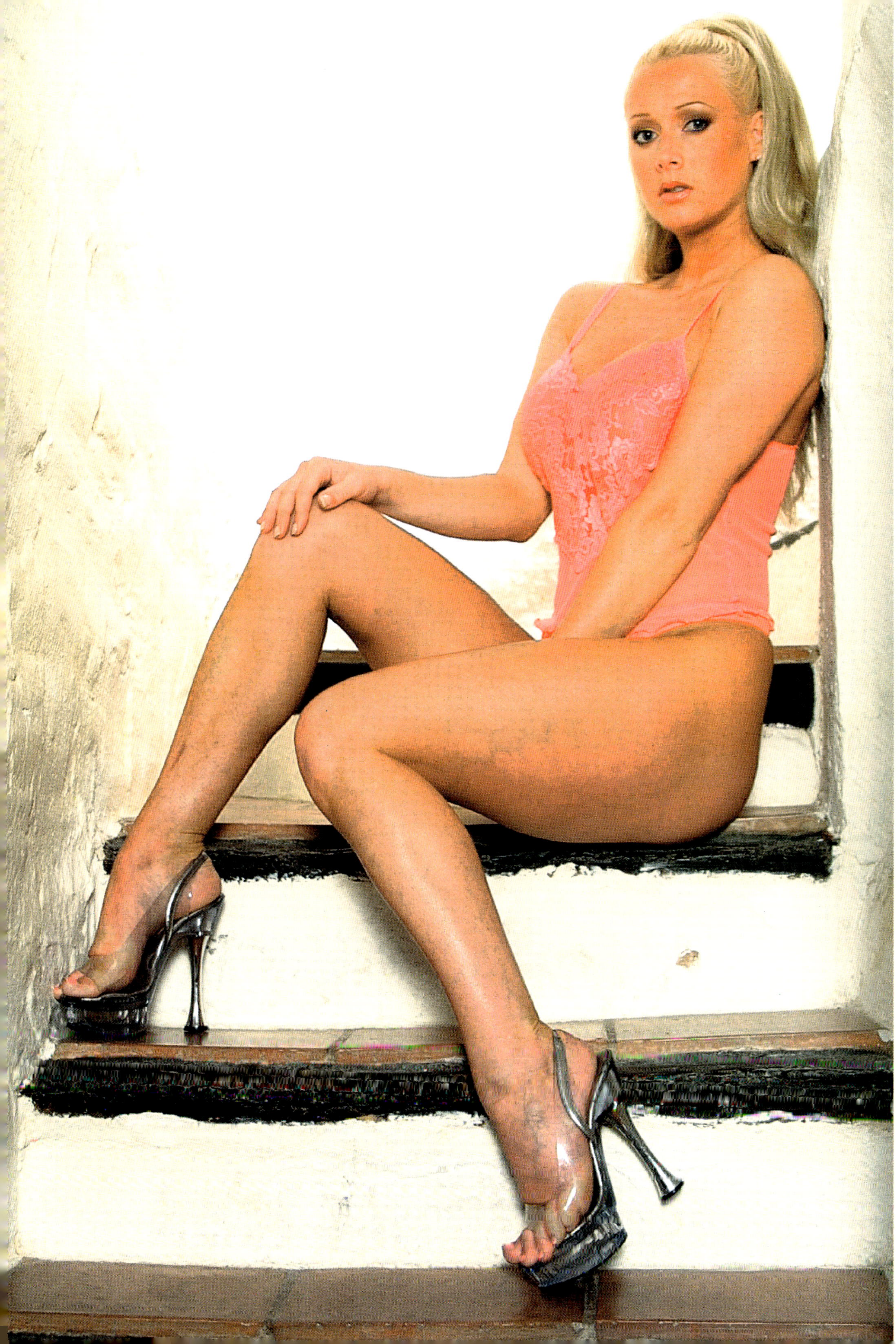

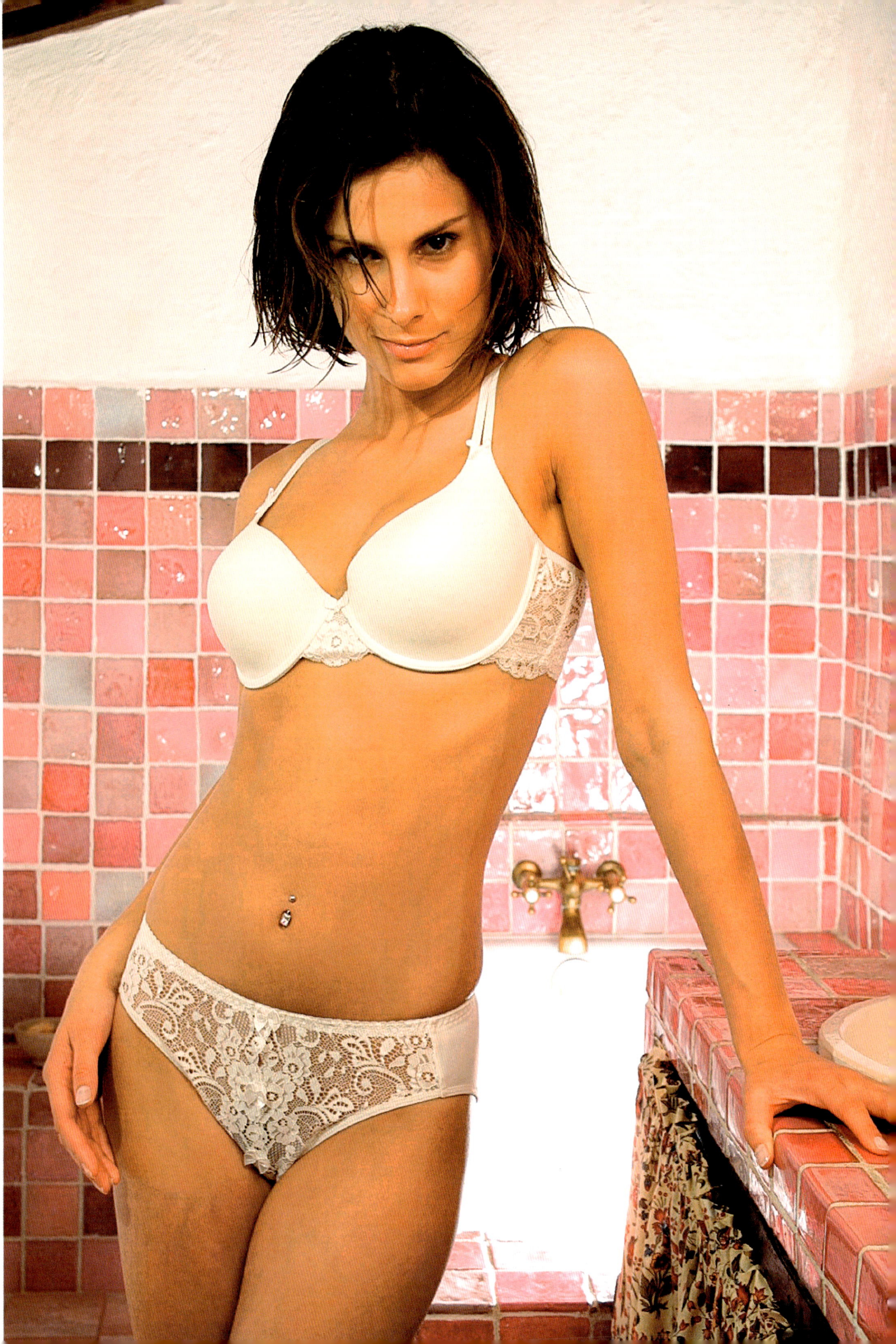

Choosing locations

From the photographer's point of view, there are many creative advantages to using interior locations. The ideal is to find somewhere that offers lots of opportunities to experiment with styling, lighting and mood, while also offering a pleasing aesthetic and atmospheric continuity. Many of the shots featured in this chapter were taken in a cottage in Provence, southern France, which had a good choice of interesting rooms to use as settings, and also gave a pleasing rustic ambience to the whole story of the shoot, with white-plastered walls, exposed wooden beams, old-fashioned fireplaces and washbasins and so on.

Other memorable interiors that I have shot in include Mentmor, a mansion in Hertfordshire owned by the Maharishi (guru to The Beatles), which was used in Stanley Kubrick's last film *Eyes Wide Shut*. This offered a fantastic range of lavish interiors, with massive gilded mirrors and endless corridors. I have also shot in a colonial house in Ocho Rios in Jamaica, where I was inspired by the unique architectural features of the house – white window shutters and wooden verandahs – and the bright, vibrant colours of the interior walls and furnishings, including four-poster beds hung with vivid-coloured drapes.

Getting the most out of the setting

One of the most exciting things about shooting in interior locations is using what you find there. There's a real buzz to be had from finding interesting props and accessories at the location and incorporating them into the shoot. Keep an eye out for features such as mirrors, balconies, mantelpieces and items of furniture when you first check out the location. Other things may turn up by chance during a shoot, such as the cat in the image on page 123; my assistant lay on the floor with strips of meat to persuade the cat to keep its pose!

Pitfalls of location shooting

One drawback of shooting in interiors is getting carried away by the interest of the settings. Some locations can be busy, with a lot of distracting detail, and you have to be careful to strike a balance: it is best to keep shots simple, so you get a flavour of the location and its unique atmosphere, while placing sufficient attention on the subject. Remember that you are not shooting the interior itself: you are using it as a setting or backdrop. Focus on a simple, strong detail – use a corner or a small part of a room, an interesting mirror or part of a bay window – rather than trying to capture the feel of a whole room. A good tip is to use a longer lens on the camera, which will put the background out of focus so you can capture the essential mood of the setting while not detracting from the model.

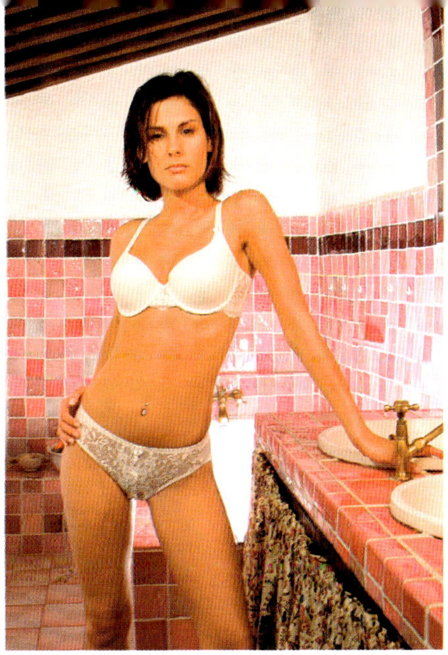

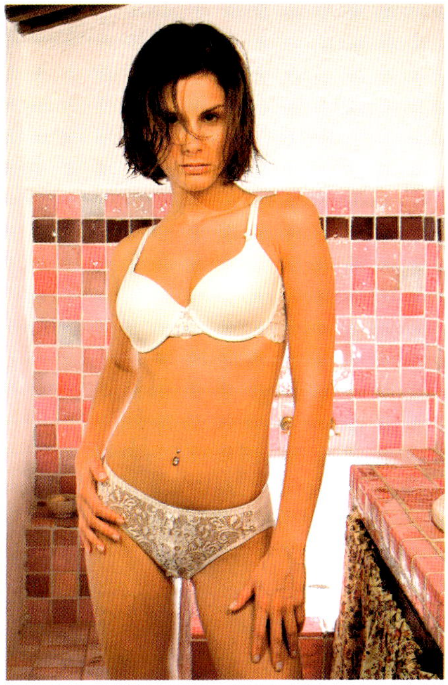

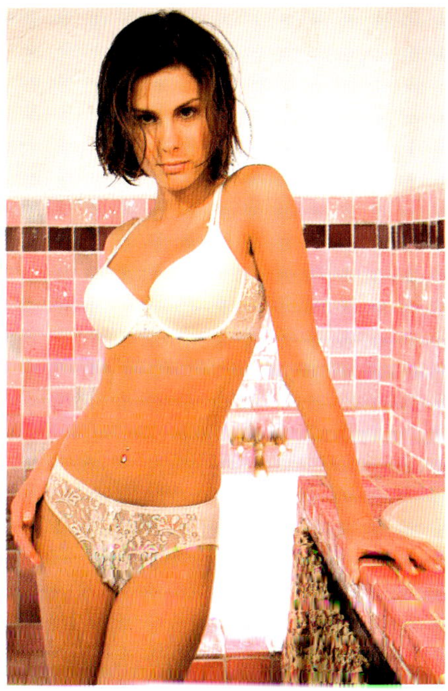

OPPOSITE AND RIGHT: Using this location was quite challenging because the bathroom was so small. The main difficulty was getting a main light source into such a confined space (there was no available light to exploit). Using an umbrella was out of the question given the size restrictions. I used a small softbox to light the model, and put a small Metz flash gun into the bath to illuminate the background. Metzes are very useful in small spaces because you can put them in places where normal flash guns can't go! In conditions such as these it is best to get in close to the subject, particularly when you have quite a busy and colourful background, as was the case here.
Mamiya RZ 6/7cm; 1/125 sec at f/11, 110mm lens; Fuji Provia 100

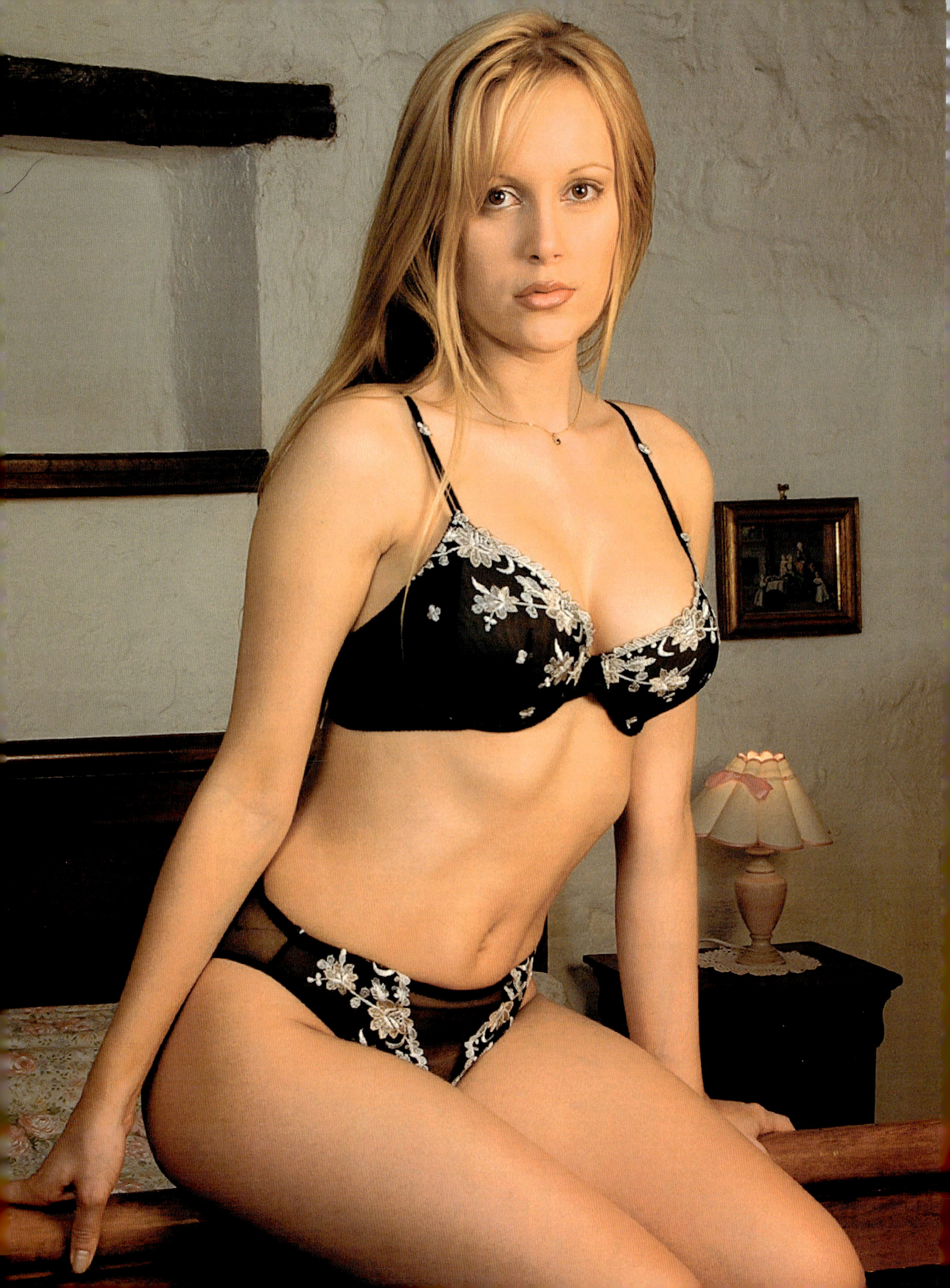

Lighting conditions

Using available light

When shooting in interior locations, it is an advantage to use available light wherever possible, as this kind of light helps to impart the atmosphere of the place. It is softer and more natural, it creates a good ambience, and it is possible to capture a lot of detail with it.

Available light often creates an artistic and evocative mood that is very pleasing. The images on pages 124 and 125, for example, were taken using only available light; the effect is toned-down, subtle and sophisticated.

Using available light often produces a creative look to an image, but it also lends itself to commercial purposes – it can help to put the required focus and emphasis onto the subject while overexposing or bleaching out the background. This may lose the detail of the backdrop or setting, which might be distracting and over-busy anyway, while maintain enough of it to convey a feeling of the spirit of the place.

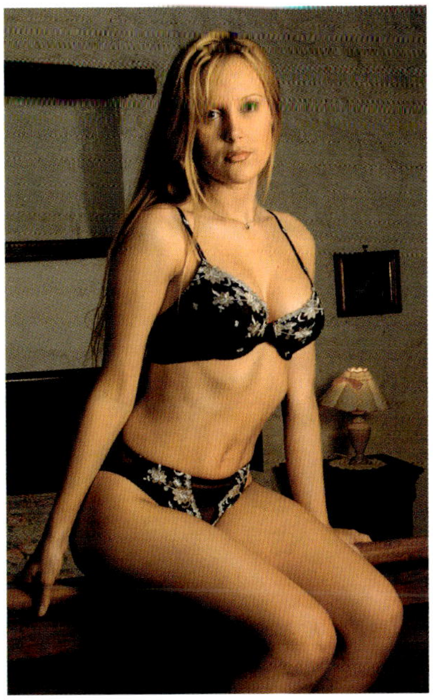

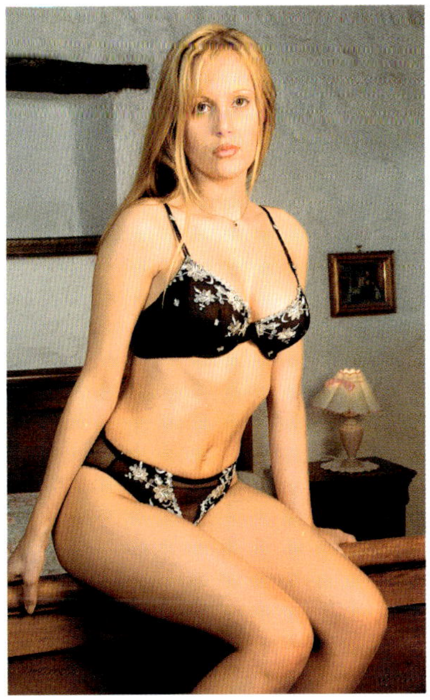

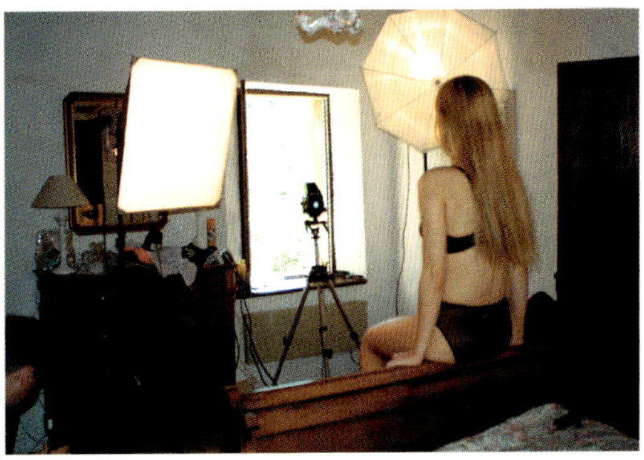

OPPOSITE, ABOVE AND LEFT: The shot left reveals the lighting set-up used for this picture. The shot above left was taken with available light only. To enhance this, I brought in some studio lights and used a small softbox and an umbrella with a flash head behind it (above right). The use of a warm gel on the flash head introduced a pleasing sunlight-type glow into the image (opposite). **Mamiya RZ 6/7cm; mainlight f/11; fill-in light f/8; background light f/8.5; 110mm lens; Fuji Provia 100**

Enhancing natural light

In many circumstances you can use available light in conjunction with studio lights. Introducing artificial lights into a setting produces various challenges: you have to strike the right balance between natural and artificial light, or you risk 'studioizing' the shot, making it look flat and dull.

In the images on these pages, I used available light from the bedroom window together with some studio lights. There wasn't quite enough available light in the room to create the effect that I was after, so I needed to enhance and warm up the natural light. I positioned a small softbox to the left of the model and an umbrella to her right, and placed a flash head behind the umbrella. Using flash in interiors can result in a picture that looks rather flat and uninteresting and cold, particularly when shooting in a bedroom: you can overdo it and kill the atmosphere that you are trying to capture. To combat this, I used a warm-up filter on the flash head, which puts a glow on the whole image, almost as if it were bathed in sunlight, and helps to warm up the model's skin tones.

The images on pages 114–116 of a model standing in a window give some idea of the many different effects that can be achieved using only available light and available light in conjunction with studio lights. I personally prefer the main image on page 115, which I find more artistic and creative. Using available light only helps to preserve the mood and atmosphere of the setting and creates strong shapes, the semi-silhouetted image of the model's body framed against the window shutter. Many commercial clients might find this image too artistic and moody, and would prefer the image below, as it is cleaner and shows more of the detail of the model. This picture was taken with available light and flash, and the balance between natural and artificial light had to be precisely controlled so as not to lose too much atmosphere. This image still imparts the feeling of daylight coming in through the window, but also puts more emphasis on the model because she is lit as well. Compare this with the bottom photograph on page 116: this image is still acceptable from a commercial point of view, but in my opinion it is rather overlit, with the result that much of the natural atmosphere of the setting has been wiped out.

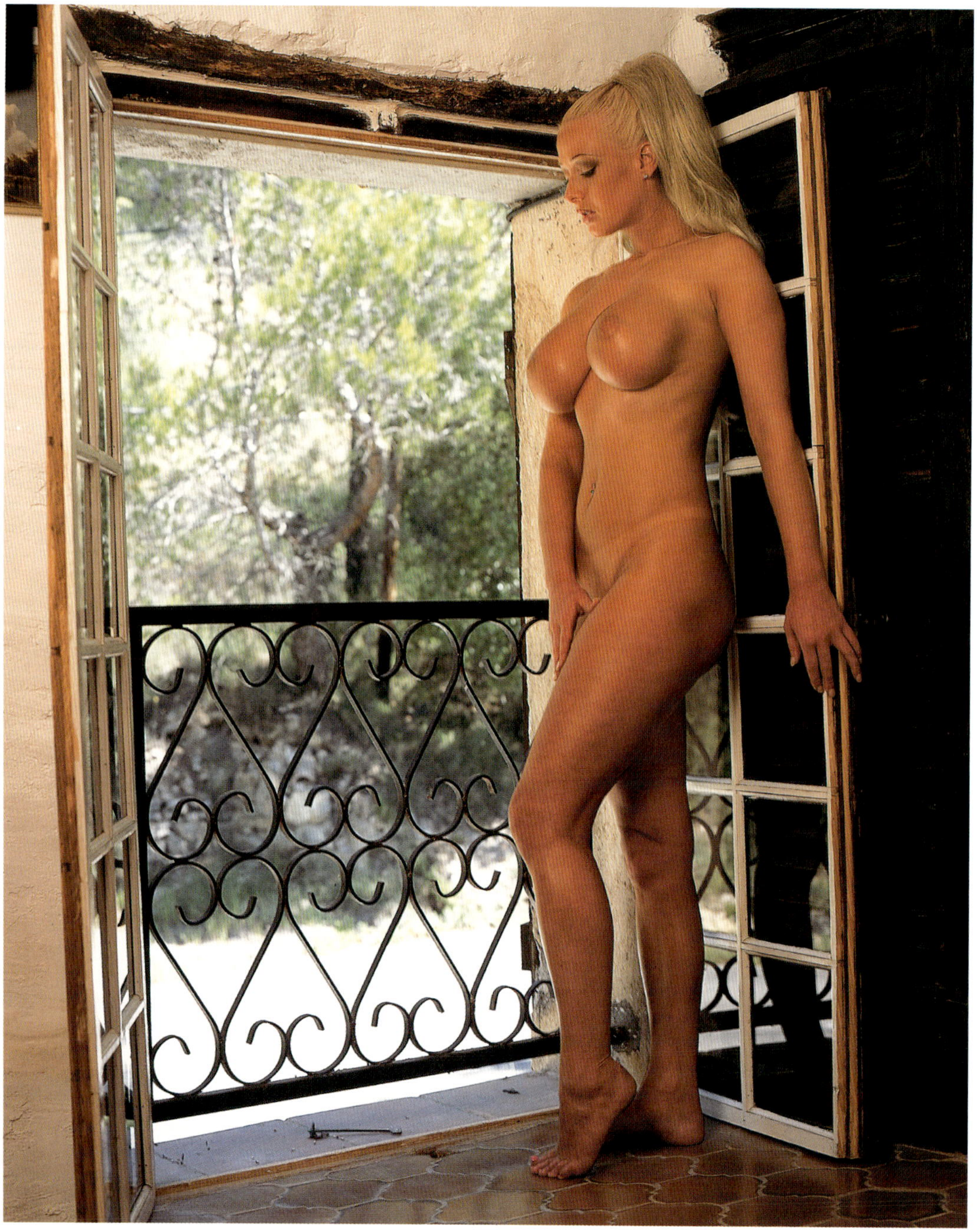

LEFT AND OPPOSITE: Available light often produces the best results, but only when there is an adequate light source – in this case, a very large window. To my mind, the image opposite is more artistic and effective than the picture on the left, where I introduced flash in conjunction with the natural daylight. **Mamiya RZ 6/7cm; 1/125 sec at f/16 for image opposite; 1/125 sec at f/11 for image on left; 110mm lens; Fuji Provia 100**

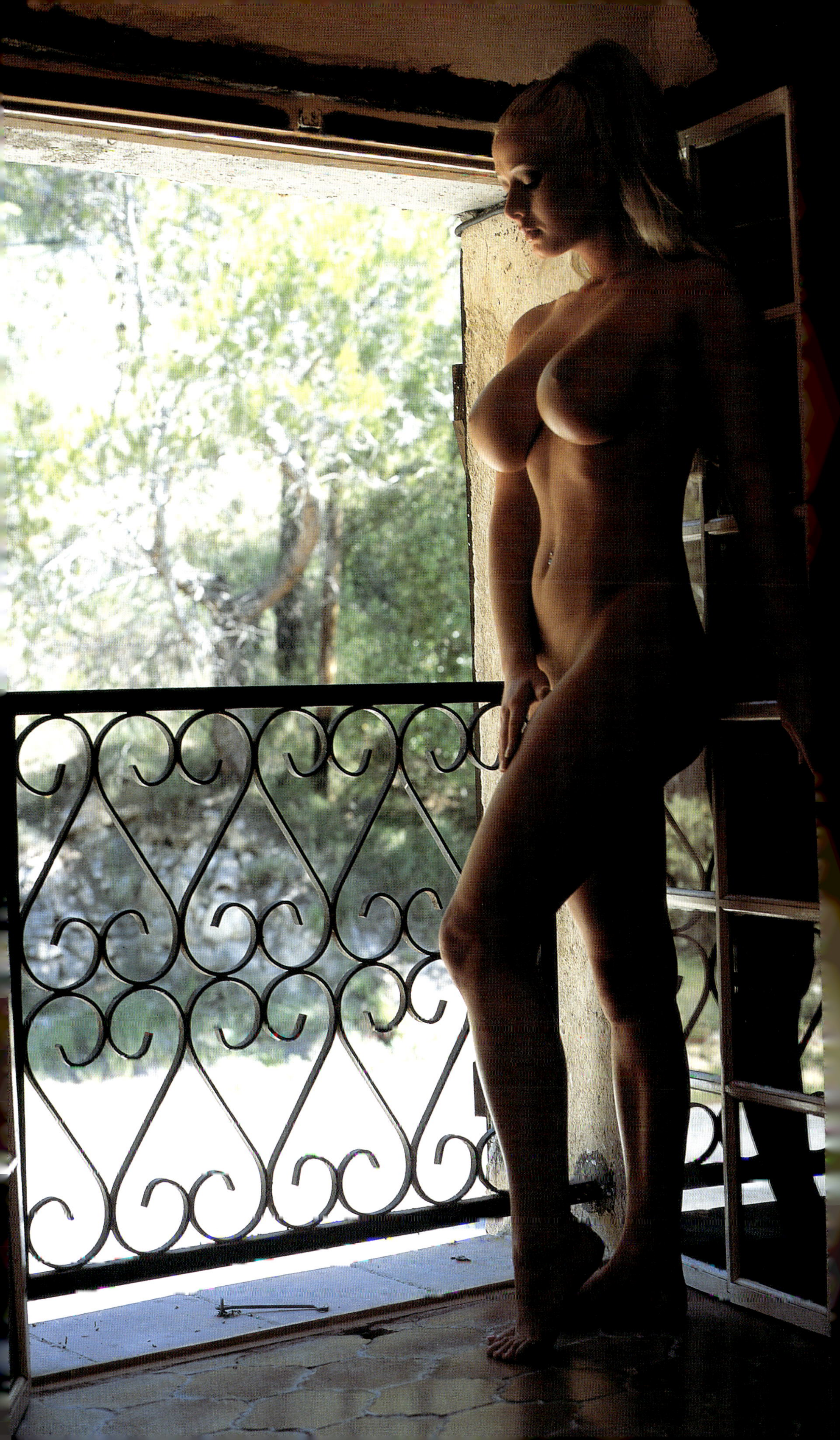

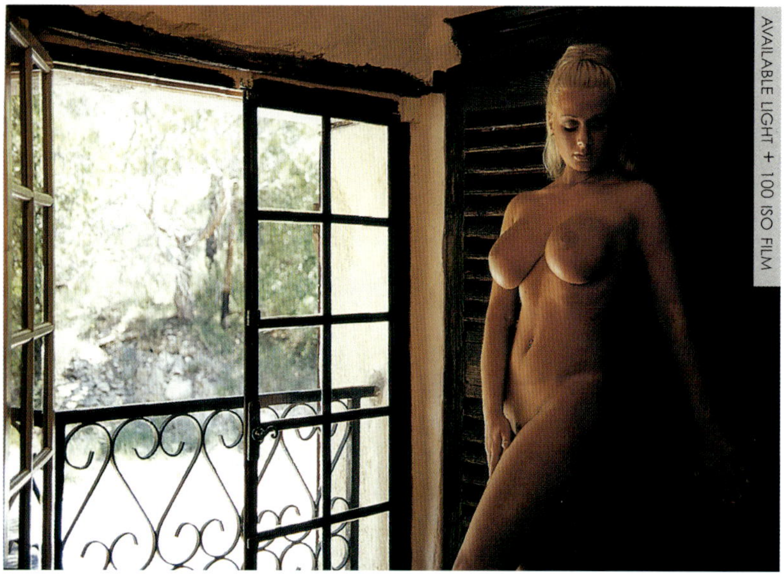

Reproducing natural light

If there is little or no apparent available light in a setting, then you can create the impression of natural light, that is, of light coming from a particular direction as if shining in through a window. This is what I have done in the image on page 122, which was taken for a poster company.

The client requested that there be a warm orange light to illuminate the back of the model's head, as if she were bathed in natural sunlight from the window. The window in the bathroom was fairly large, but it looked out onto another house and therefore allowed little daylight into the room. It also didn't help that the day on which we were shooting was particularly grey and rainy! The room we were working in was fairly small and confined, and was on the first floor of the house. My solution was to simulate sunlight from outside by hanging a light out from the floor above and dropping it down on a telescopic stand to light through the window below.

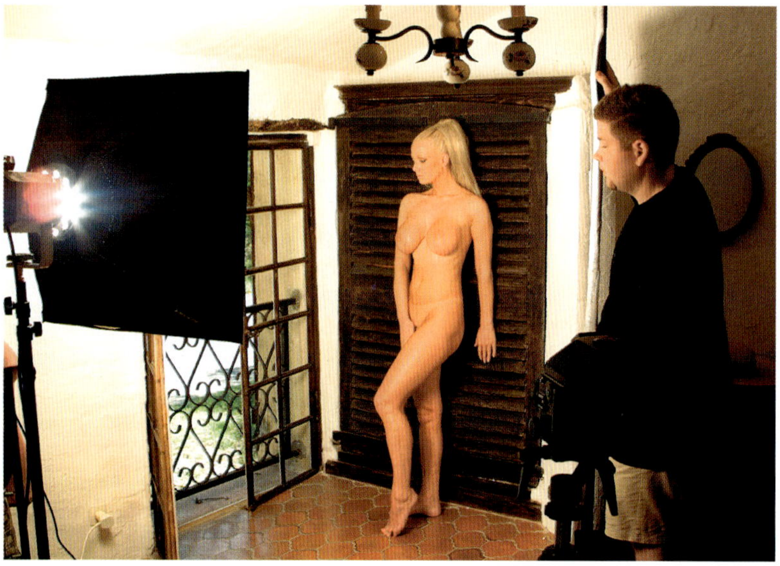

LEFT: This shot reveals the lighting set-up that I used to create the image shown below. To enhance the natural light coming through the window, I used a small softbox with a reflector, which helped to retain detail in the model's skin tones.
Mamiya RZ 6/7cm; 1/125 sec at f/11; 110mm lens; Fuji Provia 100

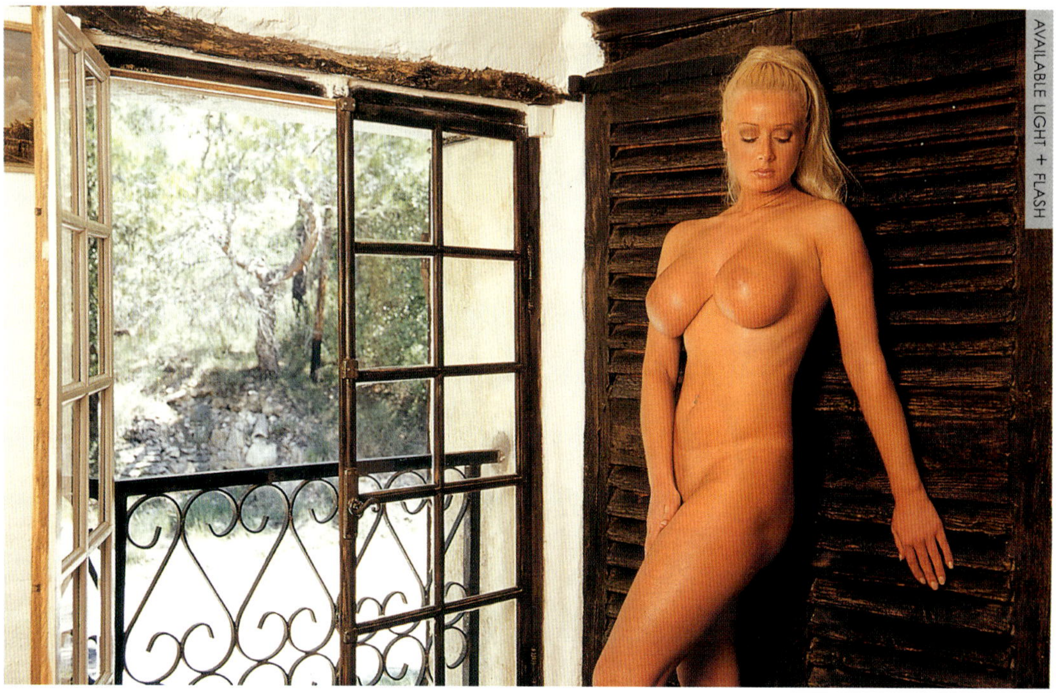

TOP AND RIGHT: The use of the softbox throws a lot of light onto the model's body and reveals more details of the room setting. The subject stands out well against the dark background of the wooden shutter. I personally prefer the shot at top, which was taken at midday using available light only, but for commercial purposes many clients would prefer the cleanly-lit shot, right.
Mamiya RZ 6/7cm; 1/125 sec at f/11 for image right; 1/125 at f/8 for image above; 110mm lens; Fuji Provia 100

Using attachments

I often use small, controllable light sources when shooting interiors, not least because I often work in spaces with little room to manoeuvre. Using attachments such as small, 60cm (24in) square soft-boxes or honeycombs means that you can direct light more on to the subject and experiment with mood. You can obtain more interesting effects than lighting flat with an umbrella, which tends to overlight the subject and spread the light very widely and evenly, creating images that are rather bland and with little depth.

The images shown right and far right were taken with a softbox and a honeycomb respectively. The honeycomb creates a strong and moody image with lots of contrast and atmosphere; I personally prefer the image taken with the softbox, which is also atmospheric and has a lot of depth, but is also warmer and softer, appearing more appropriate to the homely, rustic setting of the cottage fireplace.

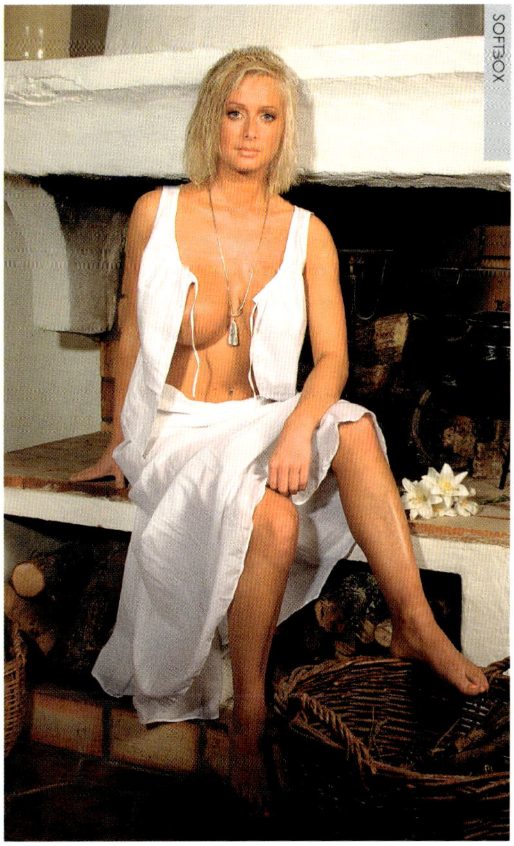

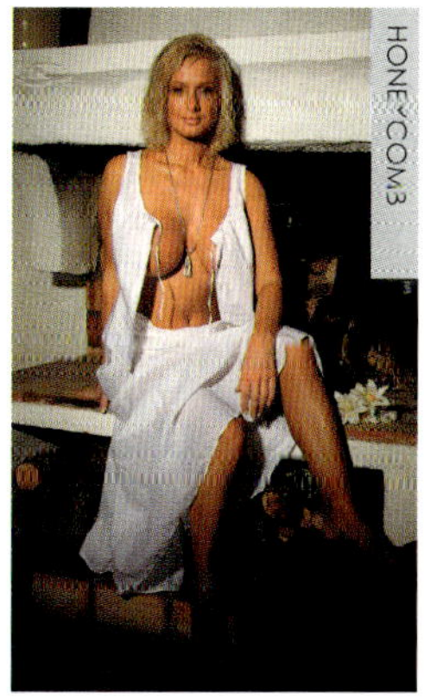

LEFT, ABOVE AND BELOW: The picture below reveals how busy the setting was. To overcome this, I focused on a small area of the room. This retained some flavour of the location without detracting attention away from the model. **Mamiya RZ 6/7cm; 1/125 sec at f/11; mainlight f/11; fill-in light f/8; honeycomb f/11; 110mm lens; Fuji Provia 100**

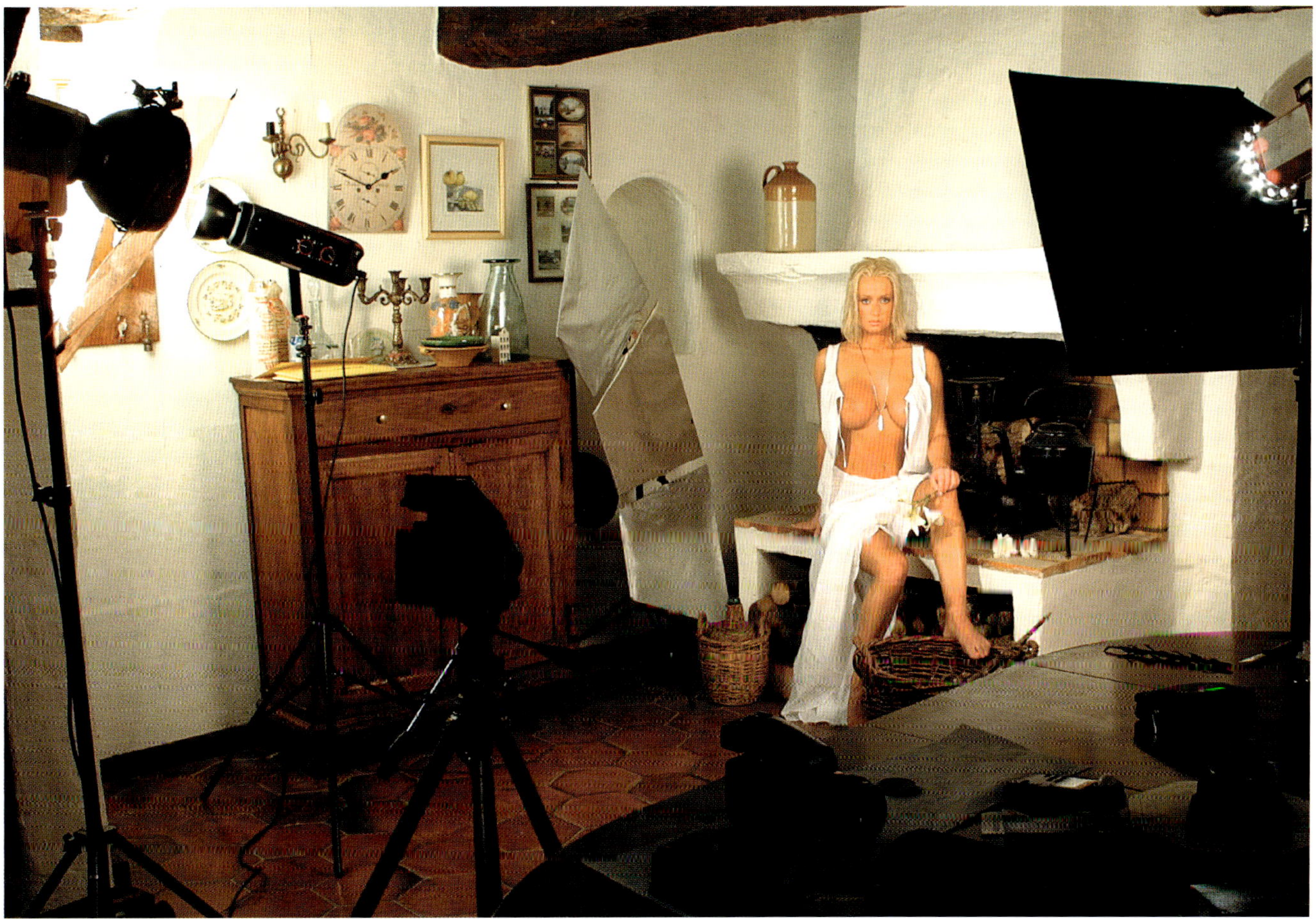

Higher-grained film

Another option to consider when shooting interiors is to use a higher ISO-rated film, which enables you to create a more atmospheric picture. In the images shown on these pages, the top picture below was shot using available light only on 100 ISO film. The window in this room was fairly small and didn't allow much natural light in, and the result is a picture that is almost silhouetted and rather flat, with very little detail. The main image (right) was shot on 1000 ISO film, and the difference is obvious – there is far more detail and far more atmosphere. The bottom image was shot with available light and flash, and is rather flat.

RIGHT AND BELOW: I think this image works well because of the muted, subtle range of colours and the composition. The reflection of the model in the mirror and in the glass of the windowpane adds extra depth and interest.
Mamiya RZ 6/7cm; 1/60 sec at f/5.6; 110mm lens; Fuji Provia 100 for images below; Fuji Provia 1000 for image right

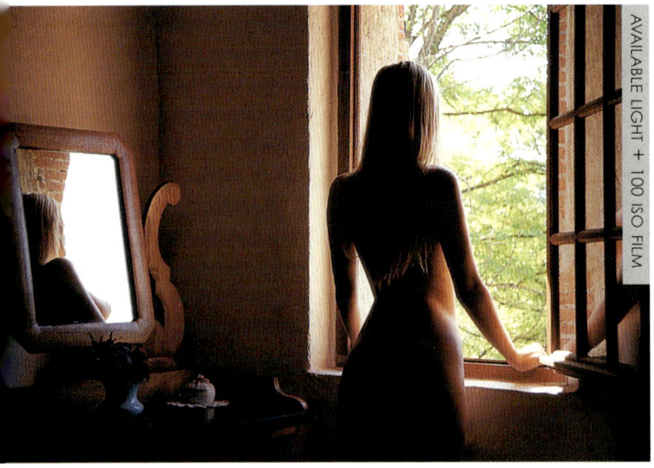

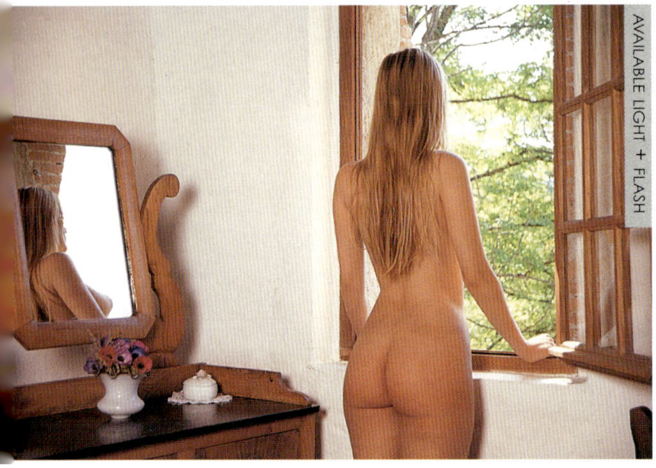

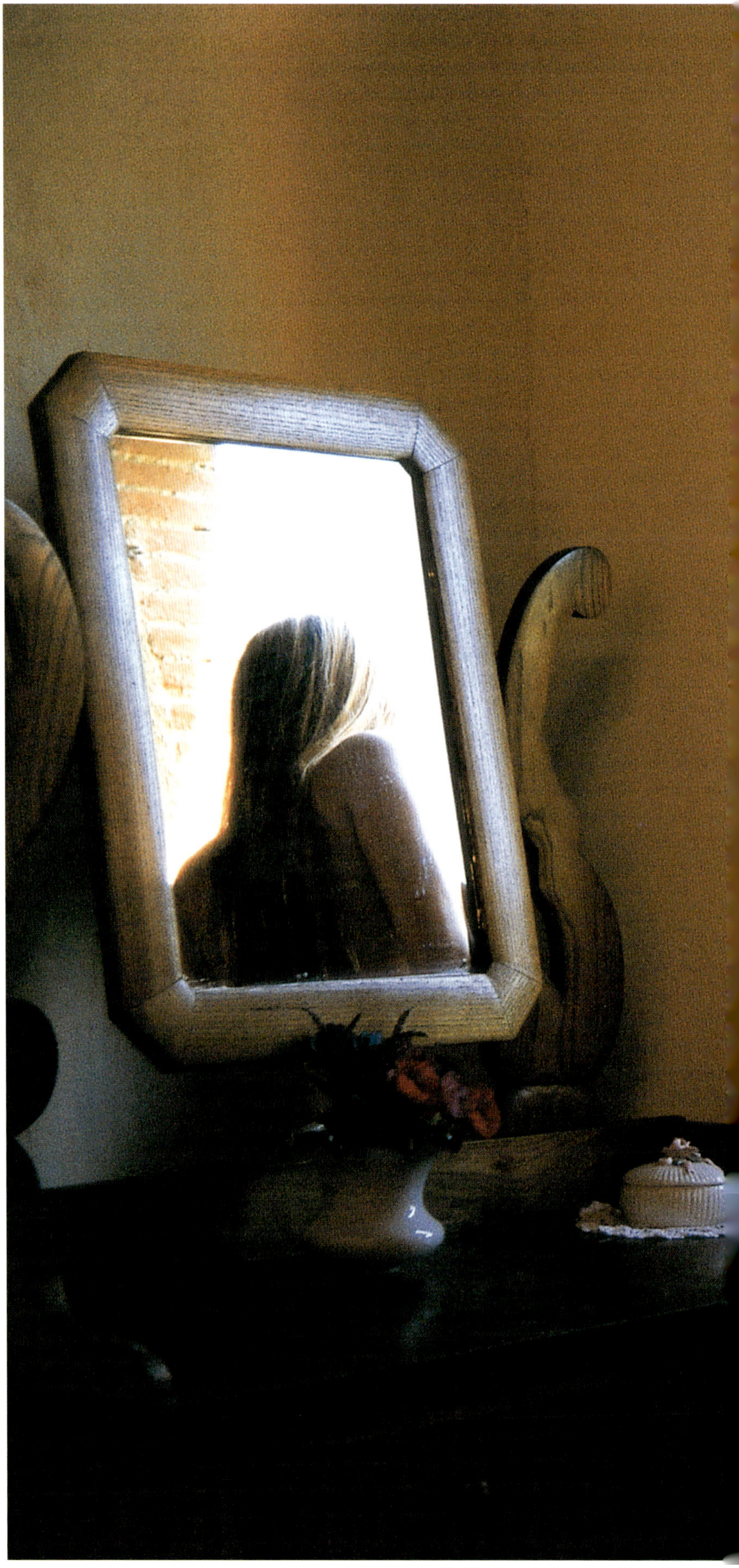

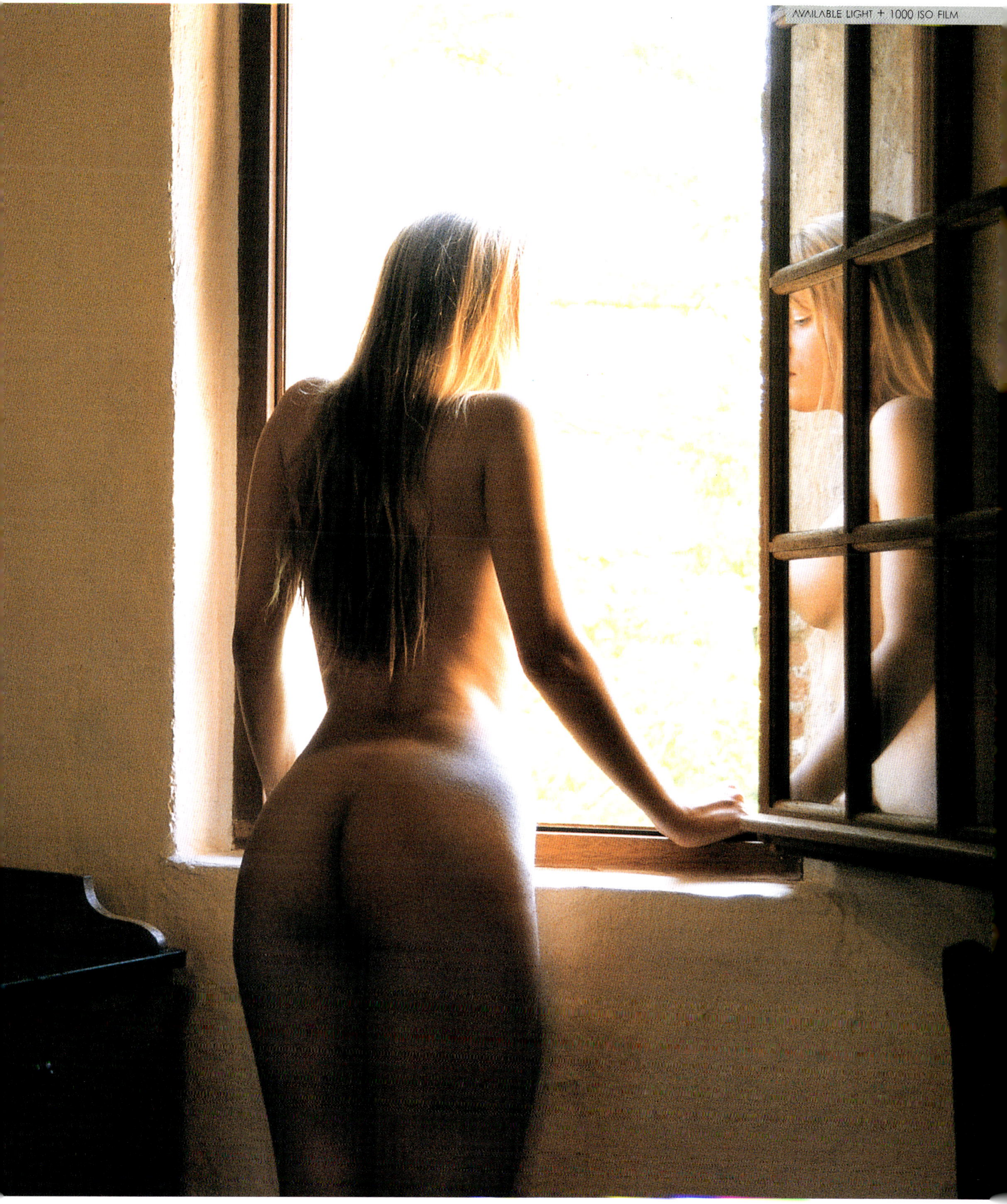
AVAILABLE LIGHT + 1000 ISO FILM

Portfolio

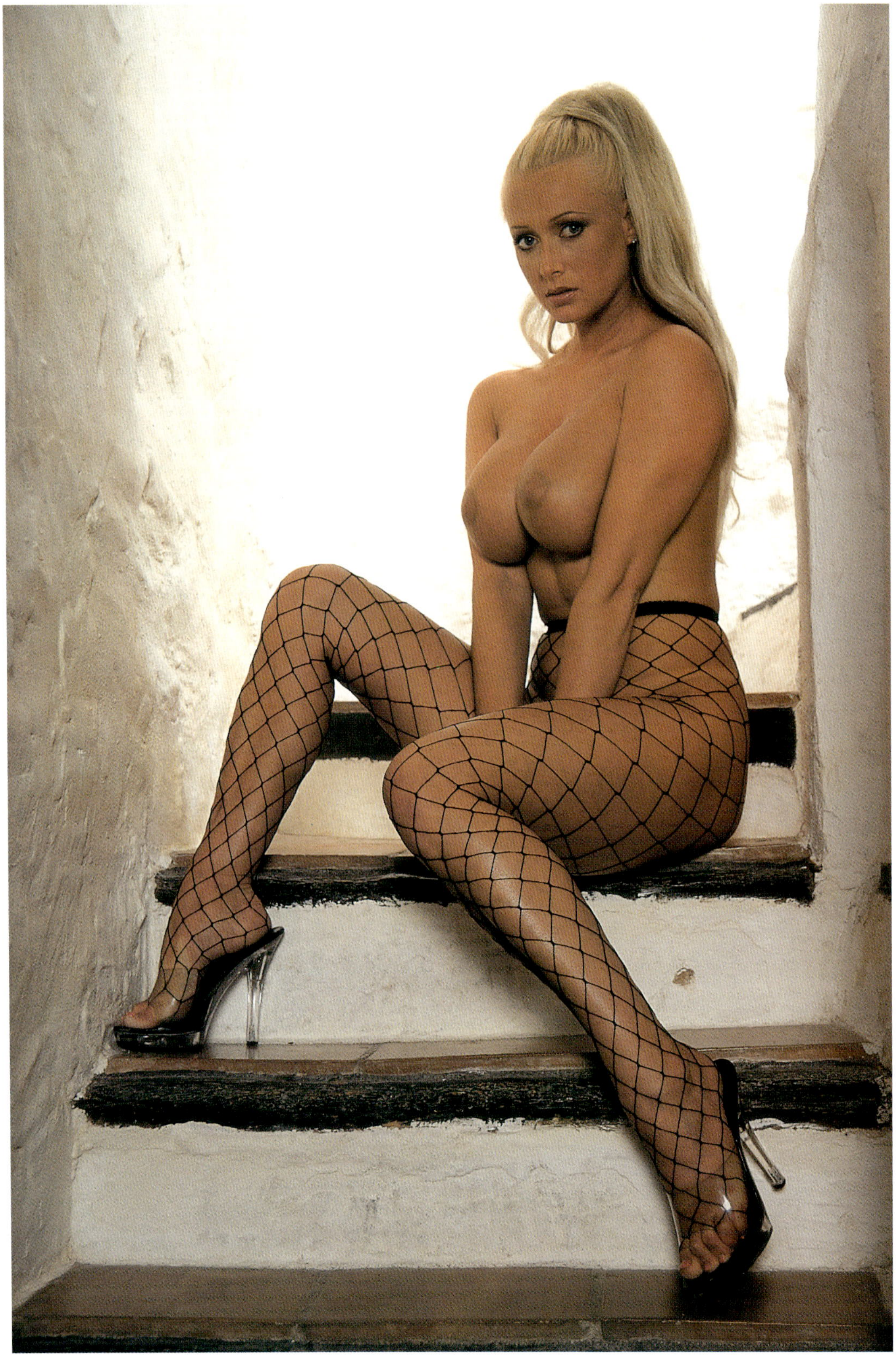

LEFT: This was taken using the same lighting set-up as for the sequence shown on pages 108–109. The model's patterned tights in this shot add a further pleasing element to the picture – the texture adds some contrast to the image, and the diagonal patterns stand out well against the verticals and horizontals of the stairwell. There is a good overall flow to this shot because of the model's posture and body language.
Mamiya RZ 6/7cm; 1/125 sec at f/8; flash mainlight f/8; background light f/8.5;110mm lens; Fuji Provia 100F

OPPOSITE: This shot, which was commissioned for a calendar, was taken in a real workshop, which gave an authentic air to the setting. We kept the props simple so as not to detract attention from the model. A small softbox was placed in front of the camera to light the model and an effect rimlight with a honeycomb attachment lit the right side of her hair and body in order to stand her out against the dark background.
Mamiya RZ 6/7cm; 1/125 sec at f/16; 110mm lens; Fuji Provia 100

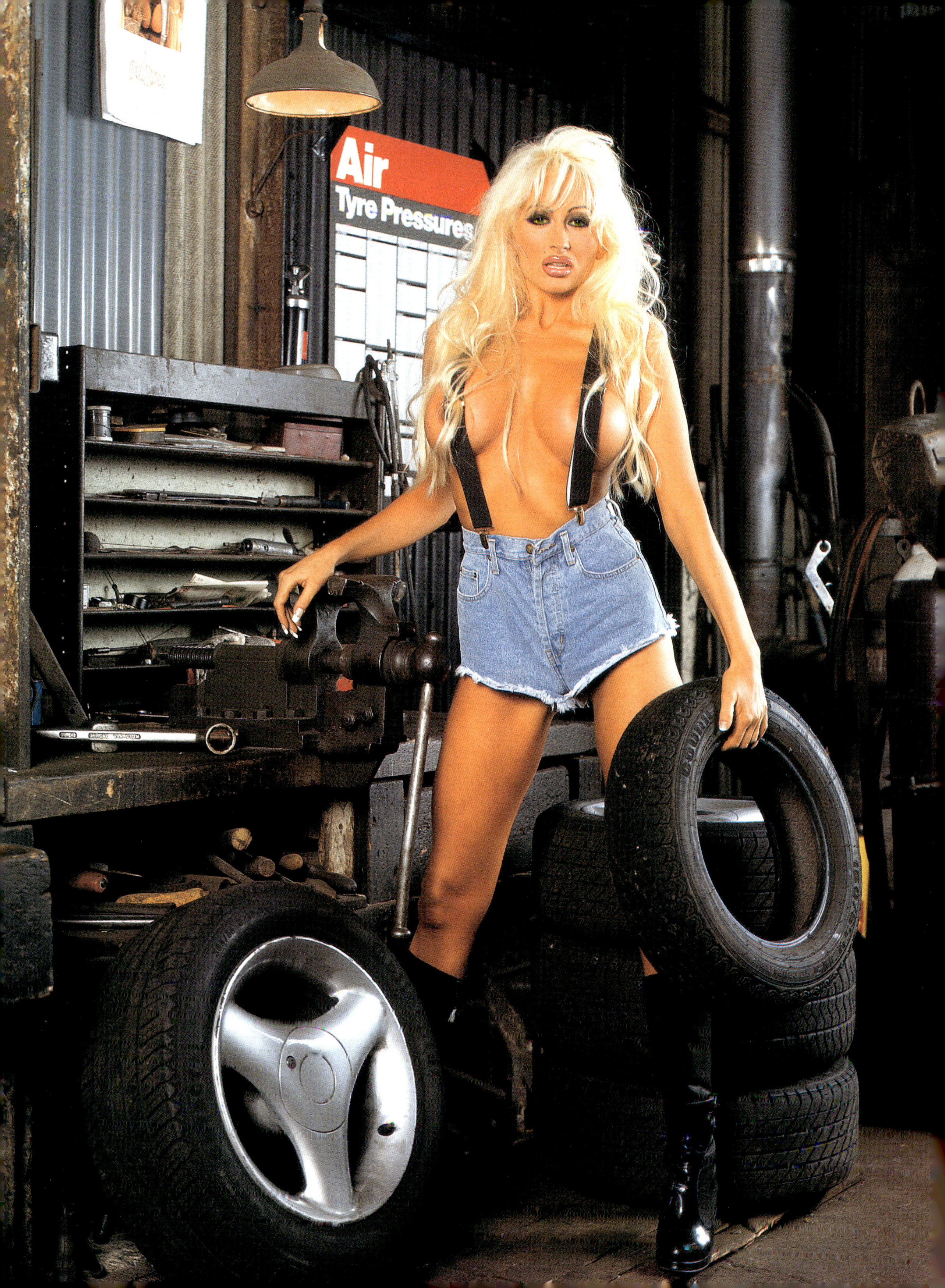
Air
Tyre Pressures

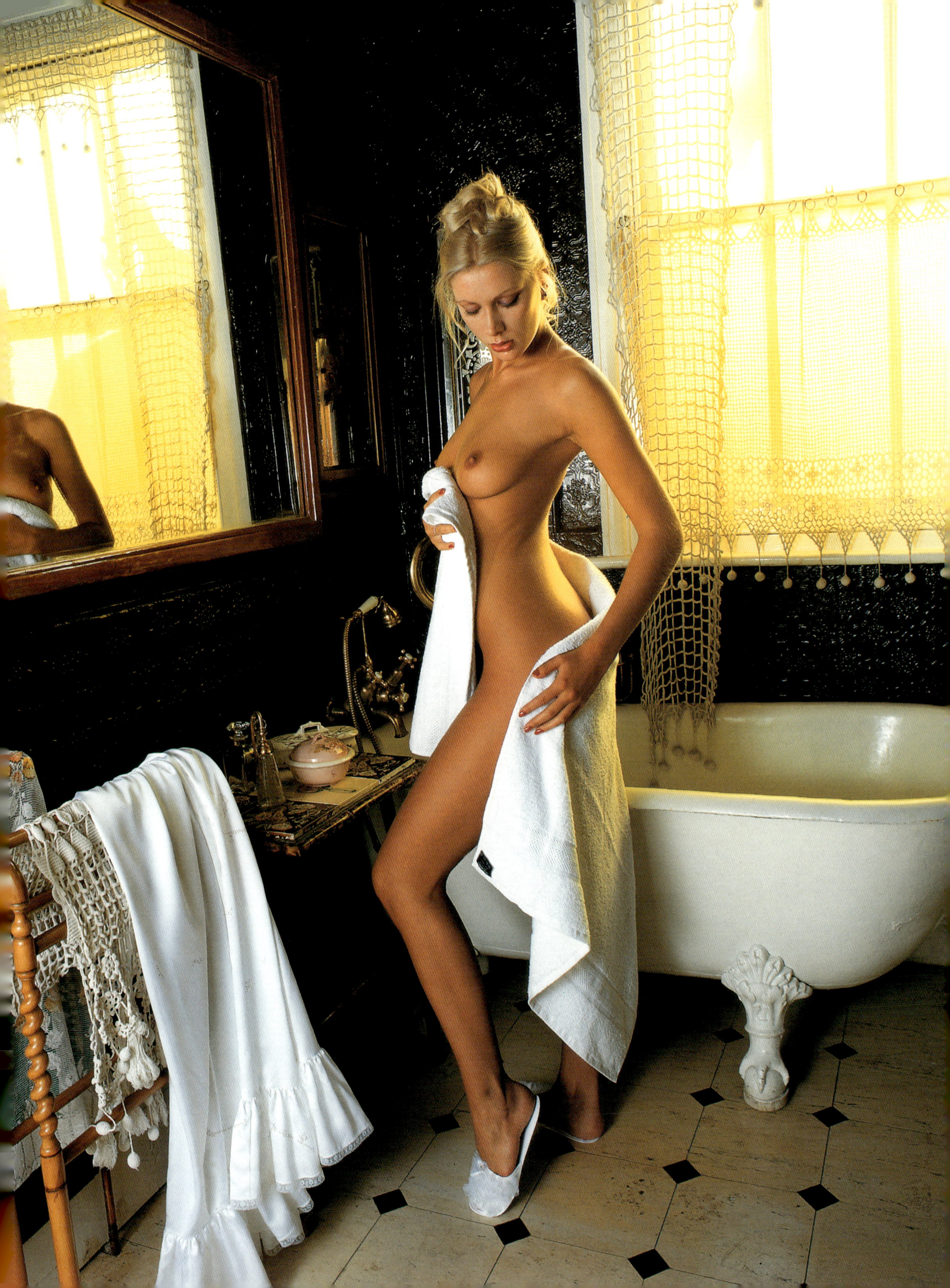

OPPOSITE: Mirrors are notoriously tricky to photograph well – you have to bear in mind that they will reflect both the subject and any light that you put on the subject, which is a disadvantage if the light flares off the mirror. However, in this image the mirror works well as it gives the shot a little more depth.
Sinar 4x5 plate camera; 1/60 sec at f/22; 40mm lens; Kodak Ektachrome 100S

BELOW: This image was taken in Jamaica for a beauty ad. I liked the simplicity of the windows, which was further enhanced by the white towels draped around the model. The presence of the cat was unplanned, but it adds a softness to the image and a pleasing balance to the composition.
Mamiya RZ 6/7cm; 1/60 sec at f/5.6; flash set at f/4; 110mm lens; Fuji Provia 100F

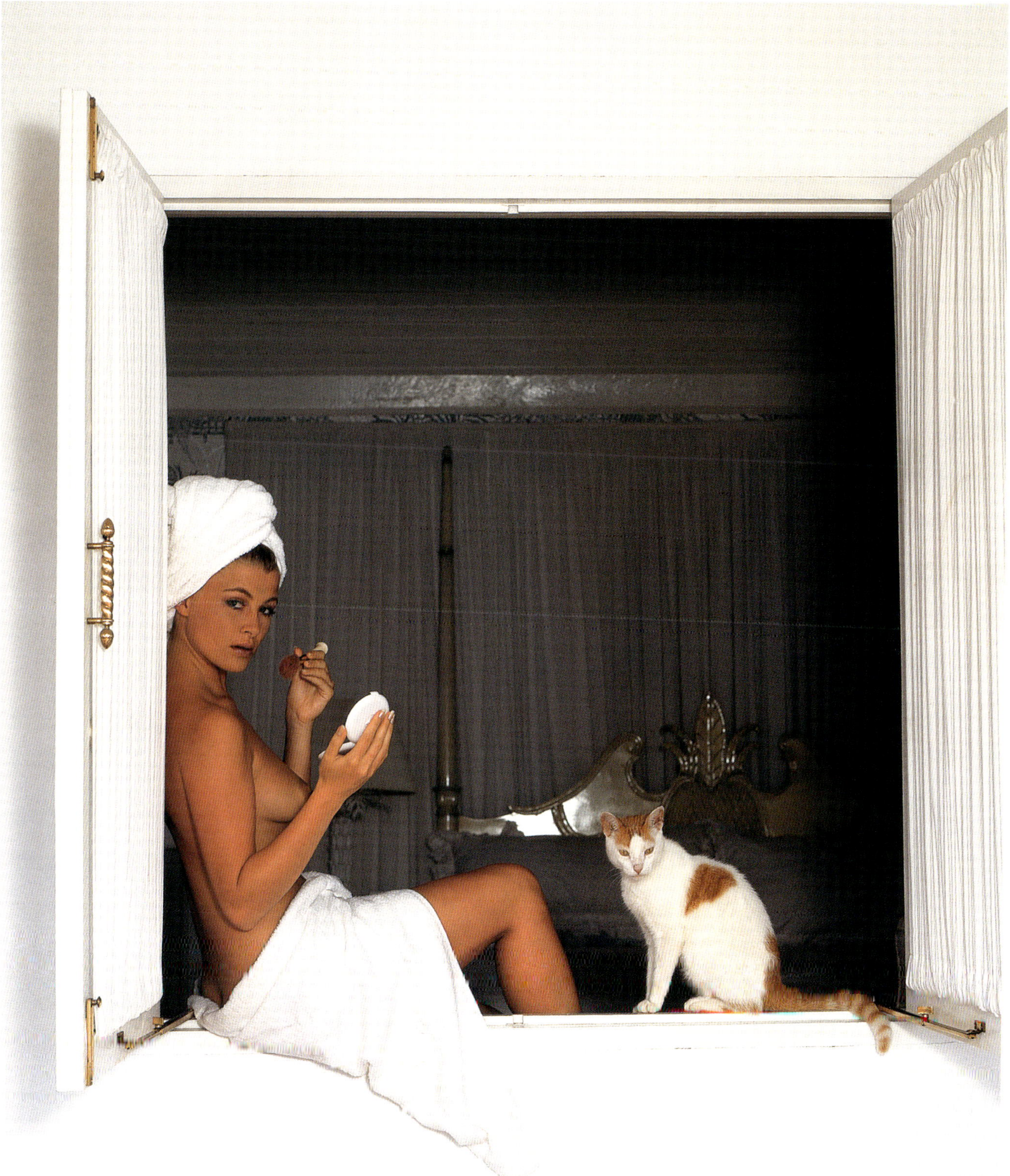

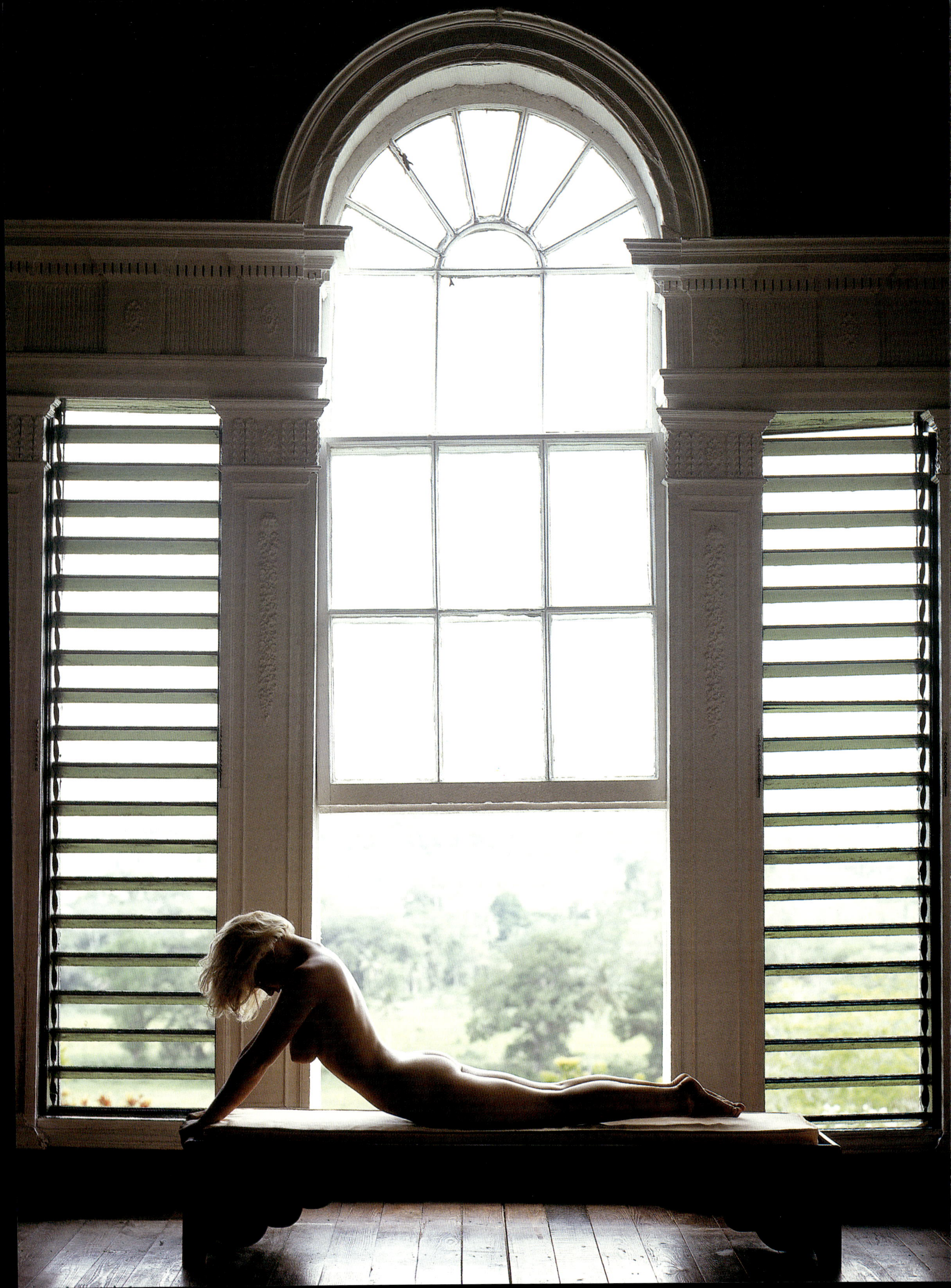

RIGHT: This image was taken for a lingerie catalogue. The shape of the drapes and the balcony help to create a graphic and interesting shot, while the intricate lines of the balcony echo the model's lace gown. This shot was taken using available light only.
Mamiya RZ 6/7cm; 1/125 sec at f/16; 110mm lens; Fuji Provia 100

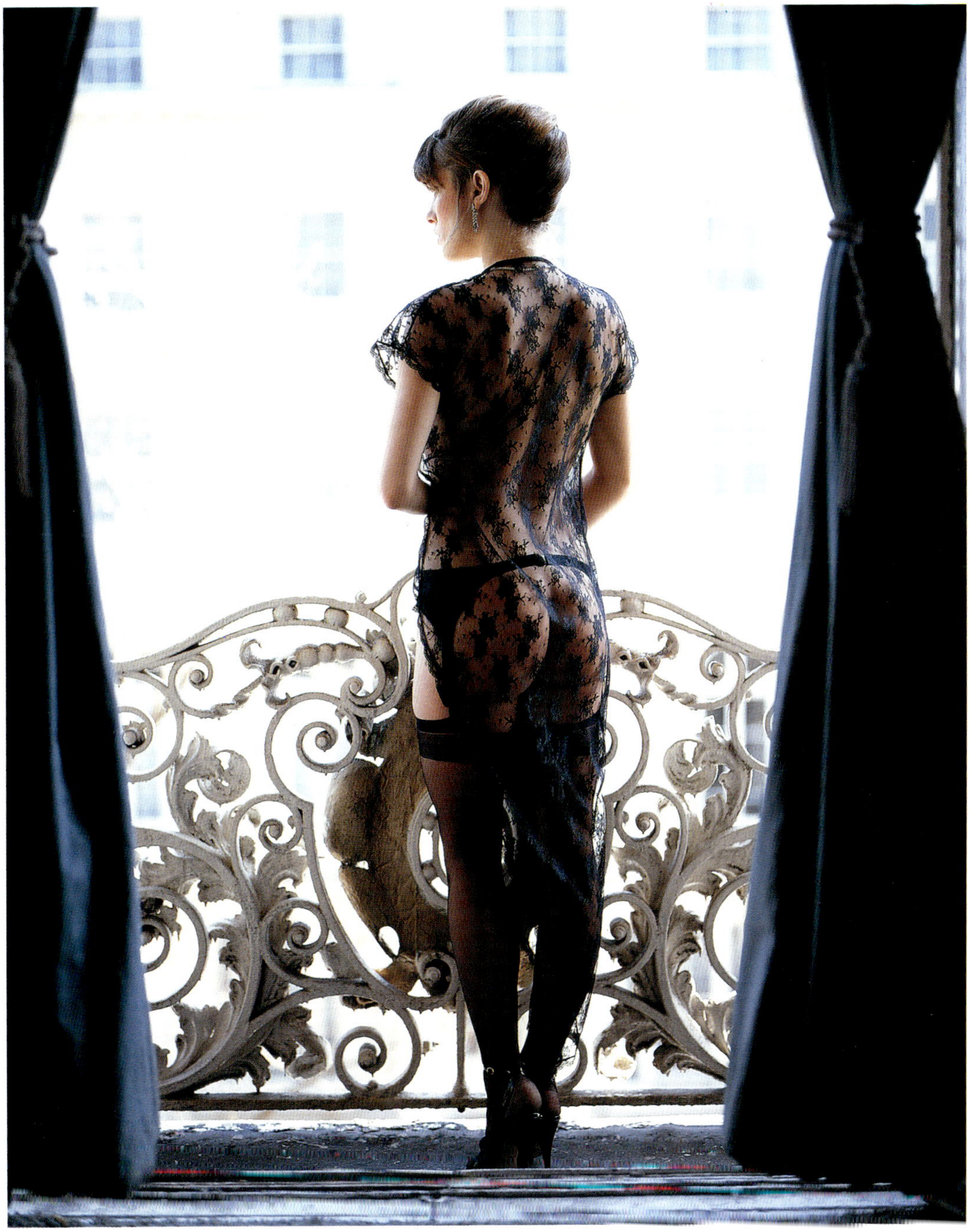

OPPOSITE: This image was taken in a colonial house in Jamaica for a calendar. What I love about this shot is the stunning shape of the window and the shutters, which works so well with the model's simple but unusual position. This picture was taken in mid-afternoon using available light only. It might have worked better in black and white, and in fact has an almost monochromatic feel as a result of the muted colours and the overall moodiness of the shot.
Mamiya RZ 6/7cm; 1/60 sec at f/5.6, 110mm lens, Fuji Provia 100

male studies

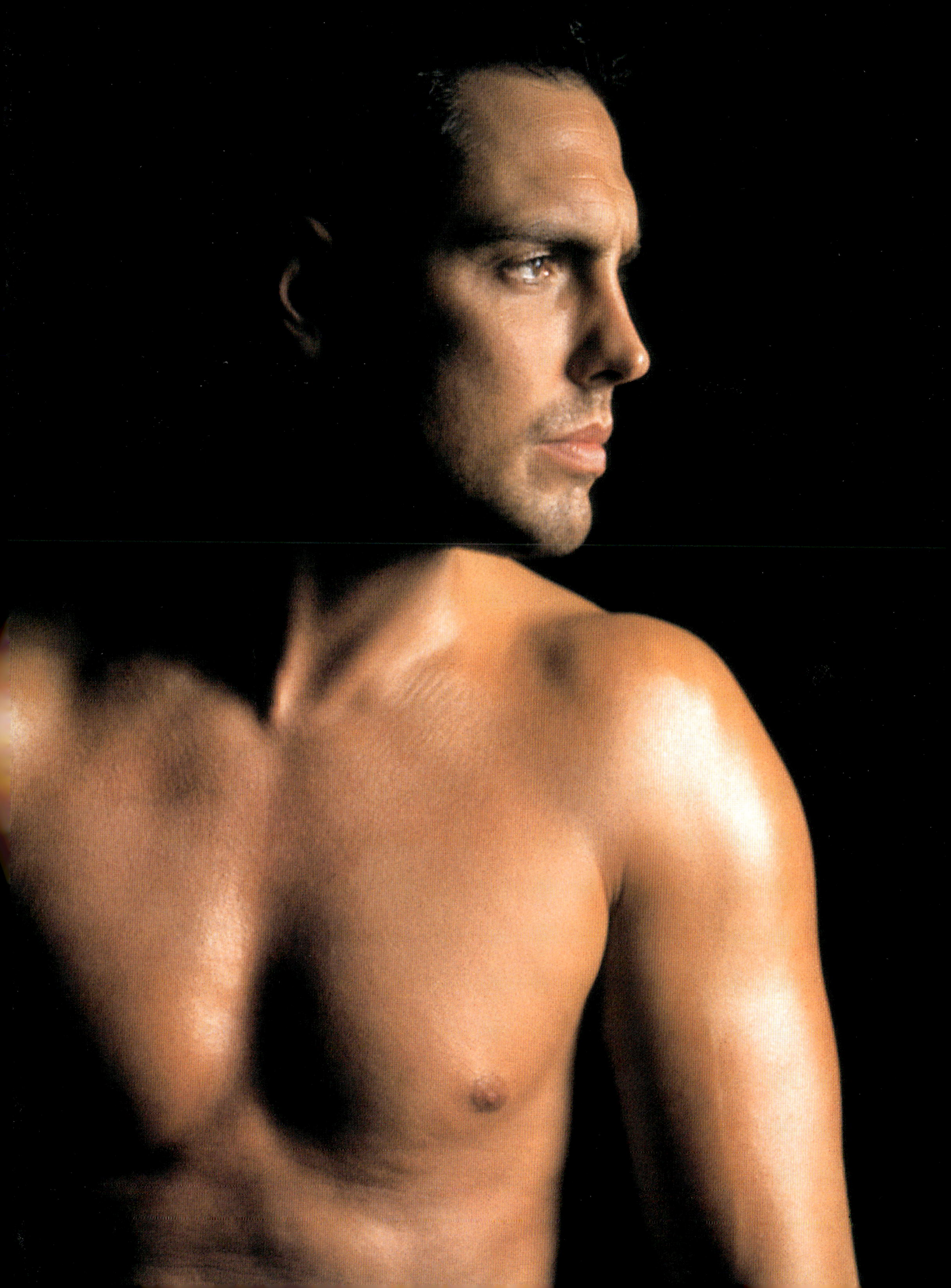

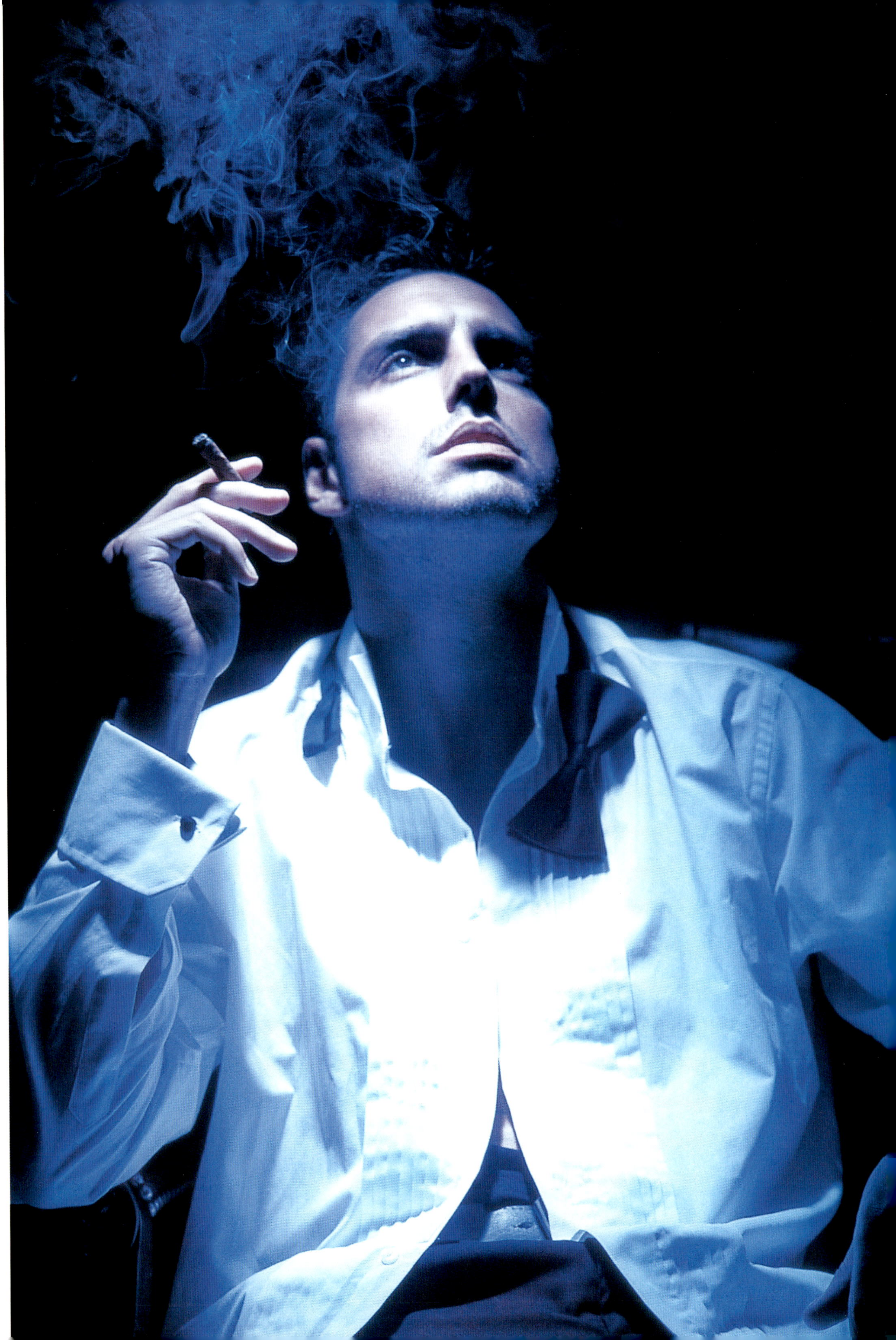

Photographing men

Glamour photography using men as subjects is still in its early days, but there is an increasing market for images of men in advertising and fashion, particularly for health and fitness, male beauty and grooming products, aftershave, underwear, fashion accessories and *haute couture*. Developments within the fashion, music and movie industries have also meant that there is an increasing market for pin-up images of men, with calendars and posters of pop stars and Hollywood actors, for example. Increasing equality between women and men also means that women are asking 'Why shouldn't we see men's bodies?' – after all, glamorous images of women have been used to sell products since the beginning of advertising.

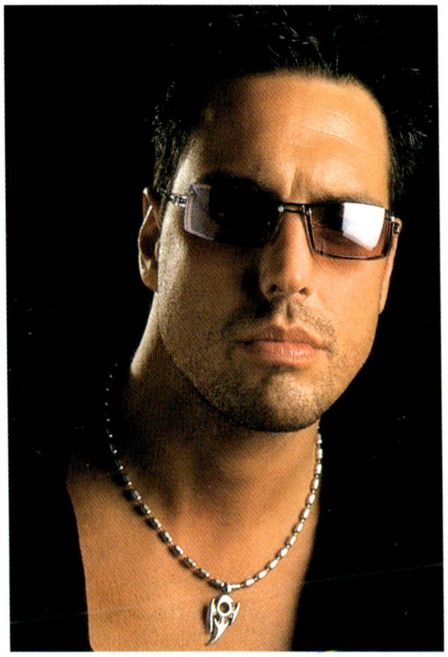

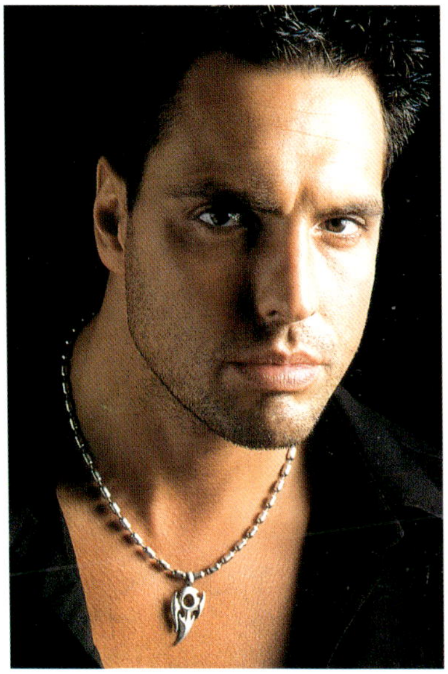

ABOVE: These images show how changing your lighting set-up can dramatically alter how your model looks. The image on the left was taken with a softbox and a rimlight with the model against a black background; the effect is strong and atmospheric. For the image on the right I used a flash with a honeycomb attachment, which created an even more harshly lit and contrasty shot.
LEFT: Canon EOS; 1/125 sec at f/8; 100mm lens; Fuji Provia 100F; RIGHT: Canon EOS; 1/125 at f/11; 100mm lens; Fuji Provia 100

Portraying masculinity

There is a market for glamorous pictures of men, but there are often quite noticeable differences between photographs of men and photographs of women. There are always exceptions, but images of women in commercial photography (in advertisements, catalogues, magazines etc) are often rather sanitized. These images tend to be idealized rather than attempting to capture the individual personality of the female model. Female subjects for glamour and beauty photography tend to be cleanly lit and presented in a way that is flattering and idealizing, smoothing out flaws and idiosyncrasies.

In the commercial environment, photographing men presents different challenges from photographing women because most clients want to convey a different mood and image. Men are not usually required to look seductive and sexually

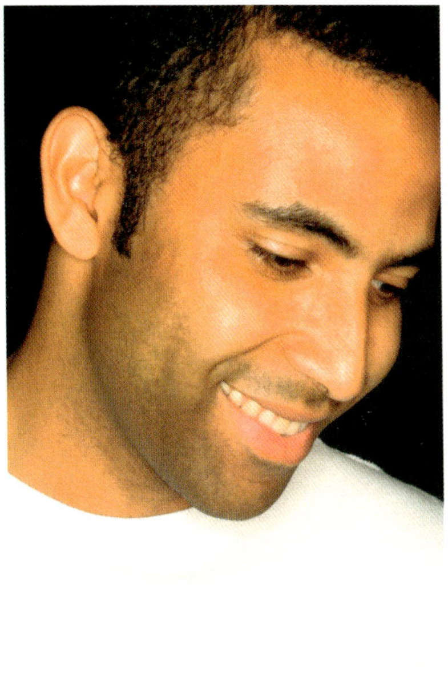

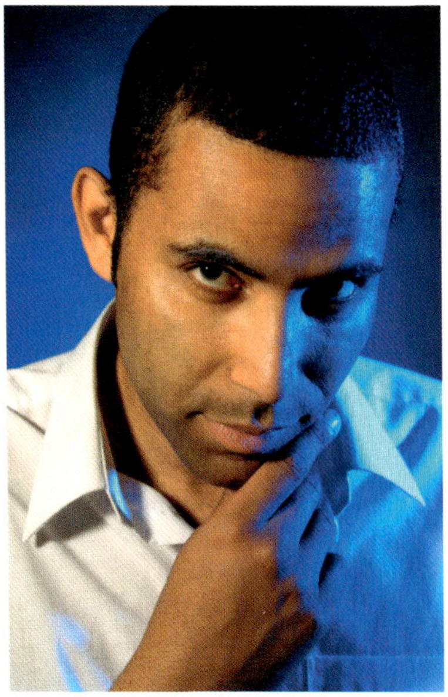

ABOVE: The image on the left was taken with ringflash, which creates quite a soft, smooth look. The image on the right was taken with a softbox to the left of the model and a honeycomb with a blue gel to his right, creating a stronger and harsher image.
LEFT: Canon D30; 1/125 sec at f/8; 100mm lens; RIGHT: Canon D30; 1/250 at f/16; 100mm lens

OPPOSITE: This shot demonstrates the sort of strong, moody lighting that is often appropriate for photographing men. I used an overhead flash with a honeycomb attachment and a blue filter.
Mamiya RZ 6/7cm; 1/125 sec at f/11; 150mm lens; Fuji Provia 100

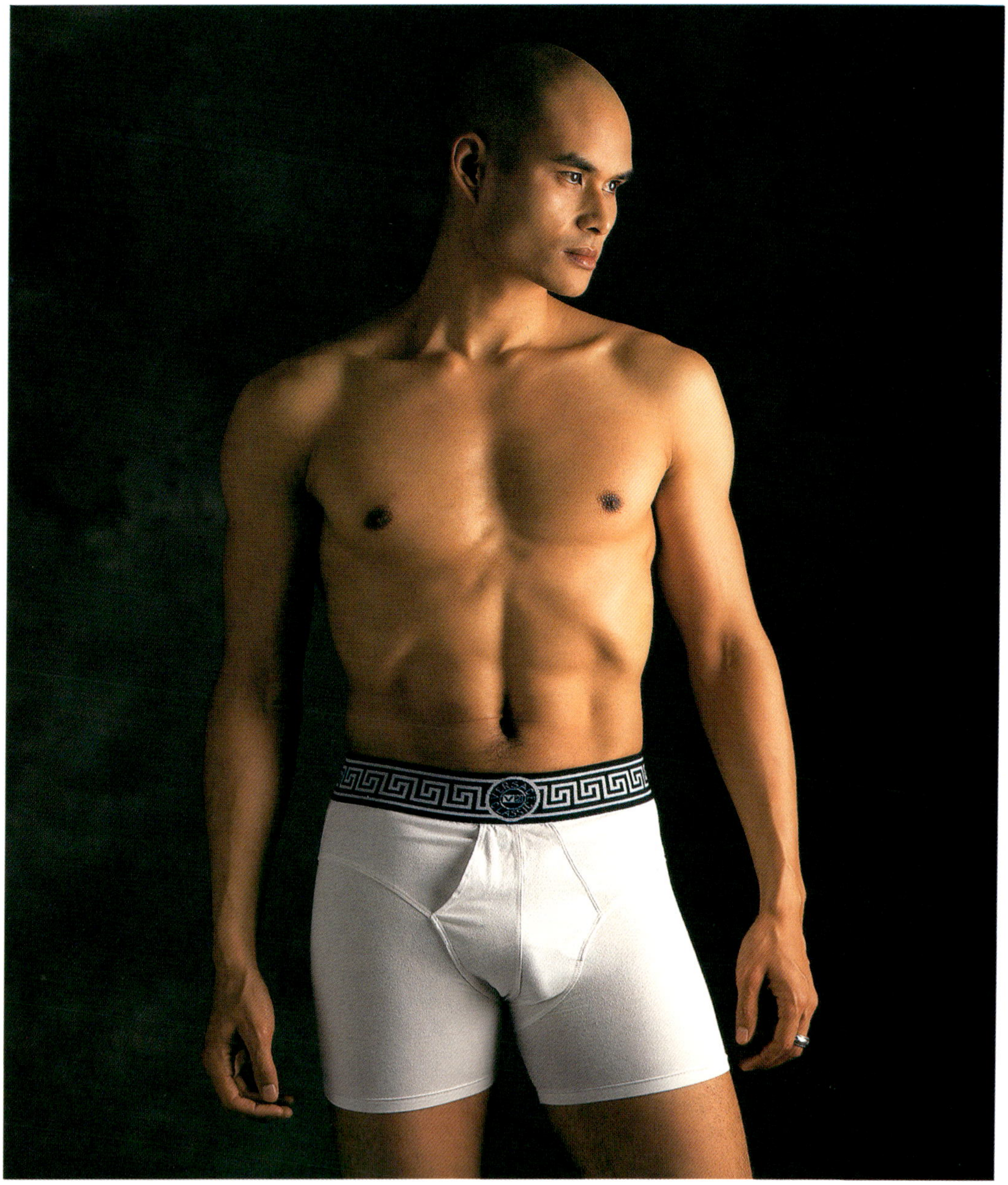

LEFT: For this image, I used a softbox at a 45-degree angle to the model, and had the model turn into the light. This lighting set-up created an effective flat, contrasty light that emphasized the model's musculature and created a strong, angular image.
Canon EOS; 1/125 sec at f/8; 100mm lens; Fuji Provia 100

OPPOSITE ABOVE: This lighting set-up is much like the beauty lighting used for photographing women – the clean, even lighting is often used for advertising male beauty and hair products. I set the model against a white background, used a softbox on a boom as the mainlight and placed a triflector below him to bounce more light in to the image.
Canon D30; 1/125 sec at f/8; 100mm lens

available, as women often are; instead, they are more often portrayed looking serious, stern, enigmatic, or purposeful rather than sexy.

Using male models perhaps gives the photographer more scope because you are freed from the constraints of lighting in only a soft and flattering manner. Men are often considered to have more character in their faces, and it is possible for the photographer to capture that character using creative lighting set-ups.

Lighting men

When you are photographing men you often have more options for lighting than when photographing women. For example, it is possible to use the sort of warm, soft, diffuse lighting sources, such as softboxes and reflectors, which are commonly used when shooting glamour and beauty images of women. This sort of lighting is often used for health and fitness images of men, where the clean, even lighting is considered appropriate. It is also used for advertising male beauty and hair products, and works well when photographing younger men or men with prettier, more feminine features, as well as fair-haired men.

It is also possible to use more controlled and harsher light sources, such as honeycombs, snoots and dishes, when photographing men. These lights create more atmosphere and more contrast in an image, which seems appropriate to capture

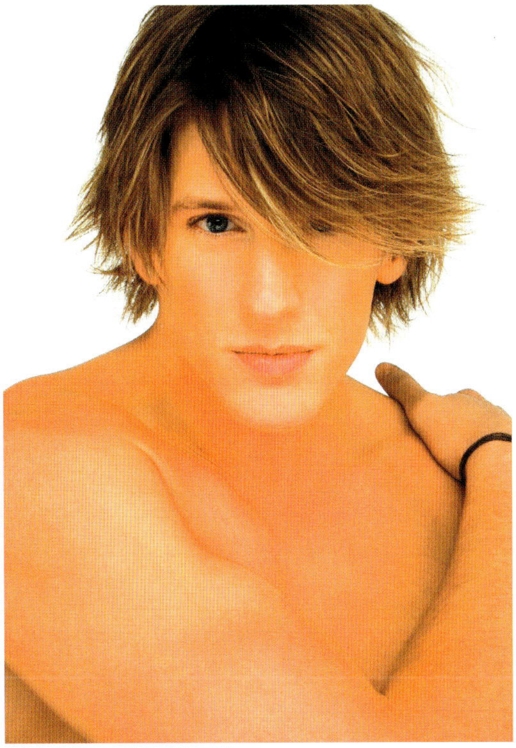

the harder, squarer, outlines of a male subject. This sort of lighting also creates a moody image that often seems appropriate when creating images to convey strength, purposefulness and the like.

You can also use softboxes as a controlled light source for photographing male models. Softboxes are more often used in conventional beauty lighting to create even and flattering light, but if you place them at an acute angle to your subject, you can create a more dramatic light.

Ringflash is another option for photographing men. Ringflash has a tendency to create a clean, slightly flat, light that could equally be used for photographing female subjects, as it tends to light out the subject, making it devoid of all shadows. Ringflash is often used as a primary light source in fashion photography, but it can also be used to create pleasing portraits. The strength of the light is often flattering due to its overlighting, which tends to smooth out features.

Colours and backgrounds

Women are often shot against softly-lit backgrounds. By contrast, it is often more appropriate and more effective to photograph male subjects against dark backgrounds. They are often shot straight-on rather than in profile, and shooting them against a dark background, with harsh, contrasty, lighting, creates a strong and effective silhouette-type image. This works well with men with well-defined physiques because it emphasises the strong, angular lines of their bodies.

When shooting women, the emphasis is often on creating warm images, using warm-up lights and gold reflectors to enhance the skin tones. This is an option when shooting men as well, but you can also use cold-coloured filters when photographing males. Blue filters create cool-toned, moody and atmospheric images that can help to emphasize the harsher contours of the male physique (see page 141).

BELOW: This shot was created using a very small softbox at an acute angle to the right of the model, who was placed against a black backdrop. This creates a dramatic, almost silhouetted, image of extreme contrasts that is mysterious and brooding.
Mamiya RZ 6/7cm; 1/125 sec at f/16; 150mm lens; Fuji Provia 100

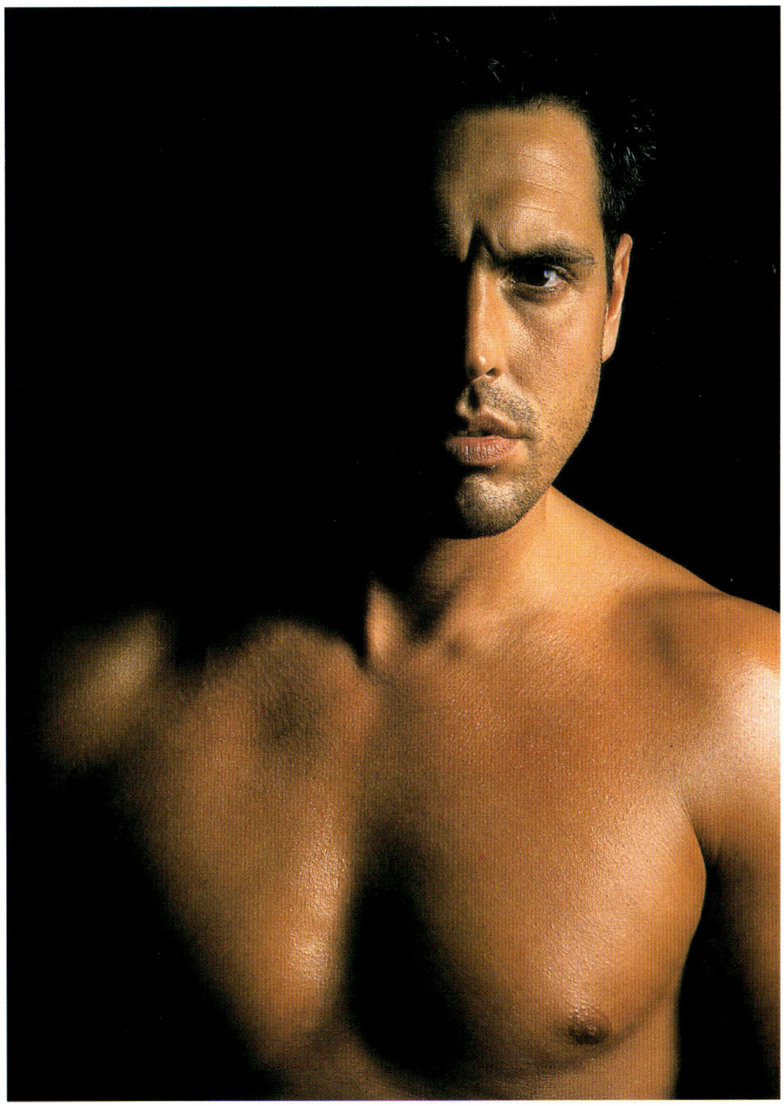

Poses

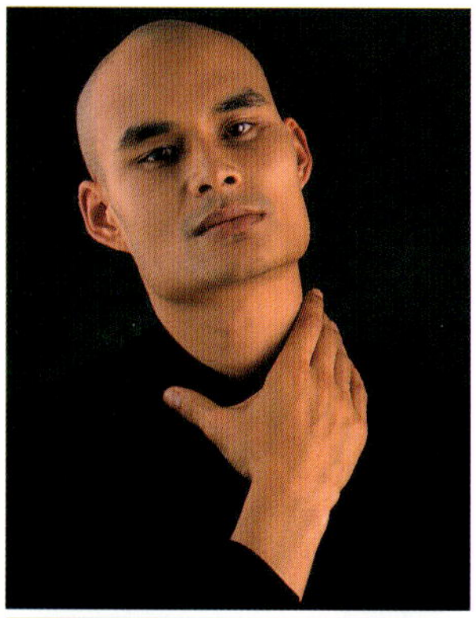

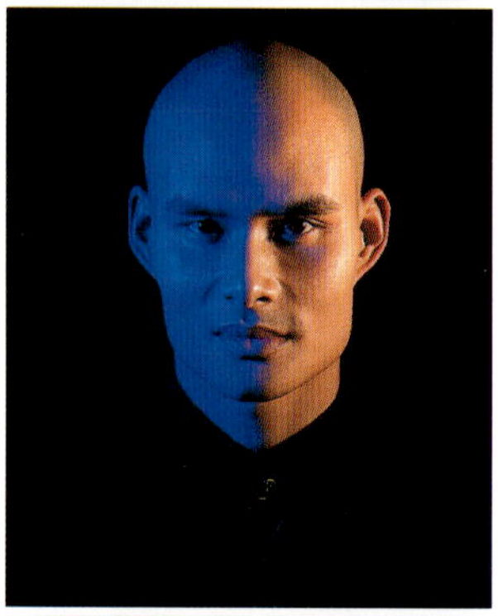

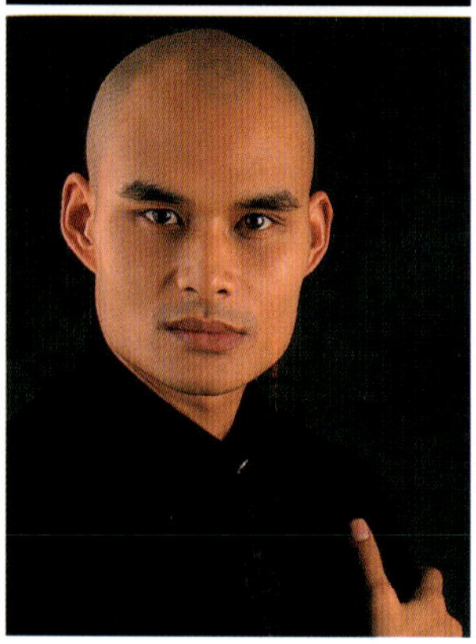

ABOVE: Simple poses often work best for male portraits, with the model straight on to camera to show off the strength of his features. You also have the option of bringing a hand in to add another strong but simple element for extra interest. **TOP AND BOTTOM: Canon EOS; 1/125 sec at f/11; 100mm lens; Fuji Provia 100F; MIDDLE: Canon EOS; 1/125 sec at f/8; 100mm lens; Fuji Provia 100F**

Posing head shots

When using male models, you will often be doing character portrait shots that focus on their faces. It is best to keep head poses of men strong and simple. One important consideration is the shape of the man's face – if he has a roundish face, it is often best to have him turn slightly away from the camera to take emphasis away from this; a three-quarter profile often works best. If he has a longer face you can usually shoot him straight on. If the model has strong features – a square jaw, for example – it is often most effective to shoot him straight on, with a strong lighting source to make the most of his bone structure.

You can then ask the model to experiment with his expression: smiling, half-smiling; looking serious; tilting his head up or down; looking directly at the camera or turning his head away. As with head shots of women, strong eye contact is an essential feature of portraits of men. But while women are often required to look seductive and alluring, men often assume expressions that are more serious and purposeful, as if conveying the strength of their personality.

Lighting head shots

The lighting that you choose will also have an effect. Flattering lighting, such as ringflash, makes the features look flatter, smoother and rounder. Stronger and more contrasty lighting creates a more moody image and will bring out the angles and bone structure of your model's face – it also tends to make the face look thinner.

Posing body shots

When taking body shots of male subjects, particularly for commercial use, you will often want to emphasise the muscularity of their physique. Shooting men's bodies offers particular challenges to the photographer. Women's bodies, because of their more rounded shape, photograph equally well straight on or in profile, and you therefore have far more variety and expression as to what poses the model can assume.

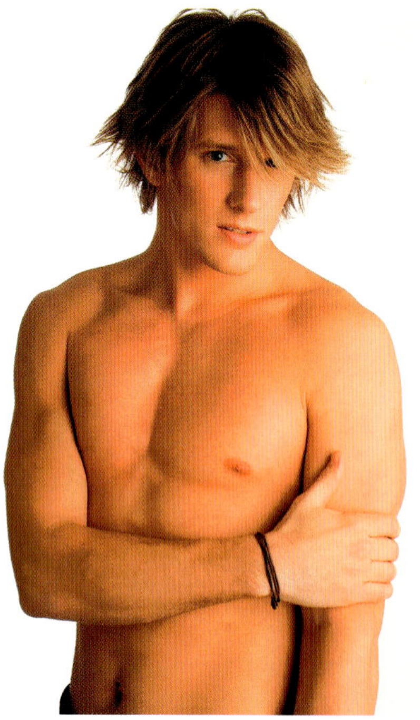

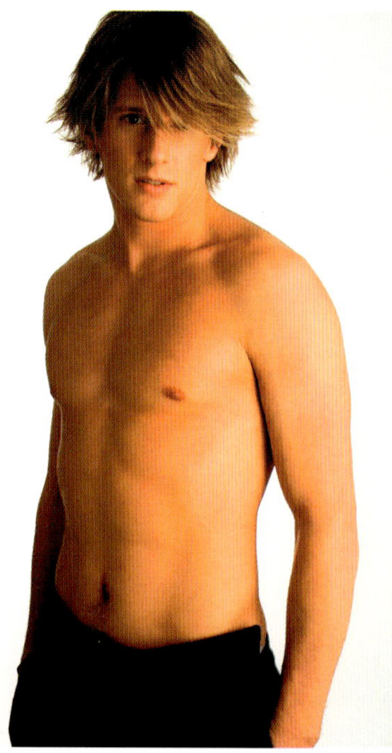

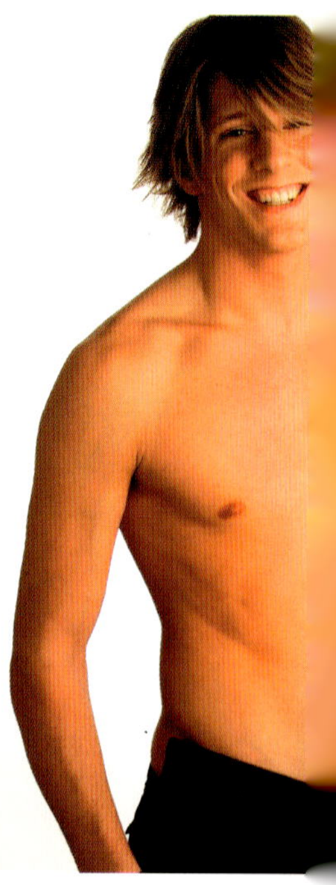

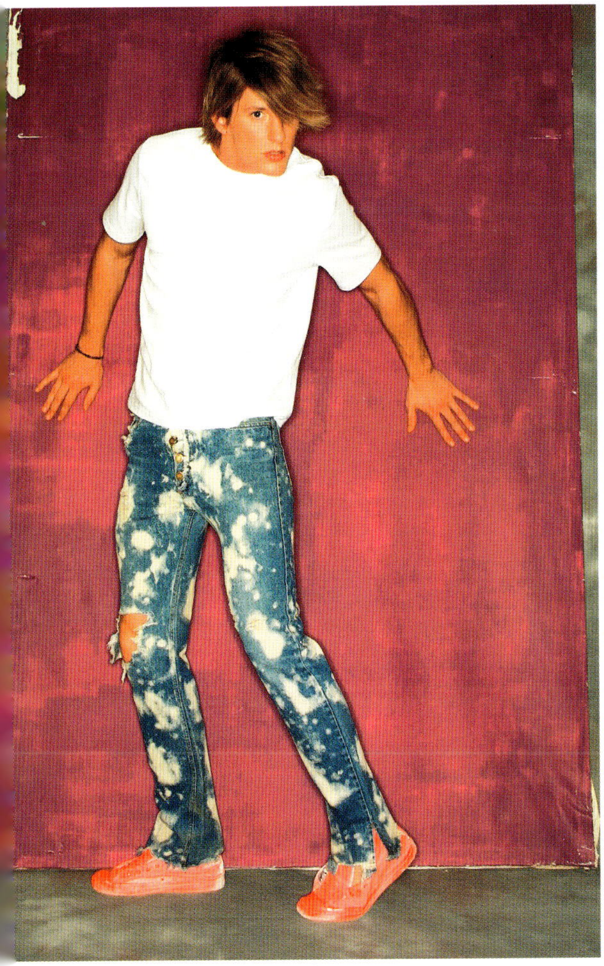

ABOVE: A quirky pose seemed most appropriate to complement the colourful and fun clothes here. I wanted to get the effect of the model being caught by surprise, as if under a spotlight. Fashion shots like this give you more scope to experiment with poses.
Canon D30; 1/250 sec at f/11; 80mm lens

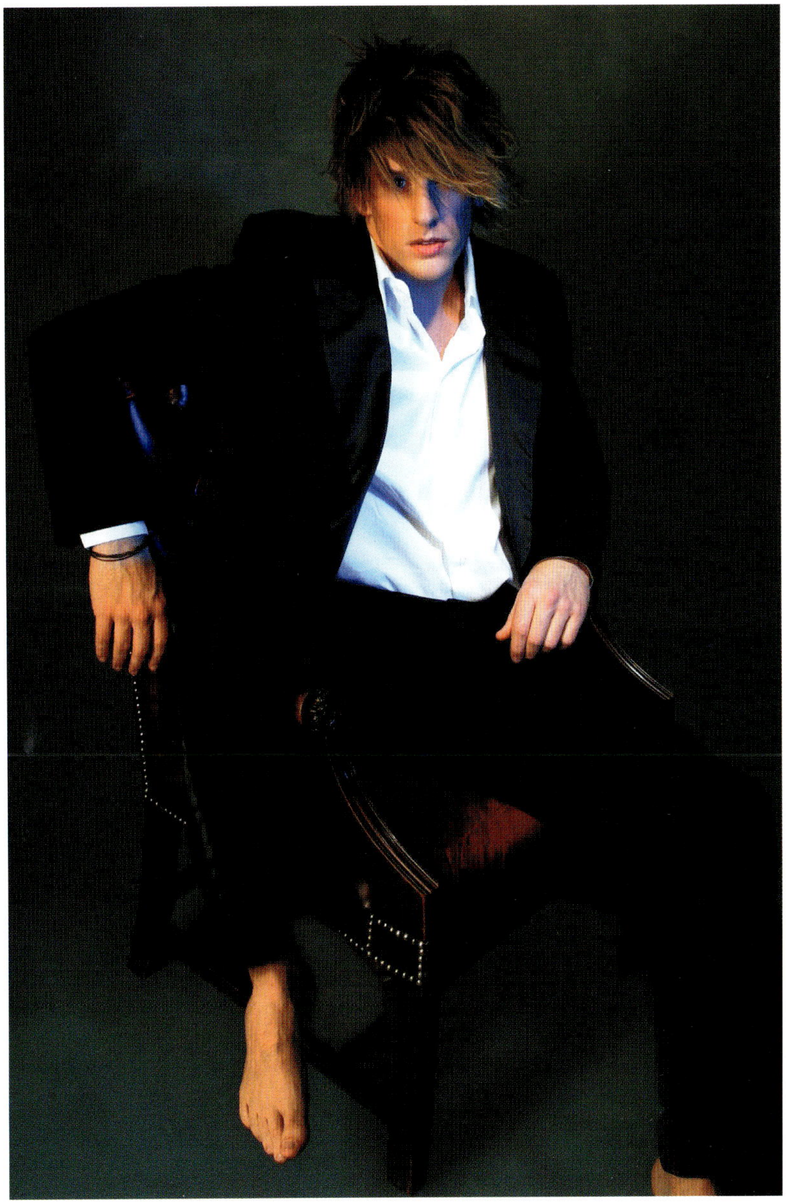

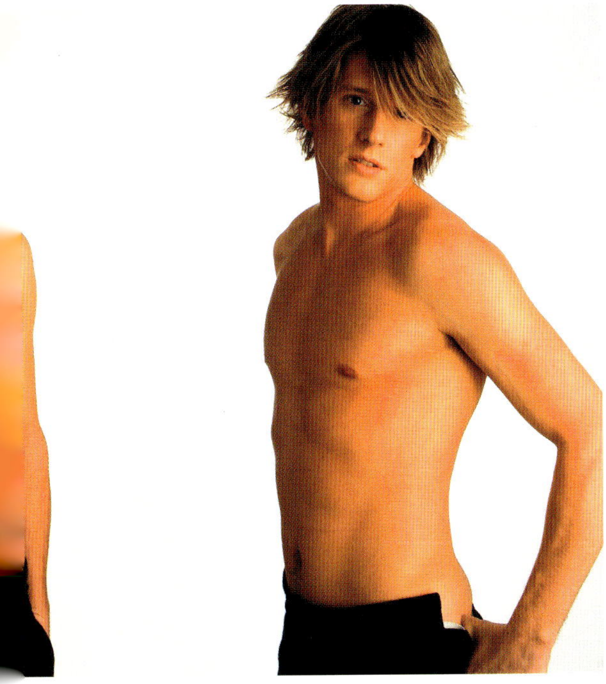

When photographing men's bodies, however, because they are more square and more angular, you are rather more restricted as to how you pose your model. Not every angle and perspective will work successfully. Simple lines and strong shapes are best. If you are trying to capture physique, particularly a 'six-pack' muscular torso, it is usually best to shoot your subject straight on, or have them turned very slightly away from the camera, to emphasise the angularity and pick out the contours of the masculine shape.

Body shots of male subjects also generally focus on the upper half of their body – simply because men's legs, even if they are muscular, tend not to be particularly photogenic!

ABOVE: It is often difficult to pose male models when sitting down to avoid them looking wooden and ungainly. The model's pose here, however, is effectively casual.
Canon D30; 1/125 sec at f/11; 80mm lens

LEFT: Simple and natural poses work best for male torso shots; here the positions of the model's arms adds a bit more shape to the composition.
Canon D30; 1/125 sec at f/8; 100mm lens

BELOW: These images show a variety of head poses. The bottom image is the most successful: there is a nice sense of intimacy between the models, with the woman's head nestling into the man's shoulder, and the close cropping and strong eye contact give a lot of impact to the shot. In the top shot, the man's eye line is slightly off-kilter, which throws the composition out of balance.
Canon D30; 1/125 sec at f/11; 100mm lens

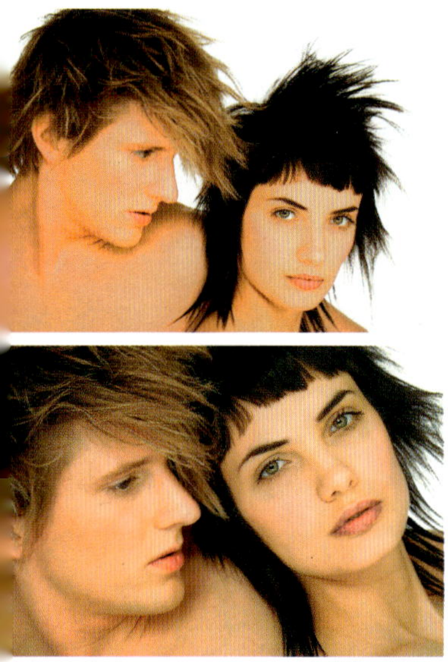

OPPOSITE: To create this sophisticated and moody fashion shot, I used honeycomb toplighting. I placed a softbox to the left of the couple, and a softbox with a blue gel to the right of the man, to create more shadows and enhance the atmosphere.
Canon D30; 1/125 sec at f/11; 100mm lens

Male/female shots

Shots of men and women together are a staple feature of glamour, fashion and advertising photography. It is usually the case that the client wants to suggest that the pair are a couple and use the suggestion of sex or romance as the selling point of the image, so the interaction between the models is a vitally important part of obtaining successful images. They should look as relaxed and convincing together as possible or their body language will look awkward and unnatural.

It is hard for people to fake intimacy with someone they have never met before, but unless the models have a good rapport then the resulting photographs will look strained, tense and unconvincing, particularly if the models are touching each other or trying to look as if they are in love. To facilitate the process, I try to create as relaxed an atmosphere as possible on a shoot: I make sure they have a tea break before they start working, so they have a chance to talk to each other, and make sure that they are both clear about what is expected of them and of the look and mood that I am trying to produce.

Lighting couples

When you are lighting men and women together, whether in a glamour or a fashion context, it is generally the case that you light for the woman. Even when the models are supposed to look like a couple, you will often want to put more attention on the woman, using the man more as a supporting or secondary element in the picture. This does not mean that you cannot use creative lighting, however. In the image opposite, a fashion shot, I wanted to create a sultry and sophisticated shot with a nightlife feel. The lighting is quite stark and moody: I lit the female model from the top with a honeycomb attachment suspended on a boom. This threw a strong and dramatic light onto the model's face, accentuating her strong features and high cheekbones.

For more straightforward beauty shots, such as the images shown left, and images with a more romantic feel, it is usually appropriate to use the sort of clean, even and soft lighting usually used for beauty and glamour images of women, notwithstanding the presence of the male model.

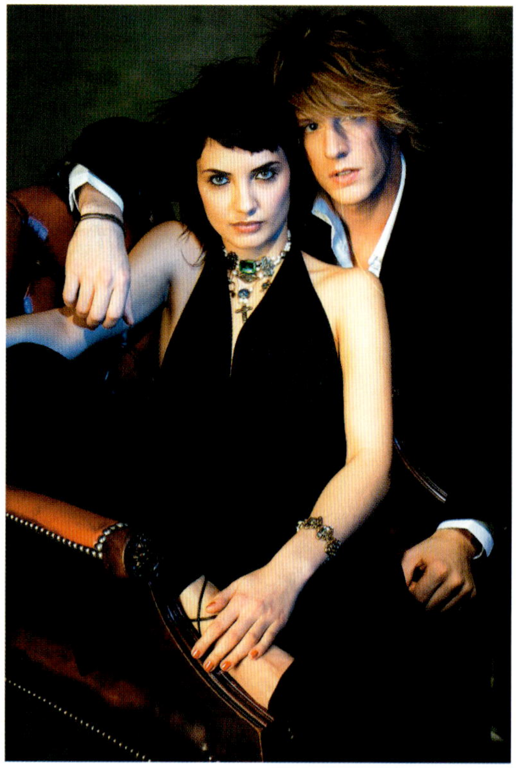

ABOVE: This image was intended to look softer, more romantic and harmonious than the picture opposite. It was lit with softboxes, which produce clean, soft lighting and no shadows.
Canon D30; 1/125 sec at f/11; 100mm lens

Posing couples

When you are trying to combine portraits of men and women, it can be difficult to get the right balance of looks and expressions from the models. It often works well to have one model (most often the woman) slightly more dominant in the picture, as in the images opposite and left. Having one model making eye contact draws the viewer into the shot, while the other model helps to balance and support the composition. When both models are looking at the camera, you need to make sure that their poses are harmonious or there will too many elements in the image fighting for attention. The image above works well, for example, because though there is more focus on the woman, the man balances the pose. They look comfortable and relaxed together.

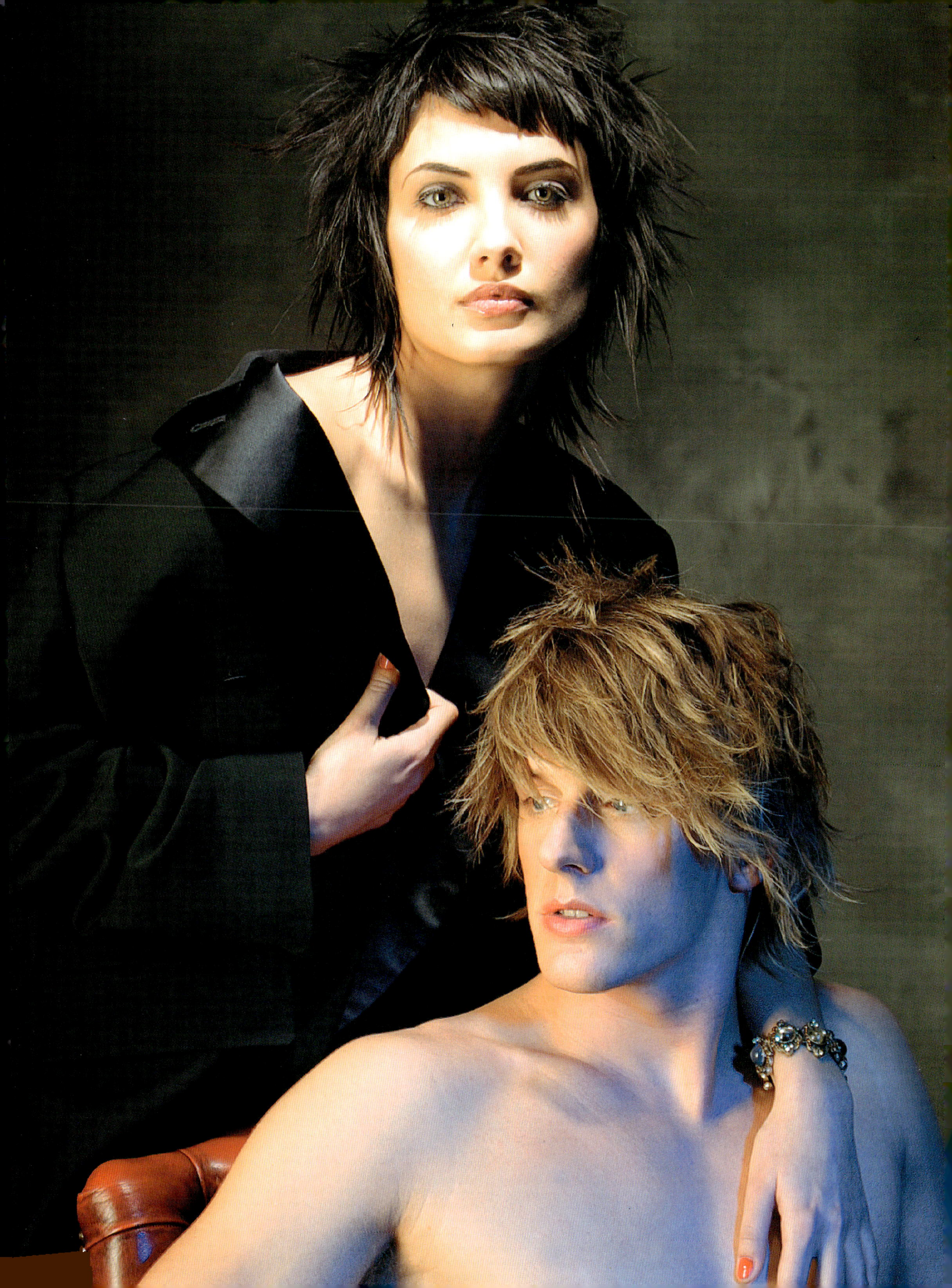

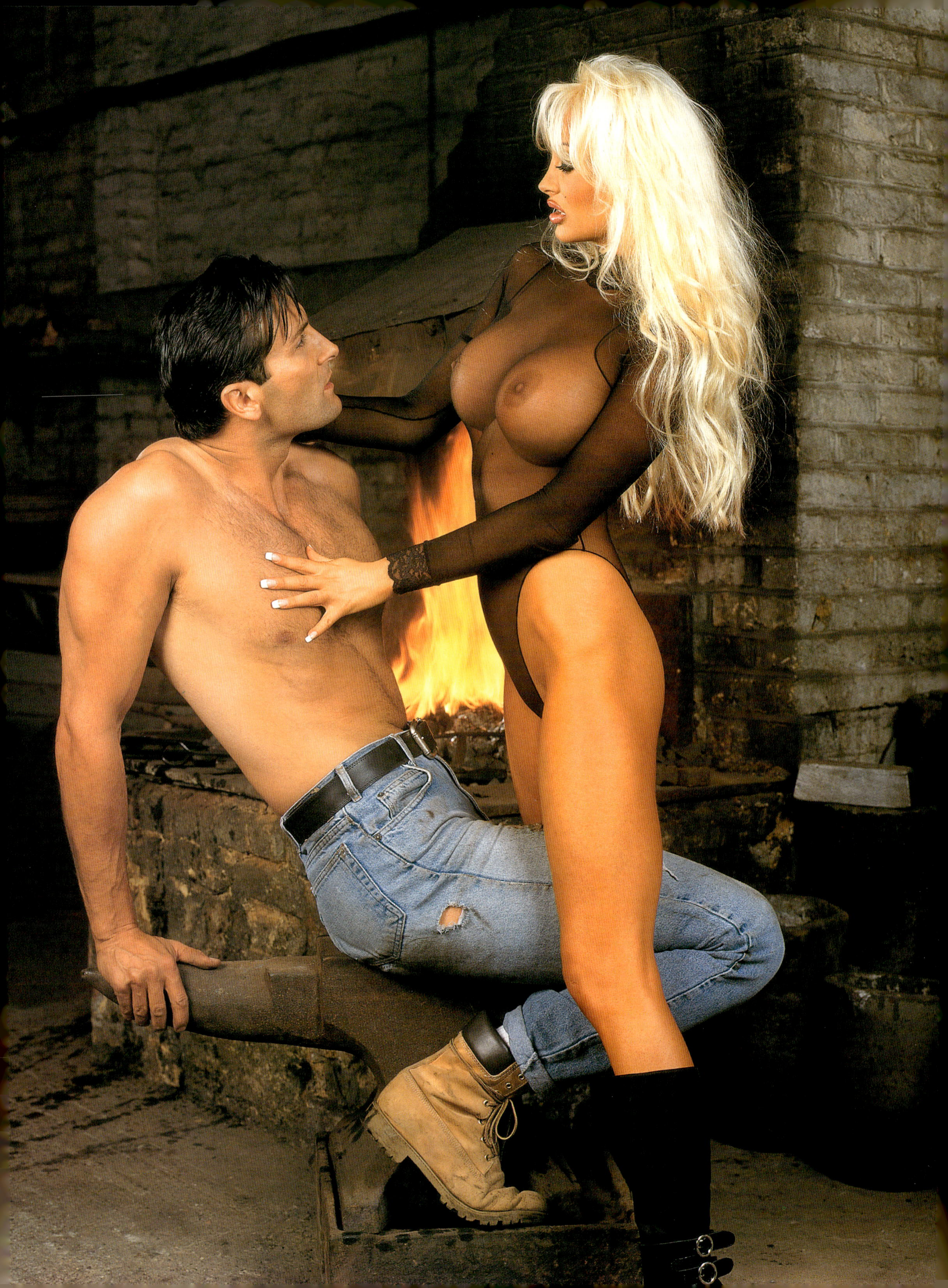

Portfolio

RIGHT: This image was shot on location in Jamaica for a calendar. It was shot in midday sun and as a result, the background has been burnt out. The model is posed in shadow in available light, and the midday sun cascades light down his body to create mood. I also used a reflector to pound some light into the image.
Mamiya RZ 6/7cm; 1/125 sec at f/8; fill-in flash at f/5.6; 110mm lens; Fuji Provia 100

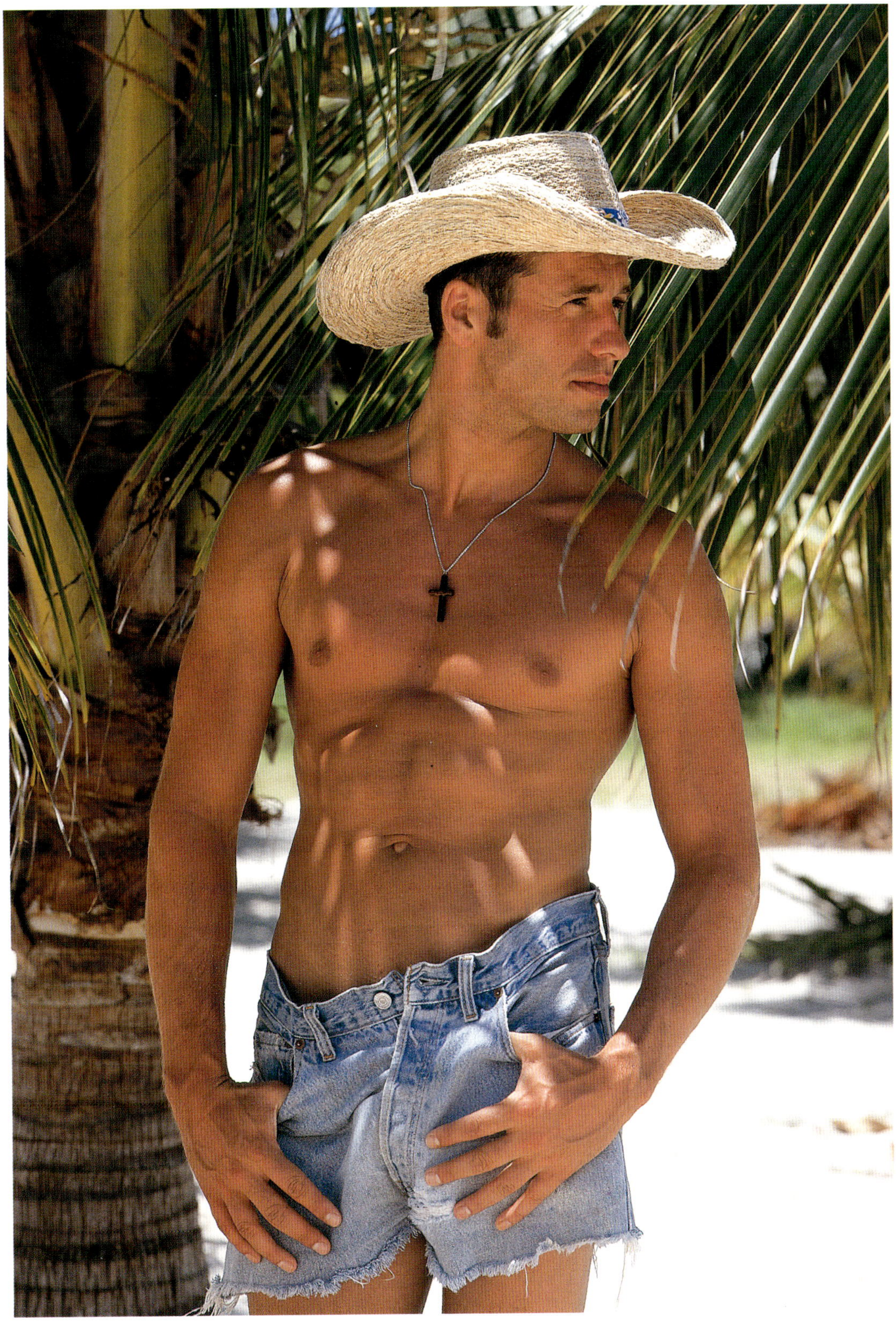

OPPOSITE: This shot was commissioned for a calendar, and was taken on location in an old foundry. The image is striking because of the dynamic shapes of the two models and the fact that the woman is the more dominant feature; the man is being used pretty much as a prop!
Mamiya RZ 6/7cm; 1/30 sec at f/8; 110mm lens; Fuji Provia 100

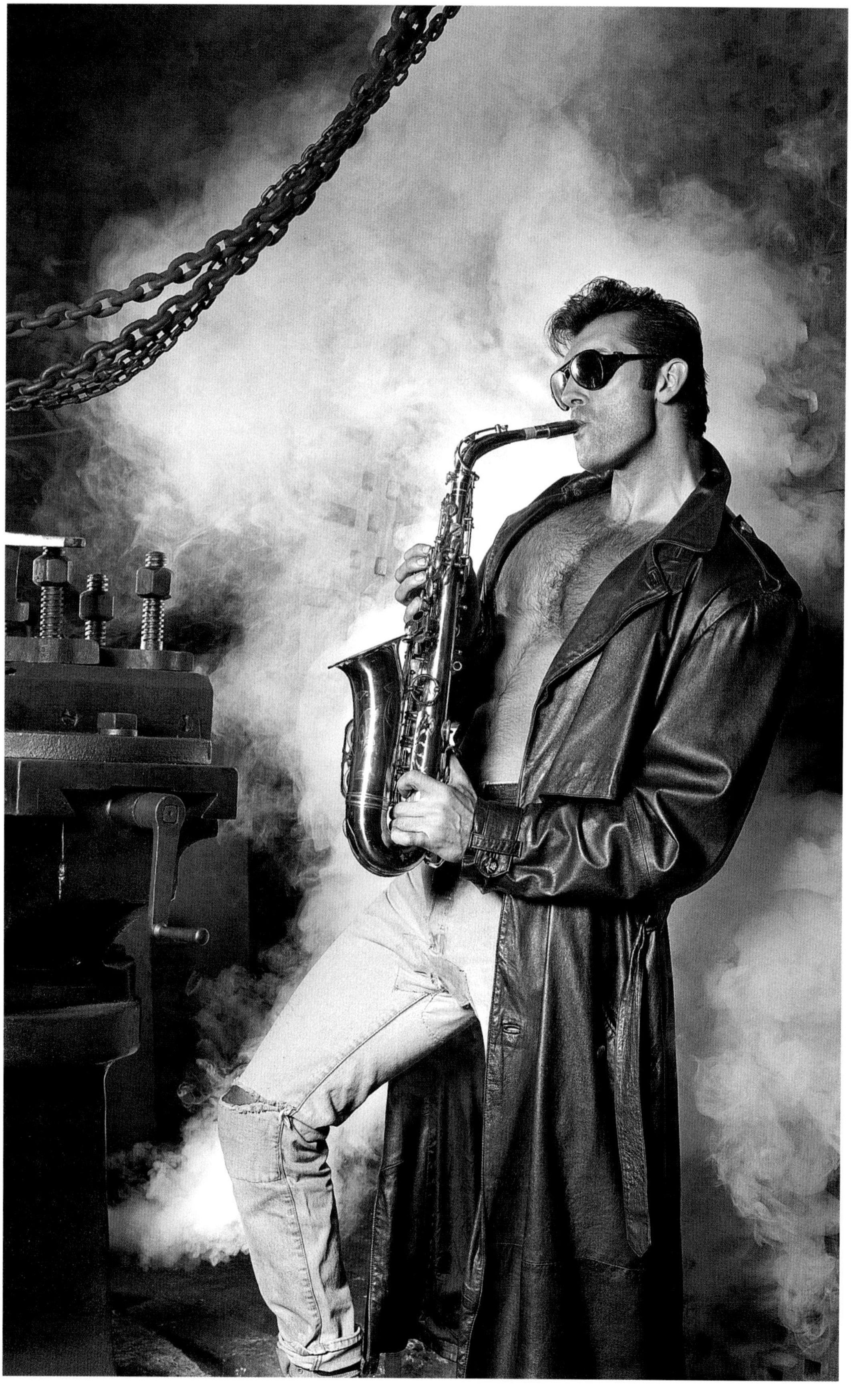

LEFT: This image, intended for a poster, was shot in an old traction engine foundry. I used a honeycomb as the main light source to give a suitably dramatic image with strong contrast. A smoke machine was placed behind the model, and I illuminated the smoke from behind with a flash light to create more atmosphere.
Mamiya RZ 6/7cm; 1/30 sec at f/8; 110mm lens; T-Max 400

OPPOSITE: This shot was taken in very late evening using available light only. The model's pose creates a simple line that is enhanced by the subdued, subtle light and colours of the setting.
Mamiya RZ 6/7cm; 1/60 sec at f/8; 110mm lens; Fuji Provia 100

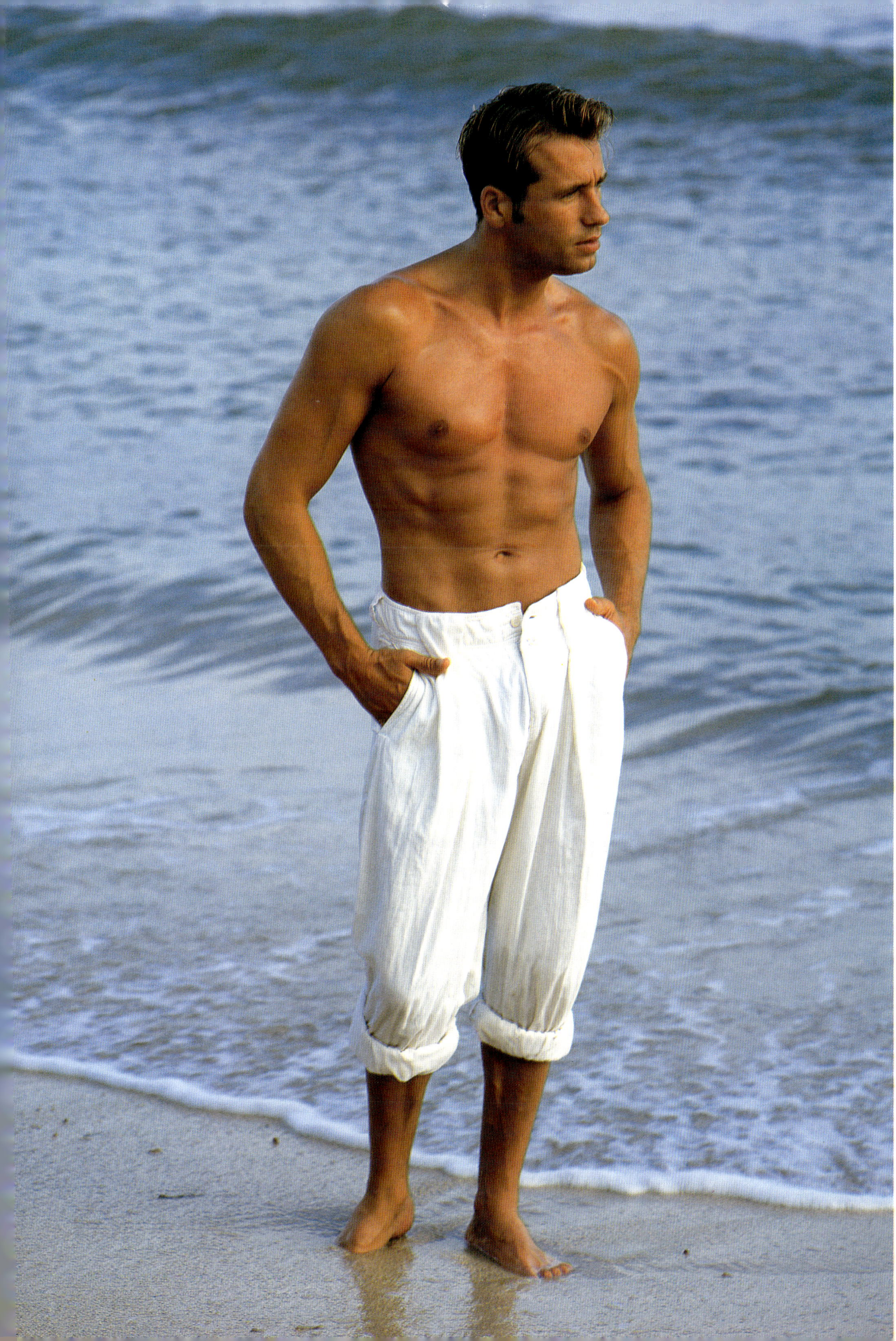

BELOW: This shot was lit very harshly from above using a honeycomb. I also used a strong backlight to highlight the edge of the model's body and the back of his hair, making him stand out from the dark background. The harsh light brought out the strong lines of the model's muscular torso.
Mamiya RZ 6/7cm; 1/125 sec at f/11; 250mm lens; Fuji Provia 100

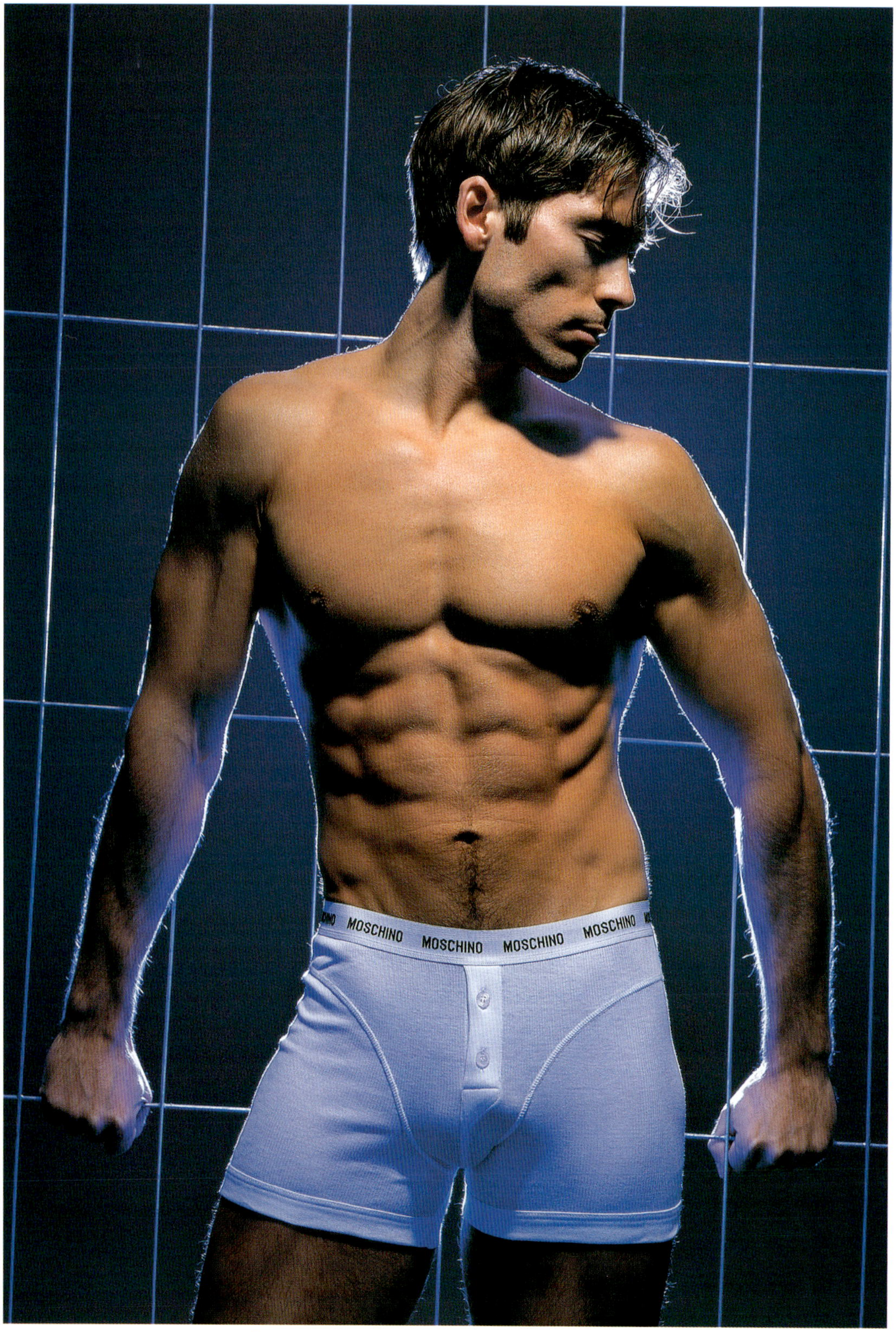

OPPOSITE: This image was created with a strong toplight with a glue gel on it. I used a rimlight with a honeycomb attachment on the right side of the model's body, and used a warm-up filter on that to contrast against the blue. The rimlight was more powerful than the toplight, and helped to highlight the line of the model's strong face and body.
Mamiya RZ 6/7cm; 1/125 sec at f/5.6; 150mm lens; Fuji Provia 100

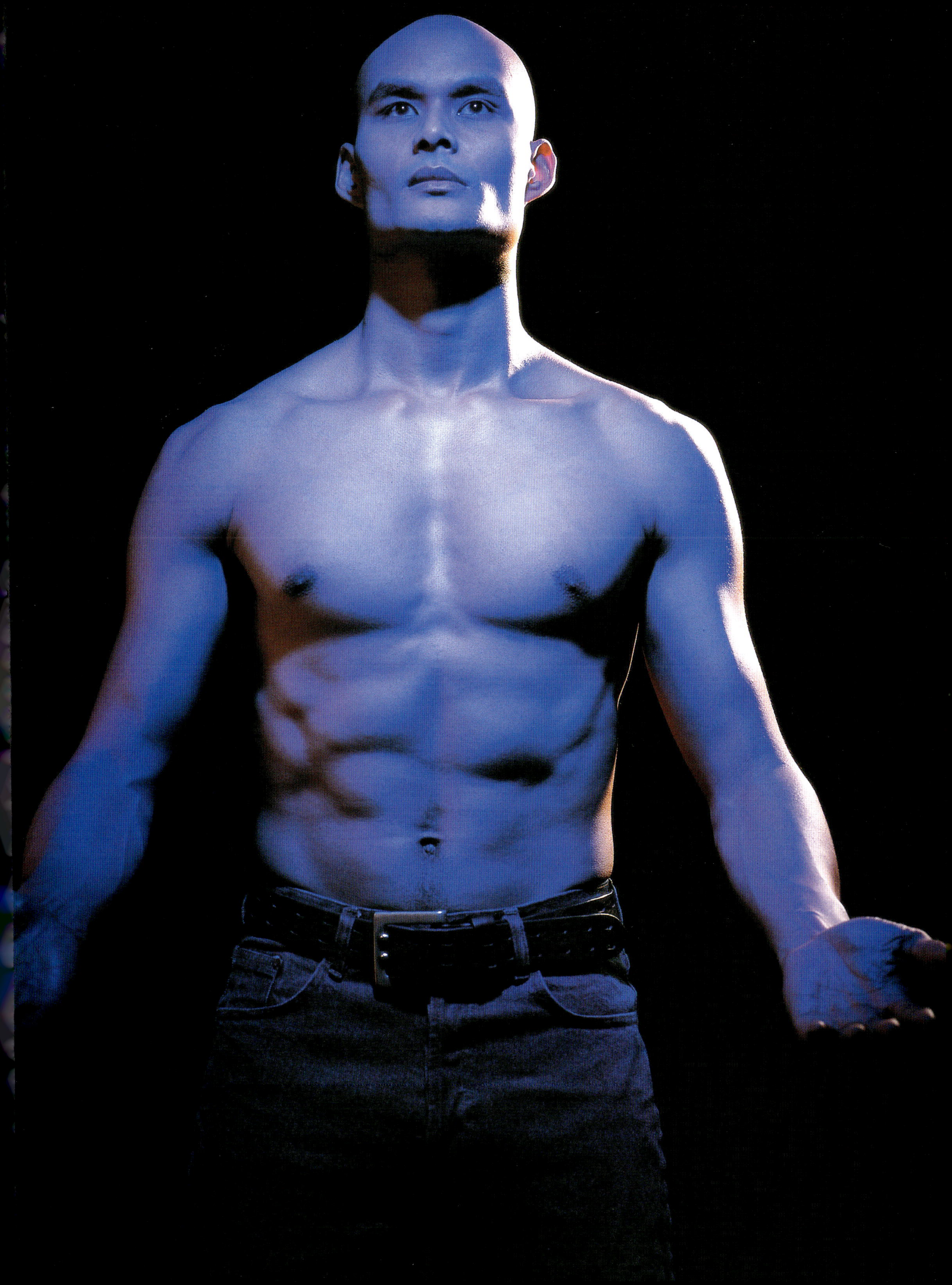

Index

Illustrations *italic*

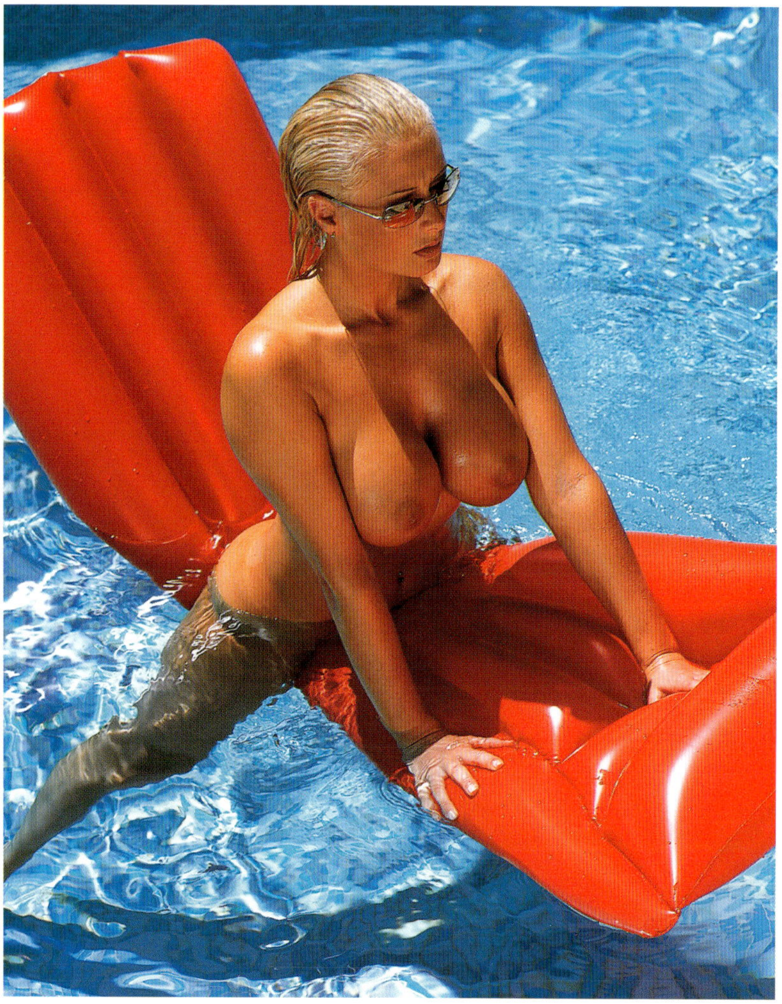

ABOVE: The camera angle, looking down on the model, and the tight cropping of this shot, along with the diagonal lines of the airbed and the model's leg, create an interesting and dynamic composition, while the red of the airbed stands out vividly against the blue of the water. This shot was taken at midday.
Mamiya 645AF; 1/250 sec at f/11; fill-in flash set at f/8; 150mm lens; Fuji Provia 100F

RIGHT: This image was taken with ringflash, which creates rich and clean skin tones and strong vibrant colours. The model's blonde hair stands out well against the dark grey background.
Canon D30; 1/125 sec at f/11; 100mm lens

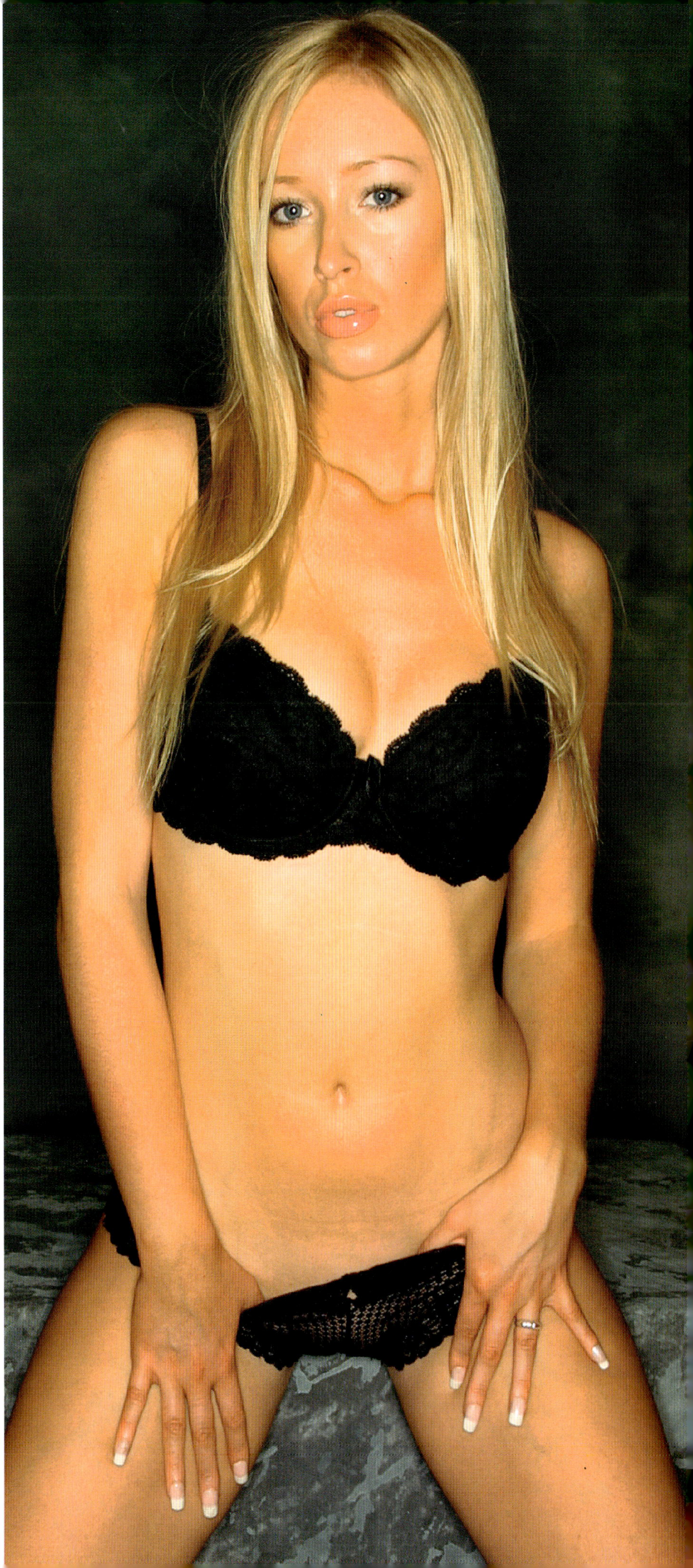

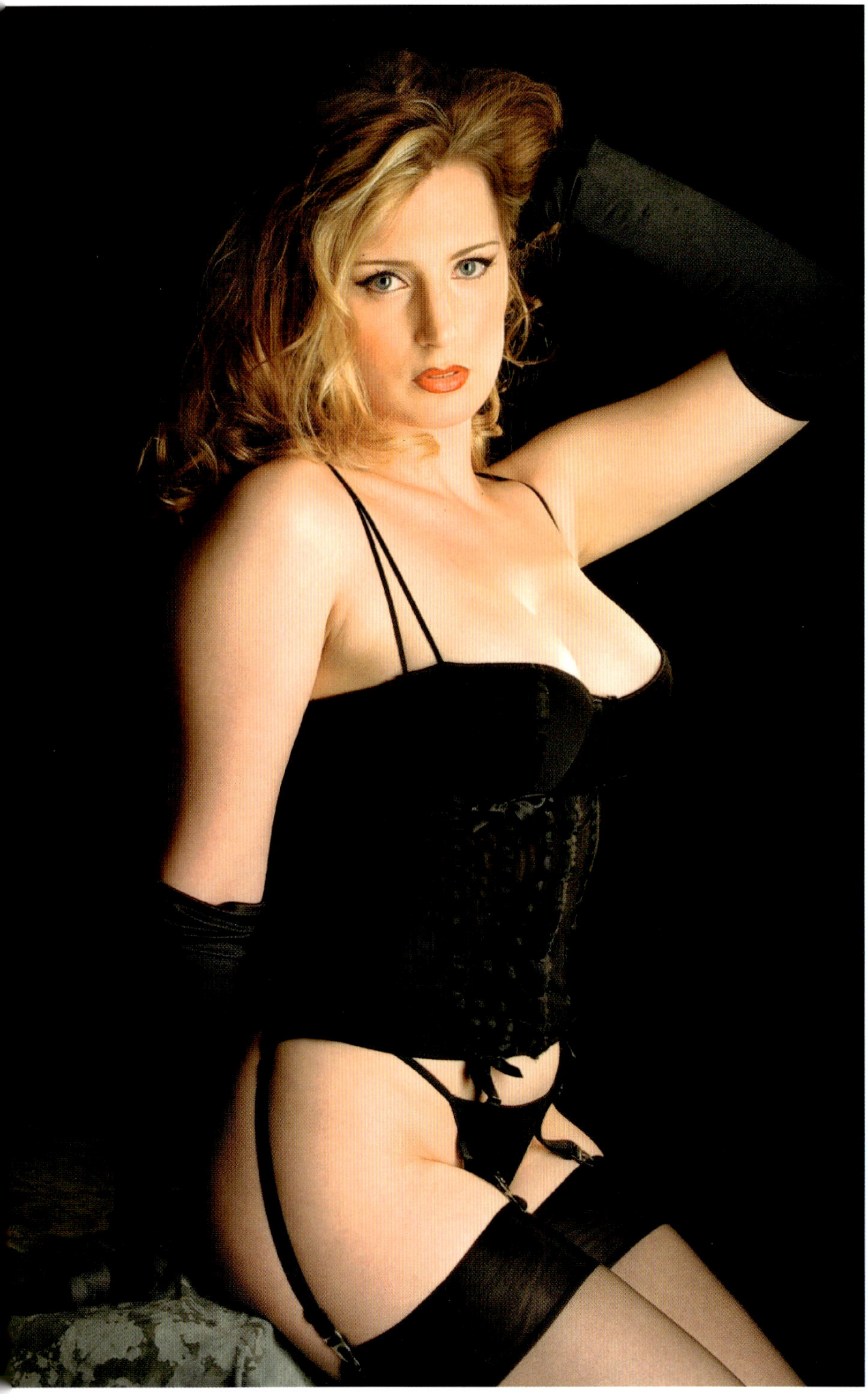

Acknowledgements

I would like to thank: all the models, too numerous to mention, used in this book; my photo library Picture Bank (www.picturebank.co.uk); make-up artist Carole and hair stylist Francesco Picardi; assistants Greg Frederick, James Brown, and Charles Glendinning; for camera equipment, Mamiya Cameras (Johnsons Photopia) and Canon Cameras; Chris Bacon at Bowens (Calumet); and for reflectors, Lastolite.

I would also like to give special thanks to Tony Stone, who inspired me in the early days of my career and who gave me the opportunity to shoot for one of best photo libraries (Getty Stone Images) in the world!

My apologies to anyone I forgot to mention!